The
Bilingual
Exceptional
Child

The Bilingual Exceptional Child

Edited by

Donald R. Omark, PhD
Joan Good Erickson, PhD

COLLEGE-HILL PRESS, San Diego, California

College-Hill Press, Inc.
4284 41st Street
San Diego, California 92105

©1983 by College-Hill Press

Library of Congress Cataloging in Publication Data
Main entry under title:
The Bilingual exceptional child.

   Includes index.
   1. Education, Bilingual—United States—Addresses, essays, lectures. 2. Exceptional children—Education—United States—Addresses, essays, lectures. I. Omark, Donald R. II. Erickson, Joan Good.
LC3731.B5525 1983   371.97   83-1896
ISBN 0-933014-88-0

Printed in the United States of America

Contents

CONCEPTS IN EDUCATION OF THE BILINGUAL EXCEPTIONAL CHILD

EXCEPTIONALITIES IN BILINGUAL POPULATIONS

NATIONAL ISSUES AND MODEL PROGRAMS

Contributors

Narciso L. Alemán, PhD Candidate
Department of Educational
 Policy Studies
University of Wisconsin—Madison
Madison, WI 53706

Gregory R. Anderson, PhD
Department of Home Economics
Bowling Green State University
Bowling Green, OH 43403

Suzanne K. Anderson, EdS
Department of Education
Phillips University
Enid, OK 74703

Effie Bozinou, PhD
Bronx Children's Psychiatric Center

Program in Bilingual Education
Teachers College
Columbia University
New York, NY 10027

J.C. Cooper, Jr., PhD
Department of Physical Medicine &
 Rehabilitation
University of Texas Health
 Science Center
San Antonio, TX 78284

Richard R. DeBlassie, EdD
Department of Counseling &
 Educational Psychology
New Mexico State University
Las Cruces, NM 88003

Joan Good Erickson, PhD
Department of Speech &
 Hearing Science
University of Illinois
Champaign, IL 61820

Joyce Evans, PhD, Director
Special Projects Division
Southwest Educational Development
 Laboratory
211 East Seventh St.
Austin, TX 78701

Juan N. Franco, PhD
Department of Counseling &
 Educational Psychology
New Mexico State University
Las Cruces, NM 88003

June Grant, PhD, Director
Special Education
Department of Education
Trinity University
San Antonio, TX 78284

Nicolás Linares-Orama, PhD, Head
Department of Communicative
 Disorders
College of Health Related Professions
University of Puerto Rico, Medical
 Sciences Campus
San Juan, PR 00936

Sharon (Mares) Merrill, M.A.,
 Consultant/Program Specialist
Communicatively Handicapped
Special Education
ABC Unified School District
16700 Norwalk Blvd.
Cerritos, CA 90701

Marion D. Meyerson, PhD,
 Speech Pathologist/Audiologist
San Francisco State University
San Jose State University

San Francisco Hearing &
 Speech Center
San Francisco, CA 94115

Njeri Nuru, PhD, Associate Dean
School of Communications
Communication Arts & Sciences
Howard University
Washington, D.C. 20059

John Oller, Jr., PhD
Department of Linguistics
University of New Mexico
Albuquerque, NM 87131

Donald R. Omark, PhD
Los Amigos Research Associates
7035 Galewood
San Diego, CA 92120

Adjunct Professor
Communicative Disorders &
  Special Education
San Diego State University
San Diego, CA 92182

Richard Pacheco, PhD, Director
Elementary Bilingual "Emphasis"
  Credential Program
Department of Elementary Education
San Diego State University
San Diego, CA 92182

Philip A. Perrone, PhD, Director
Guidance Institute for Talented
  Students
Department of Counseling & Guidance
University of Wisconsin—Madison
Madison, WI 53706

Carol Prutting, PhD
Speech & Hearing Center
University of California—
  Santa Barbara
Santa Barbara, CA 93106

Joseph L. Stewart, PhD, Chief
Sensory Disabilities Program
Indian Health Service
Department of Health & Human
  Services
Albuquerque, NM 87103

Gloria Toliver-Weddington, PhD
Speech Pathology
Department of Special Education
San Jose State University
San Jose, CA 95192

Allen S. Toronto, PhD
Educational Psychology Department
Brigham Young University
Provo, UT 84601

Barbara Tymitz-Wolf, PhD, Director
Undergraduate Training Program
Department of Special Education
Indiana University
Bloomington, IN 47401

Constance L. Walker, PhD
Department of Curriculum &
  Instruction
College of Education
University of Minnesota
Minneapolis, MN 55455

Daniel L. Watson, PhD
Los Amigos Research Associates

Special Services
San Diego County Department
  of Education
San Diego, CA 92111

Tâm Thi Dang Wei, PhD
Unit 4 School District
Champaign, IL 61820

Preface

The bilingual exceptional child presents unique problems within the educational, legal, and research arenas. The definitions and ramifications of bilingualism as well as exceptionality have been explored for many decades. Court cases have clarified the fact that nondiscriminatory assessment is imperative to avoid misidentification of handicapping conditions in minority populations. Federal mandates have encouraged implementing educational procedures that are linguistically and culturally appropriate for the handicapped child. However, the minority child who is also handicapped or gifted has yet to be appropriately served within the mainstream educational system.

Professionals in the fields of special and bilingual education, speech-language pathology, audiology, and psychology have become aware of the need to provide an appropriate education for minority children with special needs. Professionals in these fields have conjoined in order to better serve children who are variably labeled as multilingual/bilingual or limited/non-English proficient (LEP/NEP)[1] as well as different/nonmainstream/exceptional. The focus of this book is to address the issues related to bilingual special education and to provide suggestions for serving the needs of these children.

Demographics on the number of persons in the United States who speak a language other than English, coupled with statistics on the numbers of children who are exceptional, makes one aware of the number of minority children with special needs who require appropriate services. Whether in a state with a large language minority population or in a school district with small numbers of refugee children, professionals are constantly faced with pedagogical decisions related to these populations. These decisions must be based on an understanding of the uniqueness of the child who is both bilingual and exceptional.

Three facts become apparent when discussing the issues related to the bilingual exceptional child. First, there is not adequate information available regarding appropriate identification and programing procedures for these children. Second, a limited research base makes it difficult to develop educational procedures that best benefit these children. Third, personnel who are trained in bilingual education, second language acquisition, speech-language pathology *and* various aspects of special education are sorely needed.

In order to meet effectively the needs of bilingual exceptional children, it would be ideal to have professionals from the different linguistic and cultural groups adequately represented in the various disciplines. Unfortunately, this is not the current situation. While training programs focus on ameliorating this lack of bilingual bicultural professionals, nonminority professionals must become more linguistically and culturally sensitive. The editors have encouraged authors to present information which is pertinent to all professionals charged with the responsibility of developing appropriate services for exceptional bilingual/bicultural children.

In the first section, the reader is introduced to basic issues and conceptualizations regarding the bilingual exceptional child. Discussion of assessment procedures in speech, language, hearing, social, and cognitive areas provides a basis upon which to build the successive chapters.

The second section presents particular exceptionalities, varying from the handicapped to the gifted, within various cultural and linguistic groups. The authors frequently focus on a particular group such as the Hispanic, Native American, or Vietnamese children. These are presented as examples and are not exhaustive; the principles can be generalized to other ethnic groups. Specifically, the reader is encouraged to become sensitive to the needs and the uniqueness of each child.

The final section examines national organizations, alternative models, and program evaluation. It becomes apparent that diagnostic and educational decisions must be made and services provided for children in spite of the political or funding atmosphere. The changing atmosphere makes it even more important for professionals to take the initiative in developing appropriate identification and remediation services for this population. Although financial resources may disappear, the children do not.

Professionals in various areas of special education and supportive services must continue to learn about first, second, and bilingual language acquisition, the influences of nutrition, language, and community values; and the ramifications of mis- or under-identification of exceptional children from minority populations. There must be a willingness to understand other cultures, to modify tests so that they are culturally and linguistically appropriate, and to develop teaching methods that are meaningful to the child. It is also important to have support from teaching institutions, school districts, and national professional organizations. Laws and regulations will not accomplish this task. People who care about children will.

dro & jge

Note

[1]Terms continually change. These are the limited English-speaking/non-English-speaking (LES/NES) students of yesterday. Tomorrow they will be called something else.

The designations, American Indian and Native American are used interchangeably in this book.

We dedicate this book to our parents.
With deepest affection.

Ivar and Elinora Omark
and
Norman and Blanche Good

Please hear and see what I
Do not tell or show you

For I am a seed waiting to grow,
A flower waiting to open.

Only the limits of your knowledge
Keep me from blooming.

jge

Concepts in Education of the Bilingual Exceptional Child

Bilingual Exceptional Children: What Are The Issues?

Joan Good Erickson
Constance L. Walker

Children who are exceptional have been the focus of educational and legal activity for decades. Personnel in special education, school psychology, and speech-language pathology have provided services in the schools since the 1940s. Programs for bilingual children have emerged more recently having been suppressed as an educational option in the early 1900s. Indeed, for the past two decades American schooling for the child with special needs has had drastic alterations. These changes reflect education's struggle with the societal issues of *difference* versus *disorder*, *monocultural* versus *pluralistic* ideology, and the right of handicapped individuals to achieve their maximum potential.

The fields focusing on research and education of these children with special needs, whether they be gifted, handicapped, or limited-English proficient (LEP), have shared a similar course. Special education and bilingual education emerged from the awareness that being disordered or different in a mainstream society has serious educational ramifications. Both fields, prompted to action by legal activity on the federal, state, and local levels, have been required to provide appropriate identification and education for children with special and unique needs.

As the fields of special education and bilingual education developed separately, two other significant factors occurred. Initially, as services for the handicapped grew, an increasingly disproportionate number of minority children were labeled as handicapped. Children identified as culturally and, in particular, linguistically different risked being categorized as handicapped, i.e., not possessing the tools necessary for a successful school experience. Not only was there an overplacement of minority children in special education, there was a corresponding underplacement of minority children in gifted programs (Mercer, 1973).

As bilingual education grew and as administrators attempted to compensate for the high numbers of minority children enrolled in special education, bilingual education teachers began to notice an increased placement of handicapped children in their classrooms (Bergin, 1980). Thus, not only were minority children often mistakenly labeled handicapped and in need of special services, but some handicapped minority children were not correctly identified to receive necessary services to help them attain their potential (*see* Chapter 13).

Special education and bilingual education have each sought to define its territory and the characteristics of its clients. Both fields wish to deliver appropriate services to their large, distinct populations. This volume addresses these two concerns, the needs of the child who is bilingual *and* requires special services. This population requires combining professional expertise in special education *and* bilingual education in order to provide clinically and educationally sound services in a school setting. Special educators must of necessity understand the particular cultural and linguistic characteristics of exceptional minority students; bilingual educators need to comprehend the range and variability of exceptional students' characteristics within ethnic and cultural context.

This chapter will present an introduction to bilingual, exceptional, and bilingual exceptional populations and the educational services directed to them. The discussion will include data on the demographics concerning these groups, highlights of the litigation that has prompted the development of appropriate educational programs, and implications for research and teaching within a multiprofessional framework.

Populations of Bilingual Children

Results of the 1980 census (to be published in 1982) are expected to identify numbers of language minority persons in the total population of the United States with more accuracy than ever before. Following is one definition of such persons. "Language minority persons are individuals of any age whose usual or second language is not English, or, if over 14 years of age, whose mother tongue is other than English," (National Center for Education Statistics Bulletin, 1978). Until such census data are tabulated, demographic information from studies conducted since 1975 and projections anticipated from the 1980 census are utilized to determine the numbers and locations of language minority persons in the general population.

The most current projections have been collected as part of the Congressional mandate under Part C of the Title VII Elementary and Secondary Education Act (Bilingual Education). Projections indicate that the size of the

TABLE 1-1
Projections of LEP Children by Language Group Ages 5 to 14 in Thousands (NCES, 1981)

Language	Projection Years			
	1976	**1980**	**1990**	**2000**
Chinese	34.4	31.3	33.0	36.2
Filipino	36.4	33.2	35.0	38.3
French	97.6	89.0	93.9	102.9
German	97.4	88.8	93.7	102.6
Greek	29.0	26.5	27.9	30.6
Italian	104.1	94.9	100.1	109.6
Japanese	14.5	13.3	14.0	15.3
Korean	13.4	12.2	12.8	14.1
Navajo	26.6	24.3	25.6	28.1
Polish	26.3	24.0	25.3	27.7
Portuguese	26.1	23.8	25.1	27.5
Spanish	1,789.5	1,727.6	2,092.7	2,630.0
Vietnamese	27.3	24.9	26.2	28.7
Yiddish	24.6	22.5	23.7	26.0
Other LEP	154.4	140.8	148.6	162.7
TOTAL	2,520.4	2,394.2	2,795.9	3,400.0

NOTE: Due to the technique used to disaggregate LEP estimates into language groups, reported totals do not equal the sum of individual LEP estimates across languages. The reported totals are more accurate than individual language estimates because they are based on a larger sample population.

non-English-language-background population in the United States is expected to increase from 30 million in 1980 to approximately 39.5 million in the year 2000 (Fifth Annual Report of the National Advisory Council for Bilingual Education, 1980–81).

Children ages 5 to 14 of non-English-language-background are expected to increase from 3.8 million in 1976 to 5.1 million in the year 2000. Within this time period, the total number of LEP children is expected to increase from 2.5 million to 3.4 million. Table 1-1 indicates the projected numbers of limited English proficient children by language group for the years 1976 through 2000. This information is based on The National Center for Education Statistics report cited in the Fifth Annual Report of the National Advisory Council for Bilingual Education (1981).

One is impressed not only by the numbers of LEP children projected for the year 2000 but by the variety of language groups. It must also be noted that these statistics suggest a temporary decrease in LEP children in 1980 and a subsequent increase in the following decades. This temporary decrease reflects the temporary decline of younger age groups in the total population of the United States. Educational planners should, therefore, recognize that, although 1980 figures show this slight dip in population, long-term planning must take into account the projected figures for the year 2000.

The largest group of LEP individuals in the United States are of Spanish origin. Bureau of the Census (1981) current population reports give a provisional count of 13.2 million, based on population controls from the 1970 census. Of that total, 60% were of Mexican origin, 14% of Puerto Rican, 6% of Cuban, 8% of Central or South American, and 12% of other Spanish-language origin. Complete analysis of the more carefully collected language minority census data for 1980 is expected to yield demographics that are more precise.[1] It is estimated, however, that more than one-third of the language minority population and 60% of language minority school-age children are of Spanish-speaking background. The remaining 40% are composed of a variety of linguistic and cultural groups, both native-born and immigrant populations.

Large numbers of Indochinese refugees (primarily Vietnamese, Hmong, Lao, Thai, and Cambodian speakers) have settled in the United States in the past decade. For example, as of May 1975, it was estimated that approximately 50,000 Indochinese refugees in this country were children under the age of 17 (*see* Chapter 11). Add to the above statistics the numbers of speakers of other Asian, European, and Native American languages, and one is impressed with the magnitude of the population of children whose first language is not English.

Populations of Exceptional Children

Accurate statistics have been difficult to obtain on numbers of limited and non-English speaking individuals in this country due to several factors including methods of census identification, mobility, and immigration. Similar problems exist in the identification of populations of exceptional children. Data on identification of exceptional children have been available although they can be questioned due to variability of definition and inadequacy of assessment tools. Estimates indicate that 8 to 12% of the school-age population is in some way handicapped. One must keep in mind, however, that variations in disorder severity and problems in identification, particularly within the culturally/linguistically different population, affect these estimates.

With regard to severity, physical handicaps such as hearing impairment would seem to be more readily identifiable than learning disability, a more nebulous category. This is not true, however, because the extent to which a hearing, visual, or mobility impairment interferes with learning can vary with each child. For example, although it is established that transient or mild hearing loss impedes learning (*see* Chapter 7), such children rarely appear in the census for hearing impairment. In contrast, children may be categorized as learning disabled but have their reading problems *only because* they are forced to learn to read in a language other than their home language. Thus, the particular area or range of severity considered in identification of exceptional children may exclude some who would benefit from special services, yet include some inappropriately identified as handicapped. Therefore, incidence figures regarding the number of exceptional children must take into account possible inaccuracy due to over-, under-, and misidentification.

With these qualifications in mind, let us consider some estimated incidence figures of the handicapped population. Several studies by governmental agencies and other organizations have suggested various incidences for different types of handicap. Drawing from various sources, and cautioning with regard to the definition of each category, Hobbs (1975) presents the following:

Disorder	*Number of Children*
Mental Retardation	1,700,000
Emotional Disturbance	1,400,000
Visual Impairments	70,000
Hearing Impairments	
Deaf	52,000
Hard-of Hearing	350,000
Speech and Language Disorders	2,440,000

It is fortunate that learning disabilities (LD) is not included in this listing because identifying children with learning disabilities is not only problematic but also potentially affected by cultural/social bias. For example, although it was initially suggested that minority children were underrepresented in classes for the learning disabled (Harber, 1976), more recent evaluation suggests a different trend. Tucker (1980), in a study of school districts in the Southwest over an 8 year period, found that minority children continued to be classified as learning disabled or educable mentally retarded in contrast to mainstream children. He further suggests that "LD designation has provided a convenient alternative placement for disproportionately large numbers of minority students" (p. 95).

Without even considering categories such as the orthopedically disabled or other handicaps, the above five categories suggest that 6 million of the 60 million children in this country are handicapped. When one adds to this number the millions of adults who are physically or mentally disabled, one can understand the goal of the United Nations 1981 International Year of the Disabled Person to raise public consciousness to improve services and to provide equal access for the handicapped.

The incidence figures available regarding gifted children are complicated by criteria and identification procedures used to determine which children fit into this category. In 1972, the United States Commission of Education estimated that more than two million school-age children should be identified as gifted, although few were given special education. In addition, it is likely that not all gifted children were identified because the criteria for selection are often culture bound and based on IQ test norms developed on Anglo populations (Gonzales, 1974). As a broader definition of giftedness began to be recognized (academic, creative, kinesthetic, or psychosocial skills/talent), it was hoped that minority children would be identified and receive appropriate services (Sato, 1974; Chambers, Barron, and Sprecher, 1980). Therefore, if the criteria and identification procedures were adjusted to more fairly include minority children, the incidence figures on gifted/talented children would shift upward (*see* Chapter 9 and 15).

Populations of Bilingual Exceptional Children

Obtaining accurate information on the incidence of bilingual exceptional (gifted or handicapped) children is fraught with problems. Indeed, only recently has the topic become of interest to professionals. In 1976, this chapter's first author wrote to all known early childhood education programs and organizations working with bilingual handicapped children to ascertain the criteria for selecting the language of instruction for the hearing impaired or mentally retarded child who was also bilingual or limited or non-English speaking. The responses indicated there was no theoretical basis for selecting the language of instruction and there were few service delivery systems available.

Until recently there has been a dearth of literature on the topic of the bilingual exceptional child, indicating that this area of study is still in its infancy. In the past decade, pockets of interest prompted by local educational needs and state and federal litigation have resulted in sporadic publications, reports, and proposals for federal assistance (e.g., Herman, 1979; Ortiz and Yates, 1981; Texas Education Agency, 1979). Precipitating the interest in the bilingual exceptional child was the recognition that assessment approaches were discriminatory. National organizations such as the American Psychological Association, The American Personnel and Guidance Association, The Association of Black Psychologists, and The National Association for the Advancement of Colored People raised the question of discriminatory testing in the early 1970s and called for a moratorium on the use of standardized tests with minority children (Oakland, 1977; Samuda, 1975). Ensuing arguments and proposed solutions have yet to solve the problems of identifying minority handicapped children and misidentifying normal minority children.

Professional organizations that should be expected to have an interest in the bilingual exceptional child have shown varying levels of concern for the child's problem. For example, the American Speech-Language and Hearing Association, that focuses its active research, teaching, and therapy programs on communication disorders, has had minimal activity on the bilingual exceptional child, as shown from perusal of its convention programs and journal articles (*see* Chapter 17). Recently, however, an entire issue of *Asha*, devoted to the bilingual child, included an interview with a bilingual speech-language pathologist who described the needs in this field (Juarez, 1981).

Another organization that has been interested in identifying and teaching/remediating bilingual exceptional children is the Council on Exceptional Children (CEC), which held its first conference on the Bilingual Exceptional Child and the Black Exceptional Child in New Orleans in February 1981. This well attended conference was one of the first attempts on a national level to consider the issues of identification and service for the minority child who is, could be, or should be classified as exceptional. CEC continued these efforts with a conference on the Bilingual Exceptional Child in Phoenix in 1982.

Determining the incidence of bilingual exceptional children is difficult because of the lack of confidence in available measurement instruments as well as the lack of recognition and orientation to the cultural and linguistic variables of the target population (Adler, 1979; Archuleta and Cervantes, 1979; Edwards, 1979; Smith, 1980). Identifying a child who is speech-language delayed in their first language is also difficult due to the lack of acquisition and normative data on languages other than English. Furthermore, reactions to misidentification and misplacement of minority children into special education has confounded the problem of identifying NEP children who are indeed exceptional within their linguistic and cultural milieu (Bergin, 1980).

Other factors to consider when projecting incidence data of handicapped children who are linguistically and/or culturally different are the roles health and nutrition play in increasing the number of handicapped children. Factors such as poor prenatal care, low birth weight, and poor nutrition during infancy can increase the probability of learning problems (Samuda, 1975; Moore, Silverberg, and Read, 1972). The health and nutrition problems that often correspond with low socioeconomic status may contribute to more frequent handicaps among children reared under such conditions. Although the data on the relationship between nutrition and cognitive development is equivocable, the high incidence of such physical disabilities as conductive hearing loss in some minority populations is not (*see* Chapter 7 and 10).

At this point, the best estimate as to the incidence of bilingual exceptional children lies in extrapolation and projections of available data. If one were to accept the frequently stated incidence figures of 8-12% of the school-age population being handicapped and at least 2% of the same population as gifted, it is apparent that there is a significant number of bilingual children who are exceptional. Therefore, although the exact number of bilingual exceptional children cannot be explicitly identified, the size of the group is significant. Not only does it include many children who have been mislabeled but may not accurately reflect the number who have yet to be identified. The basic question still remains: How many bilingual, limited or non-English proficient children are truly handicapped or gifted and in need of appropriate educational services?

Intertwined with the need for identification of bilingual, exceptional, and bilingual exceptional children is a body of information on legal activities and federal mandates. As Arciniega (1978, p. 4) states, "A sad and regrettable indictment of our profession is the fact that it has been the civil rights lawyers and court judges who have been the true leaders in this effort. It is unfortunate that the courts have had literally to push us into doing what is right and just." An understanding of the recent litigation in regard to bilingual as well as special education is imperative to the understanding of the current and future status of bilingual special education.

Bilingual Education Litigation

Much of the impetus for bilingual education programs and the understanding of the special learning needs of language minority children can be attributed to the Great Society and Civil Rights era of the 1960s. Federal assistance to schools for poor and minority children developed from compensatory-remedial philosophies directed at *disadvantaged* populations reflected a coalescence of legal, social, and educational pressure for change. For limited-English and non-English speaking children in particular, the movement toward educational access and opportunity is characterized by a web of legislation and litigation that had far-reaching implications for American schooling.

The Civil Rights Act of 1964 must be considered the foundation for later legislative and judicial action concerning the rights of language minority children because it stipulates the right of freedom from discrimination for ethnic minorities. It applies to a wide spectrum of social and educational services, stipulating that no persons shall be discriminated against by virtue of race, color, or national origin in any service program receiving federal assistance. Many later court decisions concerning education were based on the Civil Rights Act, including the right of language minority individuals to receive services specific to their needs.

The Bilingual Education Act of 1968 recognizes the existence of language minority students and designates them as a special needs population in terms of education. It provided for demonstration programs for the development of bilingual instructional models, curriculum materials, and teacher training; and succeeded in influencing states to eliminate English-only instruction policies in schools. Individual states followed by adopting their own bilingual education legislation. The Bilingual Education Act provided federal funds for program development at the local education agency level but did not establish specific instructional strategies. Rather, it recognized *national origin minorities* as constituents who could seek differentiated services on grounds other than race or segregation. More than a decade after the right to educational equality was indicated via *Brown* v. *Topeka Board of Education* (1954), the Bilingual Education Act began the process of clarifying the concept that "equality of educational opportunity" is not the same as "equal education."

In 1970 the U.S. Department of Health, Education, and Welfare issued a policy statement referred to as the May Memorandum. This policy linked federal funds with requirements that schools meet the needs of limited and non-English speakers. The memorandum further stated that a loss of federal funds would ensue for those schools not adhering to the tenets of the Civil Rights Act.

The Supreme Court decision reached in *Lau* v. *Nichols* (1974) had the most extensive impact on the education of language minority children in the United States. A class action suit was filed on behalf of 1,800 Chinese-speaking students in San Francisco. The original case argued that students were denied meaningful instruction because they could not participate in the English-speaking classroom and thus the lack of equal access to education was a violation of the 1964 Civil Rights Act. Both the District Court and the United States Court of Appeals denied the plantiffs' demand that some remedy be provided, but, in a rare unanimous vote, the Supreme Court ruled in favor of the plantiffs. They declared, "There is no equality of treatment merely by providing students with the same facilities, textbooks, teachers, and curriculum; for students who do not understand English are effectively foreclosed from any meaningful education" (4.4 U.S. 563, 1974). This decision indicated that the San Francisco schools had, by failure to provide services, violated the rights of petitioning Chinese students under the Civil Rights Act of 1964 and suggested that some type of special language program be provided for students of limited English proficiency.

Although the *Lau* decision did not specifically mandate bilingual instruction, it was an important factor in further legitimizing bilingual education alternatives. More directly, the *Lau* decision specifies that action be taken to assess and serve the needs of non-English speakers. In 1975 the Office of Civil Rights established a task force that developed guidelines for the assessment and instruction of bilingual or non-English speaking students. Part of these guidelines specifies that action to serve non-English speakers must be taken when districts have twenty or more students in a single language group.

Later legal action reaffirms the rights of language minority children (*Serna* v. *Portales*, 1974; *Rios* v. *Read*, 1977; *Aspira* v. *New York Board of Education*, 1974) and provides for the implementation of language-appropriate instructional programs. As recently as the fall of 1981, proposed compliance regulations that would spell out specific requirements for assessment and instructional programs serving the needs of limited and non-English speakers were withdrawn by the United States Department of Education to allow for further study. Such withdrawal had *no effect* on the *Lau* decision itself, which holds that limited and non-English speaking students must be provided with teachers, materials, and curricula that allow equal access to learning.

Services provided to these children vary in scope, goals, methodology, and practice. While some states provide state funds for bilingual education programs, and school districts may elect to apply for federal bilingual money, the majority of limited and non-English speaking children receive services provided through English as a Second Language instruction. If limited-English and non-English speaking children appear in scattered numbers in a school district, they may be seen by the speech-language pathologist, who may be the only professional available with language training. Unfortunately, this professional often does not have knowledge of second language acquisition theory and processes, awareness of cultural variations, or techniques for teaching English as a second language. Many other children receive no special assistance at all.

In spite of legislation, education programs serving the needs of language minority children are dependent upon a variety of factors including administrative goals, available teaching staff, local community goals, language competencies of the target populations, and other available resources. However, within either a federal or state framework for services to language minority children, the majority of bilingual programs, compensatory/remedial in focus and transitional in nature, are characterized by the use of the native language until the learning of English is accomplished (Gonzalez, 1975). Programs and typologies of bilingual instruction are as varied as the perspectives of educators, linguists, and social scientists. They differ in such variables as community context, curricular criteria, use of languages, and program goals (Trueba, 1979). Unfortunately, the rapid development and funding of bilingual education programs at the school district level has also been far ahead of support for research, curriculum development, and teacher training.

While there exists conclusive research on the viability and effectiveness of bilingual education (Troike, 1978), very little programmatic research has been applied directly in the classroom. Thus, major problems exist in identification of students in need of special help, the assessment of proficiency in English and non-English languages, the adaptation of instructional styles for particular populations, and curriculum development for multicultural bilingual settings (e.g., Rueda, Rodriguez, and Prieto, 1981). Only recently has research begun to address the crucial questions regarding the factors that aid or diminish program effectiveness.

Germane to bilingual education and its accompanying litigation is the question of whether or not national policy in the political, social, and educational arenas has addressed the issue of cultural pluralism that underlies the theory and practice of bilingual education. Yet at the national, state, and local levels, the lack of direction in language planning and language policy (that fails to take into account the rich linguistic resources of America's language minority populations) has resulted in a continued perception of bilingual schooling as *compensatory*. The lack of language policy has resulted in a systematic lack of coordination of goals for serving limited-English and non-English speaking persons, while on the other hand calling for increased foreign language instruction in the secondary schools.

Bilingual education, as well as instruction in languages other than English, was acceptable in this country prior to World War I. The *English-only* hiatus of the past several decades has been questioned through examination of the monocultural versus pluralistic ideology. Legislation and litigation have again brought non-English language usage to the American schoolroom. The current educational practice, based on both civil rights action and on a recognition of the number and needs of language minority individuals, is beginning to reflect the realities of cultural pluralism in this country.

Special Education Litigation

Handicapped children have been treated for centuries. Cleft lips were repaired and deaf children were taught to speak in the sixteenth century. Retarded and mentally disturbed individuals have been institutionalized, separated from society, idolized, or deified, depending on their culture and the time. In the United States there has been increased attention to the education of the handicapped, initially from an altruistic perspective and currently under the direction of federal regulations.

During the past decade two federal directives, one related to educational funding and the other to the civil rights of individuals who are handicapped, have had an impact on special education services in this country. The passage of Public Law 94–142, a revision of Part B of the Education of the Handicapped Act in 1975 and Section 504 of the Vocational Rehabilitation Act in 1973 (which was in effect in 1977) have greatly affected the educational practice and civil rights of handicapped individuals and their families. These federal directives and subsequent litigation have a far-reaching effect on the future of handicapped minority children as well.

P.L. 94–142 focuses on the manner in which appropriate education for handicapped children should be implemented. This law delineates guidelines for special services provided by school systems eligible for federal support. Following are a few of the salient issues P.L. 94–142 clarified and required:

1. Children are to be evaluated in a nondiscriminatory manner.
2. Placement in programs should follow the notion of the least restrictive environment and thus encourage the concept of mainstreaming.
3. Each child must have an individualized educational program (IEP).
4. Parents or guardians are to be an integral part of the educational programing of the child.
5. If the educational program is deemed inadequate or inappropriate, parents or guardians are entitled to a due process hearing.
6. Access to school records by parents or guardians is ensured.

As state and local education agencies struggled to comply with P.L. 94–142, education of the exceptional child underwent serious consideration and, in some instances, drastic changes.

P.L. 93–112, a civil rights law, has also affected the lives of children with special needs as well as adults. Overseen by the United States Office of Civil Rights, P.L. 93–112, Section 504 states:

> No otherwise qualified handicapped individual in the United States shall, solely by the reason of this handicap, be excluded from participation in, be denied the benefits of, or be subjected to discrimination under programs or activities receiving federal financial assistance.

Thus, as a result of two landmark legislative acts, the civil and educational rights of handicapped mainstream and minority children were established.

Bilingual Special Education Litigation

In addition to the statistics presented on bilingual, exceptional, and bilingual exceptional children, a discussion of the salient litigation on bilingual and special education has provided a framework for understanding the issues regarding the bilingual exceptional child. Indeed, the major concern of this text is to explore the specific rights and educational programing options for the minority language child who is also exceptional. These children face unique problems that require unique educational solutions. As Chinn (1979, p. 1) states:

> The minority children who are handicapped are truly operating at an extreme disadvantage. Not only do these children have to cope with the common problems faced by minority children, but they must carry the additional burden of being physically or mentally different from their own ethnic or racial group. Disproportionately

high numbers of handicapped minority children also come from poor socioeconomic backgrounds. All of these factors contribute to a negative self image and low self esteem.

Given the incidence data and the realization of the social, psychological, and educational impact on the bilingual exceptional child, one is appalled that more enthusiastic attention has not been paid to the issue before this time.

Fortunately, an interaction between bilingual and special (handicapped and gifted) education is emerging in the professional arena (Gavillan--Torres, 1980). In addition, litigation is encouraging interest and compliance in state and local education agencies. A series of court cases and federal directives have provided impetus to the development of educational approaches, including assessment and intervention which are sensitive to the needs of the exceptional minority child. Some of this impetus initially was provided by research and litigation related to the Black child whose culture and language style may not be characteristic of mainstream children. In addition, the ramifications of P.L. 94–142 and P.L. 93–112, Section 504, were a turning point for children from both minority and majority ethnic groups.

Earlier court cases, such as *Diana* v. *California State Board of Education* (1970), also contributed to the movement to identify and educate bilingual handicapped children. This landmark case specified the need to assess the intellectual ability of non-English proficient children in their native language. With appropriate testing, nine Mexican American students previously identified as mentally retarded were proven to be of average intelligence.[2] Several other cases settled in and out of court have substantiated the need for appropriate identification and remediation of minority language children. Not only has litigation encouraged local education agencies to prevent inappropriate placements; it has also promoted the need to work toward appropriate assessment of and services for the minority child who has special needs.

Implications for Research and Teaching

In the movement to ensure that bilingual children are not misplaced, the need to identify and appropriately serve exceptional minority children has received less attention. Research and knowledge about exceptional children in bilingual populations is limited. Furthermore, developmental data, particularly in the area of speech and language development in languages other than English, is slow in coming and thus affects attempts to identify special needs children in their primary language. Although information on communicatively disordered Hispanic children is appearing (Dulay, Burt, and McKeon, 1980; Toronto, 1976; *see also* Chapter 8), the information about other languages is limited. This lack of normative data prevents accurate diagnosis and remediation of the child's primary language.

Various approaches to assess the communicative ability of limited-English and non-English speaking children should be considered (Erickson and Omark, 1981; Oller, 1979) along with the evaluation of their adaptive functioning (Cervantes and Baca, 1979). Pluralistic assessment using criterion referenced measures to identify the bilingual handicapped child have been suggested as the basis for individualized educational plans (Mowder, 1980). Others indicate the strengths of developing locally normed measures (*see* Chapter 6; Watson, Omark, Grouell, and Heller, 1980). One must be aware, however, that during the process of identifying exceptional children, such children in the minority population suffer from the danger of being either created (through misidentification) or ignored by the school sytem whose very duty it is to teach them. It is apparent that research on identifying the exceptional child needs to expand in order to ensure validity and reliability in diagnosing the bilingual exceptional child.

Therapeutic approaches for developing communication skills in the child can be based on normal child language acquisition processes and milestones until such time as that data sufficiently supports an alternative approach (McLean and Snyder–McLean, 1979; Bloom and Lahey, 1978). Seeing as this hypothesis is proposed tentatively for teaching language-delayed speakers of English, one is even less confident in proposing a similar approach for developing communication skills in handicapped bilingual children.

Inherent in the above suggestion is the notion that teaching exceptional children in the primary language is preferable. While it is generally accepted among bilingual educators and researchers that a child learns best through use of the mother tongue (UNESCO, 1954), can this provision also hold true for a bilingual or LEP child with a language disorder? Many programs, through their language approach for handicapped LEP children teach in English only. A limited number of programs teach handicapped LEP children in their mother tongue. Is it more effective to teach language-delayed children in their primary language only, in their primary language before introducing English, concurrently with English, or in English only? Other than the seminal Canadian studies by Bruck (1978) on French immersion programs for language disabled children, no systematic research supports any of these positions.

Evaluation of the factors that impinge upon each individual's language learning is imperative when making a decision as to which language is most appropriate for the remediation of the handicapped LEP child. One must weigh a myriad of variables in developing an educational plan for the bilingual handicapped child:

1. Age of the child
2. Severity of the handicap

3. Attitudes and goals of the family
4. Community resources
5. Potential for communication skills
6. Type of handicap
7. Physical mobility
8. Available social interactions
9. Vocational future
10. Potential for independent living

Programs that automatically assume that the language of instruction for a handicapped minority language child should be English may want to reconsider. This point is made clearly by Luetke (1976) who studied the attitudes of Mexican American parents of hearing impaired children regarding the language in which their children should be taught. The results would not be surprising to professionals who have inquired as to parent goals and attitudes. Results of Luetke's study indicate that, although approximately one-fourth of the parents preferred instruction in Spanish and one-fourth preferred bilingual instruction, both these goals were not being recognized. Would not the same inquiry be indicated if one were to develop a program for the severely retarded child from a non-English speaking or bilingual environment, particularly when family goals are for extended family care rather than independent living for the child?

Another area of research and teaching that needs consideration is that of curriculum development and evaluation (*see* Chapter 20). Bilingual education programs for normally developing children came about in part due to insight into the negative effects an inappropriate school curriculum can have on language minority children. It became evident that the school imposed learning problems occurred when there was no match between the culture of the child and that of the school. The same principle exists in curriculum planning for the bilingual exceptional child (Sanua, 1977; Milne, 1978, Nazzaro, 1981; Almanza and Mosley, 1980; *see also* Chapter 18). A rudimentary beginning is to evaluate classroom materials in terms of potential culture conflicts. As Jaramillo (1974, p. 585) indicates, "This may not be an easy task when years of tradition and our own educational background have been rigidly monocultural. It requires sensitivity, relevant training, and involvement in new perspectives." This beginning also requires that curriculum developers in the fields of special education, speech-language pathology, education of the hearing impaired, early childhood education, and allied areas take an aggressive interest.

The lack of trained personnel, proficient in languages other than English and sensitive to cultural characteristics of ethnic minority populations, continues to plague those fields that serve children with special needs. Exceptional bilingual children, appropriately identified and placed in educational programs, may not be taught by qualified professionals, due to the *lack of training programs.* Although training paraprofessionals may be an intermediary measure (*see* Chapter 21), it is not a long-term solution. The lack of bilingual bicultural personnel trained to work with the bilingual exceptional child may be due, not to training programs that do not recruit these individuals, but to a *legacy of inequality in education.*

Options for developing appropriately trained personnel for bilingual special education present a multitude of problems. Does one redirect bilingual educators into special education and similar fields or special educators into bilingual education? Should training programs infuse each specialty with the other or create a new specialty of bilingual special education? What are the risks in developing a training program that either takes an inordinate amount of time or creates a diluted version of both and thus inadequately prepares teachers? Several training models and competencies have been identified (Bergin, 1980), and a limited number of training institutions are beginning to develop programs that are designed to train students in these combined fields. Their effectiveness remains to be demonstrated.

Conclusion

The population of limited or non-English speaking children who are gifted or handicapped, misidentified or unidentified, served or unserved can be estimated and are documented to be on the increase. Litigation has prompted educational agencies to act. However, the lack of a research base upon which to pursue the education of the limited or non-English speaking exceptional child is deplorable. Professionals from several fields (linguistics, special education, speech-language pathology, audiology, psychology, and bilingual education) need to clarify the issues and provide theoretical information regarding the minority child who is both non-English proficient and exceptional. Unfortunately, those on the front line, charged with identifying and educating the bilingual exceptional child, need more immediate solutions.

The purpose of the following chapters is to assist in clarifying and solving some of the problems in the area of bilingual special education. It is *not* productive to place blame upon factors such as lack of funds, personnel, administrative support, research, or training. It *is* productive to enlist professional and community resources, to evaluate and revise assessment and curriculum approaches, and to conduct research. Most of all, it is important that we all become an advocate for the bilingual exceptional child.

Notes

[1]For example, other publicized data from the 1980 census indicates a projected Hispanic population of 14.6%. This discrepancy in figures will be resolved when complete analysis of the 1980 census is available.

[2]A student of this chapter's first author recently completed her master's degree in bilingual education. This accomplishment would be a surprise to the psychologist who diagnosed her in the fourth grade as mentally retarded one month after she arrived from South America.

References

Adler, S.: *Poverty Children and their Language: Implications for Teaching and Treating.* New York, Grune and Stratton, 1979.

Almanza, H.P., and Mosley, W.J.: Curriculum adaptations and modifications for culturally diverse handicapped children. *Exceptional children, 46*:608–614, 1980.

Arciniega, T.A.: Sociocultural imperatives in the education of young handicapped children of Spanish-speaking background. In Trohanis, P.L. (Ed.): *Early Education in Spanish-Speaking Communities.* New York, Walker and Company, 1978.

Archuleta, K., and Cervantes, H.L.: *A Manual for the Misplaced Child: Does Linquistically Different Mean Learning Disabled?* Denver, Marufa, Fulano, and Co., 1979.

Aspira v. *Board of Education of the City of New York*, C.A. No. 72 Cir. 4002 (MEF), S.D.N.Y., August 29, 1974.

Bergin, V.: *Special Education Needs in Bilingual Programs*, Washington, D.C., National Clearinghouse for Bilingual Education, 1980.

Bloom, L., and Lahey, M.: *Language Development and Language Disorders.* New York, John Wiley & Sons, Inc., 1978.

Brown v. *Topeka Board of Education*, 347 U.S. 483 (1954).

Bruck, M.: The suitability of early French immersion programs for the language disabled child. January, 1978. (ERIC Reproduction Document Service No. ED 153 460).

Bureau of the Census. *Current Population Reports: Persons of Spanish Origin in the United States*, Series P-20, No. 361, U.S. Department of Commerce, May, 1981.

Cervantes, H., and Baca, L.M.: Assessing minority students: The role of adaptive behavior. *Journal of Non-White Concerns, 7*:122–127, 1979.

Chambers, J.A., Barron, F., and Sprecher, J.W.: Identifying gifted Mexican-American students. *Gifted Child Quarterly, 24*:123–128, 1980.

Chinn, P.:   The exceptional minority child: Issues and some answers. *Exceptional Children, 45*:532–536, 1979.

Diana v. *State Board of Education*, Civil Action No. C-70 37RFP (N.D. Cal. January 7, 1970, and June 18, 1973).

Dulay, H., Burt, M., and McKeon, D.:   *Testing and Teaching Communicatively Handicapped Hispanic Children: State of the Art in 1980.* Sacramento, California State Department of Education, Oct., 1980.

Edwards, J.R.:   *Language and Disadvantage.* New York, Elsevier North-Holland, 1979.

Erickson, J.G., and Omark, D.R. (Eds.):   *Communication Assessment of the Bilingual Bilcultural Child: Issues and Guidelines.* Baltimore, University Park Press, 1981.

Fifth Annual Report of the National Advisory Council for Bilingual Education, 1980–81:   *The Prospects for Bilingual Education in the Nation.* Washington, D.C., 1981.

Gavillan-Torres, E.M.:   An interdisciplinary approach to the education of Hispanic Handicapped Children. *Education Unlimited, 2*:24–26, 1980.

Gonzales, G.:   Language, culture, and exceptional children. *Exceptional Children, 40*:565–570, 1974.

Gonzalez, J.:   Coming of age in bilingual bicultural education: A historical perspective. *Inequality of Education, 19*:5–17, 1975.

Harber, J.R.:   The bilingual child with learning problems. 1976 (ERIC Reproduction Document Service No. ED 143 149).

Herman, D.H.:   *The Identification of Bilingual Handicapped Students.* Pennsylvania Resources and Information Center for Special Education, 1979. (ERIC Document Reproduction Service No. ED 143 149)

Hobbs, N.:   *The Futures of Children.* San Francisco, Jossey-Bass, 1975.

Jaramillo, M.:   Cultural conflict curriculum and the exceptional child. *Exceptional Children, 40*:585–587, 1974.

Juarez, M.:   The bilingual professional. *Asha, 23*:635–637, 1981.

Lau v. *Nichols*, 414 U.S. 563; 39L. Ed2d 1, 94 S.Ct. 786 (1974).

Luetke, B.:   Questionnaire results from Mexican-American parents of hearing impaired children in the United States. *American Annals of the Deaf, 121*:565–568, 1976.

McLean, J.E., and Snyder-McLean, L.K.:   *A Transactional Approach to Early Language Training.* Columbus, Charles E. Merril Publishing Company, 1978.

Mercer, J.R.:   *Labeling the Mentally Retarded.* Berkeley, University of California Press, 1973.

Milne, N.M.:   Learning centers for the bilingual bicultural handicapped child. September, 1978 (ERIC Reproduction Document Service No. ED 154 434).

Moore, W.M.: Silverberg, M.M., and Read, M.S.: *Nutrition, Growth, and Development of North American Indian Children.* Washington, D.C., United States Government Printing Office, 1972.

Mowder, B.A.: A strategy for the assessment of bilingual handicapped children. *Psychology in the Schools, 17*:7–11, 1980.

National Center for Education Statistics Bulletin: Geographic distribution, nativity, and age distribution of language minorities in the United States, Spring 1976. *NCES,* 78–134, August 22, 1978.

Nazzaro, J.N. (Ed.): *Culturally Diverse Exceptional Children in School.* Washington, D.C., National Institute of Education, August, 1981 (ERIC Document Reproduction Service No. ED 199 993).

Oakland, T.M.: *Psychological and Educational Assessment of Minority Children.* New York, Brunner Co., 1977.

Oller, J.W. Jr.: *Language Tests at School.* Albuquerque, Longman, 1979.

Ortiz, A.A., and Yates, J.R.: *Exceptional Hispanics: Implications for Special Education Services and Manpower Planning.* Austin, Council for Personnel Preparation for the Handicapped, Texas Education Agency, 1981.

Rios v. *Read,* 75 C. 296 (E.D.N.Y. Jan. 14, 1977).

Rueda, R.S., Rodriguez, R.F., and Prieto, A.G.: Teachers' perceptions of competencies for instructing bilingual/ multicultural exceptional children. *Exceptional Children, 48*:268–270, 1981.

Samuda, R.: *Psychological Testing of American Minorities.* New York, Harper and Row, 1975.

Sanua, V.D.: Bilingual program for physically handicapped children: Schoolyear 1974–75. August, 1977 (ERIC Reproduction Document Service No. ED 137 448).

Sato, I.S.: The culturally different gifted child—the dawning of his day? *Exceptional Children, 40*:572–576, 1974.

Serna v. *Portales Municipal Schools,* 351 F. Supp. 1279 (D.N.M. 1972), aff'd; 499F 2d 1147 (10th Cir. 1974).

Smith, J.C.: When is a disadvantage a handicap? *Journal of American Indian Education, 19*:13–18, 1980.

Texas Education Agency, *A Position Paper on Personnel Preparation and the Handicapped Mexican-American Child.* The Council for Personnel Preparation for the Handicapped, Texas Education Agency, Austin, 1979.

Toronto, A.S.: Developmental assessment of Spanish grammar. *Journal of Speech and Hearing Disorders, 41*:50–169, 1976.

Troike, R.C.: Research evidence for the effectiveness of bilingual education. *NABE Journal, 3*:13–24, 1978.

Trueba, H.T.: Bilingual education models: types and designs. In Trueba, H.T., and Barnett-Mizrahi, C. (Eds.): *Bilingual Multicultural Education and the Professional: From Theory to Practice.* Rowley, Mass., Newbury House, 1979.

Tucker, J.A.:   Ethnic proportions in classes for the learning disabled: Issues in nonbiased assessment. *Journal of Special Education, 14*:93–105, 1980.

UNESCO, The Use of Vernacular Languages in Education. *Monographs on Fundamental Education, VIII,* Paris, 1953.

Watson, D.L., Omark, D.R., Grouell, S.L., and Heller, B.:   *Nondiscriminatory Assessment: Practitioner's Handbook, Volume 1,* Sacramento, California State Department of Education, 1980.

2

Psychological Testing and Bilingual Education: The Need for Reconceptualization

Donald R. Omark
Daniel L. Watson

Like education in general, bilingual education suffers from being tested against the models adopted by psychologists. Developed over the last few centuries, these models have been derived from particular philosophical perspectives about people and their relationship to the environment. These philosophical perspectives directly influence most present day psychological and educational research. The current approaches to educational research are in need of reexamination, especially since a large number of students, in particular bilingual minorities, drop-out of our present educational system because their needs are not being met. For example, "For Hispanic students who primarily speak Spanish, [the] drop-out rate is more than three times higher than that of Hispanic students who primarily speak English" (Federal Register, 1980, p. 52053). When so large a percent of a population fails, one should question the educational models that are employed. If these models have arisen from research, as many models have, then questions should be raised not only about the models but the manner in which the research was conducted.

The models of assessment frequently used have been applied at two different levels. At one level is the programs for bilingual students; have they succeeded in educating the students? At the other level is the assessment of bilingual students for placement in special programs; have these students succeeded at being educated? Both levels will be examined in terms of the conceptualizations about children and tests that practitioners bring to the assessment process.

Program Testing: A Reconceptualization

In the seventeenth and eighteenth centuries René Descartes in France and John Locke in England made statements that affect virtually all psychological and educational research being done today. Their statements also indirectly affect much sociological, anthropological, and linguistic research. Descartes hypothesized that the mind and body are separate entities, a notion in keeping with church philosophy that the soul is a separate entity. Locke then went on to say that the mind is a *tabula rasa*, "a blank white sheet of paper at birth," and that everything the individual comes to know is written on that paper as the child grows. In essence, these statements laid the foundation for most educational research. In other words, what is education but the filling of minds that hold nothing yet?

Cause-Effect Relationships

A cause-effect relationship existing beween adult transmitters and child receivers is the strongest implication of the theoretical perspective developed from the statements of Descartes and Locke. This relationship also appears in the physical sciences, but it is especially crucial for the education of the child. If one performs a series of actions before the child, this will *cause* within the child the *effect* of learning something. Modern behaviorists and learning psychologists have refined this approach to the nth degree, so that many assume that any number of behaviors can be taught to any organism.

What is sometimes referred to as the *medical model* (Mercer, 1979) is the cause-effect model. When medicine is the discipline making the assessment, the assumption is that some entity, e.g., germ, virus, aberrant cell, is producing the observed anomaly. At the social or psychological assessment level, such factors as divorce or death in the family may be identified as the causal agent for a child's change in behavior.

Applying the cause-effect model at the program level, education researchers have found that one effect of education is the failure of large groups of minority students. Until the *Lau* v. *Nichols* court case, the interesting result of the research was *not* to reexamine educational programs but, rather, to seek outside causal factors that interfered with the educational program, ranging from the children's English being a second language, to poverty, single-parent families, and race. Applying correlative results as explanatory causes was bad enough. Worse was the failure to change the programs.

Group Comparisons

After the mind-body and cause-effect relationships were considered, modern educational and psychological research focused upon a third concept–group responses to test situations. To see whether a particular cause had some effect, some scientific means has to be found to *prove* a cause-effect relationship.

Early in this century, Ronald Fisher laid much of the statistical framework for analyzing relationships between groups. Fisher (1930) worked in an agricultural station where he examined groups of seeds planted under various conditions. What is important to an agricultural researcher is the success or failure of treatments applied to one group compared with the success or failure of untreated control groups. Some within each group may vary because of genetic diversity, even in hybrid stocks, but the researcher is interested in each total group success or failure versus the other group.

Group statistics were initially applied in agricultural settings where few variables differed from one plot to the other; for example, the amount of fertilizer or insecticide. The same sun and rain fell on all the plots, the plants grew in the same environment, and they were usually of the same class, genetically. Such statistical models fell well within cause-effect conceptualizations of the world.

Psychologists and educators, using these models to examine animal and human reactions to a variety of stimuli, attempted to replicate the similar environments plants were exposed to before being tested. To do so, they conducted their experiments in laboratory settings where environmental conditions could be constant. The amount of time the experiment took (e.g., 15 minutes) was not equivalent to the entire growth cycle of the plants, the individuals being tested having experienced a variety of earlier environmental conditions. To overcome this problem, researchers began to randomly assign individuals to the groups in an effort to compensate for uncontrolled prior factors affecting the populations. The results were then tested to see if they could have happened by chance. If that probability was low (e.g., $p < 0.05$), then the results were assumed to be generalizable to larger or other populations.

Chance was, therefore, the equalizer that would make each group equivalent. Chance may produce roughly equivalent groups, if one is dealing with only white mice or with white, middle-class, male, college sophomore groups. However, chance does not operate so conveniently when more complex groups are being studied. For example, if one wants to compare certain individuals, e.g., exceptional children, then nonrandom manipulations have to be made.

Statistical models were subsequently developed to examine possible variables brought to the testing situation. For example, analysis of varience models (ANOVA) supposedly can examine the effect of variables such as age, sex, socioeconomic status (SES), or different classrooms or teachers. However, the more questions asked, the larger the tested population has to be.

A property of many statistical tests is that, the larger the populations tested, the easier it is to find statistically significant differences. When large populations are examined, the results may be *statistically* significant but absolutely trivial (Bakan, 1969; Carver, 1978; Omark, 1981a). For example, if two different reading programs are presented on a random basis in two sets of 20 classrooms, the results of a reading abilities test may indicate that one group is *statistically* significantly better. However, for the fourth grade teacher who sees one group performing at the 4.3 reading level and the other at the 4.4. reading level, there is little of *educational* significance to differentiate the two reading approaches.

Following from the example of earlier agricultural models, virtually all subsequent statistical models (Hersen and Barlow, 1976) depended upon group comparisons. As indicated, the factors that can be tested are limited. For instance, would you like your next salary increase to be determined entirely by your age, sex, SES, and departmental affiliation, or by any one of these factors? What you would probably prefer is a procedure that considers your worth as an individual and includes those factors that help or hinder your progress. Bilingual children would prefer similar considerations when tested. This means that we need to reexamine how children are currently being tested and conceptualized (Carver, 1978).

A start in the direction of considering individual differences could be made if test developers would stop pretending that tests standardized on representative samples of the United States census provide an adequate comparative sample. The minority groups have virtually no effect on the standardization scores (Omark, 1981a; Watson et al., 1980). Providing test norms for each race or ethnic group (e.g., Mercer, 1979) would permit initial comparisons that could then be restandardized for local populations.

The next section will examine how these philosophical perspectives influenced educational research and how different perspectives may provide new insights into how bilingual children may te tested in their classrooms. The field of bilingual education is new, so this section will not deal with final research results, but will suggest conceptualizations that may influence research.

Effect of Conceptualizations upon Research

Group Comparisons

Following directives from the Department of Health, Education, and Welfare (HEW), in 1978 the Chicago Public School System completed the initial phase of its investigation of the *effect* of bilingual education upon bilingual students as contrasted with nonbilingual, i.e., monolingual English, students. From a report on this study, one gathers that bilingual classrooms can help students progress; in eight months the bilingual students showed greater gains in reading than most monolingual students achieve in a year. The bilingual students improved their scores on a standardized English reading test by an average of 1.17 years. For several years, citywide results on the same test have shown that most Chicago public school students gained less than a year's worth of learning during a full calendar year (Suro, 1978).

Investigators found there were no solid relationships between student achievement and different kinds of instructional techniques. That is to say, the bilingual students improved their performance under a variety of teaching techniques, many of which were also presented to the monolingual English students. No particular method was outstandingly successful with either group. However, it shoud be noted that the investigators felt compelled to compare the bilingual *group* with the monolingual English *group* of students. There is no such thing as a single, homogenous, bilingual group in the Chicago Public Schools. As reported by the New York Times News Service (May 5, 1981) the Chicago schools offer "classes in seventeen languages—six more than in New York City, the historical 'melting pot' city." Other estimates of the languages unofficially used for teaching in Chicago have ranged as high as 57. This means that the public school population in Chicago comes from 17 to 57 cultural backgrounds. To expect any single teaching method to appear as *ideal* is certainly unrealistic.

The necessity felt by investigators in the above report to make group comparisons and to seek the ideal method is disturbing. Whether examining populations or educational models, half of any sample has to be below average when put to a comparative group test. When both populations and models are examined in the same study, especially where the populations are diverse, then it should be impossible to identify ideal educational methods, if such even exist. For example, suppose that children from one cultural background (ethnic, social class, or regional) expect an authoritarian approach in an educational setting. If they are then compared with children raised in a laissez-faire fashion while both are being instructed in traditional authoritarian classrooms, then one group's productivity may increase, e.g., reading level, while the other may decrease. If we then look at how well a particular authoritarian approach affects productivity in the bicultural children, we might find no difference from that of a control group, or a slight increase or decrease depending on the rise or decline within each group.

Group Identification

In order to find programs that will succeed, one may have to tailor programs for particular populations. For instance, a great deal of energy and money has been expended for those in special education (e.g., the mildly mentally handicapped) who need a slower, more concentrated approach to the basics. One of the authors, having provided individualized instruction for mentally handicapped children in high school and having seen all but one of 45 students become successfully employed, realized that modifications of educational models is worthwhile. However, the needs of the students have to be closely matched to their continually changing capabilities. In the long run, programs have to be tailored to the individual. In the short run, programs have to be at least tailored to the particular group being taught.

Educational programs that succeed with middle-class children, as many of them do, should not be rejected but should be used only with middle-class children. To do otherwise is to be insensitive to the task of discovering how minority children function. The educator has to know the group being taught. Success of the study of bilingual Chicago schools may have resulted from a variety of different teaching approaches, as well as from having teachers speaking the students' language, who could establish rapport, motivate, and accept the students' culture and learning style.

The American Institutes for Research (AIR) reports a similar contrast of bilingual students and monolingual English speaking students in various U.S. public schools. The report suggested that bilingual programs were failing in their objectives. As demonstrated by Trueba (1979), the two groups of students were poorly matched on even such elementary aspects as socioeconomic status. The AIR study also illustrates the lack of concern for individual students and their responses to particular programs. In the AIR study, bilingual students from bilingual classrooms did as well in their English reading scores as a poorly matched sample of students from monolingual English-speaking student classrooms and did better than the monolingual class in their math scores.

These two large scale studies (Chicago and AIR) suggest that when students are taught in terms they understand, they will equal or exceed typical students' rate of progress in regular classrooms. This suggestion was confirmed by the recently completed 6-year longitudinal study of bilingual programs in San Diego (Guzman, 1982). Cummins (1981) reviews additional bilingual programs he thinks were successful, because they promoted the development of the children's first language to the point of academic mastery, rather than social linquistic competence in English being used as the exit criteria. It takes time for students to become proficient in two languages, but when they do, they are better students. When minority students' dropout rate of 50% is halved, in some cases, the programs more than prove themselves. This is the real measure of the success of such programs, and the results require no tests of *statistical significance*.

The observations of students' performance have to be enhanced. What are the particular factors which most affect *each* student is the critical question. Conceptualizations, whether theoretical or statistical, have to change if more meaningful educational environments are to be produced for bilingual exceptional students.

Psychological Testing: A Reconceptualization

Evolution and Genetics

In the 1860s Charles Darwin presented his views on evolution. Two key concepts from his writings are that (a) the organism and its environment are in continual interaction, and those organisms that do not meet the pressures from the environment do not survive and that (b) there is a phylogenetic continuity from earlier to later forms of the organism. If one goes far enough back in time, one can find relationships to other species (which may or may not have descendents that still survive). Darwin saw both the mind and the body subject to the rules of evolutionary theory.

Near the turn of the century, Gregory Mendel found that the gene is the mechanism for transmitting coded instructions for the development of new organisms from generation to generation. The number of genes transmitted in each species is different, but there seems to be approximately 100,000 genes in humans. The details of what happens before and during transmission of these genes will not be developed (*see* Hirsch, 1963, 1970; Hirsch and Vetta, 1980; *see also* Chapter 16).

This transmission process makes each new individual absolutely unique. There is less than one chance in 70 trillion that siblings will be identical. This is in marked contrast to the hybrid groups studied by Fisher where some variation occurred but where all the agricultural efforts were directed toward producing plants identical for those characteristics important to farmers. If everyone basically is unique when they first confront environmental conditions, there is little likelihood that the same environment will be responded to in the same way by different individuals.

Hersen and Barlow (1976) considered individual rather than group statistics when examining clinical populations. As the reader might expect by now, most psychotherapies were found to be relatively undifferentiable from each other when examined with group tests, and only some groups of patients were slightly more amenable to particular therapies. Clinicians, of course, rejected these findings because they *knew* that some patients had been helped tremendously. After much argumentation in the literature, it was seen that some clients did improve, some remained the same, and some declined under any particular treatment program. Under these conditions, using group means to identify meaningful therapies was not an appropriate approach for such individualized procedures as psychotherapy.

Within a cause-effect model, Hersen and Barlow suggest approaches to individual statistical investigations. Their book is recommended for those interested in what is happening in bilingual classrooms from this individual perspective. From such a perspective, it will be seen that individual Chicano, Puerto Rican, Syrian, Native American, and other groups may or may not be identical to each other, either between or within groups. Until this is recognized, the investigation of *the child* will not begin in earnest.

Innate versus Learned Dichotomy

The dualistic perspective, considering the organism and the environment as distinct, is an innate (genetic/nature) versus learned (environment/nurture) dichotomy. The environment either teaches something, or the organism is able to produce particular behaviors spontaneously. Either something comes from outside the organism or it is built into the organism. This is basically the analysis of variance statistical model, with some recognition being given in the model to an interaction between genetics and the environment. This model is frequently applied to the behaviors of children, with various personal or environmental characteristics being considered on one or the other side of the model.

Instead of accepting this model, if one were to return to Darwin's thinking, then it might be seen that a holistic approach provides a workable alternative. The organism is always in interaction with its environment and never exists apart from it. First, the organism is permeable in that the environment is continually entering through the sense organs. Second, the organism is a total entity that has evolved through time to function as a unit capable of interacting with its environment. Third, evolutionary pressures continue to operate, such that organisms that successfully survive within current environments should have more successful offspring (Omark, 1980b, 1980c).

Psychosomatic Medicine and Cognitive Development

Two other sets of findings during this century have suggested that the mind and body are not separate entities and that the child is proactive rather than just reactive to its environment. The first set consists of findings from psychosomatic medicine. How the *mind* feels influences the way the *body* responds. Worrying about school, a job, or family problems can lead to ulcers or high blood pressure. Similarly, biological happenings within the body (disease, drugs, etc.) can lead to depressive or euphoric thoughts. This interaction suggests that the boundary between the mind and the body is not impermeable. That such a boundary need not be considered at all will be apparent later.

The second set of findings, which has come from Piaget and his followers (e.g., *see* Piaget and Inhelder, 1969), suggests that children in numerous cultures proceed through a series of levels of cognitive development. These levels apparently are relatively invariant cross-culturally and not particularly amenable to manipulation by learning theorists. This basically means that children view their world in ways that are determined by the interaction between biological and experiential factors (Piaget, 1971; Omark, 1980c).

Piaget's findings also suggest that the minds of children cannot be filled at will but are entities where other considerations have to be made. The major consideration is that minds are proactive rather than just reactive. Children, in large part, determine what stimuli will be attended to and how these stimuli will be incorporated into their world view (Dulay and Burt, 1980).

Holistic Perspective

What would a holistic approach mean in terms of the innate versus learned dichotomy? First of all, it would mean that the dichotomy simply does not exist. A moment's reflection will show that the organism's ability to learn has to have been selected for and, hence, is part of the repertoire of functions that the organism can perform. That the organism is attuned to acquire and assimilate particular environmental characteristics at particular ages is illustrated by initial language learning and cognitive development (Dale, 1976). There obviously is environmental information that can be acquired at any phylogenetic level but only in terms of what the organism is capable of and/or ready to acquire. This fact has been recognized within the field of special education, and individualized programs have been developed to meet the particular needs of children.

If one views the child as designed to confront and acquire environmental stimuli, one has moved far from Locke's position. One has also moved far from the position of most educational practitioners. The school cannot merely provide material that the child will subsequently acquire. This is obvious when half of the children of many minorities fail to acquire the schools' offerings.

However, rather than viewing the child as *deprived* or *deficient* because the child does not acquire the school materials, a holistic perspective suggests a different approach. The child is and has been actively acquiring cultural and linguistic rules. Before the child reaches school, many of the parents' cultural and linguistic rules have been incorporated (*see* Chapter 5).[1] The average child of any culture is not deficient or deprived but is quite capable of functioning within that child's cultural environment.

Suddenly, upon entering school, all of the rules are changed. It is similar to an adult stepping from an airplane in Addis Ababa or Moscow; one does not know how to ask where the bathroom is or how to order food. Adults as well as children would appear retarded in such circumstances. What do children do? They may withdraw, wait and watch, and slowly acquire phrases and words that are not explained in a language they understand. They want to play with the other children, so some language content is acquired faster than others, but one can imagine the task confronting each child.

At the same time, these children are also required to engage in the culture and language of the home. Some children handle the home/school cultural differences by simply ignoring the school day activities. Other children adjust to the school by finding large enough numbers of similar peers to maintain their home culture and language during school activities. Still others receive support and examples from their home for switching culture and language patterns.

The most suitable environments for the acquisition of a second language and culture are sparse for normal children and almost nonexistent for exceptional children. First, with full parental support and all the peers starting at the same level (as in the Lambert and Tucker, 1972, studies) children can acquire a second language and, almost, maintain their grade-level performance. Second, isolated minority children soon become indistinguishable from their peers, if they are immersed in a monolingual second language setting. However, children with large numbers of similar peers, and no untoward parental pressure, often do maintain their cultural and linguistic patterns (Pacheco et al., in prep). This latter fact is also obvious in any school composed mainly of minority children.

From a holistic perspective, what needs to be investigated are the salient environmental features that facilitate acquisition of a new language and culture. Parental support is one factor. However, by the time a child reaches second or third grade the child's personality and self-concept as well as the peer group assume increasing importance (Omark, 1980c). Numbers of similar versus dissimilar peers may be one of the most crucial factors. Since most children want to interact with their peers, they are forced to acquire the language necessary to do so.

Mixing children together in desegregation programs promotes this acquisition of a second language and culture. While the federal government suggests appropriate ratios of desegregation for bilingual and other programs (e.g. 40% Anglo, 60% minority), the critical ratios where the social environment is perceived by the children as necessitating change in behavior have not been examined. Research needs to be done for different age children to see when they perceive the necessity to act differently and to acquire a second language. This necessity should be the same for exceptional and average children, since all want to engage their peers. However, when conditions exist such that the minority child can readily find similar peers with whom to interact, there will be little pressure to change from speaking their native language to speaking English.

A holistic perspective places the child in continual interaction with an environment. This environment is unique to every child and has been such from birth. Environments cannot be made identical simply because the teacher, school psychologist, or researcher claim they are identical. This is one of the *myths* derived from Descartes and Locke that needs reexamination if bilingual exceptional children are to be examined for their actual capabilities.

Language is one of our most manifest capabilities as a species. It is, to some exent, apparently derived from a genetic base (Dulay and Burt, 1980).

Its particular nuances are expanded by contact with particular cultural environments. The next two sections explore some aspects of our ability to communicate and what this means in terms of various test results. The reader should keep in mind that each child can reflect nothing more than the interaction between each child's capabilities and the environmental experiences presented to that child.

Communication

While each individual is unique, the individual does not exist in isolation. In particular, it is important to remember that communication is a two-way process. Signals that are sent by one individual have to be responded to by another, if they are to have any meaning. There *has to be* some overlap between how individuals transmit signals and how individuals perceive the signals they receive, if communication is to occur. Much of the past assessment of language capabilities has not focused upon this interactional nature of communication. Instead, the assessment instruments were derived from the *introspections* of linguists and others about what constituted proper or *standard* English, Spanish, French, and so forth. Most of the currently used discrete point language tests, e.g., those that examine particular linguistic elements (Erickson and Omark, 1981), are derived from such introspections.

Labov's pioneering work on *Black English* (e.g., Labov, Cohen, Robin, and Lewis, 1968) illustrated that Black English was not a primitive, simplistic version of *standard* English. Instead, the general rules of this dialect were as complex as any *standard* English variety. The conclusion reached by Labov was that general linguistic rules would be found by observing actual behavior rather than through introspections (Omark, 1980c). The rules used by any group may differ from the rules of other groups but overlap in those areas where communication with each other is necessary.

An animal ethologist (one who watches animal behavior) would say, of course! Experiments have been conducted (Bernstein, 1975) on the overlap in communicational patterns between Old and New World monkeys (those from Africa and those from South America). While these two continents drifted apart more than 10 million years ago, monkeys from these two continents were successfully placed together: They formed a stable dominance hierarchy (nobody was killed), and they even began mating. If the ability to recognize and learn what signals made by a complete stranger from another species can mean, then it should not be surprising that general rules may be found in communicative patterns between humans.

From personal experience of the first author, humans can readily respond to primate gestures. Having neither read about nor experienced a confrontation with a baboon, when my wife and I, who were working in Africa, came upon a male (the size of a large dog) sitting five feet away, I knew at a very basic level how to act, and an attack was avoided. Similarly, my wife and I one day spent a thoroughly delightful hour discussing with ladies in the market the cultural differences between Somalis and Westerners with regard to who (the male or female) should carry what (food, materials for burning, etc.) and who should buy food and prepare it. All of this was done with less than 25 words in common.

In these examples, communication is more than being able to indicate on some test that the past tense or plural markings can be produced. Communication is the exchange of information between individuals. There has to be some common basis for this exchange for communication to occur. Perceptions, responses, ways of decoding signals, all have to have some underlying similarities if cross-species and cross-cultural communication is possible. When communication in these circumstances is possible, then the suggestion is there that a basic part of the human (or primate) communication repertoire is built into us as a species (Dale, 1976, pp. 96–99). Communication at these levels is of course minimal. We could not build an airplane but we could, perhaps, build or share a shelter.

What should be recognized is that there must be continual interplay between the individual's unique capabilities and the communicational requirements of the situation. Some individuals may have limitations (intellectually, linguistically), but these cannot be assumed *a priori* or even necessarily assumed after testing. The individual has to be observed in communicative situations to see how he or she functions, both intellectually and linguistically. Especially before a child is placed in a special education class, the child should be observed to see *how* communication occurs and *how much* is really understood (Omark, 1981b; Watson, Omark, Grouell, and Heller, 1980). In some instances, standardized tests may have to be abandoned in favor of observation, the older "scientific" approach.

In essense, the distinction between testing and permitting the child to communicate (in whatever way possible) is an *etic* versus *emic* distinction. In an etic approach (derived from phon*etics*), the behaviors, language, or test responses that will be recorded are decided beforehand. Only responses that fit this *a priori* system can be recorded. For example, the phonetic alphabet can be used to record most but not all human sounds. Responses can be recorded as data whether or not what is recorded makes any sense in the life of the individual. Using such an approach, phoneticians have learned much about the pronunciation and structure of numerous languages.

Anthropologists have learned that when one moves to the level of the *meaning* of language (or other behavior) for individuals or groups being observed, an *emic* approach is necessary (from phon*emics*). For example, humans can produce many sounds, but only certain ones have meaning within any particular language. An assessor of a child may decide that certain test responses do not illustrate how intelligent or cognitively advanced a child may be. Instead, one attempts to view the world the way the child views that world and responds to it. This means that the assessor has to know something about the child's world, linguistically and experientially.

Likewise, when testing a minority exceptional child, one can move back and forth between etic and emic approaches. Standardized tests, of any kind, are designed to assess particular behaviors of the child. They follow an etic view with *a priori* assumptions about how the child should perform. Whether testing linguistic, mathematic, or other abilities, standardized instruments serve the broad useful purpose of examining school related performance.

In general, the purpose and the design of these types of instruments are etically defined in terms of Anglo culture. To focus upon the individual child emically, one has to see first if the *purpose* of the test is reasonable, e.g., presuming that cause-effect relationships provide a solution to a test problem may be limited to certain Western cultures. Second, with many minority children, *items* and *subjects* discussed and even the manner of *presentation* may not elicit proper responses. The more *a priori* etic assumptions that we make about the way the child *should function* in the classroom, the fewer will be the emic investigations. Furthermore, there will be fewer appropriate remediations that may help children *to function* as they attempt to make the transition to a new culture and language. An emic approach requires modification of the test materials and assessment approaches so that they are culturally and linguistically relevant to the child.

IQ Testing

If everybody is different, the logical approach to testing would be to design *individual* assessments that would examine each child in terms of the child's ability to function within his or her own world. This approach obviously would be grossly inefficient; one cannot follow every child around for a day or even an hour. For children who stand the chance of being stigmatized by special placement, as in a learning disabled, developmentally delayed, or educationally disabled class, spending a few extra hours with that child may make a profound difference. This is especially true because placement frequently affects the next 10 to 12 years of the child's school life, as well as the parents' perception of the child.

However, for most children, some other approach is needed. Assessment of a potentially exceptional child typically starts with a teacher's referral. Following this referral, the routinely used *other* approach has been to test the child with group normed tests, e.g., achievement or ability tests, IQ tests, and language dominance tests. Such tests are *normed* against various populations, norming being the process of determining the *average* child's score. (By now we know that such a child does not exist.) *Per force*, most such tests are by-and-large normed against Anglo, middle-class children, since they constitute the largest and most readily available population. This means that Anglo, middle-class students, in essence, still determine what the final normed scores will be. Separate norms for the various minorities arᵢ̶ rarely obtained for national tests (*see* Mercer, 1979).

Tests are constructed generally by accumulating a set of items developed by the test constructor. These items are presented to a population of children to see how they do. Items are added or deleted as seem appropriate, with more (but generally less) attention paid to the items that actually relate to children's experiences in their world. The final form of the test is normed on some population (e.g., the Peabody Picture Vocabulary Test, Dunn, 1965, originally was normed on 4,012 white children from the Nashville area, even though it is distributed nationally).[2]

The bane of the norming results for most earlier test constructors had been that boys and girls did better on different items. The hope of all test constructors is to construct a test that is *culture fair* or *culture free*, but most tests are not even *sex free*. So-called IQ tests are notorious examples of this bias, with different norms sometimes provided for each sex. One would also expect that language assessment tests face the same problem since boys and girls from earlier than kindergarten age interact differently with their world and are interested in different aspects of their world (Maccoby and Jacklin, 1974; Omark and Edelman, 1976).

The desired goal of test constructors is to establish *general rules* for the development of an entity called intelligence (or language). Without even moving to the level of individual differences, one can see that the test constructors have problems because of differences between those individuals who receive the XX versus XY pair of chromosomes (*see* Garcia, 1972). How intelligence (or language) develops for children can never be stated, *as a general rule*, and one would not expect such statements if one knew any genetics at all.[3] Psychology, with its philosophical bent that ignores individual or species differences, led test constructors up a blind alley.

Some test constructors recognized the sex difference problem and designed their tests so that boys could produce an average IQ of 100 and so could the girls. If the boys properly answered the set of items particularly chosen for them, they could be average and if the girls answered similarly on their *separate* items, they too could be average. The trick was in adjusting the items and providing appropriate weighting so that, in general, boys and girls would score similarly at each developmental age (*see* test manual for the Stanford-Binet, 1937). In essence, the tests were designed *to prove* the *general rule* that intelligence stayed the same as the child developed, had new experiences, encountered social pressures, and so forth.

If tests have to be manipulated to show that boys and girls of a basically Anglo, middle-class background are equivalent in their intelligence quotient, then it should be obvious that additional manipulations could be made to show that any group is equivalent to or even superior to any other group. IQ tests such as the Wechsler Intelligence Scale for Children (WISC), the Wechsler Adult Intelligence Scale (WAIS), or the Stanford-Binet test, and certainly most achievement tests lost credibility as valid assessment instruments the moment the first manipulations were made. If a test constructor says a test is valid within a *general rule* theoretical framework but manipulates the items to maintain the outcome, then such a test should be immediately suspect as a valid instrument.

It has been said that the importance of IQ tests lay in their reflection of the language used in the classroom. As Mercer (1972) indicated, the level of IQ performance was testing how middle-class Anglo the students were. Since most classrooms presumably are taught by middle-class teachers, then all that is being said is that IQ tests indicate that middle-class students do best with middle-class teachers, since they both speak the same language.

The logic behind bilingual programs is to provide teachers who speak the same language as the students. The same logic can be applied to any variety of tests, as this volume illustrates (Watson, 1972). Changing the tester's ethnicity from Anglo to whatever matches the child's ethnicity may be a first step. For Black and Hispanic children at least the results of research on this method appear to be equivocal (Sattler, 1974). Establishing rapport, being "warm, responsive, receptive, but firm" may overcome some testing problems (Oakland and Matuszek, 1977). However, language barriers cannot be overcome by such approaches. The children have to understand what is being said or no amount of warmth will help them in the test situation. Similarly, *each* test given has to reflect the child's environment and language. Such changes would help in distinguishing the exceptional from the normal child (Watson et al., 1980). The next section will illustrate the interaction between language and other assessment results.

Intelligence or Language:
What Is Being Measured?

The continuing history of intelligence and achievement testing illustrates the failure of minority children to match the norms of white middle-class children. Giving the same tests to different cultural groups provides the same finding: Minority children tend to score lower than the Anglo normative group (Cronbach and Drenth, 1972). The general pattern of results indicates that other cultural groups perform very differently and generally much poorer than the groups upon which the test was developed. *If* the tests are accepted as accurate, the other groups are perceived as inferior to the normative Anglo group (á la Jensen, 1969).

When the tests are questioned, there are numerous factors both within the tests and in the test population that can be examined. For example, are the (1) test items biased? (2) norms unreliable for *this* particular population?, or (3) concepts, as presented, invalid for *this* cultural group? (*see* Watson et al., 1980, for an elaboration of these problems).

One of the factors that has only recently been brought into question is how the language used in the test relates to the child's language. If the child cannot comprehend the test language, then the test questions are meaningless. The tester might assume that when a child fails a test measuring a particular concept, the child does not know the concept, when in fact what the child did not comprehend was what was being said in English. The child may even know the concept because of previous schooling elsewhere or in the home, but just could not respond in English.

The law is quite explicit. For example,

PL 94–142 Regulation, 45 CFR §121a.532 provides that, at a minimum, local education agencies must ensure that: (a) Tests and other evaluation materials : 1) Are provided and administered in the child's native language or other mode of communication, unless clearly feasible not to do so....

Office of Civil Rights, Memorandum, May 25, 1970, states that: school districts must not assign national origin-majority group students to classes for the mentally retarded on the basis of criteria which essentially measure or evaluate English language skills.

However, this still leaves the tester with a problem. Is the *home language* the best language for testing? Peer pressure can produce rapid accommodation to another language, at least in terms of the language the child *wants* to use. Is the child proficient enough to use English, should the test be in Spanish (or some other language), or will a combination produce the best test response?

One testing procedure that might resolve these questions is the *cloze technique.* In a cloze test every 5th, 7th, or *n*th word is deleted from material that presents a complete story (Oller, 1979). The test may be presented in written form or orally (Omark and Watson, 1981). This test is a pragmatic measure in that it permits the testee to use the full context of the message to determine what the answers should be. Using cloze tests and other approaches such as dictation or conversation (Oller and Streiff, 1975), it has been found that such techniques more adequately measure language proficiency or competence than do the typically used discrete point tests (Erickson and Omark, 1981; *see also* Chapter 4).

Recent evidence extends this approach and indicates that *language proficiency* is the basic factor being measured by many achievement and intelligence tests (Oller and Perkins, 1978, 1980; Oller, 1981; Stump, 1978). For example, Oller (1981) indicates that for both fourth and seventh graders (on IQ and achievement test measures compared with cloze language tests) a large language factor accounted for "above 50 percent of the total variance." For seventh graders, the amount of the reliable variance attributable to a language factor was 60% to 90% on the two tests. These results obtained with majority Anglo children accounted for an amount of variance in test results equal to or *greater* than traditional IQ measures.

TABLE 2-1
Average Mental Ability Scores for Different Ethnic Groups

Ethnic Group	*Abilities*			
	Verbal	Reasoning	Number	Space
Jewish	58.7	52.6	54.5	52.0
Black	50.0	47.7	45.4	46.3
Chinese	48.2	54.0	54.0	54.3
Puerto Rican	43.2	45.5	46.5	47.0

Adapted from G.S. Lesser, G. Fifer, and D.H. Clark, Mental Abilities of Children from Different Social-Class and Cultural Groups. Monographs of the Society for Research in Child Development, *30*, 1965.

Subsequent research on some minority populations given the subtests of the California Achievement Tests and oral and written cloze tests reveals that "the language factor accounted for no less than 79 percent of the total variance in all of the tests. The reliable variance in every single test score was accounted for by the English language factor" (Oller, 1981). The possibility that language is the primary factor being assessed by achievement tests (rather than intelligence or achievement due to the acquisition of knowledge) goes far in explaining many past research findings. The racial and social class differences in Lesser, Fifer, and Clark (1965), and Zajonc's (1976) findings of differences in IQ scores between siblings will be discussed in terms of children's language abilities in the next two sections.

Differences Between Groups

If one considers that language competence may be the primary factor measured, rather than actual intelligence or achievement, then earlier test results take on a different meaning. For example, Lesser, Fifer, and Clark (1965) examined groups of school-age children in New York who were Chinese, Jewish, Black, and Puerto Rican.[4] Their test instrument measured purported capabilities for Verbal, Reasoning, Number, and Spatial abilities. The approximate scores for each group on each ability appear in Table 2-1.

Of interest here are the *mental ability* scores for verbal abilities. As can be seen, the Jewish children scored significantly higher statistically than the Black children, who scored slightly above the Chinese, and both of these groups scored significantly higher than the Puerto Ricans. Do the tests reflect innate capabilities that distinguish the groups or patterns of acculturation?

We can assume that Jews have most easily become assimilated into the American culture, especially the children. Their major migration to the

United States occurred long enough ago for their scores to be similar to the Italians' and Slavs' who failed the Army Alpha test in World War I, but whose children are now part of the Anglo norms. For this reason, within this study the Jewish children might be considered as representing the Anglo group.

Blacks arrived even before the major Jewish immigration but were first slaves and later restricted in their social contacts with Anglos. At the time of this study desegregation has not yet occurred (if it ever will). The Black dialect was finally recognized as both distinct and equally complex to *standard* Anglo English (Labov, 1971). That this Black dialect is significantly different is reflected in Black children's lower scores on the Lesser et al. test.

Scores for the Chinese children may reflect some of the restrictions on social contact with Anglos experienced by Blacks. However, these are Chinese who arrived at the West Coast and traveled across the United States to settle in New York City. Though they arrived much later than Blacks, their contact with Anglos may to some extent account for higher scores just as time may account for Blacks' higher scores.

In contrast, Puerto Ricans, the most recent immigrants, were not only restricted to *ghettos*, *barrios*, or to farm fields on the East Coast, but also have had less time to become acculturated and to learn *standard* English. Nothing more should be made of their scores than to assume that the test given to them was inappropriate.

The rest of the test results in Table 2–1 suggest interactions between English language acquisiton and home culture experience. Both the Jewish and Chinese family traditions stress the value of being highly educated and having respect for authority (Casamiquela, 1979). Because these traditions resemble middle-class Anglo norms, they enable these children to function within middle-class Anglo classrooms. The family training patterns of other cultures that deemphasize the value of education may limit the ability of children of such cultures to function in the classroom, and thus require changes in classroom structure, as indicated in other chapters in this book.

The rest of the Lesser, Fifer, and Clark (1965) study and a subsequent study by Stodolsky and Lesser (1967) present data showing that middle-class and lower-class children of *each* cultural group, both in Boston and in New York City, responded similarly to the same test. That is, each cultural group produced different patterns of responses for the four abilities, but *within* each cultural group the patterns were the same. However, the middle-class of each group, having more contact with *standard* English, always scored higher. The Anglo-oriented schools in the two cities did not produce different responses in the middle-class children.

If one follows the reasoning suggested, it appears that the language and cultural experience of children directly determines their test results. Other explanations are certainly plausible. However, as cautioned against in the beginning of this chapter, group data should *not* be used to fulfill the expectation that certain groups will perform better or worse on tests. English language proficiency, or any other variable, is not a suitable alternate explanation, *if the tests are measuring* what they purport to measure. The long history of testing illustrates the failure to examine critically such alternate explanations.

Differences Within Families

Among those who have sought alternate explanations is Zajonc, who developed a thesis that "Different family configurations constitute different intellectual environments" (1976, p. 227). Based upon this thesis, a number of test results from the Scholastic Aptitude Test (SAT), achievement tests, and IQ test scores were *explained*. The basic premise is that the parents provide a particular type of environmental stimulation for their children. Each new child, in turn, adds something to this environment. However, because the new child is young (has acquired less "intelligence" than the parent), when the amount of stimulation available to each additional child is averaged it is found that the environment progressively deteriorates.

For example, if the parents each have an intelligence level of 100, the amount available in the home is $(100 + 100)/2 = 100$. With the advent of the first born, the level of intelligence becomes $(100 + 100 + 0)/3 = 66.6$. If the first born matures for awhile before the next child arrives, say to a level of 40, the new environment will provide stimulation of an intelligence level of $(100 + 100 + 40 + 0)/4 = 60$. When children are spaced closer together, the environment's intellectual stimulation thus decreases even more, as demonstrated by Zajonc's data. At the extreme, twins (or other multiple births) depress the environmental stimulation the most, $(100 + 100 + 0 + 0)/4 = 50$.

The major anomaly in Zajonc's data is the result for only children. Rather than having the best-of-all-possible worlds, they tend to score lower than first borns in multiple sibling families because they have no teaching opportunties, whereas the first borns have the opportunity to develop and practice intelligence skills on younger siblings.

The following are some of the basic findings presented by Zajonc:

1. IQ increases with decreasing family size.
2. With short intervals between siblings, the early born do better.
3. Long intervals between births negate the trend in 2.
4. Long intervals generally enhance intelligence growth.
5. Multiple births have lower IQs.
6. Only children score lower because they do not get to be "teachers."
7. Last children who also suffer the handicap of not being teachers score lower.
8. Parent absent families have lower IQ children.

Differences in economic resources, linguistic habits, and other factors are raised as possible contributions to IQ levels by Zajonc, but he does not explore these factors. Similarly, before developing his thesis he sets "aside the important question of whether the various tests used are appropriate measures of intellectual ability in different populations" (p. 232).

The previous parts of this chapter suggest that this "important question" should not be overlooked. In particular, language capabilities and the patterns of language acquisition may be very important for explaining Zajonc's findings. If intelligence, achievement, and many other tests are really little more than misnamed language tests, the same data may be explainable in terms of access to appropriate language models. Taking Zajonc's findings in the same order, alternate hypotheses could be —

1. The parents provide the adult *standard* version of the language. The fewer children in a family, the more time a parent can spend talking, reading, or instructing the child.

2. Early born children do better (when there are short intervals) because the parents again have more time to interact directly with each child. With an increasing number of offspring much of the conversation becomes directives and commands, as in typical classrooms. The children also interact more with siblings who, in turn, provide non-standard linguistic models.

3&4. Long intervals between siblings mean that each additional child experiences more nearly adult language models from all of the older siblings.

5. Multiple births typically result in situations where the twins spend a great deal of time interacting with each other, so the parents interact with each one on a reduced basis. Hence, their access to adult language models is even more restricted than for single offspring. They may even develop their own language, further restricting their experience with adult forms.

6. Only children do not get to be teachers, whether of language or any other ideas (which, of course, also involves language). Here, Zajonc probably has described the right reason. In a sense, *practice makes perfect*, and the opportunities to practice on younger siblings may enhance not only language but many other capabilities.

7. Zajonc's data is less clear on last-borns who, he would like to suggest, are similar to only children. He presents some cross-cultural data. Dutch last-borns decline in IQ level, but French and Scottish last-born children increase in IQ. The French, he explains, have longer birth intervals preceding the last born, but so do those in his United States

sample, where the last-born IQ scores continue to decline. About all that is clear is that every child but the first is a *last born*, at least for awhile, and can become the *student* of the older children. Who plays with whom probably determines the level of linguistic competence to which the younger children are exposed. Some cultures require that older siblings care for the younger children. This care factor may be critical in determining what IQ score or degree of language ability to expect of any child.

8. That children from parent-absent families score lower is particularly disturbing. While Zajonc does not provide IQ scores to illustrate the differences between the average scores of Anglos and Blacks, Mercer (1979) presents IQ scores from the WISC-R: Anglos had a mean Verbal score of 104.8 and Blacks had a mean Verbal score of 90.9. Mercer also found that increasing family size correlated significantly with a decrease in IQ scores. Figures are provided by Zajonc that illustrate the increasing numbers of both Anglo and Black single-parent families for 1960, 1968, 1970, and 1974. For Anglos, the trend is 6.1, 7.7, 7.8, and 10.4% of all Anglo families. The corresponding trend for Blacks is 19.8, 27.6, 29.3, and 37.8% for Black households. Either the Zajonc or a language model suggests that a steadily increasing number of Anglo and Black children are being deprived of opportunities to experience adult stimulation.

Zajonc ends his paper with a positive hypothesis that Scholastic Aptitude Test (SAT) scores may increase from 1980 to 1986 because the number of births per family declined from 3.0 to 2.45 between 1962 and 1969. However, the increasing prevalence of single parent families should easily outweigh this birth order trend. By 1986, almost one-fifth of Anglo and three-fourths of Black families could be headed by a single parent. Given this overwhelming trend toward removal of one of the adult linguistic models in the home, our hypothesis would be that SAT and other national test scores should continue to decline.

Again, language-based hypotheses provide alternate explanations for group tests on children. Both social groups and children within families can vary in their exposure to language models. Research results that suggest that certain children *should* score lower have been common throughout the history of biased testing. When *differences* between children become *expectations*, the pattern repeats itself.

As suggested by the previous two studies, practitioners have to be very careful when applying research results to a particular child. The next section emphasizes factors that should return testing to examination of the individual child and that child's cultural experience. Each step, from the moment of referral through the choice of tests and the way they are administered, has to be taken carefully if nonbiased assessment is to occur.

Crucial Issues in Testing Bilingual Children

To Test or Not To Test?

During the mid-1960s and early 1970s a series of court cases (*see* Mercer, 1979; Oakland, 1977) indicated that the tests commonly used (e.g., WISC-R, Stanford-Binet, most scholastic achievement measures) were biased against minority children. As a result, assessors have become more reluctant to test children from cultures other than the Anglo middle class. Perhaps the decision not to test such children is a wise one, but, at the same time, not testing or not placing those children who have learning disabilities is an even greater disservice to them. Obviously, the practitioner needs some guidelines by which to operate.

The first rule of thumb is to question whether the referral for special education assessment is justified. Though several extensive lists for evaluating the appropriateness of a referral are in existence (*see* Siverman, Noa, and Russell, 1976; Watson et al., 1980), one must consider several factors when screening incoming referrals.

Has the child had enough time to become acculturated? This question is extremely important because newly arrived immigrant children are often quickly referred for evaluation for special education. Realistically, such children may need anywhere from six months to a year to become familiar with the United States educational system and its ramifications. Teachers or other referral sources must be aware that two or three weeks is not enough time to really become acculturated, especially if the individual comes from an extremely different educational system or extremely different cultural background. Often, as with some Mexican students who are new arrivals in the United States, their acculturation into the school system is dotted with periods of either being extremely active or extremely passive. The Mexican educational system follows a much more authoritarian approach than the traditional American system. These newly arrived children adjust to this new found freedom in ways that may not be adaptive within our system.

Is the referring teacher unable to deal with certain children? Many children are referred who do not meet teachers' expectations. Such teachers often have high referral rates and this may already have been noted. However, in order to deal with these individuals, the practitioner must make sure that there is awareness of the problem by the administration and that the administration is supportive of carefully examining why such children are being referred.

Has enough information been obtained? Though the teachers in the school system might be demanding that something be done about a specific child who has just recently entered the system, practitioners need to ensure that as much information as possible has been discovered about the child. This is a crucial step, for often at this point one can clarify much about the concerns of referring individuals.

A case in point was Juan Garcia-Hernandez (age sixteen) a recent arrival from Mexico, who was described as not remembering his last name. His confusion arose from the fact that the final name on the birth certificate was entered on the school records. However, in Mexico he was known by his father's last name, which was Garcia. In identifying him in the American school system, he was known by his mother's maiden name of Hernandez. He was unsure of what name was being used to identify him. A mere clarification of that problem resolved some of the doubt as to why he was having difficulty. (*See* Chapter II for further examples.)

Another very important informational category that is sometimes overlooked is referencing such children to peers who have had similar cultural experiences for an equal amount of time. If one or two children can be found who appear to come from a similar social or cultural background as the child who is being referred, then one has at least a benchmark as to how much growth in language or in academic skills one might expect from a child from that kind of environment. With that type of data, one can then begin to make reasonable estimates as to what should be expected and what is, in fact, occurring.

A second potential reference point is looking at either siblings or close relatives of the child. If the child in question has older or younger siblings who are progressing through the educational system, then one can evaluate or at least compare their progress with this individual's progress. It is not uncommon for the children of whole families to be referred for possible placement in special education. Such referrals would suggest that there is something occurring, either socially or culturally, that might be the triggering agent for referrals. However, if the other siblings are progressing at an appropriate rate, then one can eliminate, at least theoretically, any beginning concerns as to whether referral is due to social, cultural, or poverty issues.

If the teacher doing the referring, or the individual or team evaluating the referral, are very familiar with the children in the school, the environment in which those children live, and the interaction of the environment and the characteristics of this particular cultural group, then the referral will be of better quality. As a result, one would expect better or more appropriate referrals to appear before such assessment committees.

It is also a major concern, in most discussion of nondiscrimatory assessment, that one consider *at all times* the effects of poverty or extreme deprivation. Extreme deprivation may be viewed primarily as an extensive amount of absence or lack of schooling. In such cases, it is extremely hard to state clearly why a child is having such difficulties. Even though everyone may agree that the child's difficulties are due largely to poverty, special education may still be considered after exhausting all the other possibilities (e.g., Title I, bilingual education, classroom intervention, and other possible ways of intervening). Special education may be the only path by which the child might be given the opportunity to learn and profit from the educational system. At such times, one is basically balancing the stigma attached from labeling with the stigma attached from not learning.

What tests are available? The second major issue after deciding whether to refer a child, is what test instruments to use. Currently, as research done by Watson et al. (1980) indicates, most practitioners do not have a wide repertoire of psychoeducational tests. They usually continue to use the same tools they learned in graduate school. However, such practices are not necessary because there are a large number of commercial and noncommercial tests to use with bicultural children. Several test matrices that summarize these different tests provide the practitioner with clues for finding new tests.

The following is a summary of appropriate test matrices. The most thorough review of tests that has been done was by the Center for the Study of Evaluation at the UCLA Graduate School of Education. This center has developed an extensive and exhaustive review of tests that are used within the school domain. These publications (*see* Hoepfner, Nummedal, and Stern, 1976) review tests with reference to measurement validity, appropriateness for various groups, administrative useability, and normed technical excellence. This process involves a review of over 37 specific characteristics of the tests, including all types of validity and reliability measures. These reviews cover preschool, kindergarten, grade school, junior high, and high school tests.

The tests reviewed in these documents are examined subtest by subtest and area by area. For example, the WISC-R subtests are examined individually and in terms of the overall test. Similarly, the Illinois Test of Psycholinguistic Abilities has all of its subtests reviewed in detail so one can examine very closely the way that specific subtests are functioning in terms of the normal Anglo population.

Of more interest for examination of bilingual exceptional children are the matrices assembled by the Coordinating Office for Regional Resource Centers. This office has compiled two extensive lists. The first is the Preschool Test Matrix (Johnson, Marr, and Younger, 1976) that reviews 127 tests in matrix form and has individual test descriptions. This matrix examines the characteristics of a suitable administrator, the length of test time, the appropriateness of every test for each type of student, the types of responses each test needs, the types of interpretation that can be made, and technical information about the reliability and validity of each test. A second publication is the CORRC/ RRC Test Matrix (Bogatz, Johnson, Lubin, Marr, and Todd, 1976), which reviews 35 tests for higher grade levels and has a one page explanation for each test. Both of these test matrices, developed to assist in nondiscrimatory assessment, basically review those tests most commonly used in assessment.

Another very appropriate test matrix source is a work published by Pletcher, Locks, Reynolds, and Sisson (1978). This guide reviews a number of tests for native speakers of Chinese, French, Italian, Navajo, Portuguese, Spanish, and Tagalog. To be included in this review, tests must be appropriate for grades kindergarten through eighth, normed on students within the United States, and adapted and statistically debiased for use with students whose primary language is other than English. The guide consists of half-page to one page reviews of each test examined.

An equally applicable test matrix source is that presented by the Center for Bilingual Education (1978), which is a descriptive catalog of 342 oral and written tests for bilingual children. This catalog covers the various instruments that are currently being used in bilingual education and provides a page to page-and-a-half review of administration time, appropriate examinee groups, and other pertinent information. The final and last source that would be of interest to practitioners is that developed by Watson et al. (1980), which reviews over 600 tests currently being used in special education. This matrix summarizes many of the other sources that have been previously listed. Its shortcoming is that it presents only a limited amount of information on each test, although covering a wide span of tests.

The test matrix sources cited can provide the practitioner with some relatively new tests with which to approach the bilingual exceptional child. However, the practitioner must carefully examine each test and determine what is being tested, what skills one must have in order to pass or do well on the test items, and what social, cultural, linguistic, or other factors might affect a child's score on such a test.

Considerations when testing. Test assessment leads into the third major concern for those working with bilingual exceptional children: How does one approach the testing of a bilingual child who might be exceptional? Obviously, there is a great demand on the practitioner to be very sensitive to the cultural style of the child, to be very attentive to the behavior the child demonstrates in the testing situation, and to try to verify how the test results and the performance of the child reflect the way in which the child normally functions.

Though these demands on the practitioner are obviously important, there are some specific demands on the child, of which one must be aware. The first is that, to take any test, a child must have some test-taking skill. All tests demand *test-taking skills* and children who are from a bilingual background may or may not have had any exposure to taking tests. One of the primary skills important for doing well on tests is following directions successfully. If the children are unable to follow the directions or are confused by the directions, their test results will reflect confusion over the directions rather than ignorance about the subject matter.

There are some other test-taking skills that are obviously important. One of these is familiarity with games and puzzles. Almost all the tests that are given are related to solving some type of puzzle, word-type or traditional, all of which follow the basic premise that the child should find the right answer and assemble this puzzle for the person who is testing. Children unfamiliar with the test-taking situation might not realize that repeated "yes's" by the tester might in fact be an assistance. Similarly, making sure that the examiner feels happy with what the child is doing and paying attention to what is being said by the examiner is extremely important for the child when taking tests. The child has to be trained in how to take tests.

All of these factors actually reflect upon what we observe, the child's motivation to take the test. When a child takes a test there must be motivation to do so. Besides motivation, the child must realize that testing is, in essence, a competitive situation in which one should give one's all to do one's best. However, a bilingual child, especially one with any kind of a handicap, may not recognize the skills and concerns that are important in this type of situation. As a result, the practitioner may not obtain an average sample of behavior so probably will never see a superior performance from the child.

Conclusion

Any assessment procedure should recognize that culture is not a single entity that every child acquires equally, because each child is unique and confronts the environment in unique ways. The child brings past experiences to the learning situation, as well as individual ways of interacting with the world. The school adds new sets of experiences, but these experiences are uniquely assimilated by each child. The acquisition of knowledge, or cognitive development, is a phenomenon that occurs throughout the years and is not limited to the classroom.

When this broader, interactive, holistic view is taken, there are two ramifications. At the individual assessment level, the assessment process has to reflect as closely as possible the actual experience of each child. For the bilingual exceptional child the major question is not "How does this child compare with national norms?" but rather "How does this child compare with the local bilingual population?"[5] At the broader level, research investigations can move beyond asking, "Did this program help this group versus the control group?" to "Why did this group succeed or fail?" in terms of the life-styles and learning experience of the children involved. One must keep in mind that it is what the child brings to the situation that is more important than what is briefly imposed upon that child.

Notes

[1]It could be estimated that 50 to 75% of the parents' linguistic rules have been incorporated by first or second grade. For example, Spanish speaking children (4 to 7 years of age) can produce simple past imperfect, present indicative, past preterite, and compound present perfect tense sentences. Also, sentences with present, past, and future reference (although sometimes without the appropriate inflected verb form) have been produced. Passives, reflexives, possessives, etc., are also demonstrated regularly (Ortiz, 1980).

Some adult forms of language can change, e.g., regularization of verb forms, copula changes, diminished use of the subjunctive, etc., away from their appearance in *standard* English or Spanish (Reyes and Craddock, 1980; Williams and Wolfram, 1972). The problem with testing is that it starts with the *standard* version, rather than what the child has been exposed to by the parents. The above types of sentences, with their changes, are probably all that most parents produce. When one begins testing from the point of the child's cultural experiences, many deficiencies will disappear.

[2]The Peabody Picture Vocabulary Test was meant to serve only as an illustrative example. It has been revised (PPVT-R) and became available in 1980. However, the revision is based upon proportional representation of Anglos, Blacks, Hispanics, and "Others" from the *1970* Census. By the time the PPVT-R appeared, the Hispanics had grown from 3.8% of the population to 6.0% and the Other category had changed from 1.2% to approximately 1.8% of the total population. Comparable changes occurred for Blacks. No separate norms were provided for the various groups.

More importantly, proportional representation can never reflect accurately the composition of a rapidly changing population. Further, the entire concept of proportional representation means that the test is weighted in favor of Anglo children and against minority children (Omark, 1981b). The only reasonable alternative is the development of local norms (*see* Chapter 6; Watson et al., 1980).

[3]Most tests examine *surface structure* features, e.g., learned cultural and linguistic items. Such tests are based upon the false assumption that everyone has the same opportunity to learn these items. The study of genetics illustrates how unique everyone is. There may be *deep* linguistic and cognitive structures that are species-specific, but tests for these structures still need to be developed.

[4]These children were tested before desegregation and bilingual programs appeared. It can be assumed that they were being educated primarily by middle-class Anglo teachers.

[5]It should be noted that at the federal level, and in most states, there are no mandated standardized tests. The logic of test administration *requires* that the tested population match the standardization population. That matching rarely occurs, hence the necessity to develop local norms for many tests.

References

Bakan, D.:   *On Method.* San Francisco, Jossey-Bass, 1969.

Bogatz, B., Johnson, W., Lubin, M., Marr, J., and Todd, J.:   *CORRC/ RRC Test Matrix: Individualized Test Descriptions.* Lexington, Coordinating Office for Regional Resource Centers, 1976.

Bronowski, J.:   *The Ascent of Man.* Boston, Little, Brown, 1973.

Carver, R.P.:   The case against statistical significance testing. *Harvard Educational Review, 48:*378, 1978.

Casamiquela, M.:   Asian culture. In Salzman, E.G. (Ed.): *Cultural Awareness and Non-discrimatory Assessment: Trainer's Manual.* Los Angeles, Office of the Los Angeles County Superintendent of Schools, 1979.

Center for Bilingual Education, Northwest Regional Educational Laboratory: *Assessment Instruments in Bilingual Education: A Descriptive Catalog of 342 Oral and Written Tests.* Los Angeles, National Dissemination and Assessment Center, 1978.

Cronbach, L.J., and Drenth, P.J.D.:   Summary and commentary. In Cronbach, L.J. and Drenth, P.J.D. (Eds.): *Mental Tests and Cultural Adaptation.* The Hague, Mouton, 1972.

Cummins, J.:   The role of primary language development in promoting educational success for language minority children. In Dolson, D.P. (Project team leader): *Schooling and Language Minority Students: A Theoretical Framework.* Los Angeles Evaluation, Dissemination, and Assessment Center, California State University, Los Angeles, 1981.

Dale, P.S.:   *Language Development: Structure and Function.* New York, Holt, Rinehart, and Winston, 1976.

Dulay, H., and Burt, M.:   Second language acquisition. In Dulay, H. and Burt, M. (Eds.):   *Testing and Teaching Communicatively Handicapped Hispanic Children: State of the Art in 1980.* Sacramento, California State Department of Education, 1980.

Dunn, L.M.:   *The Peabody Picture Vocabulary Tests.* Circle Pines, Minn., American Guidance Service, 1965.

Erickson, J.G., and Omark, D.R. (Eds.):   *Communication Assessment of the Bilingual, Bicultural Child: Issues and Guidelines.* Baltimore, University Park Press, 1981.

Fisher, R.A.:   *The Genetical Theory of Natural Selection.* Oxford, Clarendon, 1930.

Garcia, J.:   IQ: The conspiracy. *Psychology Today, 6:*40, 1972.

Guzman, G.R.:   *Title VII Bilingual Demonstration Project: San Diego City Schools*, Publication #1-B-82-9. San Diego, San Diego Unified School District, 1982.

Hersen, M., and Barlow, D.H.:   *Single Case Experimental Studies.* New York, Pergamon, 1976.

Hirsch, J.: Behavior genetics and individuality understood. *Science, 142:* 1436, 1963.

Hirsch, J.: Behavior-genetic analysis and its biosocial consequences. *Seminars in Psychiatry, 2:*89, 1970.

Hirsch, J., and Vetta, A.: The misconceptions of behavior genetics. *Ricerche di Psicologia,* February, 1978.

Hoepfner, R., Nummedal, S.G., and Stern, C. (Eds.): *CSE-ECRC Preschool/Kindergarten Test Evaluations; CSE Elementary School Test Evaluations; CSE Junior High School Test Evaluations; CSE Secondary School Test Evaluations.* Los Angeles, Center for the Study of Evaluation, 1976.

Jensen, A.R.: How much can we boost IQ and scholastic achievement? *Harvard Educational Review, 39:*1, 1969.

Johnson, W., Marr, J., and Younger, E.: *Preschool Test Matrix: Individual Test Descriptions.* Lexington, Coordinating Office for Regional Resource Centers, 1976.

Kuhn, T.: *The Structure of Scientific Revolutions.* Chicago, University of Chicago Press, 1962.

Labov, W.: The study of language in its social context. In Fishman, J.A. (Ed.): *Advances in the Sociology of Language.* The Hague, Mouton, 1971.

Labov, W., Cohen, P., Robins, C., and Lewis, J.: *A Study of Non-standard English of Negro and Puerto Rican Speakers.* Cooperative Research Project
No. 3288, 1968.

Lambert, W.E., and Tucker, G.R.: *Bilingual Education of Children: The St. Lambert Experiment.* Rowley, Newbury House, 1972.

Lesser, G.S., Fifer, G., and Clark, D.H.: Mental abilities of children from different social-class and cultural groups. *Monographs of the Society for Research in Child Development, 30,* 1965.

Maccoby, E.E., and Jacklin, C.N.: *The Psychology of Sex Differences.* Stanford, Stanford University, 1974.

Mercer, J.R.: IQ: The lethal label. *Psychology Today, 6:*44, 1972.

Mercer, J.R.: *SOMPA: System of Multicultural Pluralistic Assessment: Technical Manual.* New York, Psychological Corporation, 1979.

Oakland, T. (Ed.): *Psychological and Educational Assessment of Minority Children.* New York, Brunner/Mazel, 1977.

Oakland, T., and Matuszek, P.: Using tests in non-discrimatory assessment. In Oakland, T. (Ed.): *Psychological and Educational Assessment of Minority Children.* New York, Brunner/Mazel, 1977.

Oller, J.W., Jr.: *Language Tests at School.* London, Longman, 1979.

Oller, J.W., Jr.: Language as intelligence? *Language Learning,* December, 1981.

Oller, J.W., Jr., and Perkins, K. (Eds.): *Language in Education: Testing the Tests.* Rowley, Newbury House, 1978.

Oller, J.W., Jr., and Perkins, K.:   *Research in Language Testing*. Rowley, Newbury House, 1980.

Oller, J.W., Jr., and Streiff, V.:   Dictation: A test of grammar-based expectancies. *English Language Learning, 30*:25, 1975.

Omark, D.R.:   The group: A factor or an epiphenomenon in evolution. In Omark, D.R., Strayer, F.F., and Freedman, D.G. (Eds.):   *Dominance Relations: An Ethological View of Human Conflict and Social Interaction*. New York, Garland, 1980a.

Omark, D.R.:   Human ethology: A holistic perspective. In Omark, D.R., Strayer, F.F., and Freedman, D.G. (Eds.):   *Dominance Relations: An Ethological View of Human Conflict and Social Interaction*. New York, Garland, 1980b.

Omark, D.R.:   The Umwelt and cognitive development. In Omark, D.R., Strayer, F.F., and Freedman, D.G. (Eds.):   *Dominance Relations: An Ethological View of Human Conflict and Social Interaction*. New York, Garland, 1980c.

Omark, D.R.:   Conceptualizations of bilingual children: Testing the norm. In Erickson, J.G. and Omark, D.R. (Eds.):   *Communication Assessment of the Bilingual, Bicultural Child*. Baltimore, University Park, 1981a.

Omark, D.R.:   Pragmatics and ethological techniques for the observational assessment of children's communicative abilities. In Erickson, J.G. and Omark, D.R. (Eds.):   *Communication Assessment of the Bilingual, Bicultural Child*. Baltimore, University Park, 1981b.

Omark, D.R., and Edelman, M.S.:   The development of attention structures in young children. In Chance, M.R.A. and Larsen, R.R. (Eds.):   *The Social Structure of Attention*. New York, John Wiley, 1976.

Omark, D.R., Strayer, F.F., and Freedman, D.G. (Eds.):   *Dominance Relations: An Ethological View of Human Conflict and Social Interaction*. New York, Garland, 1980.

Omark, D.R., and Watson, D.L.:   *Nondiscrimatory Assessment: In-Service Manual*. Sacramento, California State Department of Education, 1981.

Ortiz, M.R. de: The acquisition of Spanish as a native language. In Dulay, H. and Burt, M. (Eds.):   *Testing and Teaching Communicatively Handicapped Hispanic Children*. Sacramento, California State Department of Education, 1980.

Pacheco, R., Crespo, O., Petry, P., and Omark, D.R.:   Peer perceptions of Latino and Anglo children: A comparison of two classroom models. In preparation.

Piaget, J.:   *Biology and Knowledge*. Chicago, University of Chicago, 1971.

Piaget, J., and Inhelder, B.:   *The Psychology of the Child*. New York, Basic Books, 1969.

Pletcher, B.P., Locks, N.A., Reynolds, D.F., and Sisson, B.G.:   *A Guide to Assessment Instruments for Limited English Speaking Students*. New York, Santillana, 1978.

Reyes, R., and Craddock, J.R.: Chicano Spanish. In Dulay, H., and Burt, M. (Eds.): *Testing and Teaching Communicatively Handicapped Hispanic Children.* Sacramento, California State Department of Education, 1980.

Sattler, J.: *Assessment of Children's Intelligence.* Philadelphia, W.B. Saunders, 1974.

Silverman, R.J., Noa, J.K., and Russel, R.H.: *Oral Language Tests for Bilingual Students: An Evaluation of Language Dominance and Proficiency Instruments.* Portland, Center for Bilingual Education, Northwest Regional Education Laboratory, 1976.

Stodolsky, S.S., and Lesser, G.: Learning patterns in the disadvantaged. *Harvard Educational Review, 37:*546, 1967.

Stump, T.: Cloze and dictation tasks as predictors of intelligence and achievement scores. In Oller, J.W., Jr., and Perkins, K. (Eds.): *Language in Education: Testing the Tests.* Rowley, Newbury House, 1978.

Suro, R.: Schools' bilingual program working here, study shows. *Chicago Tribune,* Feb. 2, 1978.

Trueba, H.T.: Research, journalism or politics? In Trueba, H.T., and Barnett-Mizrahi, C. (Eds.): *Bilingual Multicultural Education and the Classroom Teacher: From Theory to Practice.* Rowley, Newbury House, 1979.

Watson, P.: I.Q.: The racial gap. *Psychology Today, 6:*48, 1972.

Watson, D.L., Omark, D.R., Grouell, S., and Heller, B.: *Nondiscrimatory Assessment: A Practitioner's Guide.* Sacramento, California State Department of Education, 1980.

Williams, R., and Wolfram, W.: *Social Dialects: Differences vs. Disorders.* Rockville, MD, American Speech and Hearing Association, 1977.

Zajonc, R.B.: Family configuration and intelligence. *Science, 192:*227, 1976.

3

Psychological and Educational Assessment of Bilingual Children

Richard R. DeBlassie
Juan N. Franco

Mexican Americans and Native Americans represent two of a number of bilingual ethnic minority groups that are presently found in the United States. There are many professionals and nonprofessionals who feel that children from these and other minority groups, especially those children in the lower socioeconomic stratum, have failed to accrue many of the advantages necessary to survive or function effectively in the American mainstream. Our educational system has not been particularly responsive to these children we choose to refer to as culturally different and who are generally bilingual. One could suggest that many of these children (including Native Americans, Mexican Americans, Puerto Ricans, and others) have been "pushed out," as opposed to "dropping out" of school because of the irresponsiveness of the educational system.

One of the most damaging and devastating practices that has been carried out by our schools is that of psychological and educational assessment and/or testing culturally different youth and using, or perhaps more appropriately *misusing*, the results of these assessment devices. Such practices have resulted in the mislabeling or misplacing of an enormous number of these youth in special education or other classes. The lack of experiential background in the areas or skills measured by most standardized tests on the part of culturally different youth is the major reason for their typical low performance on tests.

The misplacement or labeling of these youth on the basis of one, or perhaps two, psychological tests has been in practice for many years. This practice has resulted in what is tantamount to a "rape" of these children.

Nevertheless, many minority group counselors and psychologists, including the present authors, feel that for years assessment devices have served a "gatekeeping" function. The use of these devices represents one of the major elements in retarding the social mobility of the cultural different bilingual child and in blocking the path for those who are poor and deprived to share in the educational opportunities and, by extension, the goods of society.

In spite of the many injustices experienced by culturally different bilingual youth as a result of the misuse of tests and other assessment devices, it is not necessary to abandon, eliminate, or burn "those damned" tests. A positive approach entails intensifying the efforts to teach or reteach the users of assessment devices more appropriate testing and assessment procedures and methods. Of particular importance are such things as impressing upon test and assessment data users that (a) standardized tests are oriented toward and biased in favor of those individuals who are in the American mainstream of society; (b) standardized test results should be used in conjunction with other types of data, e.g., teacher observations, autobiographies, and checklists; (c) standardized tests are typically low in predictive validity when used with culturally different individuals, athough somewhat effective as diagnostic indicators of their strengths and weaknesses; (d) assessment data can and should be used to determine intervention strategies and/or teaching approaches involving corrective, remedial, and enrichment programs for these youth; and (e) assessment data should be used in positive and constructive ways to aid culturally different bilingual children in developing their potential and/or latent abilities.

Problems in Assessing Bilingual Children

Discriminatory Practices and Consequences

That many bilingual children, particularly those in the lower socioeconomic stratum, have been, in effect, shortchanged in acquiring the necessary skills to perform well in our white middle-class-oriented school system has been well established. Education is the major factor that can stand to enhance these children's chances of establishing their identity and becoming self-sufficient, contributing members of our society. However, a number of problems in the educational system have been encountered by these youth.

One of the major educational problems encountered by bilingual children is their general inability to cope with standardized tests. Mexican American children, for example, start out fairly close to Anglos in measured achievement in many areas. The two groups remain in the same relative position until the third or fourth grade, when Mexican Americans generally fall slightly behind and continue to do so until there is a significant disparity in favor of Anglos throughout adolescence. Several factors seem to influence this decline in achievement on the part of Mexican American youth. Pollack and Menacker (1971) suggest the following:

> Since English, reading, and language arts heavily dominate inter-mediate school curriculums, there is little or no attempt at solving problems of students who are falling behind in mathematics. Heavy doses of reading further handicap the child who can speak Spanish but is not instructed in his or her native tongue. The amount of work suddenly begins to increase during the intermediate grades. Teachers are concerned very much with continuity and sequential learning, and if the students do not grasp the subject matter well, they fall behind. Unless the teacher at this intermediate level can break out of this traditional teacher practice and stop viewing learning as simply a lock-step process, the result will be a compul-sion to cover the material in the curriculum guide without stopping long enough to promote mastery in students (p. 37).

Another factor that may impinge upon measurement and evaluation devices used with culturally different bilingual youth is that they are not represented distinctly in the standardization groups used by those who construct standardized tests (*see* Chapter 2). Most standardized tests have a middle-class bias that is rarely considered when interpreting the results of tests used with culturally different bilingual youth. That most of these youngsters are not of the middle socioeconomic stratum should suggest that these tests are of questionable validity for these youth. For example, the results are nevertheless widely misused in selecting, classifying, and stigmat-izing Mexican American youngsters. Jensen (1961), for example, in evaluat-ing IQ tests that discriminate between fast and slow learners, found that, although they were moderately accurate for Anglo Americans, they were inadequate for predicting performance of Mexican American pupils.

Catterall (1970), alluding to the consequences of using standardized tests with culturally different Mexican American youth, enumerates several concerns of the parents of minority group children over the testing and placement of their children in various special education programs in California. Parents of minority children, including Mexican Americans, are concerned that (a) their children are overrepresented in programs of special education; (b) education has tended to become a means of keeping their children from participating and profitting more freely in the rewards of this society; (c) group testing tends to discriminate against their children; (d) a self-fulfilling hypothesis is established so the child's level of functioning tends to be allowed to lower to meet the teacher's expectations; (e) once their children are placed in EMR classes, they are indelibly marked and can never get out; (f) districts, in order to increase their revenue, apply pressure to put children in special education; and (g) the results obtained from individually administered IQ tests are generally invalid because the psychologists do not speak or understand Spanish (pp. 145–154).

That many Mexican American children are misclassified and assigned to special education classes based on standardized test results is also suggested by Leal (1976). He points out that misclassification of Mexican American children in special education settings is not peculiar only to Texas where he did research on the problem, but a national concern as well.

The major emphasis in this chapter, therefore, revolves around the idea that there is a need for those working with culturally different bilingual students, e.g., teachers, counselors, administators, and psychologists, and for other children to understand and recognize some of the pitfalls in the use of standardized psychological and educational tests with these youth. There is no doubt that many psychological and educational tests are inimical to the development and education of Mexican American children. The tests are also middle-class oriented and, therefore, biased against lower socioeconomic level children. Notice that the emphasis is upon the questionable validity of standardized tests for lower socioeconomic Mexican American children. The authors' experience and studies indicate that middle or high socioeconomic level Mexican American children do not perform at a low level on standardized tests when compared with their lower socioeconomic level Mexican American counterparts. Middle or upper socioeconomic level children have, for the most part, become a part of the modal or dominant American cultural mainstream. Thus, they have acquired the skills and experiences that help them perform well on tests.

Since critics of the standardized test, especially its use (or misuse) with minority group children, have had little if any success in eliminating its use with such children, it is felt that such tests are here to stay for some time. If so, a better approach would be to orient and demonstrate to standardized test users (teachers, counselors, administrators, psychologists, etc.) its pitfalls, as well as what can be considered its legitimate use(s) with lower socioeconomic level bilingual children.

Assessment Instruments

While the use of standardized tests in the schools has existed for about seventy years, the testing movement has certainly not been without its critics. Criticisms of testing, however, have never been so controversial and its critics so vociferous as within the last twenty years (Oakland, 1973). One of the most recent criticisms of standardized tests is reported in the March–April 1977 issue of *Today's Education*. In this article McKenna (1977) suggests that of the social sciences, economics is known as the "dismal science." In education, he suggests, the "dismal science" has to be standardized testing. He lists six major reasons for this dilemma:

(1) its history is ominous; (2) much test content is unimportant or irrelevant; (3) the structure and formats of tests are confusing and

misleading; (4) the process of administering the tests is demeaning, wasteful of time, and counter-productive; (5) the application of statistics that result from test scores distorts reality; and (6) it is difficult, if not impossible, to ensure that test results will be used either to improve student learning or to help teachers improve instruction (p. 35).

These criticisms seem to question the usefulness of standardized tests. More specifically, they challenge the soundness and utility of educational and psychological tests as they apply to all persons. In the last fifteen years standardized tests have had an even more devastating attack by representatives of Mexican Americans, Blacks, Native Americans, and other minority or culturally different groups. Miller (1974) captures the essence of these attacks by suggesting that one of the most controversial complex issues affecting the education of minority children in America has been the role of educational and psychological testing, and further, that this controversy is the result of long and ugly racism.

Samuda (1975) also suggests that the debate concerning standardized tests, and especially the misinterpretation of the results of scores of minorities, has intensified in recent years. He feels the public has been alerted to the implications of testing that preserve the *staus quo* and thus relegate Blacks and other minorities to an inferior position in the larger society. Samuda goes on to suggest that, so far, though relatively unchallenged in their selective and censoring function, the testing organizations have been subjected to a national wave of disenchantment, skepticism, and hostility. This is evidenced by numerous lawsuits and court rulings, as well as by the positions taken by the Association of Black Psychologists and the American Personnel and Guidance Association.

The National Education Association, the popular press, the courts, civil rights organizations, state and federal agencies, and others have pointed to the failure of the test-publishing industry to consider fully the cultural and linguistic differences of minority children when constructing psychological tests (DeAvila and Havassy , 1974). They suggest, furthermore, that test publishers have responded by translating existing intelligence and nationally normed achievement tests into other languages such as Spanish, adjusting norms for ethnic groups, and attempting to construct culture-free tests. Each approach involves distinct problems that will be elaborated below.

Assessment Data: Users, Uses, and Misuses

The implications and consequences of the uses, abuses, and misuses of standardized tests by assessment data users with culturally different bilingual youth are varied and numerous. Ebel (1966), for example, enumerates four very real social consequences of testing for all youth which appear to have even more serious implications for bilingual youth. He suggests that testing may:

1. Place an indelible stamp of intellectual status on a child, thereby predetermining his or her social status as an adult and possibly doing considerable harm to his or her self-esteem and educational motivation.
2. Lead to an overly narrow conception of ability, thereby eliminating the diversity of talent sometimes associated with creativity.
3. Place testers in a position to control education.
4. Encourage impersonal, inflexible, and mechanistic processes of evaluation and determination with a corresponding loss in essential human freedoms.

In discussing the education and social consequences of psychological testing of American minorities, Samuda (1975) suggests that there seems to be a widespread belief among teachers and the general public that the learning situation is improved when classes have pupils of more or less the same level of ability (homogeneous groups). Research studies have shown, according to Samuda, that ability grouping, which is usually based on standardized test results, exercises harmful influence on the attainment and self-concept of those students placed in the lower ability classes, e.g., socioeconomic separation, mislabeling, racial discrimination, and unequal educational opportunity.

The mislabeling of culturally different children and their overrepresentation in the lowest ability classes at all educational levels is an observable and easily documented fact. The classes for slow learners, the educable mentally retarded (EMR), and the trainable mentally retarded (TMR) contain significantly greater proportions of culturally different minority youth than of Anglo youth. In Leal (1976), for example, the results of intelligence tests for Mexican American children are generally around 10 to 20 points below Anglo norms on standardized measures. As a consequence, the EMR classes in California contain a higher proportion of Spanish surname pupils. According to the preliminary analysis of the 1969 ethnic survey, Spanish surname pupils constitute 15.22% of the general nonhandicapped population yet comprises 28.34% of the EMR enrollment in California schools. The rate of labeling Mexican American children as EMR is twice as high as the rate for Anglos (*see* Chapter 13).

While the problems of mislabeling and misclassifying are apparent in the culturally different bilingual child population throughout the United States, analysis of and solutions for such problems are complex. It would be easy to suggest that cultural variation (differences) can account for some of the misclassification problems, but this is not adequately documented or researched. Objectively, the only difference between any two cultures or subcultures is cultural difference. Each culture fosters and encourages the development of behavior that is adapted to its values and demands. Thus, the bilingual (Spanish-English) child might *appear* to be developmentally retarded, having had to cope with verbal and nonverbal problems while using both a synthetic language (Spanish) and an analytic language (English). Further, it would be too simple to suggest that conflict in deciding which of two languages to use in solving problems would slow a child, since most children are competent problem solvers and adapt quite well to both their home and school environments. This is most evident in the easy shifting between Spanish and English by most Mexican American children and adults when communicating concepts and solving verbal social problems.

In a study done in Southern California, Mercer (1971) contends that the intelligence tests presently used are to a large extent "Anglocentric"; that is, they mirror the standards, values, and experiences of the white, Anglo-Saxon middle-class person. Inevitably, the results of such tests can affect persons from a different cultural background and those of lower socioeconomic status to a greater degree. Mercer's 8-year study documents the fact that public schools had been sending more chidren to EMR classes than any of the 241 organizations, e.g., law enforcement agencies, private organizations for the EMR, medical facilities, religious organizations, and public welfare centers contacted by Mercer and co-workers. Criteria for selection and placement in such classes were based on (a) the almost exclusive reliance on IQ test scores and the almost total absence of medical diagnosis; (b) the utilization of a high cutoff score (IQ of 79 or below as compared to a recommended IQ of 69 or below) in order to draw the border line between mental retardates and normal students; and (c) the failure to take into account sociocultural factors when interpreting IQ test results.

Mercer found that over four times as many Mexicans and twice as many Blacks were enrolled in the classes for the mentally retarded, a disproportionate number for their population in California. However, when Mercer used a *two-dimensional* definition of mental retardation (that takes into consideration both intellectual performance and adaptive behavior) and when IQ scores are interpreted with the knowledge that sociocultural factors contaminate them, the racial imbalance in classes for the EMR disappeared. Consequently, she argued, approximately 75% of the children enrolled in EMR classes were mislabeled, incorrectly placed, and suffering from stigmatization and lowered self-esteem in a learning environment far from optimum.

Fallacies and Issues

There are a number of fallacies and issues involved in the use of standardized tests with bilingual minority group youth. One of the major fallacies concerning the use of standardized tests with these youth is that testing is purported to be one of the most scientific means of obtaining accurate information about students. The educational system, the news media, employment agencies, and the military reinforce the attitude that standardized test results are efficient and accurate descriptions of human behavior. A standardized test is usually defined as a sample of behavior taken at a specific point in time from which certain behaviors are inferred and/or predicted about an individual. The testing agency, e.g., school or employment agency, will typically administer a standardized test and from the individual's test score infer attributes such as intelligence, achievement, or aptitude and make selection, placement, or hiring decisions based on this score. The fallacious assumption is that the derived test score is absolute and not subject to error and, therefore, precise enough to predict whether the individual will succeed for whatever purpose the test was administered. The fallacy is apparent when major decisions are made on the basis of testing instrument scores, in many cases only one test score is used. Such scores are subject to day-by-day variation as well as the experiential background the student may or may not have acquired.

Another fallacy is that standardized tests are effective predictors of individual student behavior. For example, first or second grade Mexican American children are administered a group mental ability test. From the results, predictions are made or labels are assigned to these children indicating they will have difficulty succeeding in school. In order that standardized tests be reasonably effective predictors of individual student behavior, they should have predictive validity coefficients of .90 or above. Most tests that are considered *good* tests show predictive validity coefficients ranging from .60 to .85. This range, .60 to .85, will reasonably predict the success or failure of a *group* of culturally different Mexican American youth. However, when it comes to predicting the success of a specific Mexican American student, they leave much to be desired unless used with other substantiating data. Anastasi (1976) feels that the most frequent misgivings regarding the use of standardized tests with minority group members stem from the misinterpretation of scores. If a minority examinee obtains a low score on an aptitude test or a deviant score on a personality test, she feels it is essential to investigate why the child did so.

It has been established that most standardized tests are "culturally biased" and therefore of questionable use with culturally different bilingual youth. In an effort to handle this bias, some test constructors have attempted to establish culture-fair tests that would "equalize" and/or eliminate the middle-class bias. This approach, it is assumed, would give a more accurate portrayal of the intelligence, achievement, or aptitude of the minority child. Yet Anastasi suggests that culture-free or culture-fair tests are fallacious: "No single test can be universally applicable or equally 'fair' to all cultures...Every test tends to favor persons from the culture in which it was developed...It is unlikely, moreover, that any test can be equally 'fair' to more than one cultural group, especially if the cultures are quite dissimilar" (p. 345). In addition, DeAvila and Havassy (1974) find that the testing industry has difficulty when responding to criticism of conventional IQ tests by attempting to create culture-free tests:

> Such tests are difficult to construct, and many question whether they achieve their goal of being free of cultural bias. Tests of mental ability and/or achievement attempt to determine the ability of a child to manipulate certain elements of a problem into a predetermined solution. It is difficult to conceive of test elements equally familiar to all ethnic or cultural groups especially when test developers are members of a group themselves (p. 78).

A fourth fallacy in using standardized tests with bilingual children is the assumption there is conclusive evidence that minority group children tend to do better on tests when the examiner is also of the same race or ethnicity as the examinee. Because of an apparent lack of good empirical research, the assumption that same-race or same-ethnic examiners positively affect the performance of culturally different youth comes into serious question (Anastasi, 1976).

A fifth fallacy in testing bilingual youth is the practice by some test publishers of translating existing intelligence and nationally normed achievement tests into Spanish. DeAvila and Havassy (1974) note that translating existing intelligence or achievement tests for non-English-speaking children often creates problems:

1. Regional differences within a language make it difficult to use a single translation in a standardized testing situation where examiner and examinee are permitted virtually no interaction.
2. Monolingual translations are inappropriate because the language familiar to non-English-speaking children is often a combination of two languages as in the case of Tex-Mex.
3. Many non-English-speaking children have never learned to read in their spoken language. For example, many Chicano children speak Spanish but have had no instruction in reading Spanish (pp. 77–78).

Our experience using the Spanish version of the *Wechsler Intelligence Scale for Children* (WISC), standardized in Puerto Rico, with Mexican American children in New Mexico attests to DeAvila and Havassy's notions regarding the futility of translating existing tests into Spanish for use with these youth.

A sixth fallacy is the assumption that the establishment of regional or ethnic norms can compensate for the low performance of culturally different youth on standardized tests. Such a practice leads to lower expectations for minorities, which in turn may lower children's aspirations to succeed. Furthermore, ethnic norms do not take into consideration the complex reasons *why* minority children, on the average, score lower than Anglo

American children on IQ tests (DeAvila and Havassy, 1974). Ethnic norms are potentially dangerous from the social perspective because they provide a basis for invidious comparisons between racial groups (*see* Chapter 2).

Many of the issues raised in using standardized tests with bilingual youth are related to the fallacies above. Issues of major importance have reached the courts; other issues are being dealt with by concerned parents, school officials, and psychologists in a variety of ways. The following issues have been identified as areas where changes need to be made (Brown, 1976):

1. State policies and guidelines for admission into EMR classes existed, but were not always followed.
2. Mexican American and Black children are misplaced and/or placed disproportionately in EMR classes.
3. Placements are based on only IQ tests which are biased toward Anglo, middle-class Midwestern children.
4. Misplaced children did *not* receive a challenging, intellectually stimulating education.
5. Consent for placement is not an informed, true, or valid consent.
6. Misplaced children are stigmatized for life.
7. Teachers do not interpret tests correctly or use them properly.
8. Psychological, economical, educational, and social damage results for the misplaced child.
9. Procedures for retesting are nonexistent.
10. Testers do not understand children tested, either linguistically or culturally (pp. 4–5).

Cody (1968) points out that using psychometric devices when analyzing standardized test performance with culturally different youth lead to the following conclusions:

1. The usual methods of testing and test interpretation are not likely to be of value with the culturally deprived.
2. Conservation of time does not appear to stand out as an advantage of testing the culturally deprived.
3. Paper and pencil tests that require interpretation of writing seem unsuited for working with the socially disadvantaged.
4. Personality inventories seem to render them of little value with youngsters who were predominantly from the lower class.
5. Perhaps fewer tests, selected for specific purposes, and used analytically in individual sessions with students, can be helpful.
6. Mass testing with currently available standardized instruments seems to provide little new information.

Nondiscriminatory Testing

Efficacy of Standardized Tests

In testing Mexican American youth, the authors have found that the most viable approach to using standardized tests and other data collected on these youth is what some would call eclectic. This approach, in essence, represents a distillation and integration of some of the trends referred to above. Basically, our position or approach in testing and applying test and nontest materials when working with culturally different youth assumes that both test makers and test users need to work together to improve the use and interpretation of all data.

Most standardized tests are culturally biased, favoring the middle-class mainstream, and are indeed adverse to culturally different youth if used for the purposes of predicting their probable success in academic and other settings, e.g., employment, selection for higher education. These consequences, however, are not a function of the tests themselves but more a function of the manner in which they are used and interpreted. There is a need to train or retrain those persons using tests in terms of their proper uses, delimitations, and limitations. There is also a need on the part of test makers to include culturally different youth in their standardization groups to a greater extent than in the past.

The authors would also suggest there is a greater need to train those who work with culturally different youth in the construction and use of nontest data collection devices such as rating scales, interviews, observations, and case studies. They should also be trained and encouraged to collect and use demographic data such as the socioeconomic status of the family, familial and cultural characteristics, and other information which would be an asset in understanding children totally in relationship to their environment.

Finally, we stress that the use of test and nontest data with culturally different Mexican American and other minority group youth should place emphasis on description and prescription rather than on selection and prediction. More specifically, we submit that most standardized tests, even though culturally biased in favor of the middle-class mainstream and inappropriate for culturally different bilingual children in terms of selection and prediction, can still serve a very effective function as diagnostic indicators. As such, most of these tests are good *diagnostically* in that they give a good indication of where the child is at a given point in time in terms of abilities and limitations. Once this diagnosis is made, using both standardized tests and nontest data, the test user can proceed to describe who each student is and plan and prescribe educational and/or other strategies to enhance each individual's learning potential. In short, the *predictive validity* of most standardized test scores is poor, while the *diagnostic validity* is excellent if they are used in conjunction with other data such as nontest data and demographic information.

The essence of using tests with culturally different bilingual youth is not to "burn the tests" or to declare a moratorium on their use. Their efficacious use lies in test users' prudent application and nondiscriminatory use of them. Oakland (1977) states:

> Assessment practices should be undertaken with the intentions of improving children's development and helping appropriate persons make wise and informed decisions.... It is perplexing, and disturbing, that Black, Hispanic, and other minority children are overrepresented in classes for the mentally retarded while underrepresented in classes for the physically handicapped or gifted. Many persons attribute this situation to discriminatory assessment practices and suggest that their flaws are so widespread that formal assessment practices should be discontinued altogether (p. iii).

We would hope that our approach to testing bilingual youth would be perceived as an approach that will enable test users to make intelligent and well-informed decisions as to what constitutes effective assessment-, diagnostic-, prescriptive-, enrichment-based programs so their use of tests will enhance the development and education of culturally different Mexican American and other bicultural youth and minimize scoring biases due to ethnic and/or socioeconomic characteristics. This would, hopefully, ensure that the use of tests would project and imply *nondiscriminatory* assessment and use. Testing culturally different bilingual youth demands such a nondiscriminatory approach to assessment.

A Recommended Model for Nondiscriminatory Assessment

One relatively new nondiscriminatory assessment model is offered by Tucker in an undated manuscript. He suggests that the categories of "mental retardation," "emotional disturbance," "learning disabilities," and to some extent "minimal brain dysfunction" give rise to the greatest problems in biased (discriminatory) placement, and hence in biased (discriminatory) assessment. In order to minimize or overcome bias in testing that results in biased placement, he suggests the Comprehensive Individual Assessment model. This comprehensive model or *diagnostic-intervention* process consists of (a) historical-etiological information; (b) current assessable characteristics; (c) specific treatments or interventions; and (d) particular diagnosis. In order to attain this comprehensiveness it is necessary to use a combination of any number of assessment techniques or models. It is also important to emphasize *parental* involvement, with the ongoing option of retaining the child in the regular classroom with intervening strategies provided by the regular classroom teacher(s).

Special education placement is the last option, to be utilized only after all other alternatives have been eliminated. Only then comes traditional psychological assessment. Previous test scores and other data will have an impact on its interpretation. Tucker enumerates the sources of information relevant to comprehensive assessment of a student:

1. Observational data (from teachers and others who know the child).
2. Other data available (data from cumulative records, medical exams, etc.).
3. Language dominance tests.
4. Educational assessment data.
5. Sensory-motor and/or psycholinguistic assessment data.
6. Adaptive behavior data.
7. Medical and/or developmental data.
8. Personality assessment data, including self-report.
9. Intellectual assessment data.

Tucker summarizes his model by stating: "Nonbiased testing (which we refer to as nondiscriminatory testing) simply means reducing the chance that a child is incorrectly placed in special classes and increasing the use of intervention programs which facilitate his or her physical, social, emotional, and academic development" (p. 51).

Conclusion

It is our hope that more test users carefully consider the foregoing suggestions when attempting to minimize the discriminatory testing processes and practices that have prevailed in the past. It is only through such approach that culturally different bilingual children stand a chance to develop their intellectual, social, and psychological potential. Equal opportunity to develop their aptitudes and potential is all they request. Equal opportunity to develop their potential is what they deserve.

References

Anastasi, A.:   *Psychological Testing*, 4th ed. New York, Macmillan, 1976.
Brown, C.E.:   *Testing Mexican-Americans: A Review of the Literature.* Unpublished paper, New Mexico State University, 1976.
Catterall, C.D.:   Concerns relating to the testing and special education of minority children. In Johnson, H.S., and Hernandez-M, W.J. (Eds.): *Educating the Mexican American.* Valley Forge, Judson, 1970.

Cody, J.J.: Appraisal of disadvantaged youth. In Amos, W.E., and Grambs, J.D. (Eds.): *Counseling the Disadvantaged Youth.* Englewood Cliffs, Prentice-Hall, 1968.

DeAvila, E.A., and Havassy, B.: The testing of minority children—A neo-Piagetian approach. *Today's Education,* 63:72–75, 1974.

Ebel, R.L.: The social consequences of educational testing. In Anastasi, A. (Ed.): *Testing Problems in Perspective.* Washington, American Council on Education, 1966.

Jensen, A.R.: Learning abilities of Mexican-American and Anglo-American children. *California Journal of Educational Research,* 12:147–159, 1961.

Leal, A.: The need for proper classification of Mexican-American children. In Mukherjee, A.K., Ander, S., Sluyter, G.V., and Leal, A. (Eds.): *Measurement of Intellectual Potential in Mexican-American School-Age Children.* Corpus Christi, Corpus Christi Public Schools, 1976.

McKenna, B.: What's wrong with standardized testing? *Today's Education,* 66:35–38, 1977.

Mercer, J.R.: Institutionalized Anglocentrism: Labeling mental retardates in the public schools. In Orleans, P., and Russel, W. (Eds.): *Race, Change, and Urban Society.* Urban Affairs Annual Review, vol. V., Los Angeles, Sage, 1971.

Miller, L.P.: *The Testing of Black Students: A Symposium.* Englewood Cliffs, Prentice-Hall, 1974.

Oakland, T.: Assessing minority group children: Challenges for school psychologists. *Journal of School Psychology,* 11:294–303, 1973.

Oakland, T. (Ed.): *Psychological and Educational Assessment of Minority Children.* New York, Brunner/Mazel, 1977.

Pollack, E.W., and Menacker, J.: *Spanish-Speaking Students and Guidance.* New York, Houghton Mifflin, 1971.

Samuda, R.J.: *Psychological Testing of American Minorities: Issues and Consequences.* New York, Harper and Row, 1975.

Tucker, J.A.: Operationalizing the diagnostic-intervention process. In: *Non-Biased Assessment of Minority Group Children with Bias Toward None.* Lexington, Coordinating Office for Regional Resource Center, University of Kentucky, (undated).

4

Testing Proficiencies and Diagnosing Language Disorders in Bilingual Children

John W. Oller, Jr.

This chapter is divided into two parts. The first deals with a theoretical framework and includes certain definitions and axiomatic assumptions. The second part deals with the practical side of testing and diagnosis.

For those who, as Krashen (1982) says, like to hear the punch lines early, some key points may be mentioned. It is assumed throughout that a bilingual is an *advantaged* person. It is claimed that the processes of language testing and diagnosis, though they must include evaluation of the surface forms of speech, are fundamentally deeper problems. Language is deeper, wider, and richer than speech. Further, it is suggested that a prior question for the "how-to" section is what can or cannot be tested. Related issues are: What is language proficiency? How does it differ from intelligence, school achievement, or personality? Is language proficiency divisible into multiple components? Do such components interact so as to form an integral whole, a unified system?

It is claimed that the differentiation of psychological constructs such as intelligence, achievement, personality, and language proficiency is often a matter of arbitrary judgment. The difficulty is especially acute when it comes to testing and interpreting test data. The view that language proficiency is an integral unity is in contrast with the claim that language skills can be sorted into many distinguishable and sometimes unrelated component skills. It will be seen that these apparently antithetical views are actually complementary rather than contradictory. Finally, it is suggested that evaluative procedures which focus on the use of language to convey meaning are superior to those that pinpoint particular elements of surface syntax, morphology, or phonolgy.

Theoretical Groundwork

Definitions

Test. Any instrument, technique, or interactive procedure that is used to influence decisions concerning educational or therapeutic treatment of persons, especially those procedures that give quantifiable results.

Diagnosis. The process of using tests to shape or inform a treatment in order to fit it to the needs of a person or group, i.e., the process of interpreting performances on tests.

Speech test. Any test that focuses primarily on overtly articulated elements of language—to be distinguished from a language test. A speech test in important respects is analogous to a test of penmanship. Attention is placed on surface form, with little or no regard for meaning. Perceptual tasks that require phoneme discrimination in nonsense contexts are speech tests inasmuch as they focus on surface forms without any associated propositional meanings.

Language test. Any test whose primary focus is on the manipulation of the meanings underlying overt manifestations of language in speech, sign, writing, gesture, and the like. A language test, unlike a speech test, therefore, is more like a test of comprehension, intelligence, or knowledge. It requires the use of language for the communication and expression of ideas.

Language disorders. Difficulties in the manipulation of propositional meanings which are likely to interfere with mental growth and development.

Bilingual balance or dominance. If an individual or society uses two or more languages with equal facility, the languages may be said to be *balanced.* This is a condition that rarely exists, however, even in individuals and probably never in societies. The more common condition is *dominance,* where one language is used with greater facility than the other(s). Generally, *degrees of dominance* can be distinguished.

Domains of usage and diglossia. In certain well-known cases of societal bilingualism, such as Spanish and Guarani in Uruguay and Paraguay, *domains of usage* are distinguished. Spanish is generally preferred for formal communication in such context as school and business, while Guarani is reserved for use with family or friends in informal context such as the home. In cases where the domains of usage do not generally coincide, a condition of *diglossia* is said to exist. Sociolinguists also commonly believe that relative proficiency in two or more languages will tend to differ as a function of domains of usage.

Some Basic Premises

Language is deeper than speech. If language were merely speech, there would be little or no reason to expect a high degree of correlation between performance on tasks that directly involve speech and performance on tasks that do not. For instance, there would be little or no correlation between reading comprehension and speaking ability. Similarly, the correlation between speaking and writing tasks would be nil and, even more dramatically, correlations between proficiencies across languages with radically different surface forms (speech manifestations) should be negligible. However, none of these predictions fits the facts. Studies have shown over and over again that substantial positive correlations exist in the above mentioned cases, and sound theoretical arguments can be offered to explain these correlations (*see* Oller, 1979, 1981, 1982, 1983; Oller and Perkins, 1978,1980). There is also evidence that proficiency in one's native language is a moderately good predictor of attained proficiency in a second language (Cummins, 1979, 1983).

Summing the findings of many studies, it may be said that correlations across tasks in different modalities, e.g., visual versus auditory, are apt to fall in the .5 to .9 range, while correlations between proficiencies in a first and second language fall roughly between .3 and .7. Though there remains a great deal of controversy (*see* Oller, 1983) with cautious interpretation of the evidence, it may be inferred that one general language factor pervades many language processing tasks. Moreover, some of these tasks involve speech while others do not.

In addition to the empirical evidence, there are purely logical arguments showing that language is, in principle, deeper than speech. For instance, when an infant's arms are raised, indicating a desire to be picked up, the propositional meaning does not involve speech. Normal infants engage in this sort of propositional directive behavior well before the emergence of speech. Evidence that the child is relying on a propositional form of reasoning comes from even the most cursory examination of the grammatical relations implicit in the child's actions. For instance, in reaching toward an adult the infant takes account of the potential agency, the person to whom the arms are raised. This agent is invited to perform an action on the child (who takes the place of a grammatical object, or more specifically a benefactive patient). Or, to take another example, the same child may negate a proposition concerning ingestion of food by refusing another bite during a meal. A conjoining of propositional meanings is implicit in the sequence of events that begins with a search for a certain object and ends with that object in the infant's mouth (*see* Bates, 1976).

While it is correct to reason that sensible speech entails prior language proficiency, it is not true that possession of language proficiency requires manifestation in speech. For a dramatic case of "language without speech" see the classic study by Lenneberg (1962). Also, signing systems of deaf persons constitute evidence against any argument that would equate language with speech. We may conclude, therefore, that language is more than speech even though speech is the most common and most salient manifestation of language. Uttered tokens of speech are merely the most common public manifestations of language which also include gestures, sign systems, and writing. Language, it seems, is somewhat autonomous of its manifest forms.

The totality is greater than the sum of its parts. Whether we think of language processing in terms of specific structures or in terms of systems, the totality of elements is greater than the parts taken separately.[1] Consider, for instance, the meaning of the phrase, *the red headed woman.* The word *red* has a meaning pragmatically limited to the range of colors of human hair. Moreover, the words *the, headed,* and *woman* are constrained by the grammatical relationships within the phrase as well as the lexical values of these elements. Consider the various meanings of an element such as *headed,* divorced from its phrasal context. If the phrase *the red headed woman* were viewed as the sum of its components' separate lexical meanings, it would be quite impossible to discover its ordinary interpretation.

As Ferdinand de Saussure emphasized, language is hierarchically arranged along two rather different dimensions of structure. Elements are categorically (paradigmatically) associated by virtue of the syntactic, semantic, and pragmatic classes in which they participate. They are also temporally (syntagmatically) associated with each other in the stream of speech (or in some other manifest form of language such as writing or signing). For instance, the distinctive sound represented by the letter *p* in English is paradigmatically associated with a whole class of contrasting articulatory and auditory events, e.g., those represented usually by the letters *t, k, b,* and so forth. However, in the word *pat* the letter *p* is syntagmatically linked with two other elements that, by virtue of linking, constitute a different element. Since the meaning of this newly constructed element cannot possibly be predicted from the separate values of its contributing parts, again totality is greater than the sum of its parts.

At each level of the language hierarchy, from sound features to sound segments to syllables, meaningful elements, i.e., morphemes (in linguists' jargon), words, phrases, clauses, and discourse; the elements at each higher level acquire properties that their constituent parts do not possess as separate entities. This premise has important consequences for language testing and diagnosis in general.

Not only do whole units of structure have properties not contained in their separate parts, but systems of language processing acquire properties through interaction of their subsystems that the subsystems did not possess as separate entities. For instance, presenting a talk from notes, with occasional quotations to be read, charts to be interpreted, and diagrams to be drawn on the blackboard entails a great deal of interaction between whatever subsystems exist for the skills of reading, writing, and speaking, not to mention listening, and specialized knowledge.

For this reason, it makes little sense to associate a particular component, say phonology, with only certain modalities, i.e., speaking and listening. Phonological information is undoubtedly utilized also in reading and writing. Consider that knowledge of how a word is pronounced may help a great deal in writing it, e.g., writing the correct number of syllables. Phonology enters into literacy skills in even more obvious ways if the activity of the articulators is examined through electromyographic techniques (Goodman, 1971). Even superior readers'articulatory muscles show a great deal of activity during silent reading. It may be expected that the same will be true of listening comprehension. In similar ways, knowledge of written forms may help in deciphering or remembering oral forms.

More important to the argument under consideration is that there can be similar arguments for any combination of interacting subsystems associated with language processing tasks. The chief consequence for language testing and diagnosis is that the techniques employed must reflect the relevant properties of the interacting systems and subsystems they are intended to evaluate. Because a task of listening comprehension involves complex interactions between knowledge of phonology, morphology, lexicon, syntax, semantics, pragmatics, and perhaps other skills and knowledge not yet described, it makes little sense to try to measure abilities to perform such tasks with highly focused tests, e.g., a test of phoneme discrimination. Neither would it be sufficient to sum the scores from tasks requiring phoneme discrimination, morpheme identification, word definition, phrase structure evaluation, intonation contour interpretation, etc. A mere heap of scores intended to represent all of the subtasks included in the comprehension of spoken discourse cannot in principle represent adequately one's ability to perform all of them simultaneously in ordinary listening comprehension.

A speech test is not necessarily a language test. While some speaking tasks may indeed engage the deep language capacity for negotiating propositional meanings, this is not necessarily the case. For instance, a diagnostic procedure that focuses attention on the articulation of sibilants, as opposed to the articulation of interdental fricatives—/ s /, / š /, / z /, / z / versus / θ / and / ð /—may have some use in evaluating speech but has a tenuous connection with deep language skills. For all of the reasons given supporting the premise that the whole is greater than the sum of its parts, no combination of tests aimed exclusively at the surface forms of speech can be expected to serve as a fully adequate language battery. Only in cases where the surface forms evaluated have pragmatic consequences for propositional meanings can a speech test (or battery of tests) be employed reasonably to measure language proficiency.

For instance, a phoneme discrimination task cannot be a very good language test though it may be regarded as an important part of a battery of procedures for evaluating speech perception. A speaking test which focuses on only certain morphemes such as the *Bilingual Syntax Measure* (Burt, Dulay, and Hernandez–Chavez, 1976; reviewed by Oller, 1976b), *may* be a weak test of pragmatic abilities, but must be expected to be inferior to a method that focuses on meaning (*see* the discussion of the Damico research below).

On the other hand, a task as simple as taking dictation may be a good measure of language proficiency even though it is scored by counting surface forms, i.e., in the most commonly used procedure, the number of dictated words recognizable and in the right order. A dictation score may be a measure of language proficiency because writing any of the words at all requires a great amount of internal processing of meaning. Similarly, a task such as a cloze test where examinees are asked to replace missing words in a text may serve as a good device for measuring language proficiency. This may seem surprising to some since cloze tests are usually scored for the number of words restored correctly, exactly as had been written by the original author of the text. However, even with such a method of scoring (commonly referred to as the *exact-word scoring method*) evidence shows that cloze tests require deep processing. That is, it is usually not possible to replace the missing items without understanding the author's intended meanings. When cloze tests are scored by the *appropriate word method*, the score being the number of replacements that fit the context of the whole passage, cloze tests appear to be even better indicators (Hinofotis and Snow, 1980; their references) than when scored by the exact-word method.[2]

The bilingual is advantaged. The premise that bilinguals are advantaged deserves special attention in this paper. Unfortunately, the term *bilingual* has often been associated with oppressed social groups who, in many cases, are really monolingual. For example, a ghetto in an inner city area where only Spanish, Chinese, or some other language other than English is spoken may contain a majority of permanent residents who do not know enough English to be considered bilingual at all. Still, the community may be referred to as "bilingual." Moreover, bilingual programing may be recommended for the schools that serve such communities.

Because such ghetto communities are often socioeconomically depressed, the term *bilingual* has acquired negative connotations that lead to incorrect associations. Ironically, it is the persons who are *bilingual* who know more than those who are monolingual. There is no evidence whatever that learning more than one language is a hindrance to cognitive development over any reasonable period of time. Just so, it is important to make a distinction between genuine bilingualism (knowing some significant amount of more than one language system) and simply being born into a nonmajority ethnic group or ghetto community. As Zirkel (1974, 1976) amply documented, children in schools are frequently misclassifed as bilingual on the basis of their surname or some similarly inadequate criterion.

Some years ago there was much heated discussion about the cognitive effects of learning more than one language. Some theorists held that the simultaneous acquisition of more than one language would necessarily retard mental development. Among those who held this view, however, there was disagreement as to whether the retardation would be permanent or temporary. Some believed that the bilingual would eventually attain a net advantage. Others insisted that the initial setback caused by the extra burden of having to differentiate two language systems would become a permanent lag. This argument continues today, but the current opinion of the experts is that bilinguals have certain advantages over monolinguals (Cummins, 1978).

There remains some question about whether children learning two languages develop their language ability in both languages as rapidly as monolinguals do learning a single language. However, there is strong evidence that bilinguals eventually surpass their monolingual peers in particular measurable mental skills (Barik and Swain, 1975). Earlier studies showing detrimental effects of bilingualism generally are criticized because they failed to compare bilinguals with monolinguals of similar ability and social status. Where ability and status controls have been sufficient, no research shows any negative effects attributable to bilingualism, and some show advantages due to bilingualism (*see* Cummins, 1978; Barik and Swain, 1975; their references).

Degrees of societal and individual bilingualism can be distinguished. It may be hypothesized that societies using two mutually intelligible varieties of the same language system are, in an important sense, less bilingual than those using two mutually unintelligible systems. Even finer gradations can be made where the language systems exhibit degrees of mutual intelligibility. Spanish is more intelligible to a speaker of Portuguese, for instance, than to a speaker of Navajo or Mandarin. Following the same logic, bilingualism should be more beneficial to the individual who has full command of two really diverse languages rather than two mutually intelligible varieties of the same language. Further, it may be argued that monolinguals are not categorically different from bilinguals since even monolinguals managing more than one variety of their language are more or less multilingual. Thus, monolinguals are simply less multilingual than bilinguals, and, therefore, the benefits of multilingualism are bound to be more pronounced in the person who commands a greater diversity of language systems.

However, if the term *bilingual* is used incorrectly to connote downtrodden minorities whose language may have once been something other than majority variety English, "bilinguals" are almost certain to appear inferior on any kind of standardized testing. The correct explanation for this contrast between minorities and the majority, however, must be based on social, economic, and political factors only incidentally related to any particular language system(s). As will be seen below, the claim by Jensen (1969, 1973, 1980) and by Herrnstein (1973) that persons of low intelligence naturally precipitate to the bottom of the sociocultural mix is completely inadequate as an explanation of the contrast between oppressed minority and majority school children. The process of test standardization itself defines the minority child as inferior *before the testing ever begins*.

How Can Testing and Diagnosis Be Done?

The Validity Problem

As Carroll (1980) noted, the determination of test validity (whether or not a test is measuring what it purports to measure) is a persistent problem to be grappled with constantly and never solved; at least not in a world beset by sin and error. Not only is perfect measurement an impossibility for persons whose knowledge is imperfect and incomplete, but methods of validating tests are also imperfect. Therefore, some would prefer to forget the whole business of testing and validation and just rely on recipes founded in intuitions and hunches. Surely this would be a mistake. There are better and worse ways to conduct testing and, even with imperfect methods of research, many useful distinctions can be made. On the other hand, the intuitive approach devolves into opinion polls and power plays and very often must result in wrong choices of testing techniques.

Carroll (1980) notes that research in language testing over the last several decades has made some progress, some of it attributed indirectly to advances in psychology and linguistics, but much is due to research in language testing per se. To appreciate such advances, as Piaget has pointedly remarked, it is necessary to examine the right kind of research. In his words, "when a question of psychological fact arises, psychological research should be consulted instead of trying to invent a solution through private speculation" (1970, p. 9). If the term "language testing" is substituted for Piaget's "psychology," it becomes obvious where we must begin the search for the best possible testing methods.

According to sound psychometric theory, validity presupposes reliability. That is, before a test can be judged valid, it must first be reliable. A test is reliable when it generates similar results on different occasions. Clearly, a test that produces different results every time it is used, even though the circumstances of testing and the examinees remain the same, is of no practical value. On the other hand, reliability does not ensure validity. A good yardstick may be a fine measure of spatial distances, but it is useless as a measure of object density, temperature, or cost. Therefore, demonstrations of reliability are insufficient by themselves because questions of validity must also be asked.

Traditionally, many different kinds of validity have been proposed. Among them is *face* validity. Does the test look like a test of what it is supposed to measure? The trouble with this kind of validity is that looks can be deceiving. Ultimately, *face* validity rests on the judgment of the person(s) examining the test. To its discredit, such judgments are apt to be influenced as much by the person(s)' past experience, speculation, and mere impressions, as by relevant considerations.

A related kind of validity is *content* validity—whether the test contains the right kind of tasks. If the test purports to measure language proficiency, for instance, does it require ordinary language performance? At this point it is necessary to consider what language performances are and, consequently, what language proficiency is. These considerations may be the beginning of the sort of theory that will eventually be required. The only difference between *face* validity and *content* validity is that the former is generally based on uninformed judgments whereas the latter is based on thoughtful reflection and preliminary theory building; otherwise, the two sorts of validity are quite similar.

A somewhat more empirical sort of validity is *concurrent* validity—to what extent any given test correlates with tests aimed at the same or different construct. Actually there are two types of *concurrent* validity, *convergent* and *divergent*. If the correlated measures are aimed at distinct constructs, they are expected to correlate weakly or not at all. That is, they are expected to *diverge*. On the other hand, tests aimed at the same constructs should correlate strongly, or *converge*. When the tests are identical in format or content, the measure of convergence is interpreted as an index of reliability. However, so long as the tests are regarded as distinct, either in form or in content, convergence/divergence indices are taken as measures of *concurrent* validity.[3]

All of the foregoing types of validity may be interpreted with a view to understanding the *construct(s)* one desires to measure. When attention is focused on the "object" of measurement in this sense, psychometricians speak of *construct* validity. For instance, if the construct of interest is some aspect of language proficiency, the construct validation problem is to demonstrate that a certain test (or, more commonly, a variety of testing techniques) actually yields information about just that construct and no other (*see* Carroll, 1983, p. 93 and the editor's and author's exchanges on this point). This is a difficult problem that forces an interface between theory and practice. To justify any particular testing procedure it is necessary to show how, in theory, that procedure relates to the construct of interest and excludes extraneous constructs. Furthermore, it will be necessary to appeal to *content* and *concurrent* validity in order to establish *construct* validity. Of course, this process can never be completed. However, cycling back and forth between empirical findings in practice and their explanations in theory, can progressively refine the process (Carroll, 1983).

The Language Construct(s): Apparent Antitheses

With the foregoing in mind, it is possible to address the definition of language proficiency. In one form or another, this is the principal validity problem for language testing. Investigations over the last several decades have led to apparently antithetical alternatives. The prevailing discrete point approach of the 1950s and 1960s was that multiple components of language proficiency could be clearly distinguished and that each of those components could be divided into smaller discrete elements. For instance, it was supposed that phonological capacity as one example, was distinct from lexical knowledge, as another, and that such distinct constructs would, in general, have to be assessed more or less independently. Moreover, it was urged that each item of a language test should pinpoint a single element of a particular component of language proficiency. In some quarters it was even argued that different skills implied different grammars, e.g., one grammar for speaking and another for listening.[4]

In the 1970s, the discrete point approach to language testing was discarded by many who turned to a more integrative approach. The motivation for integrative testing was that the multiplication of separate skills have no logical stopping point and that language proficiency is actually quite holistic. The proponents of integrative testing argued that much of the nonsummative information in language performance is lost when tests are designed to pinpoint single elements of hypothesized components. It was argued that even the smallest grammatical particles may have global effects on communication. Though it is difficult to say exactly what is the effect of deleting a plural marker, leveling a phonemic contrast, or overgeneralizing a particular lexical usage; there is no doubt that each distortion, if repeated over and over, will affect communication. The contribution of any particle of structure is, in principle, impossible to predict but, for instance, there is no doubt that repeatedly leveling a phonemic contrast will tend to reduce overall communicative effectiveness.

As a result of the apparently antithetical claims of the highly analytical discrete point approaches and the holistic integrative approaches, an important controversy ensued throughout the 1970s. I took the position that language proficiency could not possibly be both divisible into thousands of minute particles and at the same time be integral in nature (Oller, 1976a, 1979; Oller and Hinofotis, 1980; Oller and Perkins, 1978, 1980). As it develops, however, this view was incorrect. Both empirical evidence (Bachman and Palmer, 1980, 1983; Carroll, 1983; Farhady, 1983) and theoretical reasoning (Carroll, 1983; Upshur and Homburg, 1983) point to the conclusion that both holistic and analytical approaches are needed. They are not contradictory, but rather complementary. Just as automobile consumers are interested in global indicators such as fuel efficiency and road handling, as well as specific indicators such as engine displacement, carburation, and gear ratios; language testers will need global measures for some purposes and more specific diagnostic data for others.

In spite of significant advances in characterizing the factorial structure of language proficiency (e.g., Bachman and Palmer, 1983), there is no reason to expect a final satisfying model of the composition of langauge proficiency. However, Bachman and Palmer (1980, 1983) have convincingly demonstrated that a multiple-factor model is superior to a single, unitary-factor model. Note, however, that their research (as Carroll, 1983, indicates) does not eliminate the possible existence of a powerful general factor.

Is the General Factor Due to Language Proficiency or Intelligence?

No one can deny that language proficiency is somehow linked with a hypothesized "general" intelligence. More specifically, it would appear to be related to "verbal" intelligence. To make matters more complex, language proficiency is also related closely, perhaps inextricably, with achievement and even personality.

Gunnarsson (1978) showed that items drawn from tests aimed at such diverse constructs as intelligence, achievement, and personality were often indistinguishable from items appearing in tests designed to assess language proficiency. In a similar vein, Roth (1978) criticized "*non*verbal" IQ items because of the extent to which they seem to require propositional, i.e., *verbal*, reasoning for their solution. Gunnarsson and Roth used rather different methods to support a similar skepticism about the validity of many types of tests. Gunnarsson examined item content while Roth had examinees reflect introspectively on how they were able to solve certain items on Raven's *Progressive Matrices* (a much used test designed to assess nonverbal IQ). Both raised serious questions about the validity of the tests they examined.

On somewhat more theoretical grounds, the argument has been raised that solutions to even the purest "nonverbal" IQ items in tests such as Raven's *Progressive Matrices* and Cattell's *Culture Fair Intelligence Tests* require utilization of deep grammatical structures, including subject-predicate relations, negation, conjunction, and an abstract lexicon capable of differentiating abstract concepts and relationships (Oller, 1981, 1982, 1983). If a deep language factor does indeed penetrate even these paradigm examples of "*pure* nonverbal" intelligence tests (Jensen, 1969, 1973, 1980), will there be any aspect of knowledge or achievement that is not in some important sense dependent on language skills?

Probably any answer to the foregoing question will be controversial. An interesting proposal, hotly contested, was offered by Cummins (1979) and has since been substantially revised (Cummins, 1982, 1983). Initially, he suggests that two somewhat independent types of language proficiency should be distinguished from each other. The first type he labeled Cognitive/Academic Language Proficiency (CALP), and the second he labeled Basic Interpersonal Communicative Skills (BICS). He argued that the first type is closely related to what Spearman, in 1904, called "general intelligence," while the second is the skill that every native speaker acquires, to much the same degree, through face to face interaction. More particularly, Cummins saw CALP as related to "verbal" intelligence and distinct from "nonverbal" intelligence. He argued that all normals tend to develop roughly the same level of BICS but differ in their acquisition of CALP. He also contended that school achievement depends largely on CALP. More recently he has modified his position and sees CALP and BICS as interacting somewhat as they develop (Cummins, 1982, 1983).[5]

Another way of viewing the relationship of language and cognition is in terms of hierarchically organized levels of language capacity. At the very deep level there is the capacity for propositional reasoning, and at a quite superficial level there are skills associated with the surface forms of a particular language. In this model, the development at the deepest level may be enhanced or retarded by development of skills at the most superficial levels, and vice versa. Such a hierarchical model implicitly incorporates Cummins' suggestion (1979) that a common capacity (or cluster of capacities) must underlie the acquistion of proficiency in more than one language.

It might further be hypothesized that tasks tapping deeper levels of the hierarchy should be more strongly correlated than tasks focusing on components at the periphery. For instance, the ability to understand entailments, presuppositions, and other inferences would appear to be based on a deep capacity, while the ability to interpret phrase-structures in English would appear to be more superficial. By the same token, to distinguish phonemes in English would be more superficial still. In such a hierarchy, Cummins' CALP factor might fall at a considerably deeper level than his BICS factor although the latter probably would have an intermediate rather than superficial status. It is predicted that BICS will vary more across individuals than Cummins originally predicted and will not be independent of CALP.

Pragmatic vs. Surface Testing

A question that might well be raised in response to the preceding section is whether it is possible to have more or less holistic evaluation along with satisfactory diagnostic accuracy. Can global aspects of language proficiency be assessed to determine, for instance, which language to use in the presentation of curricula to a given multilingual community? More specifically, can appropriate judgments be made about the comprehensibility of a curriculum presented in a given language to a given child? Still more to the point for speech-language pathology, is it possible to recommend diagnostic procedures that differentiate children with language disorders from children who merely have not yet mastered some subset of surface structures of a particular language?

In general, the answers to these questions seem to be positive. With sufficient emphasis on diverse testing and diagnostic procedures, it is theoretically possible to accomplish all of the foregoing objectives with a high degree of reliability and validity. There are, however, certain pragmatic criteria to be met. Two pragmatic naturalness constraints have been proposed and discussed extensively elsewhere (Oller, 1979). First, the normal temporal development of discourse (and of experience in general) should be respected. Test items entirely removed from any temporally progressive context should probably be avoided for all but the most analytic of purposes. Second, and equally important, the linking of utterance forms or their surrogates to the ordinary contexts of experience should be taken into account. Normally test items that have no meaningful connection to ordinary experience should not be used.

The pragmatic naturalness constraints reflect respectively the temporal development and the usual meaningfulness of discourse. Tests that analyze language in ways that destroy these ordinary properties of discourse probably are not very good language tests. They may invoke *aspects* of language skills but will probably do so only superficially. More important, such tests generally will lack construct validity.

Pragmatic criteria in diagnosis. Traditionally, especially in the diagnosis of *language disorders*, and in some cases the diagnosis of other *learning disabilities*, has been based largely on the examinee's ability to use certain surface forms of speech, often the morphological and syntactic elements. A child might be referred for further diagnosis or possibly even for therapy on the basis of problems in forming plurals, using the third person marker on present tense verbs; or using irregular verbs, the possessive, or modal auxiliaries. Although it would be a mistake to suggest that surface problems are not problems at all, there is no evidence that the superficial problems usually examined are directly linked with general learning difficulties. Aside from case reports or discussions that propose certain recipes for diagnosis and subsequent therapy, there exists little evidence that diagnosis based on surface-oriented procedures is valid.

Of course, it is possible to look somewhat deeper than the surface forms of morphological and syntactic regularities, and this is exactly what Jack S. Damico, an Albuquerque based speech-language pathologist, has done.[6] Working on the basis of the pragmatic criteria summarized above, Damico developed a set of procedures for language referrals that contrast markedly with the traditional surface-criteria usually employed by speech-language pathologists. Instead of having teachers in schools look for deviations in surface syntax, he proposed looking for certain pragmatic processing problems such as poor topic maintenance or the use of indeterminate referring terms.

In order to compare the relative utility of traditional criteria with that of pragmatic criteria, matched groups of Albuquerque teachers were studied.

Group 1 was given a 45 minute training session using the traditional surface criteria, while Group 2 received a similar training session using nontraditional pragmatic criteria (*see* below; for details *see* Damico and Oller, 1980).

The surface elements taught included noun-verb agreement, possessive marking, tense, auxiliary verb usage, irregular plural formation, pronoun case and gender, reflexive pronouns, syntactic transpositions, and regular plural formation. Pragmatic criteria, by contrast, included nonfluencies, revisions, inordinate delays, nonspecific vocabulary, inappropriate responses, poor topic maintenance, and frequent need for repetition. Each problem, whether surface or pragmatic, was demonstrated during the training phase by using speech samples from one or more children. Because surface difficulties are well exemplified elsewhere (e.g., Bloom and Lahey, 1978; Crystal, Fletcher, and Garman, 1976), the following examples only illustrate the pragmatic criteria (these also appear in Damico, Oller, and Storey, in press).

(1) *Linguistic nonfluencies.* Production is disrupted by repetitions, unusual pauses, and hesitation phenomena.

Example:

"Sh...she...she...she comes at dinner."

(2) *Revisions.* The child continually revises what has already been said as if coming to dead ends in a maze.

Example:

"He's about half...he comes...he's here on me" (gestures with hand marking shoulder height)

(3) *Delayed responses.* Communicative exchanges initiated by others are followed by pauses of inordinate length at turn-switching points.

Example:

Examiner: "Well, what did you do at recess?"

Subject: "...[pauses for approximately 2.5 seconds]...Played tag."

(4) *Nonspecific referring terms.* Deictic terms such as "this," "that," "then," "there," pronominals, proper nouns, and possessives are used when neither a referent nor an antecedent can readily be inferred by the listener. Children displaying this difficulty also tend to overuse generic terms such as "thing" and "stuff."

Example:

Examiner: "...so did you help them move?"

Subject: "Yeah...but they mad cuz I drop it."

Examiner: "Oh? What did you drop?"

Subject: "That thing of Rosa's."

(5) *Inappropriate responses.* The child makes frequent turns that indicate radically unpredictable interpretations of meaning. For instance, the child understood the word "school" to be a proper noun. This interpre-

tation is so unpredictable that it gives the appearance of a complete topical shift.

Example:

Examiner: "How do you like school?"

Subject: "I don't know him yet."

(6) *Poor topic maintenance.* The child changes the topic without providing transitional cues to the listener.

Example:

Subject: "...but I missed it [a TV program] cuz I went to bed."

Examiner: "You must have had a hard day."

Subject: "Yeah."

Examiner: "What made it such a hard day?"

Subject: "The raking."

Examiner: "That's hard work, isn't it?"

Subject: "Our teacher said, uh,...whoever wins in checkers—I won—goes to McDonald's."

(7) *Need for repetition.* Multiple repetitions are required for comprehension to occur.

Example:

Examiner: "What did the little boy do?"

Subject: "..."

Examiner: "What did the little boy do?"

Subject: "He ran."

The teachers trained to look for pragmatic difficulties (Group 2), rather than surface problems (Group 1), expressed a more immediate grasp of what they were expected to do and significantly outperformed their surface-oriented peers in both number and accuracy of referrals. That is, Group 2 referred more children for further speech-language testing and a larger number of the referred children (40 for the pragmatic group, 19 for the surface-oriented group) were later judged to be language disordered according to the rigorous testing and diagnostic procedures laid down by the State of New Mexico. Furthermore, the pragmatic group recommended more than twice as many children with language disorders as the surface-oriented group. Assuming an equal distribution of disorders among the two groups of children observed (604 for the pragmatic group and 608 for the surface-oriented group), it follows that the surface-oriented group must have overlooked about 20 cases of actual language disorders.

The results clearly indicated an advantage for the pragmatic criteria, but what remained was to demonstrate a link between pragmatically diagnosed disorders and learning difficulties. It was expected that if the pragmatic criteria provided better diagnostic tools for identifying language disorders, these criteria should also provide a better basis for predicting subsequent learning problems. Further, it was supposed that children in the process of learning more than one language system would be incorrectly diagnosed more frequently by the traditional surface-oriented approach.

An opportunity for continuation of the research arose in 1980 with the referral of ten Spanish/English bilinguals for further diagnosis. As was expected, the use of surface-oriented criteria in either or both languages resulted in identification of a different set of children as language disordered than did the pragmatic criteria. It was hypothesized that the surface criteria would incorrectly identify some children as disordered who were merely in the process of learning one or both languages (*see* Selinker, 1972, on interlanguage development). Further, it was predicted that any children diagnosed as normal by the pragmatic criteria (applied to samples of data from both languages) would make normal gains in school over the course of several months, while the children diagnosed as disordered would not. For the surface-oriented criteria it was predicted that there would be no relationship between diagnosis and school achievement.

As expected, three of the ten children were diagnosed as normal by the pragmatic criteria, while seven were diagnosed as disordered. These three made normal gains over a seven month period as determined by pre- and post-testing on the *Peabody Individual Achievement Test* and the *Myklebust Pupil Rating Scale*. (All of the achievement testing was done in English and the Myklebust ratings measured only development in English.) On the average, the children judged normal by the pragmatic criteria gained 32.4 percentage points on the Peabody and 2.43 standard deviations on the Myklebust scale. The other seven children gained only 6.44 percentage points on the Peabody and lost two tenths of a standard deviation on the Myklebust scale.

When the surface criteria were employed, one of the three children diagnosed as normal by the pragmatic criteria was classified as disordered. That same child, however, made the greatest gain of any of the children on the Peabody (38 percentage points). This same little boy also had the dubious distinction of making more surface errors (in both languages combined) than any other child. Moreover, he gained two full standard deviations on the Myklebust scale. In addition, three of the children classified as disorderd by the pragmatic criteria were classified as normal by the surface criteria. Those same three showed less than one third as much growth on the Peabody as the three classified as normal by the pragmatic criteria, and they dropped a tenth of a standard deviation on the Myklebust scale (for details, *see* Damico, Oller, and Storey, in press).

Conclusion

For many reasons, therefore, it seems preferable to use pragmatic criteria that look deeper into the learner's cognitive system than do the traditional surface criteria. Of course, if there is a reason to want to know if a given child has mastered a particular element of surface syntax, perhaps it is still true that this can best be judged by looking directly for exemplars of this form on obligatory occasions in that child's speech. However, the temptation to interpret such surface deviations as indicators of language disorders should be resisted. From a good deal of research evidence it seems clear that surface deviations are normal during certain stages of language acquisition (*see* Selinker, 1972) and, on the whole, correlate weakly with the ability to manipulate propositional meanings. On the other hand, to place emphasis on meaning is not to neglect surface form, as some have contended, but simply to relegate it to its properly more superficial and less significant role.

Notes

[1] Language is *synergistic*.

[2] Other processing tasks that may be converted to scorable testing procedures are numerous and highly varied. They include oral interview procedures, essays, question-answer approaches (written and oral), command execution, reading aloud, elicited imitation of text, retelling of narrative, summarizing, and expanding. With care it is possible to convert all of these procedures to quantifiable tasks that may be used appropriately as tests (*see* Oller, 1979, pp. 262–421 for more specific suggestions). The two primary methods of quantifying such procedures include objective counting, e.g., in dictation, counting the number of words correctly rendered in the sequence dictated, and subjective rating, e.g., assigning a score referenced against some rating scale calibrated by appropriate training, such as is done with the Foreign Service Institute Oral Interview scales.

[3] There are some difficulties in saying whether tests are the same or not, but those will not be discussed here (*see* Oller, 1980).

[4] There are even a few language testers who still hold the view that distinct grammars may be involved (*see* Vollmer and Sang, 1983).

[5] He has also elaborated on his model in certain respects which have not been discussed here. However, it must be said that the modified position seems substantially strengthened over the earlier CALP/ BICS dichotomy.

[6] Damico is currently completing the requirements for his PhD in Educational Linguistics at the University of New Mexico, while he continues to serve as a consultant to the Albuquerque Public Schools.

References

Bachman, L.F., and Palmer, A.S.:   Trait and method factors in language proficiency test scores. Presented at the Language Testing Conference during the Linguistic Society of America and Teachers of English to Speakers of Other Languages Summer Institute, Albuquerque, 1980.

Bachman, L.F., and Palmer, A.S.:   The construct validation of the FSI Oral Interview. In Oller, J.W., Jr. (Eds.): *Issues in Language Testing Research*. Rowley, Newbury House, 1983.

Barik, H.C., and Swain, M.:   Three year evaluation of a large-scale early grade French immersion program: the Ottawa study. *Language Learning, 25*:1-30, 1975.

Bates, E.:   *Language and Context: The Acquisition of Pragmatics*. New York, Academic, 1976.

Bloom, L., and Lahey, M.:   *Language Development and Language Disorders*. New York, Wiley, 1978.

Burt, M.K., Dulay, H.C., and Hernandez-Chavez, E.:   *The Bilingual Syntax Measure: Technical Handbook*. New York, Harcourt Brace Jovanovich, 1976.

Carroll, J.B.:   Foreign language testing: persistent problems. In Croft, K.C. (Ed.): *Readings on English as a Second Language*. Cambridge, Winthrop, 1980.

Carroll, J.B.:   Psychometric theory and language testing. In Oller, J.W., Jr. (Ed.): *Issues in Language Testing Research*. Rowley, Newbury House, 1983.

Crystal, D., Fletcher, P., and Garman, M.:   *The Grammatical Analysis of Language Disability*. London, Edward Arnold, 1976.

Cummins, J.:   Educational implications of mother tongue maintenance in minority language groups. *Canadian Modern Language Review, 34*: 395-416, 1978.

Cummins, J.:   Cognitive/academic language proficiency, linguistic interdependence, the optimum age, and some other matters. *Working Papers on Bilingualism, 19*:198-205, 1979.

Cummins, J.:   *Conceptual and linguistic foundations of language assessment*. Paper presented at the Second Annual Language Assessment Institute, Chicago, 1982.

Cummins, J.:   Language proficiency and academic achievement. In Oller, J.W., Jr. (Ed.): *Issues in Language Testing Research*. Rowley, Newbury House, 1983.

Damico, J., and Oller, J.:   Pragmatic versus morphological/syntactic criteria for language referrals. *Language, Speech, and Hearing Services in Schools, 11*:85-94, 1980.

Damico, J., Oller, J., and Storey, M.E.:   The diagnosis of language disorders in bilingual children: Surface-oriented and pragmatic criteria. *Journal of Speech and Hearing Disorders*, in press.

Farhady, H.:   On the plausibility of the unitary language proficiency factor. In Oller, J.W., Jr. (Ed.): *Issues in Language Testing Research.* Rowley, Newbury House, 1983.

Goodman, K.S.:   Psycholinguistic universals of the reading process. In Pimsleur, P., and Quinn, T. (Eds.): *The Psychology of Second Language Learning.* Cambridge, England, Cambridge University, 1971.

Gunnarsson, B.:   A look at the content similarities between intelligence, achievement, personality, and language tests. In Oller, J.W., Jr., and Perkins, K. (Eds.): *Language in Education: Testing the Tests.* Rowley, Newbury House, 1978.

Herrnstein, R.:   *IQ in the Meritocracy.* Boston, Little Brown, 1973.

Hinofotis, F.A., and Snow, B.:   An alternative to cloze testing procedure: multiple choice format. In Oller, J.W., Jr., and Perkins, K. (Eds.): *Research in Language Testing.* Rowley, Newbury House, 1980.

Jensen, A.R.:   How much can we boost IQ and scholastic achievement? *Harvard Educational Review, 39*:1–123, 1969.

Jensen, A.R.:   *Educability and Group Differences.* New York, Harper and Row, 1973.

Jensen, A.R.:   *Bias in Mental Testing.* New York, Free Press, 1980.

Krashen, S.D.:   *Principles and Practice in Second Language Acquisition.* London, Pergamon, 1982.

Lenneberg, E.:   Understanding language without ability to speak: a case study. *Journal of Abnormal and Social Psychology, 65*:419–425. 1962.

Oller, J.W., Jr.:   Evidence for a general factor of language proficiency. *Die Neuren Sprachen, 76*:165–174, 1976a.

Oller, J.W., Jr.:   Review of the *Bilingual Syntax Measure. Modern Language Journal, 60*:309–400, 1976b.

Oller, J.W., Jr.:   *Language Tests at School: A Pragmatic Approach.* London, Longman, 1979.

Oller, J.W., Jr.:   *How do we tell when tests are the same or different?* Paper presented at the Second International Language Testing Symposium, Darmstadt, Germany, May 1980.

Oller, J.W., Jr.:   Language as intelligence? *Language Learning, 31*: 465–492, 1981.

Oller, J.W., Jr.:   Evaluation and testing in vernacular languages. In Hartford, B., Valdman, A., and Foster, C.R. (Eds.): *Issues in International Bilingual Education: The Role of the Vernacular.* New York, Plenum, 1982.

Oller, J.W., Jr. (Ed.):   *Issues in Language Testing Research.* Rowley, Newbury House, 1983.

Oller, J.W., Jr., and Hinofotis, F.:   Two mutually exclusive hypotheses about second language ability: indivisible or partially divisible competence. In Oller, J.W., Jr., and Perkins, K. (Eds.): *Research in Language Testing.* Rowley, Newbury House, 1980.

Oller, J.W., Jr., and Perkins, K. (Eds.):   *Language in Education: Testing the Tests.* Rowley, Newbury House, 1978.

Oller, J.W, Jr., and Perkins, K. (Eds.):   *Research in Language Testing.* Rowley, Newbury House, 1980.

Piaget, J.:   *Genetic Epistemology.* New York, Norton, 1970.

Roth, D.:   Raven's *Progressive Matrices* as cultural artifacts. In Hall, W.S., and Cole, M. (Eds.): *Quarterly Newsletter of the Laboratory of Comparative Human Cognition, 1*:1–15, 1978.

Selinker, L.:   Interlanguage. *International Review of Applied Linguistics, 10*:219–231, 1972.

Spearman, C.E.:   "General intelligence" objectively determined and measured. *American Journal of Psychology, 15*:201–293, 1904.

Upshur, J.A., and Homburg, T.J.:   Some relations among language tests at successive ability levels. In Oller, J.W., Jr. (Ed.): *Issues in Language Testing Research.* Rowley, Newbury House, 1983.

Vollmer, H.J., and Sang, F.:   On interpreting a general factor: a plea for caution. In Oller, J.W., Jr. (Ed.): *Issues in Language Testing Research.* Rowley, Newbury House, 1983.

Zirkel, P.A.:   A method for determining and depicting language dominance. *TESOL Quarterly, 8*:7–16, 1974.

Zirkel, P.A.:   The whys and ways of testing bilinguality before teaching bilingually. *The Elementary School Journal,* March:323–330, 1976.

5

Assessing Communicative Behavior Using a Language Sample

Carol A. Prutting

Someday there may be an alternative to the collection and analysis of a spontaneous language sample, but it does not exist today. Standardized tests serve the function of separating normal populations from disordered populations. Language samples provide an in-depth description of the individual's use of the communicative system (pragmatic, semantic, syntactic, phonologic) in natural contexts. This chapter will deal specifically with some of the main issues related to assessing communicative behavior by using a spontaneous language sample.

Communicative behavior is extremely complex and dynamic. Steiner (1975) has stated that man acts as if he were the shaper and master of language, but language remains mistress of man. Describing the nature of communicative behavior is not an easy task because of the complexities of behavior. Throughout the years we have added to our knowledge so we now have some specific guidelines for using a language sample for assessment purposes. We are still in need of determining what constitutes an adequate sample size, contextual considerations in the selection of various settings, and systematic segmentation procedures for transcription purposes. In addition, the analysis procedure will change as we learn more about the acquisition of the communicative system.

One assumes that the clinician who analyzes a spontaneous language sample understands normal communicative development before observing and describing communicative behavior for clinical purposes. Also, since communicative behavior is intimately tied to cognitive and social development, it is necessary to have a rich background in these areas in order to interpret the sample. Due to the complexity of communication and the background required to collect, analyze, and interpret a language sample, standardized tests are sometimes selected in place of the language sample procedure. It should be underscored that the clinician needs to determine what communicative rules an individual uses. Accordingly, the language sample is the only procedure which provides an opportunity to assess communication in real live contexts with real live communicative partners who need to communicate. The language sample remains a most valued clinical tool.

Collection of the Language Sample

The guidelines set forth for the collection of a language sample have been extrapolated from various investigators' experience as well as from the author's clinical experience. The three major considerations in the selection of the setting to sample—context, the communicative partner, and the goals of the communicative interaction—will be discussed individually.

Context

It should no longer be surprising to anyone that behavior is a product of the context in which it occurs. Cowan, Weber, Hoddinott, and Klein (1967) demonstrated the differential affectiveness of the communicative partner and the task upon the collection of a language sample. It is, therefore, important to select contexts that are a representative sample of the child's communicative system.

The clinician should select two communicative settings in which the child interacts frequently. That is, the settings should be natural contexts that are very familiar to the child, e.g., conversations at the dinner table or interaction during play. The selection of the contexts to sample should be made by choosing conversational interchanges that are important to the child and are part of the child's daily interactions. There may be times when it is impossible to collect samples outside the clinical situation. In these cases the clinician should try to arrange the physical properties of the room, e.g., arrange chairs, table, remove equipment, to make it appear comfortable and natural.

Communicative Partner

It is important that the communicative partner interacting with the child engage in conversation in the same manner in which he or she normally would without the presence of audio and/or videotape equipment. It has been demonstrated that various communicative behaviors do not vary in individuals when videotape procedures are utilized (Wiemann, in press). It is often necessary to explain, however, that the partners should act as normally as they would were the conversation not being recorded. This is often difficult for clinicians since we often assume a tutorial role with the child. When possible, a familiar communicative partner should be used, such as a peer or family member. Labov (1970) has written a caution to teachers and clinicians when collecting a language sample. One such caution involves what he names "*the obviousness of the obvious.*" This excerpt will illustrate Labov's point:

Teacher: *What's your name?*

Child: *Kenneth Marshall.*

Teacher: *Who's your teacher, Kenneth?*

Child: *Miss Molinda.*

Teacher: *What grade are you in?*

Child: *Miss Molinda. You know that!*

Teacher: *No, I dont. Why don't you tell me?*
         Are you in the first grade? (p. 14)

From this example it is easy to see that Kenneth knows the information requested. In order to gain the information, the teacher uses a tactic when trying to get a specific answer, i.e., providing the incorrect answer. The child is supposed to notice and provide the correct answer.

The other caution involves what Labov named the "*little old lady assumption.*" He describes it as the fallacy of misplaced concreteness and the infinite wisdom of the interlocuter. The following example depicts this caution (teacher and child are looking at a picture):

Teacher: *But how about all the litter that's on*
         the street? (pause)
         What should the children do about
         that? Hmmm? (pause)
         What should they do about all those
         papers that are on the street?

Child: *Nuttin.*

Teacher: *Nothing?*
         You don't think they should pick
         them up?

[You can clearly see the child is in trouble and the teacher is not going to let the child defy the little old lady assumption.]

Teacher: *Well, talk to me, tell me.*

Child: *Yes.*

> Teacher: *Why?* (pause)
>
> Teacher: *Well, how do you think the street will look if the children pick up all the litter? Hmmm?*
>
> Child: *Throw it in the garbage can.*
>
> Teacher: *That's right, they'd throw it in the garbage can.* (p. 19)

The teacher resorts to pressure on the child, who finally gives the desired answer. Labov refers to the arm-twisting on the part of the teacher as upholding the little old lady principle, that some answers are better than others, at all costs. As Labov suggests, the teacher usually wins in the end with height, power, and age on the teacher's side.

The important point of these examples is that the partners used in collecting a sample should not pull for a specific answer or prompt the child, but rather attempt to get a free flowing nontask conversation documented. Usually, the less the interchange is contrived, the better the sample will be. The child who is uncooperative and/or does not initiate much conversation may require a more structured prompting communicative partner. Remember, the idea behind the sample is to collect a representative sample. If prompting is required, this needs to be noted and described in the analysis section.

The Goals of the Communicative Interaction

Ideally, the goals of the conversation should reflect the nature of the relationship between the child and the communicative partner. If the child is playing with a peer, the goals might be to engage in conversation throughout the play period and the conversation may reflect changes throughout this period, e.g., to take a toy away from peer or to protest the use of a particular toy. The goals of conversation should not be imposed by the clinician, but should reflect the goals of the particular dyad.

There are occasions when the clinician will need to determine the goals by structuring the interaction. For instance, if a child's speech is highly unintelligible it may be necessary to have the child describe pictures so that the clinician can have a referent when analyzing the sample. In addition, the clinician may want to design various tasks to insure the inclusion of behavior that might not otherwise occur during a typical language sampling procedure, e.g., use of indirectives, polite forms, or interrogatives. (For particular guidelines in clinician-constructed language tasks *see* Prutting, Mulac, and Tomlinson, 1978; Leonard, Prutting, Perozzi, and Berkley, 1978. Both articles provide the clinician with specific ways of structuring the communicative interaction in order to achieve specific clinical goals.)

Final Thoughts on Collecting a Representative Sample

In collecting a language sample, it is recommended that the clinician select at least two different contexts and two different communicative partners. By so doing, it is likely that the goals of the interactions will also be different. This should permit the clinician to sample a range of communicative behaviors. One with clinical experience finds it generally takes 10 to 15 minutes to collect approximately 50 to 75 communicative acts from a cooperative child (Crystal, Fletcher, and Garman, 1976). This means that in a half hour it is possible to collect between 100 to 150 communicative acts. Some investigators advocate language samples consisting of at least 100 communicative acts (Lee, 1974; Tyack and Gottsleben, 1975), while others recommend between 200 and 300 (Muma, 1978). A minimum of 100 communicative acts should be collected. Clinicians should decide what is feasible beyond that number for the particular child and the clinician's work setting.

Analysis of the Language Sample

Segmentation

The sample should be segmented according to the criteria established by Brown (1973). Clinically, an act is often defined for segmentation purposes by the length of the pause between words or nonverbal acts. If a pause of more than three seconds occurs, the word or nonverbal act should be considered a different communicative act.

Transcription

The sample should first be transcribed including contextual information, e.g., child is pointing out window and saying, "That rain." This contextual information is often essential for analysis of the sample. The format for the transcription of the sample should be consecutive with regard to communicative partner and child.

Mother: *When will you finish that?*

Child: *I don't know.*

This format seems to make it easier to analyze dyadic interaction.

Analysis

It is recommended that clinicians utilize a stage model in making descriptions about a child's communicative behaviors (pragmatic, semantics, syntax, phonology). A stage process model is a description based on behavior acquired at various stages in the acquisition process. Each stage should consist of its own unique behavioral characteristics. These lexical descriptions are generated from investigators studying child language development such as psycholinguists, linguists, sociolinguists, and sociologists. It is beyond the scope of this chapter to provide an in-depth account of this procedure. An example of this decriptive developmental approach for children learning English as a first language is provided in Appendix A. (For a detailed description of the stage process model *see* Prutting, 1979.)

It will be necessary for researchers and clinicians to construct developmental descriptions of children learning a first language other than English. These descriptions should consist of verbal, paralinguistic, and nonverbal behavior when possible. Bloom and Lahey (1978, Appendix A2) have provided a coding system for nonverbal behaviors. This stage model gives the clinician the opportunity to compare the child being assessed with normal children and to see the child's progress.

What Constitutes Productivity and Acquisition?

Two issues are difficult to handle: (a) how to count various communicative behaviors within a language sample and (b) how to interpret these measurements once they are counted.

Phonological behaviors lend themselves to counting tactics better than pragmatic, semantic, and syntactical behaviors. When any of the three has low frequency, one cannot be sure if it is due to development or few opportunities for use during the collection procedure. Bloom (1970) stated:

> One instance of a particular behavior or a single production of an utterance type cannot be considered adequate evidence that a child has mastered the rule that underlies the form. However, if one observes several instances of a behavior in different situations, there is more than a single instance to use as evidence for inferring knowledge of the rules or other conceptual organization that was responsible for the utterance. (p. 328)

Bloom (1970) has set the criterion for productivity of semantic-syntactic relations to a frequency of five or more occurrences of a particular behavior during five or more hours of observation. It is important to keep in mind that even if a behavior occurs less than five times or is not exhibited at all, the frequency cannot be attributed to a lack of knowledge on the child's part, but may be due to the context in which the sample was collected.

One can only draw conclusions about acquisition in a context in which the behavior is obligatory for adult speakers. Brown (1973) has set the frequency criterion for acquisition in obligatory contexts at 90%. The infamous "14 morphemes" (Appendix B) as well as phonological behavior are the types of behavior from which one can determine acquisition, providing the behavior occurs several times during the sampling period.

All other behaviors that do not fit the productivity or acquisition criterion can only be referenced in the analysis procedure. These descriptions, while they often cannot be criterion referenced, are nevertheless valuable observational data that should be included in any analysis procedure. It is difficult to develop the ability to provide accurate descriptions of nonquantifiable data. It is essential to be a good observer and describer of behavior to assess communicative behavior.

Interpreting the Sample

After the child's communicative behavior is described in a stage process manner, an interpretation has to be made as to what the child knows about the communicative system. It is first necessary to determine at what stage or between what stages the child is operating. It is then necessary to decide if, for that given stage, the child has some but not all of the behaviors that characterize that stage or has the majority of behaviors that characterize a lower stage. This is important when planning remedial programs.

Remediation, therefore, can take one of two approaches: (a) vertical programing, consisting of expanding the child's knowledge at the particular stage at which the child is functioning, or (b) horizontal programing, consisting of selecting new behaviors at the next stage. The goal of vertical programing is to add and expand behavior within the stage at which the child is functioning, while the goal of the horizontal approach is to move the child beyond the existing stage to the next stage. The stage assessment procedure provides the clinician with remedial guidelines based on complexity (earlier behaviors less complex than later behaviors) of the content and sequence of communicative behavior.

Considerations for the Culturally Different Child

The rationale and principles behind using a language sample to assess communication are the same for the culturally different child as for the monolingual Anglo child. There are, however, a few other factors to consider when evaluating a culturally different child's communicative performance. First and most important, if you do not know the language your client speaks, you cannot possibly assess it. There is no way in which one can describe the regularities in a language without knowing that particular language. In cases where the language you need to assess is not known by the clinician, it will be necessary to refer the client to a professional or paraprofessional who does know the language.

The clinician must know more than the phonological, syntactic, and semantic rules as well as pragmatic behaviors. In order to assess pragmatics or the use of language, it will be necessary to know and share the child's cultural values so that one can assess whether or not language is being used appropriately within the child's language community. Anything less than this does not permit an assessment of the communicative performance.

If, however, one knows the language or languages to be assessed, then the following suggestions should be taken into consideration when dealing with the culturally different child. In sampling various contexts, it may be necessary to select communicative partners whose native language is the other language the child speaks, depending on the child's suspected linguistic capabilities. Therefore, for the culturally different child it is necessary to collect and analyze two distinct samples separately. The same guidelines should be used for collecting both samples. For the non-English speaking child, one should select communicative partners who share the rules of the child's native language.

The analysis procedure for the culturally different child should be similar to the examples found in Appendices A, B, and C for the English-speaking child. The clinician may have to combine or divide developmental data into different stages for each language being assessed. Such a procedure will need to be done for pragmatic, semantic, syntactic, and phonologic behavior. This task is no doubt burdensome; however, there is no way to simplify this procedure when analyzing and interpreting a language sample.

In interpreting the sample for the culturally different child, it is necessary to determine if the child's ability is delayed in the native language and/or the second language. In all cases, the languages have to be evaluated and compared to normative data. The child who is evaluated as functioning adequately in the native language, though delayed in the second language, will be considered less severely limited in communicative skills than the child who is delayed in both first and second languages. If the child has two native languages, coordinate bilingualism, one would expect to find that both are either developing adequately or both are delayed. It is unlikely that they will develop differentially. For educational purposes it will be necessary to determine if the non-English speaking child's communicative skills in the native language are developmentally sound or delayed.

It should be stressed that whenever a child has two languages it is necessary to assess both. Determination of communicative competence is not static. The language spoken, as well as the collection procedures, could yield differences in performance levels. Competence can be a function of the language used as well as the context in which the language is sampled. It is necessary to obtain a sufficient amount of evidence so that conclusions and judgments are made from an adequate repertoire of the child's behavior. The inferences and generalizations made about the child's communicative system are only as strong as the collection and analysis procedures.

In conclusion, Goffman (1961) has suggested that diagnosis of inappropriate or pathological behavior often becomes an ethnocentric appraisal, the diagnostician's own cultural point of view interferes in the judgment. Conduct can be judged only by the group from which it originates. It is the most important point to remember that if one does not share the child's same formal linguistic rules and cultural values, it is not possible to appraise the child's communicative performance. Referrals to professionals and paraprofessionals who know the child's language community are not only acceptable but mandatory if one respects the ethical guidelines inherent in our profession.

References

Anderson, E.S.: *Learning to Speak with Style.* Paper presented at the Stanford Child Language Research Forum, Stanford University, Palo Alto, 1977.

Atkinson-King, K.: Children's acquisition of phonological stress contrasts. *UCLA Working Papers in Phonetics, 25,* 1973.

Bates, E.: *Emergence of Symbols.* New York, Academic, 1979.

Bates, E.: Pragmatics and sociolinguistics in child language. In Morehead, M., and Morehead, A.E. (Eds.): *Language Deficiency in Children: Selected Readings.* Baltimore, University Park, 1976.

Bloom, L.: *Language Development: Form and Function in Emerging Grammars.* Cambridge, MIT, 1970.

Bloom, L., and Lahey, M.: *Language Development and Language Disorders.* New York, John Wiley and Sons, 1978.

Bloom, L., Rocissano, L., and Hood, L.: Adult-child discourse: Developmental interaction between processing and linguistic knowledge. *Cognitive Psych, 8:*521-552, 1976.

Brown, R.: *A First Language.* Cambridge, Harvard University, 1973.

Bruner, J.S.: The ontogenesis of speech acts. *J Child Lang, 2:*1-19, 1975.

Chomsky, N.: *Aspects of the Theory of Syntax.* Cambridge, MIT, 1965.

Clark, E.V.: What's in a word? On the child's acquisition of semantics in his first language. In Moore, T.E.: *Cognitive Development and the Acquisition of Language.* New York, Academic, 1973.

Cowan, P.A., Weber, J., Hoddinott, B.A., and Klein, J.: Mean length of spoken response as a function of stimulus, experimenter, and subjects. *Child Dev, 38:*191-203, 1967.

Crutthenden, A.: An experiment involving comprehension of intonation in children from 7 to 10. *J Child Lang, 1:*221-231, 1974.

Crystal, D., Fletcher, P, and Garman, M.: *The Grammatical Analysis of Language Disability.* London, Edward Arnold, 1976.

Dale, P.S.:   *Language Development.* New York, Holt, Rinehart, and Winston, 1976.

de Villiers, J.G., and de Villiers, P.A.:   A cross-sectional study of the acquisition of grammatical morphemes in child speech. *J Psycholing Res, 2*: 267–278, 1974.

Dore, J.:   Holophrase, speech acts, and language universals. *J Child Lang, 2*:21–40, 1975.

Eimas, P.:   Linguistic processing of speech by young infants.   In Schiefelbusch, R., and Lloyd, L. (Eds.): *Language Perspectives—Acquisition, Retardation, and Intervention.* Baltimore, University Park, 1974.

Ervin-Tripp, S., and Mitchell-Kernan, C. (Eds.):   *Child Discourse.* New York, Academic, 1977.

Ferguson, C., and Garnica, O.:   Theories of phonological development.   In Lenneberg, E.H., and Lenneberg, E. (Eds.): *Foundations of Language Development.* New York, Academic, 1975.

Gallagher, T.M.:   Revision behaviors in the speech of normal children developing language. *J Speech Hearing Res, 20*:303–318, 1977.

Garvey, C.:   Contingent queries. Unpublished master's thesis, Johns Hopkins University, 1975.

Gleason, J.B.:   Code-switching in children's language. In Moore, T.E. (Ed.): *Cognitive Development and the Acquisition of Language.* New York, Academic, 1973.

Gleitman, L.R., Gleitman, H., and Shipley, E.:   The emergence of the child as grammarian. *Cognition, 1*:137–163, 1972.

Goffman, E.:   *Asylums.* New York, Doubleday, 1961.

Greenfield, P., and Smith, J.:   *Communication and the Beginnings of Language: The Development of Semantic Structure in One-Word Speech and Beyond.* New York, Academic, 1976.

Grice, H.P.:   Logic and conversation. In Cole, P., and Morgan, J.L. (Eds.): *Syntax and Semantics: Speech Acts.* New York, Academic, 1975.

Halliday, M.A.K.:   *Learning How to Mean Explorations in the Development of Language.* London, Edward Arnold, 1975.

Hymes, D.:   Competence and performance in linguistic theory. In Huxley, R., and Ingram, E. (Eds.): *Language Acquisition: Models and Methods.* New York, Academic, 1971.

Ingram, D.:   *Phonological Disability in Children.* London, Edward Arnold, 1976.

Jakobson, R.:   *Child Language, Aphasia, and Phonological Universals.* The Hague, Mouton, 1958.

Keenan, E.O., and Schieffelin, D.D.:   Topic as a discourse notion: A study of topic in the conversations of children and adults. In Li, C.N. (Ed.): *Subject and Topic.* New York, Academic, 1976.

Labov, W.:   *Systematically Misleading Data from Test Questions.* Paper presented to Department of Sociology, University of Michigan, 1970.

Lee, L.: *Developmental Sentence Analysis.* Evanston, Northwestern University, 1974.

Leonard, L., Prutting, C.C., Perozzi, J.A., and Berkley, R.K.: Non-standardized approaches to the assessment of language behaviors. *ASHA, 20*: 379,1978.

Morse, P.A.: Infant speech perception: A preliminary model and review of literature. In Schiefelbusch, R., and Lloyd, L. (Eds.): *Language Perspectives—Acquisition, Retardation, and Intervention.* Baltimore, University Park, 1974.

Muma, J.R.: *Language Handbook.* Englewood Cliffs, Prentice-Hall, 1978.

Nelson, K.: Structure and strategy in learning to talk. *Monographs of the Society for Research in Child Development, 38,* 1973.

Prutting, C.A., Mulac, A., and Tomlinson, C.N.: Testing for a specific syntactic structure. *Communication Dis, 11*:335–347, 1978.

Prutting, C.A.: Process 'pras., ses N: The action of moving forward progressively from one point to another on the way to completion. *J Speech and Hearing Dis, 44*:3–30, 1979.

Sachs, J., and Devin, J.: Young children's use of age-appropriate speech styles in social interaction and role playing. *J Child Lang, 3*:81–98, 1976.

Sander, E.K.: When are speech sounds learned? *J Speech Hearing Dis, 37*: 55–63, 1972.

Shane, S.A.: *Generative Phonology.* Englewood Cliffs, Prentice-Hall, 1973.

Schvachkin, N.K.: The development of phonemic speech perceptions in early childhood. In Ferguson, C., and Slobin, D. (Eds.): *Studies of Child Language Development.* New York, Holt, Rinehart, and Winston, 1973.

Shatz, M., and Gelman, R.: The development of communicative skills: Modification in the speech of young children as a function of listener. *Monographs of the Society for Research in Child Development, 38,* 1973.

Smith, N.V.: *The Acquisition of Phonology.* Cambridge, Cambridge University, 1973.

Steiner, G.: *After Babel.* Oxford, Oxford University, 1975.

Tyack, D., and Gottsleben, R.: *Language Sampling, Analysis, and Training: A Handbook for Teachers and Clinicians.* Palo Alto, Consulting Psychology, 1975.

Wiemann, J.; Effects of laboratory video-taping procedures on selected conversation behaviors. *Human Communication Research,* in press.

Appendices 5-A, 5-B, and 5-C

APPENDIX 5-A
Summary of Stages for Acquisition of Pragmatics

Prelinguistic (birth–9 mo.)	Stage I (9–18 mo.)	Stage II (18–24 mo.)	Stage III (2–3 yrs.)	Stage IV (3+ yrs.)	Stage V (Communicative Competence—Adults)
Perlocutionary Acts gazing, crying, touching, smiling, vocalizations, grasping, sucking, laughing (Bates, 1976)	Intentions label, response request greeting protesting repeating description attention (Dore, 1975)	Functions pragmatic mathetic interpersonal textual ideational (Halliday, 1975)	Responds to contingent queries, types of revisions function of linguistic development (Gallagher, 1977)	Sustains topic (Bloom, Rocissano, and Hood. (1976)	Knowledge of who can say what, in what way, where and when, by what means, and to whom (Hymes, 1971)
Illocutionary Acts nonverbal and speech-like giving, pointing, showing (Bates, 1979)	Verbal Turn-taking procedures employed (Bloom, Rocissano, and Hood, 1976)		Rapid topic change (Keenan Schieffelin, 1976)	Systematic changes in speech depending on listener (Shatz and Gelman, 1973; Gleason, 1973; Sachs and Devin, 1976)	Behavior speakers and listeners attend to: Quality: informative but not too informative Quality: contribution should be true. Relation: be relevant. Manner: avoid obscurity, ambiguity, be brief and orderly (Grice, 1975)
Turn-taking (Bruner, 1975)	New Information coded first (Greenfield and Smith, 1976)			Productive use of contingent queries to maintain the conversation (Garvey, 1975)	
				Role-playing, ability to temporarily assume another's perspective (Anderson, 1977)	
				Indirectives and hints (Ervin-Tripp and Mitchell-Kernan, 1977)	
				Metalinguistic awareness, ability to think about language and comment on it (Gleitman, Gleitman, and Shipley, 1972; de Villiers and de Villiers, 1974)	

NOTE: Plus or minus 6 months for all age ranges reported is considered normal.

APPENDIX 5-B

Summary of Stages for Acquisition of Semantics and Syntax

Prelinguistic (birth–9 mo.)	Stage I (9–18 mo.)	Stage II (18–24 mo.)	Stage III (2–3 yrs.)	Stage IV (3+ yrs.)	Stage V (Communicative Competence–Adult)
	Semantics first-words learned are general nominals, specific nominals, action words (Nelson, 1973) Overextensions regarding shape, size, function, etc. (Clark, 1973) Functions performative indicative object negative indication volition negative volition volitional object agent action/state of agent object action/stage of object dative object assoc. with object or location animate assoc. with object or location location modification of event (Greenfield and Smith, 1976)	Semantics 2-word utterances agent-object agent-action action-object location nomination possessive attributive nonexistence rejection denial question recurrence acknowledgement (Bloom, 1970; Brown, 1973) Syntax 2-word utterances S-V-O-A clause level phrase level (Crystal, Fletcher, and Garman, 1976)	Semantics 3-4 word utterances new structures word level (Crystal, et al., 1976) Syntax 3-4 word utterances S-V-O-A new structures at clause level new structures at phrase level	Semantics word pairs–more and less, dimensional terms, before and after, verbs of expression, of causation and possession and transfer (summarized by Dale, 1976) New structures at word level (Crystal, et al., 1976) Syntax new structures at clause and phrase levels, recursion, error strategies employed (Crystal, et al., 1976) embeddings (Brown, 1973) 14 morphemes in order of acquisition: present progressive, on, in, plural, past irregular, possessive, uncontractible copula, articles, past regular, third-person singular irregular, uncontractible auxiliary, contractible copula, contractible auxiliary	Generates and understands infinite combinations from a set of finite symbols (Chomsky, 1965)

NOTE: Plus or minus 6 months for all age ranges reported is considered normal.

APPENDIX 5-C
Summary of Stages for Acquisition of Phonology

Prelinguistic (birth–9 mo.)	Stage I (9–18 mo.)	Stage II (18–24 mo.)	Stage III (2–3 yrs.)	Stage IV (3+ yrs.)	Stage V (Communicative Competence–Adult)
Discriminates phonemes during first month (Morse, 1974; Eimas, 1974)	Presented in order of acquisition first syllables CV or CVCV reduplicated	Phonological processes are employed from 18 mos. to 4 yrs. They are simplifying processes and affect classes of sounds. These are: syllable structure processes, assimilatory processes, substitution processes and multiple processes (Ingram, 1976). Hierarchically arranged constraints employed from 2 yrs.–4 yrs.	vowel and consonant harmonization	3 yrs.—/p/, /m/, /h/, /n/, /w/	Uses following rules to produce all combinations of phonemes:
Cooing—first 4 months vocalic velar or back consonantal sounds, denotes pleasure	first consonants labial most commonly /p/, /m/, /t/, and k/		cluster reduction	4 yrs.—/b/, /k/, /g/, /d/, /f/, /j/	feature changing rules
Babbling—6 months labial consonants, sound play (Ingram, 1976)	first vowels /a/, /i/, and /u/		systematic simplification	6 yrs.—/t/, /ŋ/, /r/, /l/	rules for deletion and insertion
Speech perception (in order of development) vowels presence versus absence of consonants sonorants versus stops palatized versus non-palatized consonants	homorganic fricative acquired after stop (Jacobson, 1968)		grammatical simplification (Smith, 1973)	7 yrs.—/tʃ/, /ʃ/, /z/, /dʒ/, /θ/	rules for permutation and coalescence
Between sonorants sonorants versus continuants labials versus linguals stops versus spirants pre- versus post-linguals voiced versus voiceless consonants	/h/ and /w/ first sounds acquired (Ferguson and Garnica, 1975)			8 yrs.—/s/, /v/, /ð/ 8½ yrs.— /ʒ/ (Sander, 1972)	rules with variables (assimilation, dissimilation, multiple variables, exchange rules)
Between sibilants liquids versus /y/ (Shvachkin, 1973)				7–10 yrs. comprehension of intonation (Crutthenden, 1974) 7–12 yrs. morphophonemic development (Atkinson-King, 1973)	Use of other aspects of phonological system such as stress contours, intonation patterns, pitch changes (Shane, 1973)

NOTE: Plus or minus 6 months for all age ranges reported is considered normal.

6

Developing Local Normed Assessment Instruments

Allen S. Toronto
Sharon (Mares) Merrill

Professional educators continuously find that there is a serious shortage of tests and normative information for minority groups. This problem is particularly critical for special educators. They have the responsibility of identifying children with true learning or communication deficiencies for the purpose of remediation. This identification is very difficult at present because little knowledge concerning development within minority groups is available. Educational institutions are frustrated because they are required by law to identify and treat all handicapped children but lack adequate means to do so with minorities.

In workshops and seminars concerning educational problems of minorities, the authors have encountered varying opinions and attitudes that warrant discussion in order to justify the development of locally normed instruments. The most common suggestion for testing minorities centers around the creation of a comprehensive, nationally normed test for each minority. This is an interesting proposition but is probably impossible to create such a normed test for many behaviors. To create an appropriate nationally normed test, one must have a homogenous national group to standardize it. Minority groups vary tremendously from region to region and sometimes within the same community. The linguistic components phonology and vocabulary, the targets for many tests, also vary tremendously. A national test for some behaviors such as auditory memory, nonverbal reasoning, or some visual skills may be possible. Some Spanish vocabulary items from the *Toronto Test for Receptive Vocabulary*

(Toronto, 1977a) and the *Del Rio Language Screening Test* (Toronto, 1975) have been found inappropriate for children in towns adjacent to the town in which the tests were standardized. On the other hand, nonverbal items from the *Bicultural Test of Non-Verbal Reasoning* (Toronto, 1977b) and general grammatical items on the *Screening Test of Spanish Grammar* (Toronto, 1973) appear to be fairly universal, even between ethnic groups. A national test is probably possible for the largest minorities in the United States for only some specific universal types of behavior. These behaviors have yet to be systematically determined.

Another philosophy encountered is that minorities should be evaluated with current tests standardized on the Anglo majority population to supposedly give a comparison of where a student fits nationally and indicate what the student needs in order to compete in society. There are many obvious arguments against the proposition, but mainly, that items on these tests are not valid for minorities. Students capable of answering do not because they misunderstand, are uninformed, are unmotivated to answer, or because of a host of other reasons. Such comparisons are simply unfair.

Some educators feel that formal testing should be eliminated altogether, and that criterion referenced assessment should be substituted. This type of assessment consists of determining what behaviors are normal for a particular age range and observing those behaviors in the child being examined. The child moves through a step-by-step hierarchy of predetermined criteria. This type of testing is used extensively with multiply handicapped children or brain-damaged adults. Our knowledge of normal development in minority groups, especially linguistic development, is so meager that establishing criteria is currently impossible. Here again, developmental patterns that seem universal are the only candidates for such assessment. Also, most minority children in the schools have problems that are mild or moderate, for which criterion referenced instruments are not adequately refined.

The major solution to the problem of valid assessment is to develop tests by using local resources to obtain local norms. Thus children will be compared fairly with peers in their own environment (*see* Chapter 2). Elliott and Bretzing (1980) have found local norms additionally advantageous in that, administratively, future plans can be made when reviewing curriculum and planning for program needs. The benefits of local norms have been discussed by other authors in the literature (Elliott and Bretzing, 1980; Evard and Sabers, 1979; Lyman, 1971). In spite of these conclusions, most educators needing a test do not have the expertise to construct a valid test with adequate local norms.

The purpose of this chapter is to present the basic procedures for constructing a valid and reliable locally normed test. The chapter consists of two major parts: (a) concepts of test construction and (b) steps in test construction. Although most readers may not have the statistical knowledge to adequately analyze the data they gather, competent statisticians can be found to help in this regard.

Concepts in Test Construction

The purpose of testing is twofold. First, to compare subjects with their peers and to determine placement on a scale of normal behavior. This is usually done in educational settings for the purpose of placing a child in appropriate classes. Second, to evaluate subjects' individual strengths and weaknesses regarding a particular behavior. This is done for the purpose of directing teaching or remediation.

The most useful and comprehensive tests, constructed so that both these methods of analysis are employed, usually consist of normed multiple subtests on different aspects of behavior. The *Illinois Test for Psycholinguistic Abilities* (Kirk, McCarthy, and Kirk, 1968) is the most familiar example with its subtests derived from a common model.

Types of Tests

There are several types of tests possible within the stated framework; most come in pairs. Some professionals distinguish formal from informal tests. A formal test uses normative data to compare children with their peers. The major published tests are this type, but any unpublished test using local norms for placement of students can also be considered formal. Items on these tests use broad, generic information in order to accommodate a wide range of subject knowledge.

Informal tests assess individual strengths and weaknesses for possible remedial recommendations. These range from formal publications to tests spontaneously created by clinicians seeking specific information on one child and typically examine specific information important to the learning task at hand. Formal tests have been used informally for years in testing minority children. Norms on most formal tests inappropriate for minorities are wisely ignored by professionals. A child's performance on these tests is used informally or strictly to determine a child's level of learning on a particular task.

Another distinction in evaluation is that of group testing versus individual testing. Group testing is usually used for classroom evaluation of academic skills. Group testing is not appropriate in special education because the important controls which are necessary to identify a child for remedial help are lost. A child with a learning or communication handicap has a problem that requires specific, professional analysis. A child who is a candidate for special education will probably fail a group test, but so do many children who have no special education needs. Therefore, group tests are not appropriate for use by special educators.

Another major division exists between screening tests and diagnostic tests. Screening tests are made for the purpose of testing large numbers of children quickly and identifying those who are candidates for further testing. Usually, children falling below the tenth percentile on screening tests qualify for further evaluation. Screening tests are the most common tests on the market and are the easiest to construct and standardize.

Diagnostic tests are in-depth tests usually based on some model of learning. Each component of the model has a subtest. Diagnosis of disorders is based on overall scores and comparisons of subtests. These types of tests are most difficult to construct, as they require many subtests in order to obtain a *profile* of the child's performance. Additionally, the longevity of the test depends on the veracity of the model.

A battery of screening tests is also commonly used for in-depth testing. Different screening tests of particular factors important for learning, according to each diagnostician's opinion, are used instead of a single test. This is the most common approach to testing giving diagnosticians more freedom to test according to their clinical judgment.

Norms

Norms, the end product of a test, typically determine the value of formal tests. They are the numbers by which a subject's performance is judged. Frequently they are misunderstood and misinterpreted. Simply stated, norms are averages of scores on a test for a group of subjects selected by the test originators. These subjects, called the normative group, are chosen by the examiners according to set criteria. Most professionals use criteria such as age, sex, grade, location, race, language, or handicapping conditions. These criteria are extremely important, both for the test constructors and the test users. They ensure the integrity of a test. For the clinician using the test, they indicate whether or not the norms are appropriate for the particular subject being examined.

There are two major factors to consider when using norms. First, the norms should be based on adequate numbers of children. Numbers of subjects for norms range from a handful to thousands per age group. The type of test and its purpose dictate to a large degree how many subjects are adequate. A formal test with national norms will require many more subjects from many more locations than a test developed for local use. A local test should have at least 50 subjects per one-year age group and more if one is including preschool children. The difficulty with norming on a few children is that one or two extreme performances suffice to skew the norms and invalidate them. Large numbers of subjects eliminate this influence.

Preschool children are extremely variable in their behavior so more subjects are necessary to stabilize the norms for this age group.

The second factor in using norms is to determine how appropriate they are for the children being tested. This is especially critical when testing minorities. Since we are attempting to classify or place children educationally, it is crucial they be compared to their peers, rather than another group of children with different values, motivations, and experiences. Several major factors invalidate norms obtained outside the minority community. Cultural and socioeconomic influences determine test-taking behavior of children to a large degree. Values, motivations, and competitiveness differ between ethnic groups and between socioeconomic groups. These are probably the major reasons why significant differences exist on scores between groups. Linguistic differences are another major cause of invalid items from tests normed on monolingual English-speaking children from outside the minority community. If children cannot adequately decode the linguistic input from an item, they will simply guess or not answer. Such items, common on formal tests used with minority groups, are probably the most obvious to a clinician and constitute the most frequent complaint these authors receive.

Other less obvious factors influencing the appropriateness of test items for minority children are time and geographic location. Most popular formal tests have 10 to 20-year-old norms. Many people have the mistaken idea that norms are fixed and once obtained are always reliable. Behavior, values, education, and language change with time. Old norms may be invalid, especially social and academic norms. Norms requiring nonverbal reasoning seem to be the most resistant to the influences of time. Groups from different geographic locations, even though they fit into the same ethnic group, vary considerably in their behavior.

Most people are unaware that there seems to be more variance in scores on tests for minorities. In the minority groups the authors have tested, the children are less homogenous than the children in the dominant middle-class Anglo culture. There are more individual differences linguistically, educationally, and socially within these groups, which lead to a wider range of scores on tests. Thus, the standard deviations are larger for these groups. Tests for minorities that have more variance are less predictive than those that have little variance. One cannot have as much faith in educational placement of a minority child according to the score.

An example of this phenomenon occurred when the *Wechsler Intelligence Scale for Children* (WISC) (Wechsler, 1949) was translated into Spanish and standardized in Puerto Rico. The average IQ score on the English version of the WISC is 100 compared with a standard deviation of 15 points. After the WISC had been made appropriate in Spanish and standardized, it was found that the mean IQ for Puerto Rican children was 88, with a standard deviation of 22 points (Wechsler, 1970). This difference between average scores is graphically presented in Figure 6-1.

FIGURE 6-1

United States and Puerto Rican Norms for the WISC

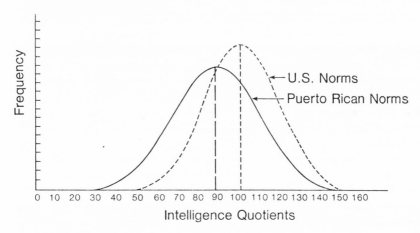

This figure demonstrates the results of testing a more heterogenous group. According to these norms, a Puerto Rican child must have an IQ score below 44 before being classified as retarded, while an Anglo child only needs a score of 70. Again, the predictive value of the score is diluted because of the increased variance in behavior of children in the same age group.

The factors involved in determining norms must be considered when interpreting test scores. Obtaining local normative data for original tests solves many of the problems that usually invalidate norms. If done correctly, the differences in culture, socioeconomic level, language, time, and geographical location are minimized. However, it must be realized that local norms are limited to use within the community. To generalize those norms to other areas is questionable.

Steps in Test Construction

Initial Planning

One of the most important activities in the construction of a new test is the initial planning and decision-making. The test developer must begin by identifying both the type of test to be constructed, e.g., screening, diagnostic, or achievement, and the behaviors to be assessed, e.g., auditory discrimination, vocabulary, or comprehension of concepts. A test should have a firm educational purpose. These activities will definitely affect the overall validity of the test. Test validity is determined by a variety of different procedures that assess whether the test measures what it purports to measure (Ingram, 1977). It is therefore essential that, prior to initiating any item development activities, the developers should determine the behaviors to be assessed, determine whether or not those isolated behaviors are *testable*, and how important those isolated behaviors are in determining ultimate educational success or failure.

The completion of this initial planning must involve the coordinated effort of those professionals who will ultimately utilize the new instrument. It is their responsibility to identify the needs for assessment, the type of assessment instrument most needed, and the target population for whom the test is intended. For example, if the need for a diagnostic test for Spanish-speaking children with potential native language deficits is identified, then speech/language specialists, teachers of severe language handicapped children, and their administrators should be involved in making decisions about the new test to be developed. The initial planning for the development of a new instrument must also encompass practical considerations such as time, money, and available personnel resources. These practical considerations will ultimately determine success or failure of the project.

Locally normed tests are usually developed so that the norming group is more precisely defined (Anastasi, 1961). Some of the major variables that affect behavior on a given test include age, grade, sex, geographic region, socioeconomic level, language, and ethnic and cultural background. The variables that define the norming group should be identified prior to development of the test during the planning of test construction. For developing tests for Spanish-speaking children, questions such as these have been considered:

1. How much Spanish do these children speak? Do they speak Spanish in the classroom, at home, and/or on the playground?
2. What instrument was used to assess their proficiency in Spanish? Were these children classified as Non-English Proficient (NEP) or Limited-English Proficient (LEP)?
3. What dialect of Spanish do these children speak: Cuban, Puerto Rican, Mexican, Chicano, mixtures with Native American, English, or other dialects?
4. Are these children permanent citizens in the community or migrants? What percentage are illegal immigrants?
5. What socioeconomic level do these children represent? How was their socioeconomic level determined?
6. What age ranges will be represented in the sample?
7. Are these children situated in regular classrooms with no bilingual instruction, in bilingual classrooms with Spanish and English instruction, or in special education classrooms?

The description of the norming group should be defined carefully during the planning phase. For a local normed test, the specific population targeted for the norming group will be dependent upon the population available. In some instances, different subgroups must be accounted for in the same community. For example, in the *Screening Test of Spanish Grammar* (Toronto, 1973), norms for both Mexican American and Puerto Rican children were gathered. The American Psychological Association (APA) stresses the necessity of clearly defining the population on which the test was normed (APA, 1974). The future test user of the locally normed and developed test will then know what individuals can be appropriately compared to the norming group. This example of a normative group comes from the *Pruebas de Expresion y Percepcion de la Lengua Espanola* (Mares, 1981): "The purpose of this test is to aid in diagnosing a language disorder among NEP/LEP Mexican American students between the ages of 6 and 10 years old from a low socioeconomic level in the Southern California area" (p. 1).

When the target population, the type of test, and the behaviors to be tested have been identified, the format for the test or subtests must be considered. The format of a test depends largely on the language skill being tested. For example, if the behavior to be tested is auditory discrimination, how will this skill be tested? One procedure for assessing auditory discrimination could be represented as a minimal pairs task. In this task, it must be decided if the words will be tape-recorded and replayed by the examiner, or read aloud by the examiner. Also, the materials to be used for this task need to be identified, i.e., tape recorder, pictures.

If the language skill to be tested is vocabulary development, the test developers need to decide if the task will involve identification of nouns, verbs, adjectives, and/or adverbs as single words or in phrases. A source for the creation of pictures will have to be identified. Will the pictures be colored, line drawings, or photographs? The specific format for each test or subtest must be decided.

When the test involves several subtests, the sequence of presentation also must be identified. In a recent test development project, five subtests were developed for a test battery in Spanish (Mares, 1981). The five subtests included Auditory Sequential Memory, Sentence Repetition, Story Comprehension, Auditory Association, and Encoding. Initially, the first subtest presented in the pilot study was Story Comprehension, which had eight stories. When the pilot study was completed, many of the field researchers complained about this arrangement. The Auditory Sequential Memory subtest was moved to become the first subtest presented, because this task utilizes toys. The presentation of the toys helped the field researchers gain rapport with the student, whom they did not know before the testing situation began.

Test Item Development

After the initial planning is completed, the test developers can begin creating the initial pool of test items from which the final test will be selected.

The sources for the creation of items will be dependent upon the type of test to be developed. The source for item content for an achievement test would be the curricular materials used by the respective district for, e.g., math or reading. This type of test is relatively easy to develop because the course content is already known. Educational objectives for the district can be amplified and used to write the test items. (For a more detailed description of item writing techniques for achievement tests *see* Roid and Haladyna, 1980.)

The opposite is true for a test of proficiency. The content for the test items becomes more subjective. The selection of items for a proficiency test usually begins with linguistic theory and statistical sampling (Davies, 1977). Basing the selection of items on linguistic theory is especially difficult when developing a test for NES students. As mentioned in the beginning of this chapter, very little developmental information is available for languages other than English.

The methods for item collection used successfully by the authors are interviewing and language sampling. In the collection of items for the *Del Rio Language Screening Test* (Toronto, 1975), native speakers of Spanish living in the area of Del Rio, Texas, were interviewed. These native speakers were mothers, classroom aides, and teachers. *Brain-storming* sessions were held with different groups to discuss the different vocabulary used in the home and at school. This combined vocabulary was used to write the test items, especially for the vocabulary subtest. This method was employed so that the vocabulary used would be appropriate for the region, both linguistically and culturally. The pictures needed for the test were then developed, and the items were pilot tested on a small population.

The item selection for *Pruebas de Expresion Oral y Percepcion de la Lengua Espanola (PEOPLE)* (Mares, 1981) also utilized the same interviewing technique. In addition, large samples of lexical items (nouns, verbs, adverbs, adjectives) were collected by bilingual speech/language specialists. These samples were collected on the playground, in the classroom, and in the language resource centers. This vocabulary was then used to write the test items for all of the subtests in the test. The initial corpus of items for the *PEOPLE* contained 500 items, which were then reviewed by consultants and reduced to 250 items which were accurate and appropriate. These remaining items were then sequenced into an order of difficulty by a panel of experts.

The Pilot Test

The purpose of the pilot test is to preview the items before they are field-tested. Only a small number of subjects are needed for a pilot test. The number of types of subjects selected for the pilot test should be in proportion to the projected number for standardization. The pilot test should include samples from the region, age levels, socioeconomic levels, and ethnic groups that will be represented in the norming sample. Several pilot tests can be completed to include the *subgroups* as time and resources permit.

All of the items of the pilot test should be presented. The examiners should keep very specific records of the responses for each item given by the subjects. It is recommended that the subjects be interviewed after each test is completed. The questions asked in the interview should center around the *errors* made on the test items. This procedure will help to identify inappropriate and ambiguous items.

The pilot test results can be analyzed by using a variety of techniques. These techniques are discussed in this chapter's section on field testing. In-depth statistical procedures are not necessary during this phase of test construction. A pilot test is very helpful, in most cases, because very poor items can be quickly identified, and the sequence of items can be readjusted. However, for some test construction projects, a pilot test may not be feasible because of time constraints.

The Field Test

Field testing involves sampling of a larger population. It is advisable to have a minimum of 25 subjects at each age or grade level per subgroup. The field test is similar to standardization, only on a smaller scale. Also, field testing the items allows the test developers the opportunity to do extensive analysis of the test. It is at this time that test items undergo vigorous editing. Otherwise, many poor items would become part of the standardized test.

The procedures for administration of the field test should be the same to be followed during standardization. The test should be administered in a standard manner by all field examiners. All of the test items are field-tested with no allowances for ceiling or basal scores. Ceiling and basal scores are reserved for the final standardized test, if they are to be used. These scores indicate top and bottom levels of performance for a child during the test to determine the level at which testing may begin or end.

After all of the subjects have been tested, the item analysis begins. This can be completed in a variety of ways, both statistically and linguistically. The minimum amount of statistical data required to evaluate test results are: mean scores of the total population by subtest, mean subtest and total test scores by age group or grade, and frequencies for correct and incorrect responses by each item for each age or grade level. Standard deviations for each group should be tabulated separately. If the test is a proficiency test, the responses for each item should be tabulated. An example of this is given in Table 6-1 (Mares, 1981). The purpose of doing this type of analysis is to identify most of the correct and incorrect responses possible on each specific test item and also to identify many dialect variations. This information will aid in editing the test item and in providing valuable linguistic data for the examiners.

TABLE 6-1

Frequency Analysis of An Item From the PEOPLE

Item	*Response*	*Absolute Frequency*	*Relative Frequency*
¿Qué usuas para	*escoba*-broom	37	27.2
limpiar la casa?	*trapos*-rags	20	14.7
(What do you	*manos*-hands	10	7.4
use to clean	*toalla*-towel	11	8.1
the house?)	*jabón*-soap	3	2.2
	aspirador-vacuum	7	4.1
	mapeador-mop	3	2.2
	garra-rag	4	2.9
	plumero-feather duster	2	1.5
	líquidos-liquids	1	.7
	cosas-things	10	7.3
	papel-paper	5	3.7
	carro-car	2	1.5
	aqua-water	13	9.6
	No response	8	6.9
		136	100

From S.L. Mares, *Pruebas de Espresion Oral y Percepcion de la Lengua Espanola.* Los Angeles, Office of Los Angeles County Superintendent of Schools, 1981.

To illustrate the type of reasoning involved in analyzing items, the item in Table 6-1 was modified for the following reasons. It was much too general. The number of correct answers should be kept to a minimum, thereby reducing the amount of subjectivity in scoring the item. By adding the word *cosa* (thing) and changing *para limpiar la casa* (to clean the house) to *para barrer el piso* (to sweep the floor), the item becomes "*¿Qué cosa usuas para barrer el piso?*" (What thing do you use to sweep the floor?) The item became much more specific, thus decreasing the number of possible answers and making the scoring of this item much easier for the examiner.

Table 6-2 presents examples of how other problem test items were identified and modified. Bilingual professionals and students can be valuable resources when analyzing test results. All items should be reviewed for cultural and linguistic content.

Frequencies gathered at every age level for every item will help identify items that discriminate between different age levels. Some items may be discriminating for young children but not for older students. Those easier items will still be needed for younger students. Other items may be very difficult for younger students yet discriminating for older students. A

TABLE 6-2
Sample Analysis of Items From the PEOPLE

Initial Item	Response	Frequency of Response	Explanation	Correction of Item After Review
¿Qué usuas para coser? (What do you use to sew?)	aguba (needle) fuego (fire) other	40% 30% 30%	Coser (to sew and cocer (to boil) are homonyms.	¿Qué cosa usuas para coser la ropa? (What thing do you use to sew clothes?)
Los árboles tienen hojas Las flores tienen _____. (Trees have leaves. Flowers have _____.)	hojas (leaves) pétalos (petals) other	46% 8% 40%	Hojas (leaves) also means petals. Item is not discriminating.	Las flores tienen pétalos. Los árboles tienen _____. (Flowers have petals. Trees have _____.)
El hombre es alto. El niño es _____. (A man is tall. A boy is _____.	chico (little) corto (short) other	75% 20% 5%	Short-tall distinction was difficult for all age levels. Item is ambiguous and inappropriate.	Eliminated.

From S.L. Mares, *Preubas de Expresion Oral y Percepcion de la Lengua Espanola*. Los Angeles, Office of Los Angeles County Superintendent of Schools, 1981.

difficulty range from simple to complex is needed to challenge the abilities of all age ranges represented in the population. There are always items 95% of the children answer correctly or incorrectly. These items have no discriminating value. They are too difficult or too easy for the population and should be eliminated. Tests that have several ethnic groups represented in the norming group will require more analysis to identify test item bias. Frequencies can be gathered for each item for each ethnic group. If an item is answered 70% correct by one ethnic group and only 30% by a different ethnic group, the item may be biased in favor of the first group (Scheuneman, 1979).

There are many statistical methods that can be utilized to analyze test items. However, a discussion of statistics is not within the scope of this chapter. The reader may wish to consult Nie (1975) for a more in-depth discussion of statistical procedures.

Once the test items have been analyzed, the pool of items should be reduced. Items that are not discriminating at any age level, are duplications, are biased culturally, linguistically, and sexually; and are ambiguous should be deleted. Some of the very simple items can then be used as demonstration items for the test. The sequence of the subtests should be changed as recommended by the examiners. The test items within each subtest should again be ordered according to statistical results or linguistic content. The test is ready to be standardized if the items are sufficient for the educational purpose identified during the planning phase. When there are not sufficient items to satisfy the original purpose, it will be necessary to create and field test more items.

Standardization

Standardization is essentially the same as field testing, except that editing items after the data is collected is not permissible. It is imperative that the procedures used to administer the test are *standard* throughout this phase of construction. Therefore, administrative directions should be clear for all who are expected to collect data. Such procedures as determining ceilings or basals, repeating test items, probing for more specific responses, arranging the testing environment, limiting time for administering certain subtests, and handling articulation errors on expressive items, should be decided before collecting. A list of considerations that are essential during the standardization process is presented by Weiner and Hoock (1973):

1. The norming group should be representative of the population which was identified during the planning phase mentioned earlier.
2. The sample size should be sufficient so that an adequate range of scores is collected.
3. The norming group should be identified by a process which is random- ized so that the results are not biased by the selection process.
4. The collection of test data should not extend beyond three months so that the results are not influenced by time. (This is especially true for preschool children whose development and growth is rapid.)
5. The statistical analysis must be rigorous and in-depth.

When the population sample is specific, it will be necessary to identify a large number of students who fit within the norm group(s) criteria, and then choose individuals within this pool of subjects in a random manner. This type of sampling technique is termed a *stratified sample* (Plakos and Russell, 1980). Stratified sampling helps assure that the data collected is representative of the population that is identified by subgroups.

The norming group should be as large as possible and practical. A small norming group will tend to be skewed by a few very good or very poor test performers or by a narrow range of scores. A minimum number of 50 subjects, ideally 100 subjects, should be sampled at each age or grade level. This may not be practical in most districts, especially when the test is individually administered. It may be necessary for several school districts to pool their resources so that a larger sample can be collected. The standardization of the *PEOPLE* test was accomplished by 35 school districts within five counties (Mares, 1981).

After standardization data are collected, it is necessary to determine test reliability and validity. Test reliability means that a test gives consistent results. The simplest method for examining test reliability is test-retest. In essense, a small number of subjects who were tested during test standardization are retested approximately one month later. The subjects are selected in a random manner so there is less bias in selection. The scores for both tests are then correlated to determine temporal consistency of results. If possible, other types of reliability should be determined through split-half procedures and analysis of variance.

Test validity can be determined in a variety of different ways; however, only one method will be discussed. For a more detailed discussion of test validity, consult references at the end of this chapter. *Concurrent validity* is one of the more convenient ways of evaluating test validity. In this procedure, another test must be identified in order to assess the same or similar criteria for the same age or grade levels. The second test is then administered to a small sample of the norming population. The results of the two tests are correlated with each other. It is essential that the second test be widely used and already accepted as a valid instrument; otherwise the newly developed test will be compared to another test of unknown potential and value.

The norms will be developed from the data collected during standardization. The test developers should determine if the norms should be represented as percentiles or as scaled scores. This determination depends on the test users anticipated. Speech/language specialists and psychologists are familiar with interpreting scaled scores. Classroom teachers, aides, and other personnel may be more accustomed to percentiles. The test norms should be easy to interpret. The number of norm tables necessary to give an accurate description of the norming population will depend upon the number of subgroups sampled. Separate tables may be needed if subgroup norms vary significantly. Subgroup norms may be formed with respect to age, grade, sex, geographic region, and socioeconomic level. The use of the test will also determine what type of differentiation between groups is needed (Anastasi, 1961).

The Test Manual

When all of the test results have been analyzed, the test developer is ready to write the test manual. A test manual should be written even if the test will be used only locally. The potential users of the test need to know how the test was developed and what its prescribed uses are. The following standards have been suggested by the American Psychological Association for inclusion in the test manual (APA, 1974).

1. Information needed to substantiate any claims by the test developer.
2. A description of the development of the test, rationale, specifications in writing items, procedures, and results of item analysis and other research.
3. Information about plans for future revisions.
4. Information which helps test users make correct interpretation of test results and warns against common misuses.
5. A statement of purposes and applications for which the test is recommended.
6. A description of the psychological, educational, or other reasoning underlying the test and the nature of the characteristic it is intended to measure.
7. A statement of any special qualifications required to administer and interpret the test.
8. A statement of evidence of reliability and validity and other pertinent data to support any claims being made.
9. Directions for administration with sufficient clarity and emphasis so that the test user can duplicate them.
10. Directions for scoring with a maximum of detail and clarity to reduce the possibility of error.
11. Norms for the test which refer with specific detail to the clearly described population.

Summary

A well developed locally normed instrument will be an invaluable tool for educational specialists faced with the overwhelming task of assessing the abilities and disabilities of culturally diverse children. However, the users of these tests must always keep in mind the limitations of locally developed and normed instruments and not use these tests for purposes for which they were not intended or on populations on which they were not normed. No test, no matter how well developed or validated, should ever be used as a sole determinant of the educational placement of any child. Davies (1977) summarizes the authors' feelings well when he states, "Testing is not an end in itself; its essential aim is to provide information which will help us to make intelligent decisions about possible courses of action" (p. 87).

References

Anastasi, A.: *Psychological Testing*, 2nd ed. New York, Macmillan, 1961.

American Psychological Association: *Standards Manual for Education and Psychological Tests*. Washington, D.C., American Psychological Association, 1974.

Davies, A.: The construction of language tests. In Allen, J.P., and Davies, A. (Eds.): *Testing and Experimental Methods* (Vol. 4) London, Oxford University, 1977.

Elliott, S.N., and Bretzing, B.H.: Using and updating local norms. *Psychology in the Schools, 17*:196–201, 1980.

Evard, B.L., and Sabers, D.L.: Speech and language testing with distinct ethnic-racial groups: A survey of procedures for improving validity. *Speech and Hearing Disorders, 44*:271–281, 1979.

Ingram, E.: Basic concepts in testing. In Allen, J.P., and Davies, A. (Eds.): *Testing and Experimental Methods* (Vol. 4). London, Oxford University, 1977.

Kirk, S.A., McCarthy, J.J., and Kirk, W.D.: *The Illinois Test of Psycholinguistic Abilities*, Rev. ed. Urbana, University of Illinois, 1968.

Lyman, H.B.: *Test Scores and What They Mean*, 2nd ed. New York, Macmillan, 1971.

Mares, S.L.: *Pruebas de Expresion Oral y Precepcion de la Lengua Espanola*. Los Angeles, Office of Los Angeles County Superintendent of Schools, 1981.

Nie, N.H., et al.: *Statistical Package for the Social Sciences*. New York, McGraw-Hill, 1975.

Plakos, J., and Russell, D.M.: *Measuring and Evaluating Affective Growth in School Programs*. Sacramento, California State Department of Education, 1980.

Roid, G., and Haladyna, T.: The emergence of an item-writing technology. *Review of Education Research, 50*:293–314, 1980.

Scheuneman, J.: A method of assessing bias in test items. *J Educational Measurement, 16*:143–152, 1979.

Toronto, A.S.: *Screening Test of Spanish Grammar*. Evanston, Northwestern University, 1973.

Toronto, A.S.: *Del Rio Language Screening Test*. Austin, National Educational Laboratory, 1975.

Toronto, A.S.: *Toronto Test for Receptive Vocabulary*. Austin, National Educational Laboratory, 1977a.

Toronto, A.S.: *Bicultural Test of Non-Verbal Reasoning*. Austin, National Educational Laboratory, 1977b.

Wechsler, D.: *Wechsler Intelligence Scale for Children*. New York, The Psychological Corporation, 1949.

Wechsler, D.: *Escala de Intelligencia Wechsler para Niños.* New York, The Psychological Corporation, 1970.

Weiner, P.S., and Hoock, W.C.: The standardization of tests: Criteria and criticism. *J Speech and Hearing Research, 16*:616–626, 1973.

7

Audiological Screening and Assessment of Bilingual Children

J.C. Cooper, Jr.

Introduction

Preparing a discussion of audiology in a text as far ranging as this poses several problems, not the least of which is defining the level of discourse. Specialists from a wide variety of fields might scan, if not study, a chapter as comprehensive as this. This chapter will address those who have little, if any, prior knowledge of audiology. An audiologist may find generalization and omission of detail. Some information for nonaudiologists intimately involved with the hearing impaired has been excluded in this chapter. A volume devoted entirely to hearing loss will supply more detailed information (*see* Northern and Downs, 1974). This chapter will provide some insight into audiological considerations for the bilingual child.

Effects of Hearing Loss on Language

Hearing loss is the most devastating of disabilities. A deformed limb or blindness reduces mobility. Mental retardation reduces potential for intellectual achievement. Disease shortens life span. None of these operates like a hearing loss. To one degree or another, hearing loss isolates an individual from the most important contact with the world—other human beings. This occurs because the bulk of social interaction is spoken. To be unable to hear is equivalent to being unable to communicate. Beyond social isolation, the hearing impaired are underachievers. Consider that those with severe hearing loss have a normal distribution of intelligence, yet, after completing schooling, 30% are illiterate (Vernon, 1970). Less than 5% achieve at a higher level than tenth grade. A major reason is that the human nervous system is somehow geared to language learning during the first years of life (Lenneberg, 1967). If language is not heard (or otherwise encountered) during this period, then it will unlikely be developed. If it is heard imperfectly, it will unlikely be mastered. From the point of view of underachievers, it has been demonstrated that those with learning disabilities fail hearing screening tests three times as often as those without disabilities (Katz and Illmer, 1972).

For present purposes, it is important to note that there is evidence that hearing loss is more prevalent among certain bilingual cultures and those with low socioeconomic status, commonly correlated with bilingualism in the United States. As many as 38% of preschool children may have hearing losses (Cooper, Gates, Owen, and Dixon, 1975), although that the majority came from Mexican American homes was stricken from the original report by the editors (*See* Chapter 10 regarding hearing loss in the native American population.) Reports of hearing loss in other large bilingual groups in the United States could not be uncovered. Whenever hearing loss and bilingualism (or the need for acquiring a second language) occur together, a child is doubly damned. Underachievement can then occur in both languages.

Physiology of Hearing

Before considering the specifics of identifying, assessing, and compensating for hearing loss, a review of the function and likely malfunctions of the auditory system is appropriate. It is convenient to think of the auditory system in terms of five distinct functions. The first is amplification of environmental sounds before they reach the sensory cells. The anatomy involved is called the conductive system and extends from the external ear through the eardrum to the last of the three bones of the middle ear, the stapes. The second function, analysis of the intensity and tonal composition of sound, is carried out in the inner ear. Here the complicated vibrations delivered by the stapes are sorted out in a manner not unlike transcribing a tune onto sheet music for piano. The third function is detection of the analyzed signal and is carried out in the inner ear by hair cells, which, continuing the simple analogy, are like the keys on a piano. When stimulated, they activate nerve fibers that can be likened to the piano strings. The fibers serve the fourth function, transmission of the analyzed signal to the brain. The last of the five functions is the interpretation of the signal by the brain.

Although there are disorders that affect analysis, transmission, and interpretation, they are rare in comparison to other defects, and their consequences are so dramatic that they are unlikely to go unnoticed. Because they are more prevalent and because their effects can be far more subtle, discussion will be limited to two types of hearing loss: conductive and sensory impairment. The latter category is usually labeled *sensorineural* hearing loss or *nerve* deafness, although nerve fiber damage is seldom the primary problem.

Conductive Hearing Loss. The effect of conductive hearing loss can be best understood as a reduction of loudness. Although the effect can be dramatic, as in the case of a child with a congenital defect that obliterated the entire system (no external ear, canal, or eardrum), the majority of conductive hearing losses involve congestion, not unlike a stuffy nose. These conditions are generally labeled *otitis media* and may be modified by adjectives such as *chronic*, *serous*, or *purulent*. The effects are mild and may go unnoticed because they are generally not painful, they may be overcome by increasing the intensity of the voice, and because the effects may be minimal when engaging in face-to-face conversation.

An appreciation of the effect of conductive hearing loss can be had by considering the following example. If, late at night, when there would be little noise, two normal hearing people stationed themselves at opposite ends of a football field and one spoke in a normal conversational voice, the other would be able to understand approximately half of the words from a standard speech threshold test. The listener with a maximum conductive hearing loss would have to advance some 10 yards from the speaker to understand half the words. The point to remember is that the person with a conductive hearing loss is subject to sensory deprivation by virtue of the fact that his or her auditory *area* has collapsed to 1% of normal (area is a function of the radius squared).

A further complication of conductive hearing loss is that its degree can vary, literally, from day to day. In effect, the child ceasses to be able to rely on the auditory environment in the same sense that one would cease to rely upon traffic lights that blinked rapidly and randomly from one color to another. This kind of distrust of the auditory environment by hearing impaired children has been demonstrated experimentally (Gaeth, 1966). More concretely, a variety of studies have shown that chronic conductive hearing loss reduces language level, level of performance on mechanical arithmetic and reading tasks, and amount of verbal responses (Forcucci and

Stark, 1972; Holm and Kunz, 1969; Ling, 1972). Even short-term (as little as five hours) conductive hearing loss has been shown to affect the task of detecting a soft tone (Katz, 1965). Furthermore, the effects of chronic conductive hearing loss are not self-correcting after the hearing loss has been resolved. It would appear that educational intervention is necessary to restore normal progress (Ling, 1972).

Beyond any educational consequences lies the spectre of permanent disfigurement and life-threatening disease. Suffice it to say that unattended conductive hearing loss can lead to facial paralysis or death (Glasscock, 1972). If there is a bright spot in this dismal picture, it is that the vast majority of conductive impairments can be medically corrected. The earlier the intervention the easier the medical and educational remediation will be.

Sensorineural Hearing Loss. If conductive hearing loss can be conceptualized as a defective volume control of a hi-fi set, then sensorineural hearing loss can be thought of as a combination of defects in the volume and tone controls. Since the sensors for the bass end of the tonal scale are generally less affected than those for the treble, one can approximate sensorineural hearing loss by turning the bass control to maximum, turning the treble control to minimum, and reducing the volume control until the sound is barely audible. Perhaps the most important aspect of this analogy is that a portion of the melody of speech is simply unavailable for transmission to the brain. It is also important to note that the consonant sounds are represented in the treble range. It is as though someone had erased many of the consonants from a manuscript. The remaining letters lend little information regarding the message.

Fortunately, severe sensorineural hearing loss, or *deafness*, is exceedingly rare, no more than 1 per 2,000 (Northern and Downs, 1974). The mildest forms do not exceed 4% of school-age children (Hull and Mielke, 1971). The dark side of the picture is that sensorineural loss can rarely be corrected. Amplification, by a hearing aid, is often necessary to ensure that even a minimal auditory signal reaches the brain.

Graphic Representation of Hearing Loss. This brief summary of the two major types of hearing loss in the above discussion can be supplemented by examining their graphic representations. The first is what is usually called a performance-intensity function of speech discrimination. Figure 7–1 represents three such functions.

The normal curve on the left demonstrates what is obvious: as speech gets louder the ability to understand improves until complete understanding is achieved. Beyond that point, speech simply becomes louder. Notice that normal individuals can achieve 100% understanding at levels somewhat

FIGURE 7-1

An abstraction of the relationship between understanding and the
intensity of speech for normal hearing and two types of hearing loss
subjects. Conversational loudness is 50 dB.

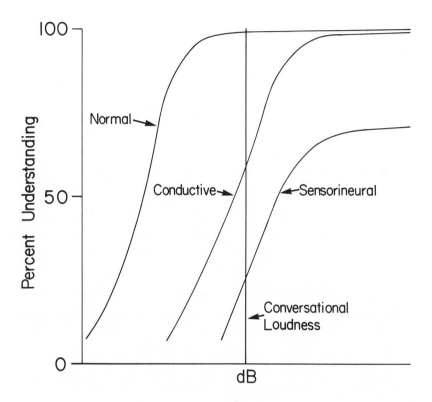

below the conversational level indicated by the vertical line. At conversational levels, persons with both conductive and sensorineural hearing losses
suffer the same disability, reduced understanding, as speech is not loud
enough. When speech is louder than normal, the conductive hearing loss is
overcome and complete understanding is achieved. However, this is not the
case in most sensorineural hearing losses. To one degree or another, some of
the speech is simply not converted into a signal that can be sent to the brain.
Complete understanding may not be achieved, no matter how loud speech
level is.

This can be better understood by examining the second of the two graphic
representations, the audiogram presented in Figure 7-2.

FIGURE 7-2

A hypothetical audiogram illustrating the selective effect of hearing loss on understanding speech. Sounds above the line of connected dots cannot be heard.

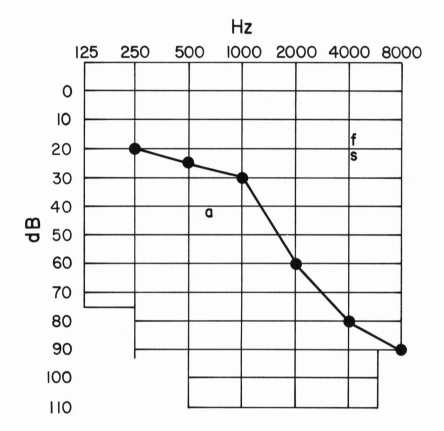

For orientation, 250 Hz on the *x* axis is approximately middle C on the piano, and 4000 Hz is close to the last note on the right hand end of the piano. Zero dB on the *y* axis represents the softest sounds heard by a normal hearing individual, and 110 dB is close to the loudest sounds that can be tolerated. This standard audiometric representation is atypical of most graphs, in that louder sounds are increasingly lower on the page. It is convenient to remember that the lower the graphic representation, the louder the sound for a normal person. The line connecting the dots represents a hypothetical case of hearing loss. The dots indicate, for example, that sounds of 20 dB are required so that middle C is just barely audible. The lower the dots, the poorer the hearing. The person is only aware of sounds below the line.

Notice the letters placed on the audiogram. These letters indicate the frequency range and intensity of that speech sound spoken in a normal conversational voice. Notice that this hypothetical individual can hear the vowel *a*, but is unaware of consonants such as *f* and *s*. The impact of this audiogram is that while the individual may be aware of speech, it is unlikely that understanding of the word *safe* will take place. Further, it is important to note that the degree to which understanding takes place will vary as a function of the precise composition of the speech sounds involved in the message. Thus, a hearing loss may present itself as inconsistent or intermittent understanding of the spoken word. The parallelism between the effects of hearing loss and the consequences of bilingualism or first/second language learning is obvious.

Screening for Hearing Loss

It might be assumed that intimate contact with a child would disclose hearing loss. This is probably not so in the case of parents and certainly not so in the case of teachers. It has been demonstrated that teachers detect only 62% of children with confirmed hearing losses and that only 12% of suspected losses are confirmed (Geyer and Yankauer, 1956). Moreover, since most conductive losses and virtually all sensorineural losses occur without the child suffering any large amount of pain or discomfort, such indications of loss are less than reliable. Therefore, screening is necessary to ensure that the *majority* of hearing losses are detected.

The qualifier *majority* is used to emphasize that no screening technique is perfect. For example, consider that the efficiency of vision screening is such that only 80% of young children who fail are found to have poor vision (Hatfield, 1967). A definitive statement about the status of a person's vision or hearing can only be made after a thorough evaluation. However, evaluations are expensive and impractical for an entire population. The rationale for screening is based on economics: detect the most hearing losses at the least cost. It can be demonstrated that early detection of hearing loss should reduce the cost of rehabilitation (Cooper, 1978) as well as easing the possible suffering of the individual so afflicted. Thus, hearing screening is a viable economic endeavor above any humanitarian reason. Screening should be conducted on all individuals who enter an educational program, no matter what their ages.

Techniques

The two major types of techniques used to screen for hearing defects are audiometric and impedance. The basis of audiometric screening is the presentation of relatively soft sounds (20 to 25 dB) at a variety of frequencies whose combinations are included in the range from 500 to 6000 Hz. Specific tones depend on the agency recommending screening. It is assumed that if a child can hear these very soft sounds, hearing is likely to be normal. The technique has been found to be satisfactory in estimating hearing sensitivity (Melnik, Eagles, and Levine, 1964) and, hence, in the detection of sensori-neural hearing losses because they involve significant reductions in sensitiv-ity. However, the technique is totally inadequate in detecting conductive hearing losses, many of which produce only small decrements in sensitivity. Depending upon the particular study, up to 76% of conductive hearing losses requiring medical attention may go unnoticed by audiometric screen-ing (Cooper, Gates, Owen, and Dixon, 1975).

The alternative, impedance screening, has only recently come into wide-spread use; thus the criteria for failing remain in a state of flux. The problem does not lie in the technique itself, rather because it is sensitive to changes that may escape a physician's notice being either minor or possibly transient. Since conductive hearing losses fluctuate, a child may have a mild defect at the time of screening that may resolve by the time of a physician's examina-tion. Nonetheless, it is noted that impedance bridges detect more than 90% of conductive problems which are confirmed by a physician's immediate examination (Cooper, Gates, Owen, and Dixon, 1975). It is convenient to summarize the comparative efficiency of the two techniques detecting conductive hearing loss by saying that the use of audiometers will dramati-cally under-refer patients while the use of impedance bridges will moder-ately over-refer. A serious limitation of impedance technique is that it fails to reliably detect sensorineural hearing loss. This shortcoming cannot be ignored.

The selection of a specific screening technique and its implementation should be left to an audiologist. There are several reasons for this admoni-tion; the following example may bring some insight into the problems associated with screening, in this case, giving appropriate instructions. One objective of any screening program is to approximate an individual's ability to hear very soft tones. In the case of an adult, the instructions would be similar to the following:

> You will be hearing a series of tones, some high pitched and some low. Some will be clear and easy to hear, and others will be so soft that you may not be sure you have heard the tone. Please respond (raise your hand, push a button) every time you hear a tone no matter how soft it may be. You do not have to be certain that you heard the tone since some will be so soft that you will hear them only half of the time that they are presented. For that reason you are urged to respond even if you think you have heard a tone.

One can imagine the difficulty in conveying those instructions to a two or three year old child, whether bilingual or not.

A Recommended Screening Technique

It is recommended that screening be conducted with a combination of audiometric and impedance measures. Such a combination involves three distinct steps, the first two using an impedance bridge and the last using an audiometer. Most screening equipment includes both functions in a single device. Initially, a narrow rubber tipped probe is placed in the entry to the ear canal. The tip must be seated firmly enough to prevent any air leakage from the canal. The canal is then pressurized and the air pressure varied in positive and negative directions. During the pressurization a tone is continuously presented via the probe. The amount of sound reflected from the eardrum is monitored by a microphone which provides an indication of the condition of the middle ear. The second step involves presenting a loud tone to one of the ears. This loud presentation causes a reflex contraction of one of the muscles of the middle ear, which is detected by the microphone since the contraction alters the amount of reflected energy.

The first two steps should take no more than 45 seconds per child. It should be noted that no cooperation whatsoever is required from the individual being screened. This is what makes the impedance technique so attractive for screening young children. However, excessive movement or vocalization creates noise that is detected by the microphone, preventing an accurate measurement of the energy reflected from the eardrum. The third step is to present at least one soft tone (25 dB at 4000 Hz) through an earphone. The child is instructed to respond when the tone (or tones) is heard. An allusion has already been made to the difficulty in adequately completing this portion of the examination.

If there is an indication of a conductive hearing loss either in the pattern of energy reflected from the eardrum during pressure variations or by failure to observe the acoustic reflex, the child is failed. Such failures should be either referred to a physician for possible medical management or, depending on the degree of severity of the possible conductive loss, scheduled for rescreening within six to eight weeks, the typical duration of transient conductive problems (Brooks, 1976). Rescreening of children with indications of mild conductive hearing loss is desirable because the loss may be only temporary. It would be inefficient and costly to refer for immediate medical management. Referral occurs if the child fails the rescreening.

Failure to respond to the tone indicates either that the child may have a sensorineural hearing loss or, in the presence of a conductive hearing loss, will give some indication of its severity. If the only failure is not responding to the tone, then a sensorineural loss is present or the child has misunderstood the task. If misunderstanding is suspected and the screening team has the experience and knowledge necessary for testing a child's ability to hear soft tones, an audiogram may be obtained. However, if such experienced staff is not available, or if the child has clearly understood the task, referral should be made to an audiologist for evaluation.

Periodic Rescreening

Diseases, noise, or drugs can cause sensorineural hearing loss, and exposure to these hazards does not follow a calendar. Conductive loss can occur at any time. Therefore, rescreening, particularly for conductive hearing loss, should be part of a hearing conservation program. Although annual rescreenings are generally recommended (American Speech and Hearing Association, 1975; 1979), the intervals may be shortened, depending upon the likelihood that hearing impairment will occur within the particular group being managed. Because the onset of a hearing loss is unlikely related to rescreening schedules, any indication of less than expected increases in language proficiency may be reason for immediate rescreening, particularly among those with past, presumably resolved, hearing loss.

Evaluation

The following is intended to provide an overview of the capabilities and limitations of an audiological evaluation. Because of the nature of this text, the steps of medical evaluation of a conductive hearing loss will not be detailed. Suffice it to say that an examination can range from a relatively simple visual examination of the ear canal to radiographic and immunological studies. The audiological evaluation encompasses two major processes: determination of the *site of lesion* (for present purposes conductive or sensorineural) and *communication function* (the efficiency of present ability and the potential for improving efficiency).

Site of Lesion

The foundation for determination of site of lesion has already been provided in Figure 7–2, the audiogram. In an evaluation, the audiogram is more detailed, involving presentation of tones by two pathways. These pathways are referred to as air conduction and bone conduction. In the first case, an earphone is placed over the ear, and the overall sensitivity of the auditory system is measured in octave steps from 250 Hz through 8000 Hz. Each ear is measured separately at each frequency, with the right ear represented by O and the left ear represented by X. Bone conduction involves presentation of tones by a mechanical vibrator placed behind the ear. For most purposes, thresholds obtained in this manner represent the sensitivity of the hair cells without being affected by any malfunction of the conductive system. Symbols for bone conduction are not well standardized.

However, every audiogram carries a legend that indicates the meanings of the symbols used.

A person with a conductive hearing loss would have better sensitivity (symbols placed higher on the audiogram) by bone conduction than by air conduction. The magnitude of difference between bone conduction and air conduction thresholds would describe the magnitude of the conductive hearing loss. Detailed impedance studies would be conducted to provide additional information about the nature and extent of any conductive hearing loss.

A person with a sensorineural hearing loss would have air conduction symbols located lower on the audiogram than the range of normal (0 to 20 or 25 dB), and bone conduction thresholds would approximate air conduction. There are a wide variety of tests that could be used in the presence of sensorineural loss. However, since these studies are primarily aimed at more specific determination of the site and extent of hearing loss, they will not be discussed here.

Communication Function

Before discussing the two major types of tests used to estimate a person's efficiency with speech, some general comments are appropriate. The ability to understand the spoken language is obviously complex. It depends on the listener's vocabulary, the speaker's abilty to articulate properly, the particular words used, and the degree to which noise interferes, to list a few of the more important factors. The most important factor in evaluating bilingual children is the nature of the vocabulary used to develop test word lists.

As in American English, there are regional differences in the vocabulary of other languages. However, the differences may be greater because of the relative isolation of the groups involved. For example, Spanish spoken in San Antonio is likely to be more different from that spoken in Los Angeles than differences in American English between two comparatively distant cities. There is evidence that even vocabulary differences between regions within a state may be sufficiently large to prevent standardization of test lists (Ickes and Brown, 1976). The impact of such information is that lists may only be standardized city-by-city.

Age of the person tested is another important factor since children are likely to have a different vocabulary than adults. For example, standard audiological American English test word lists for adults are different from that for kindergarten children. While children's lists have been developed for American English, no such lists are available for bilingual populations. It is clear that more research is needed in this area. Since the reader is unlikely to be involved in the audiological evaluation of communication function, no further mention of particular test materials will be made. However, if there is any question about the adequacy of a particular child's vocabulary, close cooperation between the educator and the audiologist will be necessary to accurately evaluate communication efficiency.

Pure auditory communication function is evaluated using two types of tests. The first involves establishing a speech threshold by using familiar spondaic words. Such words are two-syllable, spoken with equal stress on each syllable, and each of the two syllables constitutes a word, for example, *baseball*. The words are generally presented through earphones, and the patient is asked to repeat them. The level of presentation is varied and the level at which approximately half the words are repeated is called the speech reception threshold (SRT). While useful in several ways, the SRT is of little interest when examining communication function.

The more important measure is speech discrimination, expressed as the percentage of words correctly identified when presented at some level above the SRT. As suggested in Figure 7-1, the percentage of words correctly identified varies as a function of the level of presentation. Two levels of presentation are commonly used. The first is repetition of a test list at conversational level. That measure gives some insight into the person's present auditory discrimination ability. The second speech discrimination measure, when communication at normal conversational level is impaired, is made at 30 to 40 dB above the SRT. That range is necessary for maximum discrimination of a wide variety of patients. The value in establishing these two measures is that when the score of the second measure is larger than the first, then amplification can be of value in remediating the hearing loss. Speech discrimination testing is usually conducted in quiet. As has been suggested, noise many influence a person's discrimination ability. Therefore, to more accurately assess the child's ability to hear in a classroom, speech discrimination testing may also be conducted with a background of noise.

If communication efficiency cannot be brought into the range of normal by amplification, the additional step permitting the patient to listen to the auditory signal while viewing the speaker's face is normally taken. The addition of lipreading cues can often assist a defective auditory system in restoring normal communication. Lipreading skill alone can also be assessed although it is important to realize that visual cues are seldom sufficient to permit complete understanding because many sounds are not readily visible or are easily confused. For example, the words *back* and *pack* begin by putting the lips together and releasing them suddenly. Therefore, on the basis of no more than visual observation, the two cannot be distinguished. At most, with no contextual or auditory cues, lipreading is a 50/50 proposition.

Recommendations for Rehabilitation

The air conduction audiogram provides the initial information for estimating communication potential. While the tones from 500 to 2000 Hz are commonly called the *speech frequencies*, there is evidence (Cooper and Owen, 1976) that hearing loss above 2000 Hz can contribute to difficulties in understanding speech. This is particularly true when listening to female voices which tend to be higher pitched than male. Because communication normally occurs in environments which provide other than auditory cues, the effect of poorer hearing in the high frequencies cannot be precisely gauged by simple examination of the audiogram. It is clear that normal hearing across the entire audiometric range precludes the possibility that hearing is contributing to poor communication. If poor auditory communication can be documented in the presence of normal hearing, it is likely that the problem involves those rare cases of malfunction of the neural transmission system or the cortical interpretation system. There is little that can be done in the way of audiological rehabilitation of such cases. A thorough neurological examination is warranted.

In the presence of an abnormal audiogram, the speech discrimination scores are far more important than tonal thresholds in understanding the effects of hearing loss and considering measures for rehabilitation. When it can be shown that increases in performance are achieved through amplification, a hearing aid is indicated. Advertising claims not withstanding, a hearing aid is nothing more than a portable amplifying system. A hearing aid can be thought of as a public address system operating in reverse. While a public address system is employed when many listeners require amplification to hear a speaker, a hearing aid is employed when the listener is required to hear one or more speakers. Thus, hearing aids can improve communication by raising the level of conversation, but cannot increase the discrimination potential.

Comparison of communication efficiency under conditions of auditory and audiovisual stimulation provide additional guidance in the selection of rehabilitation measures. Since it has been demonstrated that even normal hearing individuals utilize visual cues for understanding under difficult listening conditions, it should be expected that the hearing impaired will do so as well. If no improvement can be found with the addition of visual cues, then lipreading instruction may become part of a rehabilitation program. Auditory training may be recommended as well, particularly when the hearing loss is of early onset, so the child has had little experience with sound. This involves training that may begin with tasks as simple as distinguishing between high and low pitch tones or sounds of short or long duration.

Two seemingly innocuous types of hearing loss bear particular comment when dealing with children: unilateral hearing loss and mild conductive hearing loss. It may be easy to assume that a single normal ear is sufficient for auditory interaction and edcuational progress. It is not so for two reasons. The first involves what is known as the head shadow. In addition to the normal quieting of sound as it travels from the speaker to the listener, there is some 10 dB of additional quieting as sound passes from one side of the head to the other. What is adequate loudness when speaking toward the normal ear may become inadequate when speaking from behind the head shadow. Thus, the child with a unilateral hearing loss may be at a disadvantage whenever the bad ear is toward the source of information. A unilateral hearing loss also creates a distinct disability in the listener's localization of sound. The ability to localize the speaker's voice and separate it, in a quasi-spatial manner, from background noise provides the normal hearing individual with an additional advantage over the person with the unilateral hearing loss.

A person with mild conductive hearing loss may be able to function normally under ideal conditions, i.e., when communicating face to face in quiet. However, the educational progress of a child with a mild loss may be impaired during the process of language acquisition because of the reduced scope of auditory input. While an adult with a 15 dB conductive hearing loss is unlikely to experience any significant disability, children with such losses have been shown to have retarded language acquisition (Forcucci and Stark, 1972).

Educational Evaluation of Those with Hearing Loss

Hearing loss does not automatically qualify a child for special education intervention without concrete evidence of less than optimal achievement. This is particularly true with mild losses where the impact is variable. Thus, children with hearing loss should be evaluated to determine academic potential whenever educational progress is unsatisfactory. Because language may be impaired, nonverbal test instruments may need to be used. (It is understood that there may be some difficulty in selecting an instrument to gauge the academic potential of a bilingual hearing impaired child.) Standardized tests should also be used to determine the child's actual achievement. Comparisons between the two tests will provide an index for the need of remediation.

The periodic use of standardized tests as an independent gauge of educational progress is recommended to prevent any halo effect from masking the absence of progress. In the absence of satisfactory educational progress, reevaluation for possible modification or additional amplification or review of the current educational placement is necessary. The important thing to remember is that without documented evidence of educational progress, efforts devoted to screening and evaluation are rendered meaningless.

Classroom Management of Hearing Loss

Classroom management of the child with hearing loss conveniently falls into three categories: those without hearing aids, those with, and those with handicaps in addition to hearing loss, with or without the use of a hearing aid. If a child with a hearing loss has not been fitted with a hearing aid, it may be assumed that the child has either a mild, a transient, or a unilateral hearing loss. Failure to recommend the use of amplification does not under any circumstances imply the child's hearing loss is not causing a disability. A hearing aid may not be recommended for a variety of reasons, mostly financial. For example, if a child's hearing loss is conductive, it may fluctuate and is likely to be corrected eventually through medical management. Under such circumstances it would be difficult to justify the expenditure of as much as $500 for a hearing aid when there are alternatives to using a hearing aid. Hearing-impaired children without hearing aids are more likely to be encountered in nonspecialized classrooms (the typical reader is more likely to encounter them) than those with hearing aids or additional handicaps. Although children with hearing aids may be encountered in nonspecialized classes, their initial education is likely to have been in a specialized classroom. It is inconceivable that children with multiple handicaps are supervised by teachers whose training would make the comments in this chapter necessary.

Children without Hearing Aids

There are four basic rules that should be followed by any teacher communicating with a hearing impaired child not wearing a hearing aid.

1. Come close.
2. in a quiet place while
3. facing the child and
4. writing new information.

The first rule has its roots in the earlier example of hearing over the length of a football field. Since speech gets progressively less intense as the square of the distance between two individuals, communication should be conducted at distances as short as practical. What is adequate hearing at three feet may be inadequate if a child is located at the back of the classroom and the teacher is at the front. It is important to emphasize that the child's location in the classroom is not relevant. What is relevant is his or her location with respect to the source of information. For example, if the teacher moves to the side of the classroom for a demonstration, a child sitting at the front on the opposite side is at a disadvantage. As another example, the loudspeaker of most film projectors is located with the projector at the back of the room. When the teacher is showing films, the child should be near the loudspeaker.

Since the presence of noise in a communication situation works to the detriment of the listener, there is good reason to reduce extraneous noise to an absolute minimum in any situation where communication must be conducted with a hearing impaired person. Speaking to a hearing impaired child across a classroom where there is small group activity is foolish. Similarly, communicating in a noisy cafeteria is begging for misunderstanding to take place.

The suggestion that the listener should always have access to the visual cues from the speaker's face is a particularly difficult one to follow. It is all too easy to turn one's head while, for example, pointing out a feature of a chart or writing on a blackboard. It should be remembered that the addition of visual cues under difficult listening circumstances can be worth a 20 to 30% improvement in communication efficiency even with normal hearing individuals (Cooper and Langley, 1978).

Even though a teacher may follow all communication precautions, a hearing impaired child may still miss critical information. To guard against this probability, any new information, such as the introduction of vocabulary, should be presented in a visual or written form. While omissions of familiar information can be overcome by guessing (e.g., the unheard word was *cows* when discussing a photograph of a Jersey herd), it is improbable the word *stapes* will be understood in an introductory lecture on the anatomy of the auditory system.

The student can assist in ensuring information transfer by requesting written confirmation in those cases where the harried teacher may momentarily forget to provide such information, by being given the freedom to change classroom position whenever the teacher moves away (presuming that the child has the prerequisite maturity to do so) and by being encouraged to request supplemental assistance whenever necessary.

Children with Hearing Aids

The four rules take on added importance whenever a child is wearing a hearing aid. The use of a hearing aid implies that the hearing loss is more than mild and is likely to be permanent. The detailed management of a child who wears a hearing aid in a special classroom is beyond the scope of this text. However, since the goal of any program for hearing-impaired children is placement in a normal environment, it is possible that a teacher in a regular classroom will be faced with a hearing aid user. This should not be done without having available the consultation of an educational audiologist or a teacher of the hearing impaired.

An additional burden placed on the classroom teacher who has a child with a hearing aid is to ensure that it functions properly. It is unfortunate, but true, that less than 50% of the hearing aids in use are functioning adequately (Gaeth and Lounsbury, 1966). While the classroom teacher cannot be expected to become an expert in hearing aid maintenance, several steps can be taken. The first is to ensure that the hearing aid is providing adequate amplification by an easy, daily test. In its simplest form, the test involves asking the child to respond to a series of questions without benefit of visual cues. When auditory discrimination is poor, the teacher simply requests that the child raise a hand whenever the teacher's voice is heard. By using normal conversational voice some 5 to 10 feet behind the child, it will become quickly evident whether or not the aid is functioning.

Because hearing aid batteries can function at near normal levels for a long time and then suddenly fail, two additional steps are appropriate. The first is to ensure there is a spare battery in class at all times. The second is to repeat the daily test whenever it appears that the child is no longer hearing. Replace the battery if hearing is worse. If this does not correct the problem, the child should be referred immediately for repair of the hearing aid. While this step is seldom possible, the teacher should remember that no auditory information is likely to be effective in the educational progress after hearing aid malfunction. To continue to use oral communication is analogous to continue to write after a child's glasses have been taken away. It is readily acknowledged that virtually no classroom teacher has a responsive repair system available. The teacher is faced with an insoluble dilemma. It is necessary that the teacher acknowledge that the educational process is no longer continuing.

Summary

Hearing loss is unique among human disabilities in that it may reduce communication efficiency. In the young, hearing loss may lead to language retardation, particularly when mild hearing loss produces variable responses to normal auditory stimuli, not unlike the effects of bilingualism. Further, hearing loss may occur without the visible manifestations or clear-cut complaints normally associated with disease. Thus, whenever language skills are below what is expected, the possibility of hearing loss must be considered. A bright note in an otherwise dismal picture is that the dominant type of hearing loss, conductive, is amenable to medical intervention.

The only effective way to detect hearing loss is by screening all individuals in question who enter the system. It must be remembered that screening techniques do not identify or quantify hearing loss. They simple isolate a group in which the likelihood of hearing loss is high. Only an evaluation of hearing can establish the presence of a loss and measure its degree. The evaluative process addresses itself to two questions: (a) Where is the lesion? and (b) of greater concern to those involved in education, what is the level of communication efficiency? Such determinations may include both purely auditory as well as audio-visual tests. When a hearing loss has been identified, an educational evaluation should be completed to determine the degree of educational retardation; hence the need for educational intervention.

Hearing-impaired children may or may not be required to wear a hearing aid. To ensure that a child without a hearing aid continues to make educational progress, communicate with such children in as close to an ideal manner as possible: at short distances, in as quiet an environment as possible, with maximum opportunity for lipreading, and with visual supplementation for new information. The same guidelines apply for those who teach children wearing hearing aids, with the additional burden of ensuring that the aid is functioning.

This chapter has attempted to provide a brief overview of hearing loss. Of necessity, it has glossed over many details essential to the daily management of the hearing impaired child. The reader faced with such a child must not assume that there is little more to do, but should consult with colleagues who have expertise in dealing with the hearing impaired or study the available literature more extensively to adequately confront the real disability that results from hearing loss.

References

American Speech and Hearing Association: Guidelines for identification audiometry. *Asha, 17*:94, 1975.

American Speech and Hearing Association: Guidelines for acoustic immittance screening of middle-ear function. *Asha, 21*:283, 1979.

Brooks, D.N.:   School screening for middle ear effusions. *Ann Otol Rhinol Laryngol, 85*:Supp. 25: 223, 1976.

Cooper, J.C., Jr., Gates, G.A, Owen, J.H., and Dixon, H.D.:   An abbreviated impedance bridge technique for school screening. *J Speech Hear Res, 40*:260, 1975.

Cooper, J.C., Jr., and Owen, J.H.:   Audiologic profile of noise induced hearing loss. *Arch Otolaryngol, 102*:148, 1976.

Cooper, J.C., Jr.:   Hearing screening. In Singh, S., and Lynch, J. (Eds.): *Diagnostic Procedures in Hearing, Language, and Speech.* Baltimore, University Park Press, 1978.

Cooper, J.C., Jr., and Langley, L.R.:   Multiple choice speech discrimination tests for both diagnostic and rehabilitative evaluation: English and Spanish. *J Acad Rehab Audiol, 11*: No 1, 132, 1978.

Forcucci, R.A., and Stark, E.W.:   Hearing loss, speech-language and cystic fibrosis. *Arch Otolaryngol, 96*:361, 1972.

Gaeth, J.H.:   *Verbal and nonverbal learning in children including those with hearing loss.* Part II, Project No. 2207, Contract No. SAE OE-4-10-1033. Detroit, Wayne State University, 1966.

Gaeth, J.H., and Lounsbury, E.:   Hearing aids and children in elementary schools. *J Speech Hear Dis, 3*:283, 1966.

Geyer, M.L., and Yankauer, A.:   Teacher judgment of hearing loss in children. *J Speech Hear Dis, 21*:482, 1956.

Glasscock, M.E., III: Complications of otitis media.   In Glorig, A., and Gerwin, K.S. (Eds.): *Otitis Media.* Springfield, Thomas, 1972.

Hatfield, E.M.:   Progress in preschool vision screening. *Sight Sav Rev, 37*: 194, 1967.

Holm, V.A., and Kunz, L.H.:   Effect of chronic otitis media on language and speech development. *Pediatrics, 43*:833, 1969.

Hull, F.M., and Mielke, P.W., Jr.:   National speech and hearing survey: preliminary results. *Asha, 13*:501, 1971.

Ickes, W.K., and Brown, J.:   A translation of the Peabody Picture Vocabulary Test into Tex-Mex. *Tejas, 1*: No. 1:15, 1976.

Katz, J.:   Temporary threshold shift, auditory sensory deprivation, and conductive hearing loss. *J Acous Soc Am, 37*:923, 1965.

Katz, J., and Illmer, R.:   Auditory perception in children with learning disabilities. In Katz, J. (Ed.): *Handbook of Clinical Audiology.* Baltimore, Williams and Wilkins, 1972.

Lenneberg, E.H.:   *Biological Foundations of Language.* New York, John Wiley and Sons, 1967.

Ling, D.:   Rehabilitation of cases with deafness secondary to otitis media. In Glorig, A., and Gerwin, K.S. (Eds.): *Otitis Media.* Springfield, Thomas, 1972.

Melnik, W., Eagles, E.L., and Levine, H.S.:   Evaluation of a recommended program of identification audiometry with school-age children. *J Speech Hear Dis, 29*:3, 1964.

Northern, J.L., and Downs, M.P.:   *Hearing in Children.* Baltimore, Williams and Wilkins, 1974.

Vernon, McC.:   Potential, achievement, and rehabilitation in the deaf population. *Rehabilitation Literature, 31*:258, 1970.

Exceptionalities in Bilingual Populations

8

Management of Communicatively Handicapped Hispanic American Children

Nicolás Linares

Immigration policies in the United States encourage the entrance of people of various cultures and languages into its territory. A significant portion of these immigrants comes from countries of Hispanic origin. People from Puerto Rico, a commonwealth associated with the United States, constantly move to and from the Mainland. These individuals bring with them the Spanish language (with dialectal variations) and their very own cultures, which, in the case of the Puerto Ricans, is a blend of Spanish, "Taina," Black, and Anglo American. These linguistic and cultural contacts affect the persons involved. Their offspring become a new breed of Hispanic Americans who, to fill their needs, hope for (and sometimes achieve) social, economic, educational, and linguistic changes in the society that receives them (John and Horner, 1978).

There are 15 million Hispanic Americans living in the continental United States and Puerto Rico. In California, Hispanic American children represent nearly 15% of the students attending public schools (Castaneda, 1976); they also comprise 40% of the handicapped children in New York City (U.S. Office of Education, 1978). These individuals are entitled to all appropriate services mandated by law for the handicapped. Thus, professionals in communicative disorders, special education, bilingual education, and related fields are often called to serve these persons.

An estimated 5% of school-age children have speech and language disorders (Wood, 1969). A probably similar, if not larger, percentage of

Hispanic American children may have difficulty in communication. They need to receive communicative and educational services from professionals who consider their biculturalism and bilingualism. In this chapter, information is provided that will assist professionals in rendering such services. Although most of its content pertains to the Puerto Rican child, the reader is encouraged to study its applicability to other Hispanic American children.

Basic Concepts

It is necessary for the professional to understand some fundamental concepts if quality educational or clinical services are to be offered to the bicultural communicative impaired child. For example, speech/language pathologists and audiologists should understand the culture and language to which the child is exposed and the idiosyncracy of the Hispanic American child's communicative development. A professional must also be cognizant of services available for communicative disorders so that appropriate referrals can be made.

Latin American Culture and Language

It is necessary for the professional to ascertain the cultural and linguistic behavior of Hispanic American children who are seen for services. Many variations can be encountered, e.g., Puerto Rican Spanish-speaking children living in Puerto Rico, and Puerto Rican English-speaking children living in New York. After spending some years in the Mainland they become Puerto Rican American, Cuban American, and the like. Comprehensive descriptions of these variations are scarce in the literature; thus the professional must develop strategies to determine what characterizes a particular child's culture and language.

The Spanish language has some peculiarities that make it very different from English. The characteristics of the phonological system of Spanish are different from, and in many ways simpler, than English. On the other hand, the inflectional morphology of Spanish is more complex than that of English. Considering these facts will assist the professional in avoiding a communication barrier with the Hispanic American child.

Normal Communicative Development of the Spanish Speaking Puerto Rican Child

Hispanic American children vary in their use of the Spanish language. A monolingual (Spanish) Puerto Rican child raised in Puerto Rico, for

TABLE 8-1
Manners in which Puerto Rican Children Normally Produce Some Spanish Phonemes

Spanish Phoneme	Variations
d	Omitted in last syllable of descriptive verbs: "El niño está parad(d)o"
j	Produced glottally
ll	Produced with tongue blades against sides of palate
r	Sometimes produced as "l" when in the middle and end of word: "Voy a coltal el papel"
rr	Produced either with vibration of tip of tongue or with contact of back of tongue with velum
s	Aspirated in middle and end of word: "¿Lo pusihteh?"
v/b	Produced as b
z	Produced as s

example, uses the language in ways different from the bilingual (Spanish and English) Puerto Rican child raised on the Mainland. With this in mind, some information about the communicative development of children born and raised in Puerto Rico follows. These data are useful when evaluating the language status of a child with communicative disorders.

Hispanic American children learn to use the specific vocal intonation patterns of their community, e.g., Cuban, Puerto Rican, and Mexican. This is one of the most variable aspects of the dialects of the Spanish language. Puerto Rican children, for example, use an ascending vocal tone to ask, and keep the intonation uniform to declare. Children from rural areas in Puerto Rico learn to use a soft vocal volume when talking to an adult stranger because of respect or subordination; they also have a tendency to speak at a faster rate than those from urban areas. It has been observed that this increased speed causes some of the children to be very dysfluent.

The few studies on the development of articulatory skills of Puerto Rican children (González, 1981; Ramírez, 1977) indicate that by five years of age they are able to produce nearly 90% of the phonemes of Spanish. Blends are completely mastered by age six. Table 8-1 contains information about the articulatory characteristics of Spanish-speaking Puerto Rican children.

There is scant empirical normative data about the language development of Puerto Rican children. However, based on the author's direct experience with normal children 2-6 to 3-0 years of age, the following table has been developed. It can be used for identifying Puerto Rican children who have the risk of presenting language problems.

TABLE 8-2

Language Performance of Normal Puerto Rican
Children 2-6 to 3-0 Years of Age

Aspect of Language	*Appropriate Performance*
1.0 Vocabulary (a sample)	1.1 Identification of: "bola" – ball "carro" – car "tenedor" – fork "cama" – bed "sapo" – frog "pan" – bread "zapato" – shoe "abanico" – fan "inodoro" – toilet "elefante" – elephant "correr" – to run "brincar" – to jump "tirar" – to throw "prender" – to put on an appliance "llorar" – to cry "gordo" – fat "triste" – sad "feo" – ugly "debajo" – beneath "encima" – on
2.0 Inflectional Morphology	2.1 Article-noun number and gender agreement
	2.2 Article-pronoun number and gender agreement
	2.3 Article-adjective number and gender agreement
	2.4 Noun-adjective number and gender agreement
	2.5 Pronominalization of first, second, and third person singular
	2.6 Noun-verb singular person agreement in regular, com- pound verbs with "estar" (to be) in present and past tense
	2.7 Noun-verb singular person agreement for regular simple verbs in past tense

	Aspect of Language		*Appropriate Performance*
3.0	**Mean Length of Utterance in Morphemes** (Linares-Orama, 1975)	3.1	An average of 6.50 with a standard deviation of 2.0
4.0	**Conjunctions**	4.1	Uses "como" (as), "porque" (because), "y" (and)
5.0	**Interrogative Words**	5.1	Understands and uses "qué" (what), "dónde" (where), "por qué" (who), "a quién" (to whom), "cúando"(when)
6.0	**Syntax**	6.0	Simple sentences with ninety percent of required elements and up to eleven words in the right order
		6.1	Conjoined sentences with "y" (and), "porque" (because)
7.0	**Developmental Sentence Score** (Toronto, 1972)	7.1	An average of 5.7 with a standard deviation of 1.5

Communication that is transmitted through gestures and body movements, as with other languages, is a salient aspect of the Hispanic American culture. Understanding the production of nonverbal messages is basic to effective clinical and educational services provided to Hispanic Americans. Eye contact, or the lack of, is related to the Puerto Rican child's sense of obedience. The professional should not interpret absence of eye contact as lack of interest. This same child may be willing to bring the body near to the person with whom a relationship is being built and often has some kind of body contact with the individual. In addition, the Puerto Rican child moves the arms constantly while speaking.

Communicative Disorders

This section contains general information about speech and language disorders with some reference to Hispanic populations. It is aimed at the reader who is not trained in speech/language pathology but is interested in basic services for communicatively handicapped Hispanic American children. Later, information and considerations in assessment and remediation of communicatively disordered Hispanic American children will be discussed.

Data on the prevalence of communication disorders in the Hispanic American child population are limited. For the Puerto Rican, Fábregas (1979) found that nearly 26% of children in kindergarten through second grade in metropolitan San Juan had some kind of communication handicap. Language disorders were most prevalent, followed by voice, articulation, and fluency disorders.

Some conditions associated with communicative handicap include organic, psychological, environmental-social, and functional factors. Damage to the central nervous system can affect language processing and movements of the musculature involved in speech production. Hearing loss can impede language acquisition and processes. Psychological disabilities that impair a child's ideas about space, time, causality, and adaptation to the environment could also be associated with speech and language disorders. On the other hand, if a child does not feel that communication is rewarding, the child's efforts to engage in speaking will be reduced. For those communicatively handicapped children with no apparent associated conditions, some clinicians believe the children learned deficient communication and call the children's speech difficulties functional. Finally, although speech and language disorders can occur as a result of the above various factors, they in turn can be the cause of other conditions; for instance, a child who stutters could develop emotional disturbance.

Disorders of Speech

Definitions of disordered speech imply that the production of speech follows social rules and that any deviance from these affect the exchange of messages between members of the community (Perkins, 1977; Van Riper, 1972). Speech difficulties comprise disorders of voice, fluency, and articulation. According to Boone (1971), most difficulties in voice production are due to forced or tensed use of the respiration, phonation, and resonance mechanisms. This alters voice intensity, quality, and pitch. Voice pathology can be categorized as volume disorders (too soft or too loud), pitch disorders (too low or too high), and quality disorders (harshness, hoarseness, breathiness, hyponasalization, or hypernasalization). Most classifications of vocal impairments depend on the listener's judgment. For example, what one culture might regard as extreme nasality another may interpret as normal.

Fluency disorders are those that interfere with the *smooth* production of speech at an adequate rate. They may be classified as either hyperdysfluency or stuttering; in addition, rapid or slow speech may occur. Hyperdysfluent persons speak with many fluency breaks and usually have no apparent consciousness of these breaks or their effects. In the case of children, preventive measures need to be implemented to avoid habit formation. Stuttering is characterized by interruptions or blockages in the production of utterances (Bloodstein, 1969). These may take the form of repetitions, fixations, prolongations, long periods of silence, or pauses filled with stereotyped words. Stuttering is the most frequent disorder of fluency. It is often accompanied by fear and secondary body movements, a feature not encountered in hyperdysfluency.

A disorder of articulation is present when the person has difficulty in producing phonemes of the language. It may be described as misproduction of phonemes in isolation or in words. Some speakers may be able to produce phonemes consistently in some phonetic environments but not others—or with ease in isolation but not in connected speech. Errors may be described in terms of substitutions, omissions, distortions, or insertions of phonemes or sounds. They may also be explained in relation to the contrastive features involved in phoneme articulation. For example, if a Spanish-speaking child says "caba" for "cama," or an English-speaking child says "baba" for "mama," it could be inferred, among other things, that the child does not perceive the contrastive feature of nasality between segments present in these two words.

Disorders of Language

A language disorder exists when children's comprehension and/or expression does not compare favorably to the language used by their peers. In this case, the language comprehended or expressed departs from linguistic norms to such a degree as to interfere with communication. The language disordered child may present moderate to severe difficulties in one or more aspects of the language, that is, its lexicon, semantics, morphology, syntax, or pragmatics. With the Spanish-speaking child, special considerations should be given to the inflectional morphology of the language which is a very complicated aspect of Spanish. To illustrate, consider the possible ways English and Spanish conjugate the verb *to run—correr*:

I run	Yo corro
We run	Nosotros corremos
You run	Tú corres
You run (plural)	Ustedes corren
He, she runs	El, ella corre
They run	Ellos, ellas corren

An English-speaking child needs to learn two inflectional forms while the Spanish-speaking child needs to master five.

In the past, speech/language pathologists in Puerto Rico primarily managed children with language disorders due to minimal brain dysfunction and hearing loss. At present they serve, not only these, but children with language disorders associated with mental retardation, cerebral palsy, infantile autism, neurological disorders, blindness, and childhood schizophrenia.

Intervention for Children with Communicative Disorders

A child with a speech and/or language disorder needs a professional who can be both a scientist and an artist. Intuitive, creative, empirical, and objective judgments of the clinician assist in appropriate decisions in each of the components of clinical management, that is, identification, evaluation/diagnosis, prognosis, referral, intervention, and prevention.

Screening tests are often administered to language populations in order to identify individuals with possible communicative handicaps. These are, hopefully, concise instruments that are administered in a short period of time. However, as human communication is the product of a multiplicity of variables, sampling becomes difficult and results often become doubtful when only a short test period is possible.

In evaluating a child with a suspected communicative disorder, the examiner compares the patient's performance in structured and unstructured situations with normative data or criterion-referenced measures. This process needs to be comprehensive and objective with emphasis being placed on the individual, not on the difficulties presented (Emerick and Hatten, 1974). In emphasizing the child's reality, the clinician needs to consider all interactive organic, psychological, environmental, and communication variables. Intervention for communicative disorders is as efficient as their evaluation.

The evaluation process should start with a preliminary collection of the client's data which is used in planning and organizing a systematic and comprehensive examination. Based on this information, determinations about applicable evaluative methods and the client's testability are made. Following this, the communication examination is undertaken for the purpose of describing the child's abilities and disabilities. This description is then conveyed to parents and interested professionals. Should the client present symptoms of associated conditions, referrals need to be made to other professionals in medicine, psychology, and education. Their findings are also incorporated into the therapeutic process.

The therapeutic design and intervention is based on diagnostic findings. Usually clinicians base management on particular models of clinicial interaction that can range from strictly behavioral to cognitive procedures. Regardless of the philosophy selected, the general intervention goal is to assist children in becoming as good communicators as their abilities permit.

Preventive activities in speech, language, and hearing comprise early identification and intervention strategies for children at the risk of communicative disorders. These activities are undertaken to prevent speech, language, and hearing disorders from causing greater damage to the child's emotions.

Special Provisions in the Management of the Hispanic American Child with a Communication Disorder

In the first part of this chapter, information was presented aimed at providing a broad view of concepts basic to the communicative-disordered Hispanic American child. This section contains specific information based primarily on the author's experience with this type of child.

Evaluation Procedures

When evaluating the communication abilities of a bicultural child, it should be asked whether or not instruments and procedures used for this task really measure this child's speech and language skills. Items of tests should represent the child's language and culture. Direct translation into Spanish of English language tests should be avoided since English and Spanish vary in syntax and morphology, and in the number of syllables and phonemes for words that represent particular referents. It would seem more valid to construct new tests, albeit following English test formats as often as possible. Should the child lack contact with certain elements of a culture, those should not be included in the methods and tests used. For example, most Puerto Rican children in Puerto Rico have never been exposed to cold winter clothing; thus, including the word "abrigos" (coats) as a vocabulary test item would be unrealistic.

Areas of Preliminary Observation

Initial observations of a child's behavior need to be undertaken in a controlled fashion. The observer should focus on specific kinds and types of cognitive, social, and communicative behaviors and should separate them from irrelevant ones. In observing a bicultural child, the professional looks for evidence of linguistic use (Spanish, English, or Spanglish) and the adopted predominant culture (American, Hispanic, Hispanic American). This information assists the clinician in selecting appropriate evaluative methods and tests for this child.

Regarding the languages used by the child, the professional should seek evidence on the comprehension and expression of English and Spanish morphology, syntax, and vocabulary, and in addition, the child's pronunciation of both languages. When it comes to the child's culture, observations are to be made on the individual's manners, dress style, and parent-child relationship.

Interview with Parent or Custodian

Preliminary observations will help the clinician in deciding the language to be used when interviewing and the proper way to relate to Hispanic parents or custodians. Should Spanish be the predominant language, this language needs to be used by the speech/language pathologist or audiologist who converses with the parent. An alternative for this would be a competent interpreter. Most of these custodians may demonstrate a passive behavior, in which case the professional should not adopt an extremely imposing attitude, either in the social relationship or in both verbal and nonverbal messages.

Obtaining Information from Other Professionals

When so indicated, the client should be referred to physicians, psychologists, occupational therapists, and social workers in order to gather a comprehensive description of the child's status. The clinician should know whether the tests they use to evaluate the referred child are valid for the child in terms of language and culture, as one still finds cases of failure to control for cultural differences in intellectual assessments, for example. It is often useful to obtain information about the child from the Hispanic country of origin of the child. These data may be more valid because tests may already have been administered in the child's mother tongue.

Evaluation of Communicative Skills

When evaluating a Hispanic American child, the clinician needs to rely heavily on controlled observations because there is a lack of standardized communication tests for this population. If the child is also bilingual, an assessment of comprehension and production in both languages should be included. (For further discussions of tests for Spanish and English *see* Erickson and Omark, 1981.)

Evaluations of voice and fluency are undertaken without specific tests; rather, they consist of evaluation of these features in conversation or connected speech during free play. The professional will determine whether or not the child presents vocal problems in intensity, quality, pitch, and/or resonance.

Pertaining to fluency, it is necessary to describe dysfluent speech in terms of repetitions, prolongations, insertions, and/or silent blocks. Reactions to speech situations are assessed and observations of secondary behaviors are made. For the Hispanic American child who has not had an adequate opportunity to learn a language, the clinician should not confuse lack of vocabulary with a fluency disorder, for the term *fluency* refers to the rhythm of speech and not to language problems related or unrelated to second language learning.

Articulatory behavior can be evaluated through spontaneous or imitative speech samples. Paynter and Bumpas (1977) found that the results of these two approaches used with three-year-old children did not differ significantly. With older children, however, it is important to obtain spontaneous production. Whatever method is selected, the aim is to describe the child's phonemic and phonetic behavior. When testing Hispanic American children for articulatory proficiency, one must consider the possibility of intra- or interlanguage learning errors. Erickson and Omark (1981) provide discussions of this phenomenon and the different merits of both contrastive and error analysis.

The Austin Articulation Test. This is one of the few tests developed for Spanish-speaking children (Learning Concepts, 1974). Since its stimulus vocabulary items and illustrations are for Mexican American children, however, modifications have to be made to apply this test to Puerto Rican American or Cuban American children so that phonological targets are prompted in these populations.

Children's language behavior depends so much on their specific community of residence that it is practically impossible to find a single national test that can be validly and reliably administered to all children (*see* Chapter 7). With Hispanic American children, the situation is more difficult because there are various kinds, types, and degrees of bilingualism and biculturalism. Thus, the speech/language pathologist or audiologist needs to be certain a test instrument is applicable to a particular child, or, when this is not the case and no other instruments are available, that criterion-referenced procedures are to be developed. A visit to the child's neighborhood or a talk with parents should give the clinician an idea of the kind of language to be assessed with such methods.

The evaluation of language should yield information on the child's comprehension and expression of the vocabulary, morphology, syntax, use, and semantics of the language. The *Toronto Test of Receptive Vocabulary* (Toronto, 1977) has been developed with norms for Mexican American children. Some of its contents, however, are not useful with Puerto Rican children, e.g., words such as *borrega* and *llanta* are not used by Puerto Rican children (*see* also Toronto, 1973a, and consider its contents).

To measure the child's understanding of Spanish structures, the Spanish version of the *Test for Auditory Comprehension of Language* (TACL) (Carrow, 1973) can be useful. Again, some lexical items need to be changed so that Puerto Rican children can take the test. Also, as few syntactic constructions on the test are not frequent in Puerto Rican Spanish, minor modifications are needed. This instrument was applied to a sample of 123 Puerto Rican children by students of the University of Puerto Rico and the data presented in Table 8–3 resulted.

TABLE 8-3

Some Norms on the TACL for Middle-Class Puerto Rican
Children Living in Puerto Rico

Age	Total Score & S.D.	Lexicon Score & S.D.	Morphology Score & S.D.	Syntax Score & S.D.
3-6 to 3-11 (n=33)	55.30 (8.25)	25.12 (3.60)	25.09 (4.50)	5.33 (2.10)
4-0 to 4-5 (n=40)	61.15 (10.16)	26.00 (4.11)	29.00 (5.49)	6.00 (2.26)
4-6 to 4-11 (n=50)	66.64 (7.83)	28.86 (3.57)	30.04 (4.60)	6.86 (1.94)

Another useful standardized instrument is the *Screening Test of Spanish Grammar* (Toronto, 1973b). It screens both receptive and expressive Spanish of Hispanic American. Some vocabulary items need to be changed, though; for instance, item 11 contains the word *helado*, which for Puerto Rican children should be *mantecado*.

Unfortunately, no instruments for evaluating pragmatics, semantics, and comprehension of meaning of connected speech have been published for Puerto Rican children. The professional will have to adapt methods proposed for English speakers in the literature (*see* Hopper and Naremore, 1978; Leonard, Prutting, Perozzi, and Berkley, 1978; McLean and Snyder-McLean, 1978; and Chapter 5).

Spoken language formulation of the Spanish-speaking child, as with the English speaker, is mainly evaluated by analyzing a transcribed corpus of elicited and spontaneous speech taken from the child in various settings and situations, and with different people. To undertake analyses of uttered speech in terms of syntax and morphology, the clinician can use the *Developmental Assessment of Spanish Grammar* (DASG) (Toronto, 1976) as well as the rules for calculating mean length of utterance (MLU) in morphemes (Linares, 1981). Both are useful in discriminating language deviant from that of language normal children (Linares-Orama and Sanders, 1977). Table 8-4 contains data on these measures for Puerto Rican children. Care should be taken in comparing these values with those for English-speaking children because Spanish and English differ in syntax and morphology.

Should the clinician suspect the child possesses some bilingual skills, the administration of language tests in both languages is recommended. This may assist the professional in determining whether or not the child's communicative problems are related to second-language learning. Based on the child's performance in the evaluation, the clinician interprets results in light of expected behavior according to age, social environment, and standards of communication. A child has a communicative problem when

TABLE 8-4
DASG and MLU for Three-Year-Old Puerto Rican Children

Age	DASG Score & S.D.	MLU Score & S.D.
3-0 to 3-5 (n=15)	5.91 (1.51)	7.03 (1.54)
3-6 to 3-11 (n=15)	6.92 (1.47)	8.62 (1.33)

there is a relative difficulty in understanding what others say or when others find it hard to comprehend what the child tells them. This is important to consider, especially concerning Hispanic American children who have been exposed to both English and Spanish. Some of these children may have heard parents misproduce either language and are just repeating what they have heard. The speech/language pathologist must then distinguish among language-different, language-disordered, and language-delayed children.

A prognostic statement should be made considering the severity of the problem, the presence of maintaining factors, available treatment frequency and intensity, and parent involvement in therapy. This is not an easy task, but one often required by administrators in order to establish priorities in patient programing.

The language evaluation of a child must include analyses of both spontaneous and elicited verbalizations. Miller (1981) has reviewed many possibilities for this kind of assessment. Verbatim transcriptions of these utterances are studied in terms of phonemics, morpho-syntax, lexicon, semantics, and pragmatics.

Regarding Spanish-speaking children's oral syntax and morphology, it is important to consider quantitative as well as qualitative analyses. In addition to MLU, for example, data on errors in inflectional morphology should be obtained. These may include verb construction as well as number and gender agreement. For oral syntax assessment, the clinician should include types of syntactical constructions and errors made. These errors may be described in terms of word substitutions, omissions, transpositions, and reversals.

The evaluation must contain an assessment of the child's hearing, at least in response to pure tone audiometric screening by air conduction or impedance screening audiometry. If speech audiometry is done, the stimuli must be appropriate in vocabulary frequency and speech pronunciation. Martin and Hart (1978) developed a prerecorded speech threshold procedure for testing Spanish-speaking children that can be used by clinicians who do not speak Spanish (*see* Chapter 7).

The speech/language pathologist must also evaluate the oral and respiratory mechanisms involved in the child's production of speech. With Hispanic American children, the clinician may face difficulties in having them open their mouths because they may be shy with a non-Hispanic professional. In this case, parent assistance is indicated.

Therapeutic Intervention

Communication therapy is the process by which a speech/language pathologist assists the client in achieving specific therapeutic objectives aimed at making the person a better communicator who uses the community rules for voice, fluency, and articulation production, and language comprehension and expression. This process depends on the particular individual being served, which makes speech and language therapy difficult to standardize. Nevertheless, there are some steps used in many programs for communication therapy.

Selection of Aspects for Therapy

Depending on the child's needs and learning capacities, the clinician chooses one or more aspects for intervention. It is more efficient to select basic aspects first, those upon which the client may build others. For example, attention skills are necessary before developing any speech and language behavior, and in language therapy, concept formation precedes verbal labeling.

When a Hispanic American child requires language intervention, the professional should determine which language (English or Spanish) to develop or modify. The primary basis of this decision should not be the relative complexity of each language, but the language that the child needs in order to communicate with more persons in the social environment.

Application of Therapeutic Methods

The speech/language pathologist develops a therapeutic design that specifies stimuli to be presented, manners of stimuli presentation, and techniques and activities for assisting the child in giving the desired response to stimuli. Consequences of the response, and procedures for stabilizing and automatizing the response should also be part of the overall design.

Voice therapy is aimed at eliminating misuse of the laryngeal mechanism and arriving at vocal characteristics most appropriate for the client. Intervention for fluency disorders seeks to assist the child in controlling, consciously and later unconsciously, the rhythm and velocity of speech. Voice and fluency therapy for Hispanic American children can be provided with the same methods, techniques, and activities that have been developed for American children. The clinician needs only to be able to speak sufficient Spanish to convey general suggestions to the Hispanic client and family.

Therapy for articulation disorders purports to help the child produce the phonemes of the language. Intervention usually starts with phonemes in isolation, then in syllables, words, phrases, and, finally, in connected speech. For the treatment of the Spanish-speaking Hispanic American child with articulation problems, the speech/language pathologist should have adequate skills in pronouncing Spanish, otherwise the clinician would be an inadequate model for the child.

Language intervention is aimed at assisting the child in developing or changing the use, both for comprehension and expression, of the pragmatic, phonemic, morphemic, syntactic, and semantic aspects of language. Language therapy must be an extensive and intensive activity if it is to produce significant effects. Parents and teachers should collaborate in order to make language therapy an all-day endeavor. To provide adequate language therapy to limited English Hispanic American children, the speech/language pathologist must be fluent and correct in the use of the Spanish language. Should this be unrealistic, other therapeutic alternatives, such as using Spanish-speaking assistants, should be sought. The clinician will have to use applicable data on normal communication from studies of children who speak languages other than Spanish in order to provide language therapy to Hispanic American children. However, it is a relief to know that there seem to be cognitive and language universals (Slobin, 1970) that can be of use for these therapeutic activities.

Generalization of Communicative Skills

Speech and language behavior developed in the clinic or classroom needs to be used consistently in the child's natural environment. Therefore, the speech/language pathologist must involve parents, teachers, and other significant community members in language intervention so the child understands that newly acquired skills are very useful to fulfill needs. When involving Hispanic parents, the clinician must learn their ideas about life, health, human development, and handicapping conditions. Some Hispanics are very firm believers in the "unavoidable rules of destiny" and accept as God-given their children's conditions. Obviously, these children do not progress as they might otherwise because their parents are resigned.

Conclusion

This chapter has covered a broad range of topics essential for effective management of Hispanic American children who have difficulties communicating. The reader will have recognized that additional normative and clinical data are needed for assisting clinicians and educators in providing better services for these children. One urgent necessity is that of understanding the acquisition of competence for verbs in Spanish, as this is a complicated element of the language. In addition, information about similarities and differences in pragmatic and semantic development of American and Hispanic children needs to be obtained. New therapeutic alternatives such as involving nonprofessional Spanish-speaking aides in language intervention for Hispanics are also needed. Speech/language pathologists and teachers who serve handicapped Hispanic American children should participate in educational activities that enhance their knowledge of the Spanish language and Hispanic cultures. In this manner, they will become true helping *amigos* of these children.

References

Bloodstein, O.:   *A Handbook on Stuttering*. Chicago, National Easter Seal Society, 1969.

Boone, D.:   *The Voice and Voice Therapy*. Englewood Cliffs, Prentice-Hall, 1971.

Carrow, E.:   *Test for Auditory Comprehension of Language*. Austin, Learning Concepts, 1973.

Castaneda, A.:   Cultural democracy and the educational needs of Mexican-American children. In Jones, R. (Ed.): *Mainstreaming and the Minority Child*. Minneapolis, Leadership Training Institute, 1976.

Emerick, L., and Hatten, J.:   *Diagnosis and Evaluation in Speech Pathology*. Englewood Cliffs, Prentice-Hall, 1974.

Erickson, J.G., and Omark, D.R. (Eds.):   *Communication Assessment of the Bilingual, Bicultural Child: Issues and Guidelines*. Baltimore, University Park, 1981.

Fábregas, Z.:   *La prevalencia de trastornos comunicológicos en una escuela pública en San Juan, Puerto Rico*. Unpublished master's thesis, University of Puerto Rico, 1979.

González, A.:   *Phonological development of southern Puerto Rican preschoolers*. Unpublished doctoral dissertation, Pennsylvania State University, 1981.

Hopper, R., and Naremore, R.:   *Children's Speech: A Practical Guide to Communication Development*. New York, Harper and Row, 1978.

John, V., and Horner, V.:   Bilingualism and the Spanish-speaking child. In Williams, F. (Ed.): *Language and Poverty*. Chicago, Rand McNally, 1978.

Learning Concepts: *Austin Spanish Articulation Test.* Austin, Learning Concepts, 1974.

Leonard, L., Prutting, C., Perozzi, J., and Berkley, R.: Nonstandardized approaches to the assessment of language behaviors. *ASHA, 20*:371–379, 1978.

Linares, N.: Rules for calculating mean length of utterance in morphemes for Spanish. In Erickson, J.G., and Omark, D.R. (Eds.): *Communication Assessment of the Bilingual, Bicultural Child: Issues and Guidelines.* Baltimore, University Park, 1981.

Linares-Orama, N.: *The language evaluation of pre-school Spanish-speaking Puerto Rican children.* Unpublished doctoral dissertation. University of Illinois, Urbana, 1975.

Linares-Orama, N., and Sanders, L.J.: Evaluation of syntax in three-year-old Spanish-speaking Puerto Rican children. *J Speech Hearing Research, 20*:350–357, 1977.

Martin, F., and Hart, D.: Measurement of Spanish-speaking children by non-Spanish-speaking clinicians. *J Speech Hearing Disorder, 43*:255–262, 1978.

McLean, J., and Snyder-McLean, L.: *A Transactional Approach to Early Language Training.* Columbia, Charles E. Merrill, 1978.

Miller, J.F.: *Assessing Language Production in Children.* Baltimore, University Park, 1981.

Paynter, E., and Bumpas, T.: Imitative and spontaneous articulatory assessment of three-year-old children. *J Speech Hearing Disorders, 42*:119–125, 1977.

Perkins, W.: *Speech Pathology: An Applied Behavioral Science.* St. Louis, C.V. Mosby, 1977.

Ramírez, M.: *El Desarrollo fonémico de niños puertorriqueños entre las edades de tres a cinco años.* Unpublished master's thesis, University of Puerto Rico, 1977.

Slobin, D.: Universals of grammatical development in children. In Flores d'Arcais, G.B., and Lenelt, W.J. (Eds.): *Advances in Psycholinguistics.* Amsterdam, North-Holland, 1970.

Toronto, A.: *A developmental Spanish language analysis procedure for Spanish-speaking children.* Unpublished doctoral dissertation, Northwestern University, 1972.

Toronto, A.: *Spanish Syntax Screening Test.* Evanston, Northwestern University, 1973a.

Toronto, A.: *Screening Test of Spanish Grammar.* Evanston, Northwestern University, 1973b.

Toronto, A.: Developmental assessment of Spanish Grammar. *J Speech Hearing Disorders, 41*:150–171, 1976.

Toronto, A.: *Toronto Tests of Receptive Vocabulary.* Austin, Academic Tests, 1977.

U.S. Office of Education: *Application for grants under handicapped per-sonnel preparation program*. Washington, D.C., Department of Health, Education, and Welfare, 1978.

Van Riper, C.:   *Speech Correction*. Englewood Cliffs, Prentice-Hall, 1972.

Wood, N.:   *Verbal Learning*. San Rafael, Dimensions, 1969.

9

The Exceptional Native American

Gregory R. Anderson
Suzanne K. Anderson

The first Americans, Native Americans, are the last ethnic group when one examines their level of education, income, and employment (U.S. Bureau of the Census, 1973). Native Americans frequently have numerous problems in academic performance (Cazden and John, 1971) with a large percentage not graduating from high school (Owens and Bass, 1969; Cherokee National Planning Department, 1977). Other problems include cultural conflicts with the educational system (Dumont, 1969; Nelson, 1972, Pepper, 1979; Cazden and John, 1971), language difficulties (Cazden and John, 1971; Kaplan, Downing, and Clark, 1979), teen-age marriage and pregnancy (Oklahoma State Department of Health, 1980), and limited access to or influence in determining educational opportunities (Fuchs and Havighurst, 1973; Thomas and Wahrhaftig, 1971). These factors lead to Native Americans' lower academic performance, lower levels of formal education, and excessive representation in special education programs.

The incidence of various handicaps among Native Americans will not be examined, for this information has been compiled by Ramirez (1976, 1978) and others from the Council for Exceptional Children. Instead, the focus will be on the cultural and language differences that have led to problems in school performance and exclusion from programs for the gifted. Also addressed will be the physically disabled or mentally retarded Native American, issues related to gifted education, and legal aspects of Native American education.

Conditions and situations found in Oklahoma, the state with the largest Native American population, will provide most of the examples. In many ways, the situation in Oklahoma mirrors the national picture, with one exception: in Oklahoma, the Native American population does not live on reservations but was given land allocations. Therefore, Native Americans and Anglos attend the same schools and often live side-by-side. In addition to reporting findings in the literature, this chapter will provide information gathered from on-site visits with members of the following tribes: Arapahos, Caddos, Cherokees, Cheyennes, Choctaws, Creeks, Kickapoos, Kiowas, Pawnees, Poncans, and Seminoles.

Classroom Cultural Conflicts and Exceptionality

Many Native American students are labeled exceptional due to cultural differences rather than true handicapping conditions. For this reason one needs to examine the effects of culture and tribal language variants upon school performance. This section will address the cultural differences that lead to difficulties in academic performance, including communication styles, behavior patterns, and assessment issues.

Cultural conflict has long been a part of the education of Native Americans. From early years, the federal government has viewed education as the primary means of acculturation. J.D.C. Atkins, the commissioner of Indian Affairs from 1885 to 1886, cited a report submitted to him stating that "in the difference of language today lies two-thirds of our trouble....Schools should be established, which children should be required to attend; their barbarious dialect should be blotted out and the English language substituted" (Atkins, 1887). This attitude led to inevitable conflict between the educational system and Native Americans. As an agent of acculturation, the school enforced *speak English* policies, refused to acknowledge Native American culture, and forced at least tacit acceptance of the mainstream culture and values by all. In addition, this policy led to limited knowledge of the Native American culture by Anglo teachers and a subliminal belief in the superiority of Anglo mainstream culture (Torrance, 1974a).

Another factor contributing to the conflict is that, even in Bureau of Indian Affairs (BIA) schools, few of the teachers are Native Americans themselves or have a thorough knowledge of the Native American culture. Fuchs and Havighurst (1973) found that only 11% of the BIA teachers were themselves of Indian ancestry and only 10% had a good understanding of, sensitivity to, and respect for the Indian community. More recently, Ramirez (1979) found that only 14% of the teachers in Native American classrooms had any Indian heritage. The situation is the same in Oklahoma, where, in schools with very high tribal enrollment, the teachers are almost all non-Indian and are not able to answer several basic questions regarding the Native American culture or language.

Among the cultural behaviors that lead to lower teacher evaluations of Native American children are the following characteristics:

1. Valuing of cooperation over competition (Davis and Pyatskowit, 1976; Dumont, 1969, 1972; Pepper, 1974; Phillips, 1972)
2. Avoiding public recognition (Dumont, 1972; Youngman and Sardongei, 1974)
3. Producing a lower level of language in Anglo-dominated classroom settings (Dumont, 1972; Fuchs and Havighurst, 1973; Youngman and Sardongei, 1974)
4. Valuing individual autonomy (Dumont, 1972; Fuchs and Havighurst, 1973)
5. Refusing to defend oneself against accusations made by Anglo authority figures (Davis and Pyatskowit, 1976; Pepper, 1979)
6. Responding to authority figures by looking down or away (Pepper, 1974; Saville, 1972)
7. Valuing an orientation toward the present rather than the future (Davis and Pyatskowit, 1976; Fuchs and Havighurst, 1973; Phillips, 1972)

Probably one of the most significant learning characteristics of Native Americans is their visual motor coordination ability. Most educators and anthropologists agree that Native American children show a definite preference for visual learning experiences (Cazden and John, 1971). Feldman and Dittman (1972) found that 5-year-old Native American children handle scissors as well as third grade Anglo children, and Native American preschoolers demonstrate advanced fine motor coordination.

Native Americans are similar to many minority groups and individuals in the culture of poverty as documented by Sigel (Sigel, Anderson, and Shapiro, 1966; Sigel, 1971), and tend to be visual rather than auditory learners (Bell, 1979). This learning style contributes to problems in reading and language arts performance.

The authors have frequently observed that Native Americans show visual preference in academic settings. Native American students also demonstrate superior visual memory performance. For example, they spent an extensive amount of time examining pictures and illustrations in books. Teachers reported that their Native American students do not easily comprehend verbal instructions; therefore, visual demonstrations are given to ensure that academic tasks are completed satisfactorily.

The visual learning style preference might be traced to the Native American lifestyle and parental teaching techniques. The Native American people often live close to nature and fully utilize their tactile and visual sensory modalities to abstract information from the environment. Indeed, such visual awareness and keen observation skills play an important role in the traditional learning of complex tasks.

Phillips (1972) described a three-step sequence in this traditional learning process demonstrated by Native Americans on the Warm Springs Indian Reservation in Central Oregon. The first step requires young children to watch and listen as an adult performs a rather complicated duty such as tanning a hide. In the second step an adult teaches the child a simple skill that is a component of the entire task, supervising the child as the subskill is practiced. After that subskill is mastered, additional subskills are modeled, taught, and supervised. The third step involves self-initiated independent practice and testing. Speech plays a minimal role in this process. Adults limit their verbalizations to corrections and answering questions. Likewise, the final achievement of a skill does not require the child to verbalize, since concrete products or physical demonstrations serve as success criteria. Traditional background experiences such as these reinforce the visual learning style that continues to be the Native American's primary mode of acquiring information.

In our verbally-oriented educational system one must refrain from labeling the Native American child as intellectually deficient simply because the child's strengths lie in the visual rather than the verbal modality. It is true that many educators and psychologists believe that language is an essential process required in cognitive development. However, others, such as Gestalt theorists, have stressed the role of other perceptual processes in thought as equally important (Cazden and John, 1971). Indeed, mental visualization plays a valuable part in numerous academic learning activities such as reading, mathematics, spelling, writing, and memorization tasks, to name a few. Such a skill should be appreciated, reinforced, and built upon, not denigrated. The apparent visual modality preference among Native Americans may actually be a natural coping behavior due to a deficiency in the English language. With limited language abilities, this type of behavior might be expected. Nevertheless, teachers of the Native American should be aware of this mode of learning and use it in teaching.

Many blocks to education, such as truancy and low motivation, have been attributed to the Native American's apathy towards formal education (Pepper, 1974; Northeastern Oklahoma State University, 1975). Such resistance is not toward education itself but toward Anglo values and customs forced on these children in the schools. Native American parents want their children to succeed in school, to learn English, and to acquire skills which will earn a living. Dumont (1972) reports a parent's comment: "All I am asking is to have a good teacher in our community school where our children go, because they sure do have a hard time in school.... We send the children to school to read and write and talk English not just to get punished" (p. 363).

Indian children value their education, and academic success is important to them. Frequently, older boys and girls will teach their younger siblings after school. Dumont (1969) notes that children sit for hours in their chairs absorbed in study without talking to anyone.

The apathy develops when the school curriculum fails to prepare Native American students for anything they see as relevant, i.e., skills necessary for a living or for an occupation. In discussing the culturally relevant priorities in Native American education, Pepper (1974) cited a need to develop vocational programs suited to the specific skills used in different Native American settings and cultures (*see also* Baca and Lane, 1974). There is also a need for evaluation of education for occupations not available in the tribal area. Often, schools force the young Native American to choose the tribe, job, or education. If Native American students realistically are not able to find jobs suited to their academic preparation, then attending school, for them, is pointless.

Native American Language Performance

Throughout the authors' interviews with educators of Native American children, one response was consistent: the greatest problem of Native American students falls in the area of language performance. The Native American's language difficulties in the classroom have also been documented in sources such as the Coleman Report (Coleman, 1966). These difficulties have arisen from a number of factors: cultural constraints on language production in Anglo-dominated classrooms, difference in learning styles, pidginization of Native American languages, and the existence of Indian dialects, several of which have been studied and are referred to as Indian or Red English.[1]

Cultural constraints on language production in the Anglo cultural setting are evident in most classrooms enrolling Native American students. Reduced language production of Native American students, documented by Dumont (1972) and others, leads to both a lower evaluation by the teacher and a lack of opportunity for the student to obtain feedback or develop acceptable school language usage. Most educators and tribal leaders questioned in the preparation of this chapter referred to the sparing use of language and the simplification of syntax by Native Americans. This sparing use of language tends to restrict language development.

The rapid pidginization of Native American languages has added to problems in English performance. The Tucson Program and others have found that facility in the native language is highly correlated with facility in English (Lavatelli, 1971; *see* Chapter 4). Today, however, many tribal languages are rapidly losing lexicon and undergoing a simplification of syntax. Native American bilingual educators have related many incidences of such change. One Choctaw bilingual educator stated that the Choctaw spoken by tribal members in Oklahoma, the first language of many Choctaws in Oklahoma, is now considered *children's speech* by tribal members in Mississippi (Jacobson, 1979). Those students with simplified Choctaw as a primary language base could be severely handicapped in learning English as a second language.

It has been found that English variants tend to be far more pronounced in their morphological and syntactical variants (grammatical variants) than in their phonology or lexical variants (pronunciation, systems or vocabulary omissions, combinations, or variants). Indeed, many of the early assessments conducted to evaluate Title VII Bilingual Education programs were merely tests of morphology. Middle- and upper-class Anglo society frequently sees nonstandard morphology as a mark of poor education or poor performance in school. Therefore, the student speaking and writing in Indian English is often viewed as a failure in the academic setting.

Oklahoma is an especially interesting place to examine the role of Indian English in children's education and culture. As previously stated, unlike most other states, the Native American population lives not on reservations but beside the Anglo population and in very close proximity to many other tribes. With a decrease in the number of native speakers, intermarriage with other tribes, and greater movement into nearby cities or towns, some method of group identity is needed. In this setting, Indian English plays a major role in tribal identity. For tribal Indian English to define group membership is perhaps nowhere more important than among the Cheyenne-Arapaho. In Oklahoma, Cheyenne-Arapaho is probably the most nonstandard Indian English dialect spoken by the majority of the members of a tribe. Cultural membership is more often defined by dialect than by the official one-eighth blood quantum. The relationship between distinctiveness of the dialect and degree of identity was made apparent by a Cherokee who accurately identified the tribal affiliation of several individuals by their dialect. Therefore, Indian English dialects appear distinctive and carry an important identity role.

What may be of greater significance, especially for those working with Native American children, are the differences among tribal languages. The importance of these differences can be viewed in the studies of Leap (1973), who depicted Isleta Indian English as having an English lexicon and a Tiwa syntax. Though this was an overstatement (admitted as such by Leap, 1976), it points to the prominence of native language entrants into Indian English dialects. Many Native American language differences that puzzle teachers are contrastive in nature, such as the omission of the pronoun gender among the Cherokees. Pulte (1978) identified numerous syntactic and phonological errors in Creek children stemming from native language remnants in Creek English production.

Among Choctaw children, the authors found that most of the phonological differences seemed to be normal developmental errors. However, some omissions and substitutions that were not developmental in nature could have been predicted due to the phonology of Choctaw. Similar results were obtained by examining the results of Cherokee children's school speech assessment. In rural Cherokee schools it was noted that characteristics of the students' Indian English production, e.g., the stops and intonation, closely resembled Cherokee.

Educational service providers need to realize the important role played by the dialect of Indian English. There must not be the strict *speak proper*

English demands in the classroom reminiscent of the destructive rule to *speak only English* in BIA schools of the past. There needs to be the realization that dialect production does not represent a lack of understanding of Standard English but a culturally dictated mode of interaction. Knowledge of the local Indian English dialect can be of value to education professionals who need to understand student language and the reason for nonstandard production so they may be more likely to view nonstandard language as a difference rather than a deficit.

Education professionals need to be trained to assist the Native American child in the production of Standard English when society and employers demand it. However, it is imperative that educators still accept Indian English when the culture demands. Indeed, the interpretation of the Ann Arbor Decision regarding Black English (Joiner, 1979) has direct relevance for teachers who encounter Indian dialect. Finally, professionals need to be alerted to the importance of Indian English for cultural identity; the student forced to speak Standard English may be viewed as "less of an Indian."

The Physically Disabled or Mentally Retarded Native American

Due to the lack of research and data presently available about physical or mental handicaps among Native Americans, many comments in this section are limited to informal surveys and interviews conducted by the authors. (For information on hearing impairments *see* Chapter 10.) Obviously, well organized studies are needed before many generalizations and conclusions can be made.

Attitudes toward the handicapped and access to services varies greatly among Native Americans. Historically, many tribes held the handicapped, especially the mentally retarded, in awe. Today, many attitudes are far less positive, although there still seems to be the feeling that the handicapped should be accepted members of the tribe. The local community or tribal unit feels some responsibility, but the family seems to assume most of that responsibility. This attribute often leads to overprotection and isolation.

People from twelve tribes in Oklahoma were interviewed regarding tribal attitudes toward handicaps. Results indicated that physical handicap was viewed fairly uniformly; the tribal groups attitudes were protective. The physically handicapped are seen in the local community and are not isolated or hidden.

There is a reluctance, however, on the part of families to obtain treatment for physical handicaps through the Indian Health Service. Several children were observed with unrepaired cleft lips or minor untreated orthopedic difficulties in rural Head Starts and kindergartens. All, however, seemed to have received treatment in the early elementary years. A number of Native American parents are now willing to have high risk infants sent to neonatal intensive care units. For many, however, the trauma of birth defects and hospitalization of the child far away from the Indian Health Service hospital is immensely difficult. The high risk infant was rarely visited until returned to the Indian Health Service hospital from the neonatal intensive care unit.

Mental handicap seems to be viewed, and thus handled very differently among various tribal groups with different levels of acculturation. In most tribes, the mentally retarded are hidden from view and only reluctantly, if at all, placed in training settings. Among many tribes, the mentally retarded are regarded negatively. However, in the very traditional tribes, a handicapped member is seen as possessed by the gods, very close to the gods, or a messenger from a god (Patterson, 1979).

With greater acculturation, Native American views of the handicapped are becoming similar to those held by the Anglo community. A good example of what one might find in a school setting was related by a Poncan school counselor. Youngsters often tried to bring the physically handicapped into their play, making a concerted effort to ignore the condition. However, the response to a mentally retarded student was quite different. Generally, Native American peers would go to great lengths to avoid the retarded student. There was little acceptance of mental handicaps among the Poncans (Headman, 1979).

An important area of concern is the frequent lack of services for the handicapped child in the traditional Native American community. As a large percentage of Native Americans live in sparsely populated areas, services are not usually available. Stories of Native Americans having to leave tribal communities to obtain services for a child are frequently heard (*see* North American Indian Women's Association, 1978). Ramirez (1976) has documented the inadequate amount of special education opportunities available to Native Americans in all types of educational settings. Numerous rural, predominantly Native American, schools have no special services other than limited speech therapy or an occasional special reading program. In many of these schools, numerous children were observed by the authors who would have been more appropriately placed in programs assisting the retarded, severely disturbed, or learning disabled.

Several handicapping conditions are more prevalent in some Native American populations than among the population in general. Probably the greatest amount of documentation exists regarding conductive hearing loss (*see* Chapter 10). High incidence of otitis media among Native Americans in Oklahoma was related by several speech pathologists and audiologists.

Alcoholism is high among many Native American groups. The North American Indian Women's Association (1978) has expressed fear of a rise in the fetal alcohol syndrome, which could increase the incidence of handicaps. Other abnormalities have been noted such as the congenital hip deformity present in Navajo.

Indian Health Service personnel suggest that a high incidence of handicapping conditions is largely due to poor prenatal care and pregnancies at an early age (Lundsford, 1979). Related to this is the poor nutrition of Native American mothers. Native American children's weight norms are below those of Anglo children. High infant and childhood morbidity and mortality rates have been documented by the Oklahoma State Department of Health (1980).

Identification of Handicapped Native Americans

It is unfortunate that so little data is available regarding the education of handicapped Native Americans. The data that does exist covers only students in BIA supported schools. No published information on those outside of BIA schools in Oklahoma is presently available. The lack of data could in part be because no blood quantum is required under Title IV to identify an Indian. The Native American is defined by the Office of Education as being a person regarded as an Indian by the local community. In collecting data on exceptional Native American children, it was found that the Muskogee District BIA office had been totally unsuccessful in its attempts to obtain such information (Patterson, 1979). Therefore, a discussion of the exceptional Native American children cannot be based on statistical data other than that from a few tribes.

In recognition of the need for accurate data, a program has been developed entitled American Indian Special Education Policy (AISEP) Project (funded January 1979 by the Bureau of Education for the Handicapped and the Bureau of Indian Affairs). The purpose of this project's initial phase is to develop a survey of existing and needed policy concerning the delivery of special education and related services. This project examined conditions in or near Indian reservations or on restricted lands in twenty-six states (Pages, 1979).

Currently, the data from this project are undergoing analysis. The results of the survey will indicate the methods used to identify exceptional Native American students, categories of exceptionality being served, methods of delivering special education services, total Indian enrollment, and the number of Native Americans enrolled in special education. Information will also be available regarding the attitudes of special education teachers and administrators toward the exceptional Native American student. Unquestionably, this project will contribute significantly to better education of the handicapped Native American student and will, hopefully, set a precedent for further investigation in this area.

The Gifted Native American: A Neglected Population

Educators are just beginning to consider the needs of culturally different children and to develop appropriate experiences for them (*see* Chapter 15).

Many of these efforts are directed toward compensatory education and acculturation. Very little attention has been given to the education of the gifted minority child; indeed, many people use the terms *minority* and *disadvantaged* interchangeably. In addressing this subject, Torrance (1974a) made the following comment regarding the American attitude toward culturally different gifted students: "We could never quite admit it, but we....held that there was a superior set of cultural characteristics to be emulated and against which all members of our society must be evaluated" (p. 471). Unfortunately, extensive interviews conducted with educators and others responsible for the education of Native Americans substantiate Torrance's statement.

The small amount of literature that does exist on minority gifted students deals mainly with Black and Mexican Americans. It comes as no surprise that the general public is not aware of gifted Native Americans since professionals have rarely addressed this population. In a literature search conducted by Bruch (1978), only six journal articles were located on Native American gifted students between preschool and college.

Before hoping for a change in societal attitudes, one must deal with several issues. First, the public must become aware of the existence of gifted Native Americans. As obvious as it may seem that gifted Native Americans do exist, many gifted programs in areas with a high proportion of Native Americans include few, if any Native Americans. Those gifted programs that do have Native American students include only the most highly acculturated ones. Second, one must recognize the current difficulties in identifying gifted Native Americans and look for alternative methods (*see* Chapter 2). One must acknowledge the relationship between appropriate programing for culturally different gifted students and their feelings of success. Finally, there is a need to examine the problems in educational programing for culturally different gifted students in order to make necessary improvements. Intelligence and giftedness are usually defined according to Anglo middle-class cultural norms. Therefore, the assessment of giftedness becomes culture-bound and does not recognize attributes of talent and/or giftedness valued by other cultures. Western cultures tend to value success, striving, tenacity, and pragmatic problem-solving, whereas Native American cultures value the ability to help others and cooperative problem-solving. The community and educators must develop an appreciation of how cultural norms determine characteristics valued as giftedness.

An accurate perception of the tribal culture is a necessity before the educator can develop an awareness, an assessment procedure, and an appropriate education program for gifted Native Americans. Most Anglo middle-class teachers hold rather stereotypical views of Native American cultures, values, and aspirations. Torrance (1974b) found this to be true in preworkshop assessments of teacher perceptions of Native American expertise. These findings demonstrate the need for accurate information to be delivered to the teachers of Native American students.

An awareness of which specific Native American students are gifted cannot come from an examination of standard achievement tests for several reasons. For example, these tests rely heavily on verbal abilities, so typically most scales are heavily weighted in terms of reading comprehension and related factors (*see* Chapter 4). In a study that utilized an achievement measure with Cherokee adolescents (Anderson, n.d.), it was found that the only scale that did not have a large part of its variance accounted for by reading comprehension, was a mathematical computation scale. The rest of the test was primarily a reading comprehension test. Gonzales emphasized that we must not be blinded by English language competency when deciding if a child is gifted or retarded. "Minority children gifted in one area may still not be proficient in standard English. This is particularly true if the child has been reared in a language environment that is linguistically different from that of standard English" (p. 568).

Most of the standardized measures of giftedness are not only culturally irrelevant for Native Americans but have been developed and normed on Anglo middle-class populations (Torrance, 1974a; Bruch, 1974; Watson, Omark, Grouell, and Heller, 1980). No consideration is given to the life experiences of the youth being assessed. Most Native Americans are residents of isolated rural communities or the inner city and have had limited exposure to many of the test items included in the measures. Even in Oklahoma, where Anglos and Native Americans attend the same schools, more Native Americans tend to live in isolated rural communities while more Anglos tend to live in town. The differences in experience become apparent in a study by Anderson (n.d.). Career knowledge of Native Americans was assessed utilizing the measure Planning Career Goals (AIR, 1977). It was found that Native American youth perform more poorly than Anglos on questions assessing knowledge about activities of occupational groups. This difference was independent of achievement level.

A federally funded project conducted by the Cherokee Education Center assessed potentially gifted and talented Native Americans and their Anglo classmates. The assessment included a teacher checklist, a biographical inventory, an achievement test, an artistic evaluation form, a career inventory, and other measures. Though differences were not great, some measures, such as the achievement test, identified more Anglos as gifted than Native Americans. The teacher checklist also tended to include more Anglos than Native Americans on criteria such as having larger vocabulary, long memory, persistence, ability to work independently, ability to initiate, concern for world affairs, and an orientation toward setting high goals. Teachers nominated Native Americans more frequently only in the areas of fine or performing arts. Native Americans performed far above Anglos on the art evaluation and far below Anglos in career development.

It may be better to reach outside the classroom for assistance in identifying gifted Native American students. Bruch (1978, p 317) cited Bernal who suggested that "members of a particular ethnic group can identify their own smartest." Obviously, a member of a child's own tribe is going to be more qualified to judge whether a child is gifted or not in relation to tribal peers than a teacher from another culture. This statement is made for two reasons. First, the tribal member will be familiar with the behavioral customs particular to that tribe. Second, the tribal member will understand the language used by the child.

Peer pressure also affects assessment. According to Gonzalez (1974), the gifted child has to mask giftedness to conform to peer pressure phenomena because in school being gifted means behaving in ways that are valued by the mainstream culture rather than behaviors that are valued by the tribe. Being identified as gifted draws excessive attention to the child, an unpleasant situation for most Native American children (Witty, 1978). Lack of motivation is still another stumbling block to proper identification of the gifted Native American. This can be caused by tests designed for Anglo middle-class children that lead the Native American child to expect failure. It can also be caused by fear of additional academic pressure placed upon the student identified as gifted.

The emphasis in identification should be on divergent production, transformations, and implications rather than verbal performance. Examiners should be aware of alternative valid responses, response styles, and culturally relevant procedures for each group. Approaches which are not norm referenced may also prove fruitful. Biographic inventories are evidence of creative behaviors within the culture (Renzulli, 1973).

Successful experience is essential for any program involving Native Americans. Several studies have found that Native American students demonstrate a lower level of self-esteem than do Anglo children when assessed on standard measures (Church, 1977; Coleman, 1966; Heaps and Morrill, 1979; Martin, 1979; Tefft, 1967). Any program needs to make the Native American students feel positive about their ethnicity and their culture. Programing must avoid cultural violations that disregard the tribe. Rather, elements and artifacts valued by the culture should be brought into the classroom. Studies have found that the more the students are able to feel a part of their traditional culture and the more that traditional culture is accepted, the greater the feelings of positive self-esteem (Boggs, 1958; Kupferer, 1966; Lefley, 1975; Tefft, 1967). Therefore, the classroom teacher who desires to have Native Americans view themselves in a positive manner and have favorable feelings about their ability to succeed needs to help them feel positive about their culture.

Problems for the gifted Native American exist in educational programing as well as in identification. Even if a sensitive, well-trained person identifies the gifted Native American child, the child probably will be placed with an Anglo middle-class teacher who is unaware of the child's special cultural assets or the motivation that inspires these particular talents. Witty (1978) suggests that most school systems reflect the values of mainstream culture such as "the concepts of rule, conformity, regularity, normality, control, egocentricity, closeness, consistency, standardization, ... being focused, and rigid order" (p. 348).

In response to this apparent cultural conflict, many people advocate a compromise. Davis and Pyatskowit (1976) propose what they call bicognitive education—education enabling effective functioning in the world of the tribe and the world of the Anglo. This approach allows the child to use tribal experiences to respond to situations one might encounter in the mainstream culture. Torrance (1974a) also recommends melding the child's tribal and mainstream experiences.

An effective curriculum would also include a counseling program to assist the Native American students in establishing their tribal identity and functioning in the mainstream culture (Witty, 1978). These counseling programs should help the child develop particular learning styles, talents, and related responsibilities and should be catalysts encouraging the child to assess available resources and gain access to them for use in special projects. If gifted children from various cultural groups have difficulty with interpersonal relationships, this should be a concern of the counseling program. Finally, the program will be most effective when parents and community members are actively involved. Parents of culturally different gifted students often have adjustment problems and need as much guidance and support as does the child.

Native American Special Education and the Law

The advent of legislation that has provided support for Native American education is quite recent. Responsibility for providing educational services to Native American students has been and continues to be haphazardly handled by federal, state, local education, and tribal agencies. Due to this multiple educational delivery system, it is difficult to determine where the responsibility for specific educational services lies.

In 1972, the Indian Education Act proved to be a turning point for the education of Native Americans (Demmert, 1976). Of particular interest with regard to the exceptional Native American are the Education Amendments of 1974 that adds two sections to part B of the Act. Part B provides for parent and community involvement in Native American education. One of the amendments authorizes the development of grants for special education programs for teacher training and Native American pupils.

Another law that has affected the education of exceptional Native Americans is the Education of all Handicapped Children Act (P.L. 94–142). Section 611 (f)(1) authorizes payments to the Secretary of the Interior for the education of handicapped Native American students on reservations (Ramirez and Smith, 1978). A committee report (No. 94–168) that accompanies the Senate version of P.L. 94–142 provides the same rights and protections for handicapped Native American children and their parents that are provided for other handicapped children served by state and local education agencies. These include:

1. child-find programs
2. individualized education programs (IEPs)
3. personnel development
4. appropriate evaluation materials and procedures
5. placement in the least restrictive and most appropriate environment
6. safeguards for confidentiality of information (Ramirez and Smith, 1978)
7. advocacy for children's and parents' rights

The Bureau of Indian Affairs (BIA) does not presently conduct special education programs for all tribes. If the Indian Education Act and P.L. 94–142 are to be implemented for Native Americans, the BIA must accept responsibility for the development of official policy statements demanding appropriate identification procedures and educational programing for handicapped Native American children. There are some cases where public, BIA, and tribal-controlled schools serve Native American children within the same geographical area. In these situations, written agreements must be developed designating specific educational responsibilities to assure that no children will be lost in the shuffle between agencies.

Requirements for personnel development and inservice programs are also outlined in P.L. 94–142. These require that BIA and state education agencies initiate training programs for teachers, administrators, and other special service personnel in preparation for intervention with handicapped Native American students.

Legislation on the education of Native Americans also addresses the issue of advocacy with advocacy groups to protect the rights provided for in P.L. 94–142. This is particularly important for Native American families who in many cases are unaware of their rights to appropriate free education and the administrative procedures needed to procure it.

Conclusion

Native American education has progressed from the days of the BIA "speak English" policy, though little of the Native American cultures and languages is allowed into the classroom today. Educational professionals need to become more aware of the cultural differences that lead to conflict and lower teacher evaluation of these students. In the same vein, there needs to be a greater appreciation of the Native Americans' languages, including an awareness of their values, origins, and forms. Greater attention must be paid to assessments and services that can be more specifically focused on Native American cultures. Finally, more research and development is necessary in the area of demographics, identification, service delivery, and culturally appropriate intervention if the needs of the exceptional Native American child are to be met.

Notes

[1] *See* the Trinity University series of Papers in Southwestern English (Leap, 1976).

References

American Institutes For Research: *Planning Career Goals.* Monterey C.T.B./ McGraw Hill, 1977.

Anderson G.: *Native American Career Development*, Urbana, University of Illinois, dissertation in process.

Atkins, J.D.C.: *House Executive Document.* Fiftieth Congress, 2:18, 1887.

Baca, L., and Lane, K.: *Exceptional Children, 41*:552–562, 1974.

Bell, A.: Personal communication, October 1979.

Boggs, S.T.: Culture change and the personality of Ojibwa children. *American Anthropologist, 60*:47, 1958.

Bruch, C.B.: Assessment of creativity in culturally different children. *Gifted Child Quarterly, 19*:164, 1974.

Bruch, C.B.: Recent insights on the culturally different gifted. *Gifted Child Quarterly, 22*:374, 1978.

Cazden, C.B., and John, V.P.: Learning in American Indian children. In Wax, M., Diamond, S., and Goeting, F. (Eds.): *Anthropoligical Perspectives on Education*, New York, Basic Books, 1971.

Cherokee National Planning Department: *Cherokee Nation Comprehensive Plan: Base Studies.* Talequah, October 1977.

Church, A.G.: Academic achievement, IQ, level of occupational plans, and self-concepts for Anglo/Navajo high school students. *Psychology, 14*:24, 1977.

Coleman, J.S.: *Equality of Educational Opportunity.* Washington, D.C., Health, Education, and Welfare, United States Office of Education, 1966.

Cowen, A.D., and Coker, J.: *A Study of the Contribution of Diagnostic Test Data to Maturity in the Career-Decision-Making Process.* Washington, D.C., Health, Education, and Welfare, United States Office of Education, 1978.

Davis, T., and Pyatskowit, A.: Bicognitive education: a new future for the Indian child. *J American Indian Education, 16*:14, 1976.

Demmert, W.G., Jr.: Indian education: where and whither? *American Education, 12*:6–9, 1976.

Dillard, J.L.: *Black English: Its History/Usage in the United States.* New York, Random House, 1972.

Dillard, J.L.: *All-American English: A History of the English Languages in America.* New York, Random House, 1975.

Drechsel, E.J.: Historical problems and issues in the study of North American Indian marginal languages. In Leap, W.L. (Ed.): *Papers in Southwestern English II: Studies in Southwestern Indian English.* San Antonio, Trinity University, 1976.

Dubois, B.L.: Spanish, English, and Mescalero Apache (1845–1880). In Leap, W.L. (Ed.): *Papers in Southwestern English II: Studies in Southwestern Indian English.* San Antonio, Trinity University, 1976.

Dumont, R.V.: Cherokee children and the teacher. *Social Ed., 33*:70, 1969.

Dumont, R.V., and Wax, M.L.: Cherokee school society and the intercultural classroom. *Human Organization, 28*:217–226, 1970.

Dumont, R.V.: Learning English and how to be silent: Studies in Sioux and Cherokee classrooms. In Cazden, C.B., John, V.P., and Hymes, D. (Eds.): *Functions of Language in the Classroom.* New York, Columbia Teachers College, 1972.

Feldman, M., and Dittman, L.: Curriculum for Indian children. In Cazden, C.B., John, V.P., and Hymes, D. (Eds.): *Functions of Language in the Classroom.* New York, Columbia Teachers College, 1972.

Folb, E.: Rappin' in the vernacular. *Human Behavior, 2*:16, 1973.

Fuchs, E., and Havighurst, R.J.: *To Live on this Earth: American Indian Education.* New York, Anchor/Doubleday, 1973.

Gonzalez, G.: Language, culture, and exceptional children. *Exceptional Children, 40*:565, 1974.

Haas, M.: What was Mobilian? In Crawford, J. (Ed.): *Studies in Southeastern Indian Languages*, Athens, University of Georgia, 1975.

Headman, L.: Personal communication, May, 1979.

Heaps, R.A., and Morrill, S.G.: Comparing the self-concepts of Navajo and white high school students. *J American Indian Education, 19*:12, 1979.

Jacobson, B.: Personal Communication, June, 1979.

Joiner, C.W.: Memorandum and Opinion. Civil action No. 7-71861, 1979.

Kaplan, D.W., Downing, C., and Clark, B.: *Prevalence of Speech and Language Deficits in American Indians Aged 4-8 Years.* Oklahoma Childrens' Memorial Hospital, Oklahoma City, 1979.

Kupferer, H.J.: *The Principal People 1960: A Study of Cultural and Social Groups of the Eastern Cherokee. Anthropological Papers #78,* Washington, D.C., Bureau of American Ethnology, *196*: 1966.

Lavatelli, C.S.: The Tucson method of language teaching. In Lavatelli, C.S. (Ed.): *Language Training in Early Childhood Education,* Urbana, ERIC, 1971.

Leap, W.L.: Language pluralism in a Southwestern pueblo: Some comments on Isletan English. In Turner, P.P. (Ed.): *Bilingualism in the Southwest,* Tucson, University of Arizona, 1973.

Leap, W.L. (Ed.): *Papers in Southwestern English II: Studies in Southwestern Indian English,* San Antonio, Trinity University, 1976.

Lefley, H.: Different self-concepts in American Indian children as a function of language and examiner. *J Personal and Social Psychology, 31*: 36, 1975.

Lundsford, J.: Personal Communication, September, 1979.

Martin, J.C.: Locus of control and self-esteem in Indian and white students. *Bureau of Indian Affairs Educational Research Bulletin,* 7:22, 1979.

Nelson, M.: Problems Indian students face. *Indian Historian, 5*:2, Summer 1972.

North American Indian Women's Association: *Special Needs of Handicapped Indian Children and Indian Women's Problems.* Washington, D.C., Bureau of Indian Affairs, 1978.

Northeastern Oklahoma State University Department of Education and Psychology: *Teacher, There's an Indian in Your Classroom,* mimeo, 1975.

Oklahoma State Department of Health: *Oklahoma Health Statistics 1978.* Oklahoma City, 1980.

Owens, C.S., and Bass, W.P.: *The American Indian High School Dropout in the Southwest.* Albuquerque, Southwest Cooperative Educational Laboratory, 1969.

Pages, M.: Personal Communication, June, 1979.

Patterson, T.: Personal Communication, June, 1979.

Pepper, F.: Interview conducted by Baca, L., and Lane, K.: Dialogue on cultural implications for learning. *Exceptional Children, 40*:552, 1974.

Pepper, F.: *Educational Characteristics of the Native American Student.* Paper presented at Council for Exceptional Children National Convention, Dallas, 1979.

Phillips, S.U.: Participant structures and communicative competence: Warm Springs children in community and classroom. In Cazden, C.B., John, V.P., and Hymes, D. (Eds.): *Functions of Language in the Classroom.* New York, Columbia Teachers College, 1972.

Pulte, W.: Memo to Factor, S., Maxwell, R., and Creek-Seminole Title VII Bilingual Education Project, East Central Oklahoma State University, Ada, 1978.

Ramirez, B.A.:   *Background Paper on American Indian Exceptional Children.* Paper presented to the National Advisory Council on Indian Education, Reno, 1976.

Ramirez, B.A., and Smith, B.J.:   Federal mandates for the handicapped: Implications for American Indian children. *Exceptional Children, 44*: 521, 1978.

Ramirez, B.A.:   *The American Indian Special Education Policy Project.* The Council for Exceptional Children, Washington, D.C., 1979.

Renzulli, J.S.:   Talent potential in minority group children. *Exceptional Children, 40*:437–444, 1973.

Saville, M.R.:   *Linguistic and Attitudinal Correlates in Indian Education.* Paper presented at the American Educational Research Association Convention, Chicago, 1972.

Sigel, I.E., Anderson, L.M., and Shapiro, H.:   Categorization behavior of lower- and middle-class Negro preschool children: Differences in dealing with representation of familiar objects. *J Negro Education, 35*:218, 1966.

Sigel, I.E.:   Language of the disadvantaged: The distancing hypothesis. In Lavatelli, C.S. (Ed.): *Language Training in Early Childhood Education.* Urbana, ERIC, 1971.

Tefft, S.K.:   Anomie, values, and culture change among teenage Indians: An exploratory study. *Sociology of Education, 145*: 1967.

Thomas, R.K., and Wahrhaftig, A.:   Indians, hillbillies, and the education problem. In Wax, M.L., Diamond, S., and Gearing, F.O. (Eds.): *Anthropological Perspectives on Education.* New York, Basic Books, 1971.

Torrance, E.P.:   Are the Torrance Tests of Creative Thinking biased against or in favor of disadvantaged groups? *Gifted Child Quarterly, 15*: 75–80, 1971.

Torrance, E.P.:   Differences are not deficits. Teachers College Record, *75*:471–482, 1974a.

Torrance, E.P.:   Readiness of teachers of gifted to learn from culturally different gifted children. *Gifted Child Quarterly, 18*:137, 1974b.

U.S. Bureau of the Census: *Subject Reports, American Indians in the U.S. 2*:IF, 1973.

Watson, D.L., Omark, D.R., Grouell, S.L., and Heller, B.:   *Nondiscriminatory Assessment: Practitioner's Handbook*, Vol. 1. Sacramento, California State Department of Education, 1980.

Witty, E.P.:   Equal educational opportunity for gifted minority group children: Promise or possibility. *Gifted Child Quarterly, 22*:344, 1978.

Youngman, G., and Sadongei, M.:   Counseling the American Indian child. *Elementary School Guidance and Counseling, 9*:272, 1974.

10

Communication Disorders in the American Indian Population

Joseph L. Stewart

While you would expect that everyone has a commonly accepted definition of what constitutes an *American Indian* or *Native American*, such definitions appear to be almost as numerous as the Indian people themselves. For the purposes of this chapter, an American Indian is considered to be a person so recognized by a tribe or other constituent group recognized by the federal government and, further, resides on or near a federal Indian reservation. For the sake of brevity, Alaska Natives are also considered within this definition. Best estimates to date indicate that, using broader definitions, there are somewhere in the vicinity of one million American Indians, of which approximately one half fits this definition.

If you take these 500,000 American Indians, scatter them thinly in the predominantly rural areas of 27 states stretching from Maine to California on one dimension and from Alaska to Florida on another, place them, unequally, among more than 260 tribes and 200 Alaska Native villages, and then assign them one of 217 native languages, the extent of the problem of defining and remediating communication disorders affecting American Indians becomes more apparent. Added to this is the further complication that the population distribution by states ranges from about 400 in Louisiana to over 100,000 in Oklahoma.

To further confound and confuse the issue, many of these children are not, strictly speaking, bilingual; the decline in use of an ancestral language in one area, however, seems to match the increased awareness and stress of an ancestral language in another community. Many Indian languages are now having an orthography invented for them, and, even in areas where the language has essentially died, cultural awareness expressed through overview courses on the language are gaining in popularity. While not all Indians are bilingual in a strict sense, available data do indicate that many are nevertheless limited in their use of English and therefore fit the criteria of this book.

Hearing Disorders

Middle Ear Disease

Based on available data, the leading communication disorder affecting American Indian children is conductive hearing loss. For every year since 1961, when it was first listed as a reportable disease in the Indian Health Service, otitis media has been at least the second highest reported health condition; for most of those years, it has been the leading reported condition. The term *otitis media* is used to refer to any inflammatory condition of the middle ear and covers several different but related conditions. The infectious stage of the disease can be caused by a variety of pathogens and may or may not be accompanied by hearing loss. Most commonly, inflammations in the middle ear cavity are the result of an infection in the nose and nasopharynx, so that common respiratory infections are the underlying source of middle ear diseases and their subsequent complications.

In the Indian population, the acute state of the disease is most often seen before the age of two years, the child suffering earlier episodes being most susceptible to repeated infections and development of the chronic stage of the disease. In the acute stage, inspection of the ear drum of the affected child reveals an inflamed drum accompanied by such symptoms as a feeling of fullness in the ear, the possibility of a slight hearing loss, and intermittent or continuous pain of varying severity. When acute suppuration (formation of pus) occurs, severe pain is the leading symptom and is usually accompanied by high fever and definite indications of hearing loss. If the pressure increases, the ear drum may rupture, leading to an immediate relief from pain. Chronic suppurative otitis media is more commonly found in persons with a history of acute childhood ear disease, and the term itself implies a perforation of the ear drum. Hearing loss may vary from negligible to severe.

The most complete epidemiological research has been conducted in Alaska as a result of clinical data collected in the middle and late 50s indicating unusually high incidence and prevalence of this disease. A study begun in 1970 by Maynard and Hammes indicated that 38% of a cohort of Eskimo infants had at least one episode of draining ear during the first year of life. Brody, Overfield, and McAlister (1965) found that 31% of Eskimo children surveyed had a history of a draining ear. A study by Reed, Struve, and Maynard (1967) found 62% of Eskimo children with one or more episodes of draining ear from the time of birth, and Reed and Dunn (1970)

TABLE 10-1

Comparison of Perforations and Overall Ear Problems

Service Unit Site	*% Perforations*	*% Overall Ear Problems*
Florida	1.9	29.2
Idaho	5.0	23.8
Nevada	0.2	5.2
South Dakota	2.5	16.7
Utah	2.0	28.7

found 63% of children in six Eskimo villages with past or present evidence of otitis media. In 1973 Kaplan, Fleshman, Bender, Baum, and Clark reported a ten-year cohort study of Alaskan Eskimo children in which they found that 76% of 489 children had experienced one or more episodes of otitis media since birth; 78% of these had their first attack before the age of two. Perforations or scars were found in 41% of the children and half of these had bilateral defects. These findings were highly correlated with histories of otitis media. Audiometrically, 16% showed a hearing loss of at least 26 dB and another 25% had a measurable air-bone gap even though they were within the normal range. Similar results are reported among the Canadian Eskimo and Indian population by Cambon, Galbraith, and Kong (1965); Ling, McCoy, and Levinson (1969); Schaefer (1971); and Graham (1975).

While all the disease rates are higher in Alaska, disproportionately high rates are also seen for Indians elsewhere in the United States. In an early study on the Navajo Reservation, Johnson (1967) found a chronic otitis media rate of 7% among a sample of three thousand Navajo children enrolled in boarding schools. Of those, 25% had bilateral involvement. More recently, a survey conducted among selected schools on the Navajo Reservation reported by Stewart (1977) showed chronic otitis media rates varying from 1.8 to 9.3% depending upon the school surveyed, with boarding schools generally showing the highest rates. In 1968 Zonis reported results from a prevalence study of chronic otitis media at the White Mountain Apache Indian Reservation in which 505 people were examined and 8.3% had chronic otitis media.

The most recent epidemiologic study of the extent of the hearing problem was conducted by McCandless and Parkin (1976) at five sites throughout the United States: Hollywood, Florida; Lapwai, Idaho; Ft. Dushesne, Utah; Owyhee, Nevada; and Sisseton, South Dakota. The results of this study comparing percentage of perforations and overall ear problems are summarized in Table 10-1.

While the prevalence of chronic middle ear disease at the five study sites was lower than had been expected, it was still much higher than in the population at large for which the National Health Survey (March, 1972) found the perforation rate in children to be less than 1%. Nearly 30% of the subjects from all areas showed some type of hearing loss or ear pathology, a figure which is again much higher than in the general population.

Starting in 1970, the Indian Health Service initiated a special program to combat otitis media in the American Indian population. Over the first six years of the program, a total of some 237,000 patients, mostly children, had been seen. Of this number who had audiometric screening, 26% were screening failures, and 48% were found to have a confirmed hearing loss. No data are available to indicate the breakdown between conductive and sensorineural losses.

Sensorineural Hearing Loss

For a variety of reasons, data on the prevalence of sensorineural hearing loss in the Indian population are less readily available. The Indian Health Service program above has been oriented largely toward active and chronic middle ear disease affecting children, so that statistics on sensorineural and mixed hearing losses are less frequent. In the case of adults, statistics are unreliable since the built-in bias is that an adult seeking services probably suspects a problem prior to the time the service is provided.

In New Mexico, Watrous (1978) reports that there are 25 school-age Indian children known to have sensorineural hearing losses sufficient to require amplification out of a population of 16,721 (.01%). This recent intensive survey in New Mexico of at least six hundred children between the ages of birth and four years revealed two with sensorineural hearing losses of this extent (.3%). McCandless and Parkin (1976) found that sensorineural hearing loss first became significant in the age range between 18 and 21 years where it was 4.4%, with a rapid increase beginning in the forty to fifty-year-old age group, which was largely attributable to the aging process and is similar to what is found for the general population.

In Montana, over a two-year period (1976–1977), Lewis (1978) found sensorineural or mixed hearing losses in a population of 925 children as follows: 112 (12%) unilateral and 100 (12%) bilateral. The severity of the losses reported was not indicated.

Identification and Intervention

Testing Procedures

Given that otitis media strikes the very young child, program directions are undergoing change at the present to emphasize the earliest possible identification and intervention. The additional need for extending the testing procedures downward—to younger children—are inferred from the relatively recent research on the effects of early and intermittent otitis media. The resultant minimal and fluctuating hearing loss has significant effects on the speech and language development of the child and on subsequent learning, educational achievement, and social problems (*see* Chapter 7).

The earliest study of fluctuating hearing loss on the ultimate educability of children was that of Holm and Kunze (1969). This study found children with a history of intermittent otitis media to be significantly deficient in most of the tests in the battery requiring reception and processing of auditory stimuli or producing verbal responses. The more recent study by Kaplan et al. (1973) is more pertinent to the scope of this chapter. In that study, those children with a history of otitis media prior to the age of two years with a hearing loss of 26 dB or greater were significantly poorer in verbal ability and rated retarded on a total reading, total math, and language scores. Those with a hearing loss of less than 26 dB but with a history of early otitis media showed lower achievement and verbal scores than the normal group against which they were compared.

Similar results were found among the Australian Aborigines by Lewis (1976) who studied the effects of chronic middle ear disease on the development of auditory processing skills. His experimental group of fourteen Australian Aboriginal children with histories of chronic middle ear disease was compared with two control groups, one European and the other Aboriginal, each consisting of eighteen children with normal middle ear function. He interpreted his findings to show that chronic middle ear impairment restricts the development of certain auditory processing skills and distorts integrational patterns. He notes that chronic ear disease is not the sole cause of the linguistic incompetence found in these children, but that ear disease is related to a variety of other factors such as malnutrition and social-cultural inequality.

Population Distribution

The territory served by the Indian Health Service is divided into 10 constituent Areas, each of which serves an Indian population that may consist of (a) residents in a single state, such as Alaska or Oklahoma; (b) residents of a widely disbursed group of states, such as the area serving Maine, New York, North Carolina, Florida, and Mississippi; or (c) a single tribe of Indians such as the Navajo. An Area may also serve only a portion of the Indians in the state, such as the Albuquerque Area that serves those Indians in the States of New Mexico and Colorado not served through the Navajo Area that extends into the State of New Mexico. Given the diverse nature of these breakdowns and the variability of other programs to provide services within a state, there is a high degree of diversity in the identification programs throughout the country. In many places audiologic screening in the schools is a state program and covers all the residents of that state. In other states, rudimentary or no hearing screening programs are provided in the schools so that those provided by the Indian Health Service are the only ones available. Also, a given state may have Bureau of Indian Affair (BIA) schools within its boundaries which serve Indian students, while other students attending public schools adjacent to or remote from the reservation have less chance of being served.

In general, the Indian Health Service program first stressed identifying those children of school age with active ear infection or residual damage from previous ear infection and hearing loss. Typically, such a program tests children in the Head Start program, and in kindergarten, first, third, sixth, and ninth grades, as well as special education pupils, teacher/ parent/ physician referrals, and newly enrolled students. The children failing the screening are then retested, preferably within two months from the original test. Referrals for medical treatment, where appropriate, are made at this point, and the child is rescheduled for evaluation following medical and/ or surgical intervention.

The tests routinely administered in the school programs are audiometric, usually using a portable audiometer, and tympanometric, using a portable acoustic impedance meter. Typically, the audiometric test is administered through 500, 1000, 2000, and 4000 Hz and the impedance test compliances measured and recorded for pressure points at +100, +50, +25, -25, -50, and -100 millimeters (H_2O) relative to the point of maximum compliance. Acoustic stapedial reflex is administered routinely at 1000 Hz, and afterwards at 2000 and 4000 Hz if there is no response at 1000. The child who fails any part of the acoustic impedance or the pure tone screening is administered a pure tone threshold test and is scheduled for a recheck. All children failing the initial test are seen again during the next school year regardless of the retest performance.

Most Indian children attending school present a relatively *captive* population for a screening program. The at-risk infant, the one most susceptible to ear infections and impaired later development due to auditory deprivation is most difficult to test if accessible, presenting a more complex set of problems. Efforts to locate these children are currently underway.

Geographic and political considerations, among others, influence the program's effort to find these children. In Arizona, for example, the University of Arizona has been conducting research to determine the impact of intensive efforts to prevent successive episodes of otitis media among persons at high risk. The research also studies how familial, environmental, behavioral, and other factors associate with the rate of occurrence of otitis media among groups with contrasting incidence rates. Incorporated also is a retrospective study of factors associated with hearing loss and other related sequelae of otitis media.

Trained Indian technicians are stationed at three different Service Units which serve four different Indian tribes. Each encounter of otitis media is followed by home visits, during which care is provided in addition to data collection. In this manner, any child seen medically for any stage of disease is entered on a roster and followed for an appropriate period of time. Since evidence indicates that otitis media seems to "cluster" in families, follow-up visits by the technician have a secondary beneficial effect of keeping the parents and other family members aware of the early symptomatology of disease and the availability of services to provide for immediate care. The technician can also follow the course of disease throughout the year in each individual family constellation.

A similar program has been started in the northwest portion of the United States. Here pediatric nurse practitioners and nurses are trained in otoscopic examination of children who are seen both as patients in the various medical facilities and those attending well baby clinics. This approach assures regular routine examination of children in the target population, giving the opportunity for preventive education to mothers and other family members at the same time.

Future Directions

A deficiency of these programs serving American Indian students is their lack of attention to hearing loss, due largely to the time and training necessary for the administration of audiometric tests, particularly those suitable for the very young. Over the past two years, a pilot project on early identification and early intervention for the diagnosis of both sensorineural and conductive hearing loss has been under way. The project has established appropriate follow-up for every Indian child, including medical treatment, amplification, and language and speech stimulation. The project stresses that early identification and intervention are desirable not only from the humanitarian and educational standpoint, but from the economic standpoint as well.

The feasibility of testing children below the age of four was proven by two pilot programs in New Mexico. Early identification testing techniques and equipment were field-tested and evaluated. Various interview techniques and assessments of development skills were used and evaluated in these clinics for early identification.

The equipment used for the early identification/early intervention program was either purchased or designed according to the following criteria: (a) portability, (b) appropriateness for the young, (c) durability, (d) availability to purchase, and (e) suitability for field work. For newborns and infants, the Neometer was selected. This device generates a 3000 Hz warbled tone at 70, 80, 90, and 100 dB. Battery operated, it is used only when audiometric sound field testing equipment is not available. The criterion for passing is a response to 90 dB in each ear.

The taped sound screening series developed at Bill Wilkerson Hearing and Speech Center in Nashville is used as a slightly more refined and sophisticated technique. This electronic calibrated cassette tape contains sixteen stimuli with the following filtered conditions:

1. All of the stimuli below 500 Hz unfiltered
2. All stimuli below 1000 Hz unfiltered
3. All stimuli above 1000 Hz unfiltered
4. All stimuli above 2000 Hz unfiltered

The tester operates a tape recorder with a remote hand switch and scores responses by observing orienting and location-seeking responses of the child. This equipment has been found to be successful with children as young as five months and can be used until the age of three years, at which time pure tone audiometry is usually the test of choice. As with the Neometer, the Wilkerson test is used when no sound field facilities are available.

A technique found to be particularly useful for children, especially those difficult to test, has been tangible reinforcement operant conditioning audiometry (TROCA). The particular TROCA used in this project has a portable audiometer and is designed so that by depressing one switch, both the tone and the reinforcer switches are activated. The types of reinforcement available—dispensing a small candy, illuminating a toy located within the unit, or activating a mechanical toy—gives considerable versatility to the test procedure. Children are screened at 20 dB at 1000, 2000, and 4000 Hz and at 25 dB at 500 Hz. Children must pass the screening frequency for both ears. The TROCA, found to be useful in clinical testing in sound fields and under earphones, has been of great assistance in diagnosing preschoolers' hearing losses and in fitting their hearing aids.

The impedance bridge is a vital piece of equipment used for all ages in this program. The ease of operation on even very young children can be inferred from Watrous' (1978) findings: of 567 children tested, only 6% could not be tested the first time; these children were rescheduled and the second time only 1% could not be tested.

At the present, based upon the early findings that an extremely high test failure rate was coupled with a very low rate of confirmed cases of ear pathology, a retest in six to eight weeks is done when either of the following conditions are found: (a) peak pressure is more negative than -170 mm (H_2O) and less negative than -300 mm (H_2O), or (b) a reflex is not observed at 100 dB at 1000 Hz. Medical referrals are made if the peak pressure is -300 mm (H_2O) pressure or greater, or no peak pressure is obtained (flat tympanogram .2cc equivalent volume). Using these criteria, the failure rate dropped from 30 to 10% in the recheck category and from 37 to 23% in medical referrals.

The combination of tests to be performed varies with the age, location, and physical state of the child at the time of test. In all cases audiometric as well as impedance screening is appropriate.

Use of Paraprofessionals

Paraprofessional personnel to test the hearing abilities of American Indian students evolved from two related problems: (a) the scarcity of fully trained audiologists willing to work on reservations and (b) the lack of local acceptance of non-Indians doing the testing in Native Indian communities. Throughout Indian reservations, a large number of paraprofessionals are used in a variety of roles requiring varying degrees of experience and competence. The core training for a paraprofessional technician consists of three weeks intensive study of anatomy and physiology of the ear, the operation of audiometric and impedance equipment, the establishment of referral channels, and follow-up procedures for once persons are evaluated and referred.

A number of other persons receive far less training to acquaint them with the problems of middle ear disease, its distribution, and procedures to be followed when hearing loss and/or middle ear disease is suspected. At the present, nearly 400 persons have received at least this basic information.

Given suitable and appropriate audiologic background, supervision, and surveillance, the Indian paraprofessionals have been fully functional members of the hearing health teams and at the local level their work is far more acceptable than that of the more highly qualified non-Indian professionals (*see* Chapter 21). It must be emphasized that both the professional and paraprofessional are necessary in this program and that the professional's acceptance and credibility in the local community has increased as the use of paraprofessionals has been extended.

Sensorineural Auditory Deprivation

Since the deprivation of auditory stimulation is at least as critical (perhaps more so) in the child with a sensorineural hearing loss as for the child with a conductive loss, every effort is being undertaken to identify these children as early as possible so that appropriate remedial programs might be initiated. As a matter of policy, every Indian child found to be in need of hearing amplification is provided binaural hearing aids at as early an age as possible. In addition, an individual program has developed that stresses maximum use of the child's hearing residual.

Available research indicates that the languages are learned most efficiently through the auditory channels and that the physiologically critical period for learning is probably before the age of one year. Hence, aural programs for these children have the highest priority. Residential schools for the deaf, *total* communication programs, and manual communication programs available at some distance from the child's home, are scrupulously avoided unless the child cannot be provided an aural program or that the child has not progressed in such a program.

Cultural-Social Factors Regarding Ear Disease, Hearing Loss, and Prostheses

A lesson learned early by the non-Indian health practitioner and educator working on the reservations is that many accepted definitions, standards, and assumptions previously held are not necessarily valid in this new environment. Often differences in cultural perceptions are determined by the community's local and past history over which the Indian may have no control. The numerous documented instances of young Eskimo mothers bringing their infants to the clinic to find out why the child's ears had not yet started to drain validates the assumption that anything as common as a draining ear, that occurs as frequent as losing deciduous teeth, must be normal, and any deviance from that norm must be cause for concern. Such instances raise several questions: What is regarded a problem in each locality? What problems do the people involved know firsthand? How are problems conceptualized? What services do people perceive to be available to deal with a problem once identified?

In various communities, a number of local remedies for draining ears seem to predate the arrival of Europeans. Either these same remedies were discovered independently, or they were transmitted throughout the groups. Among the Sioux, for example, the common treatment for earache was to have tobacco smoke blown in or warm badger oil poured into the ear. The Sioux child feeling the badger oil bubbling in the ear would be told that it was the sound of the digging of a badger and that the treatment involved the spirit of the badger digging the sickness and ache out of the ear.

Similar indigenous treatments are reported from the Zuni Pueblo, many hundreds of miles from the Sioux country, including putting hot packs on the ear and putting pinion gum, garlic juice, warm honey, or tobacco smoke into the ears. Harding and Boyer (1976) observed that in Zuni these treatments for pain are all associated with keeping the ears warm. This association between pain and heat applied to the ear was made by all respondents. Indigenous treatments that work are not likely to be replaced by more modern practices, even though the tendency is for indigenous and modern medical treatments to exist simultaneously.

Harding and Boyer note that the Zunis had developed one of the most elaborate systems of health treatment in North America many centuries before the first European contact. Their extensive knowledge of plant medicines made it possible for the Zuni medicine men to use antiseptics and to induce unconsciousness in patients while performing basic operations, both prior to the use of antiseptics and anaesthetics in Europe. Zuni knowledge of anatomy and medicine was demonstrated in their ability to set fractures, treat dislocations, make simple incisions for the removal of pus, treat diseases of the uterus, and conduct other operations. Today even government doctors refer many fracture cases to indigenous Indian "bone pressers" who specialize in treating fractures without the use of casts.

Like other Indian people, the Zunis worry a great deal about witchcraft, and many believe that some people in the tribe have the ability to cast a spell that can cause sickness, an accident, or other misfortunes. The person who feels subjected to witchcraft usually consults the local medicine man, traditionally a spiritual leader as well as a medical practitioner. Harding and Boyer (1976) related one example of a woman who felt her otitis media was induced by witchcraft. Persons who attribute their communication disorders to witchcraft present an entirely different problem than those who assume other etiologies and therefore seek alternative sources for relief (*see* Chapter 16). This is the case only when the problem is perceived as a problem not only by the individual involved but also by the community.

Availability of services to remediate a problem probably influences the local perception of whether or not there is a problem. Thus, a condition for which no treatment is available must either run its course or gain community acceptance in the absence of effective treatment for it.

While hearing loss and deafness seem to be generally recognized in Indian communities as problems, the traditional solution to the problem was highly dependent on the availability of services. In the past the absence of institutionalized forms of treatment necessitated more acceptance of deviance; this appears to be undergoing change. However, the tendency among many Indian communities still is to absorb the handicapped or otherwise "different" person within the structure of the society.

Any reliable estimates of the number of deaf persons in rural reservations such as the Navajo, for example, have been difficult to obtain since many Navajo known to be deaf spend their entire lifetime as sheep herders, a vocation they are capable of pursuing that has a great deal of value in the community. While there are Navajo and other Indian children enrolled in various state schools for the deaf, such enrollments are not easily achieved, since Indian parents, by and large, are extremely reluctant to send children away for prolonged periods.

It appears that today many Indian groups are more accepting of *deviance* than society at large. Many times a child born with a handicap is not regarded as deviant in the usual sense. It is assumed that children have, before birth, the choice of deciding in what condition they wish to be born; if handicapped, the children do so by choice. Some Indian languages take problems into account in a more sophisticated fashion than does English. The Ute Indian term *n'kvat* ("can't hear so can't talk") is much more descriptive of the condition than is the corresponding English expression "deaf and dumb."

There is no question that the handicapped person within the Indian community is recognized as being different but, for the most part, such differences have a wider range of tolerance. Prosthetic devices such as eyeglasses and hearing aids do not seem to have the same acceptance in all Indian communities. While perhaps only a reflection of general children's behavior, ridicule of Indians for using such prostheses is common. The ridicule does not seem to be associated with the condition requiring the device but with the device.

In Harding and Boyer's (1976) research, 53 attributes for ear treatments and the services available were described; approximately half of these related to hearing aids. Only five attributes regarded as positive related to such factors as improving hearing and the ability to communicate, improving a person's social life, and improving involvement in family life by improved communication. The 23 attributes regarded as negative fell into two broad categories: (a) such problems as function, care, and maintenance of the apparatus, i.e., hearing aid distortion, static, battery life, and breakability and (b) problems related to personal appearance such as embarrassment, being teased about wearing a prosthetic device, and its being noticed by other people. The negative attributes, not limited to responses from younger people, indicate that concern about appearance and self-image are not determined by age.

Habilitation/Rehabilitation

It might be inferred from the foregoing that programs for the habilitation and rehabilitation of the hearing impaired Indian are not abundant even today. As with other rural populations, professional personnel at clinical facilities that provide such services are not readily available. Indians with a communication disorder are as eligible as other citizens to receive such services. The uneven geographic distribution of the population, coupled with the long distances many Indian families need to travel for even rudimentary services, make it necessary to either develop alternatives to available services or accept the lot in life of afflicted persons.

Early identification and intervention programs for the infant and younger child currently are being developed. These are coupled with home-training programs in which the parents and family members are instructed in procedures to follow in the home to ensure maximum relevant auditory stimulation for the child and to maintain the child's hearing aid. The newness of these programs is such that no evaluation of its effectiveness has been undertaken at present. For hearing-impaired children, the resources are usually obtained in the nearest community where they are available. As more and more Indian children attend public schools, more and more receive the services that are available in these locations. Residential schools for the deaf in states with an Indian population do have Indian students enrolled.

For the adult hearing-impaired Indian, available services on the reservation are generally limited to the case-finding of the persons in need of services, the selection of a hearing aid, if appropriate, and the involvement of persons in the community who check the hearing aid's use, functioning, and need for repair. Preliminary data tend to indicate that hearing aid use is a direct function of battery availability and related maintenance and repair facilities. Using such a criterion for evaluation as battery use, information collected by community health representatives during home visits, and direct questioning of the user, it is estimated that 80% of the hearing aid users are getting part- to full-time use from their hearing aids. This range is from approximately 60% use on the Navajo reservation, where battery availability and related services are crucial factors in nonuse, to approximately 95% in the areas served by Albuquerque, where such services are readily available.

Speech and Language Disorders

In view of the extent of middle ear disease and concomitant hearing loss, it follows that this may be a factor resulting in a higher incidence of speech and language deficiencies in the Indian population. The problem is further compounded by bilingualism or nonstandard dialect use with all its ramifications (*see* Chapter 9). In some locales, Indian children enter schools knowing only their respective ancestral languages and rudimentary English.

The absence of a balanced bilingual educational program in school environments has been presumed to result in emotional stresses, educational insufficiency, and a significantly higher dropout rate than exists in the general school population. In some instances, the dropout rates run as high as 25 to 50%. Many of these children in school have been identified as having "deviant" speech and "insufficient" language. Field observations indicate that these behaviors are reflected and, in many instances, the children do require the combined service talents of competent speech/language pathologists and special educators.

No single or combination study or survey of the American Indian population has answered the critical issue of the *number* of speech and language impaired. We are not now in a position to obtain reasonably accurate data on the prevalence of speech and language disorders in this population. The availability of such data have to await the development of nondiscriminatory tests and evaluation procedures. This is a formidable task, considering the diversity in the numerous American Indian and Alaska Native cultures and languages, the cost of developing such instruments, and that most of these native languages do not have a written form. Such information as is available shows, as in the case of hearing disabilities, that the proportionate number of children so affected is much higher than in the population at large.

Except for the survey cited above, very little data are available on the extent of the problem, other than information presented as part of clinical programs and private studies initiated to determine service needs. In the latter category, a recent report of the speech and language screening project at Shawnee, Oklahoma, by Clark and Downing (1978) shows a high incidence of speech, language, and hearing dysfunctions. The study, conducted on a group of four through eight-year-old children showed: (a) deficits in receptive language—13.6% of the sample; (b) deficits in expressive language—19.2%; (c) deficits in articulation—19.3%; (d) failures on hearing screening—11.4%; and (e) voice deviations—7.4%. The national average of all speech and language problems combined is 8%. Most recent information from certain New Mexico pueblos (Miles, 1976) shows from 34 to 35% of the Head Start children evaluated at these sites in need of speech and/or language therapy with from 27 to 50% of those tested requiring follow-up testing to determine whether they may also warrant speech therapy.

While the extent of the problem affecting American Indians seems and is overwhelming, it does not differ from reports from other areas of the world with aboriginal populations. Clearly, total eradication of the problems presented is beyond the financial resources of the United States. The program described has recognized this problem by focusing on the health aspects, stressing prevention to the greatest extent possible. Problems of lesser priority can be solved as funds become available and as the extent of disease diminishes. All such programs, however, must be viewed in terms of their desirability and acceptability by the Indian people.

References

Brody, J., Overfield, T., and McAlister, R.:   Draining ears and deafness among Alaskan Eskimos. *Archives of Otolaryngology, 81*:29, 1965.

Cambon, K., Galbraith, J.D., and Kong, G.:   Middle ear disease in Indians of the Mount Currie Reservation, British Columbia. *Canadian Medical Association J, 93*:1301, 1965.

Clark, B., and Downing, C.:   Personal communication, December, 1978.

Graham, M.D.:   Prevalence of middle ear disease among the Indian population of Coastal British Columbia. *Hearing Instruments, 26*:26, 1975.

Harding, J.R., and Boyer, J.:   Determination of Zuni perceptions of otitis media treatments and attributes: A methodology and some pilot results. Unpublished final report, Indian Health Services, December, 1976.

Holm, V.A., and Kunze, L.H.:   Effect of chronic otitis media on language and speech development. *Pediatrics, 43*:833, 1969.

Johnson, R.L.:   Chronic otitis media in school age Navajo Indians. *Laryngoscope, 77*:1990, 1967.

Kaplan, G.J., Fleshman, J.K., Bender, T.R., Baum, C., and Clark, P.S.: Long-term effects of otitis media: A ten-year cohort study of Alaska Eskimo children. *Pediatrics, 52*:577, 1973.

Lewis, C.:   Personal communication, March 24, 1978.

Lewis, N.:   Otitis media and linguistic incompetence. *Archives of Otolaryngology, 102*:387, 1976.

Ling, D., McCoy, R.H., and Levinson, E.D.:   The incidence of middle ear disease and its educational implications among Baffin Island Eskimo children. *Canadian J of Public Health, 60*:385, 1969.

Maynard, J.E., and Hammes, L.M.:   A study of growth, morbidity, and mortality among Eskimo infants of Western Alaska. *World Health Organization Bulletin, 42*:613, 1970.

McCandless, G.A., and Parkin, J.L.:   Otitis media among various Indian populations. Unpublished final report, contract number HSM-110-73-377, Indian Health Service, 1976.

Miles, M.:   Personal communication, May 24, 1976.

National Health Survey, Vital and Health Statistics, 11, No. 114:DHEW, PHS, HSA, March, 1972.

Reed, D., and Dunn, W.:   Epidemiologic studies of otitis media among Eskimo children. *Public Health Reports, 85*:699, 1970.

Reed, D., Struve, S., and Maynard, J.E.:   Otitis media and hearing deficiency among Eskimo children: A cohort study. *American J of Public Health, 57*:1657, 1967.

Schaefer, O.:   Otitis media and bottle feeding: An epidemiological study of infant feeding habits and incidence of recurrent and chronic middle ear disease in Canadian Eskimos. *Canadian J of Public Health, 62*:478, 1971.

Stewart, J.L.:   Otitis media annual report, FY 1976. Indian Health Service, April, 1977.

Watrous, B.:   Personal communication, August 28, 1978.

Zonis, R.D.:   Chronic otitis media in the Southwestern American Indian. I. Prevalence. *Archives of Otolaryngology, 88*:40, 1968.

11

The Vietnamese Refugee Child: Understanding Cultural Differences

Tâm Thi Dang Wei

In the past decade, thousands of Indochinese refugee families came to the United States to settle in various cities and rural communities. Initially, many group sponsored families were scattered throughout the country, some say for ease of assimilation. However, as families sought cultural ties, a more acceptable climate, and/or familiar occupational resources such as fishing, there has been a tendency toward the development of ethnic clusters. Large populations of Vietnamese individuals now reside in states such as California, Louisiana, Minnesota, and Texas.

These populations (as well as other Indochinese groups from Cambodia, Laos, and Thailand) vary greatly in educational and occupational background. This variation is often related to the political atmosphere in their native country that prompted immigration to the United States. Therefore, it is impossible to make statements about Vietnamese refugee children that will be characteristic of each child. There are some general considerations, however, in regard to adjustment, cultural conflicts, and educational evaluation that professionals should consider. The information in this chapter is part of a more extensive report (Wei, 1980) that also describes the Vietnamese cultural heritage regarding religion, value systems, customs, and behavior expectations (*see also* Thuy Vuong, 1976). The purpose of this chapter is to summarize these considerations and assist the professional in differentiating between those children who are normal but in the process of adjustment and those who are indeed handicapped and in need of special services.

Adjustments and Conflicts

The Vietnamese child who has recently immigrated to the United States is faced with many adjustment problems. The child has to learn sufficient English to be able to communicate with teachers and peers. New ways of behaving, thinking, and learning have to be acquired. This child must compare, sort out, and eventually decide what parts of Vietnamese cultural heritage to retain, what parts to modify, and what parts to replace in order to function effectively in the new society. There are three general areas of conflict and adjustment that a Vietnamese refugee child may encounter: (a) emotional, (b) cultural-social, and (c) educational.

Emotional Conflicts

The emotional adjustment is the most difficult for the Vietnamese child to make because the child is totally unprepared for the new situation. In Vietnam, the child was faced with war and evacuation. In the United States, the child has had to adjust to changing family roles and a new environment.

The effects of war and evacuation. Vietnamese children were born during war and witnessed its brutality. Many Vietnamese rufugee children appear very serious compared to their American counterparts. The war has affected them by causing some of them to become introverted, unstable, unfriendly, or distrustful.

During the evacuation process, refugee children are faced with the real dangers of death, separation, and deprivation. Many children are separated from their parents, their siblings, or their relatives. Many have been through tragic experiences and all of them are faced with the fear and anxiety of an unknown future. These experiences are very traumatic. The depth of their imprint on the child is hard to measure; however, it is certain that they are sources of many nightmares and fears.

Changing roles and lifestyles. In Vietnam, the child was very secure in the family circle where each member had a defined role. Once in the United States, these roles change. The father is no longer the authoritarian head of the family. He often is unemployed or underemployed. He is no longer the sole support of his family. The changing role of the father, whom the child respects the most, is confusing, causing the child conflict and insecurity.

Many of the refugee parents cannot give their children the moral support they gave them in Vietnam because they also are faced with their own emotional adjustments. They often feel lonely, homesick, or isolated in their new environment. This isolation causes adults to become depressed and children to lose motivation in school. These feelings are compounded by physical differences and the inability to communicate.

Although these adjustment difficulties are quite real, they are not completely insurmountable. It has been observed that many Vietnamese refugee students are making good adjustments and progress in American schools. When the Vietnamese child has strong moral support at home and understanding from teachers and school administrators, there is a very good chance to adjust quickly and adequately to the new life and to the new school situation.

Cultural and Social Conflicts

These conflicts arise when cultural and social expectations differ. Vietnamese refugee children experience conflicts when they try to meet the different expectations of their parents and their American teachers. If the child wants to conform to the expectations of the parent, the child must work hard, do well in school, and be respectful and obedient to elders and authority figures. This will require that the child ignore or reject the Western values of independence and individualism because such values are incompatible with the parental and cultural expectations of the Vietnamese.

Behavioral differences. The Vietnamese child is expected by the parents to be quiet, polite, modest, and humble. These characteristics cause the child to seldom express wishes and opinions. This behavior often is interpreted by American teachers as being withdrawn, unmotivated, or uncooperative. Westerners also view the humbleness of the Vietnamese as derogatory, and interpret their modesty as a form of self-degradation.

A Vietnamese child who has been taught to respect and obey elders and persons in authority, often is confused and bewildered by the direct, spontaneous behavior of American peers towards adults and teachers. The Vietnamese child would consider such "free" behavior to be disrespectful. On the other hand, the gestures that the Vietnamese child uses to show respect, e.g., bowing the head to the teacher, or handing papers to the teacher with both hands, are often laughed at by American classmates. The polite response of the Vietnamese of not looking someone in the eye while talking may be interpreted by Americans as a symptom of an insecure, even emotionally disturbed person.

Cultural differences. Differences in foods, eating habits, clothing, and weather also can affect the newly arrived refugee child. A little girl did not eat her lunch because she was not accustomed to using a knife and fork. Some Vietnamese children become ill from different water and food. Others, affected by cold weather, are either overdressed or underdressed by their parents, making it easy for them to catch colds. These are just a few of the cross-cultural problems that a Vietnamese child will experience in the United States.

Educational Conflicts

In addition to emotional, cultural, and social differences, the Vietnamese child must also adjust to differences in the American and Vietnamese educational systems. There are three categories of educational differences that the Vietnamese child must face: (1) different learning styles and classroom activities; (2) a change in the student-teacher relationship; and, most of all, (3) the language barrier.

Differences in learning style and classroom activities. The Vietnamese educational system promotes a passive type of learning where the students learn by listening, watching, and imitating their teachers. The open type of classroom common in many American schools is perceived by the Vietnamese as confusing and disorganized. Since Vietnamese students are used to a lecture method, team teaching and active class participation are uncommon and strange to many of them. They are not familiar with group activities and do not know how to react. Independent projects or library research are foreign to them, and they need to be guided with patience.

The student-teacher relationship. The friendliness and informality of American teachers is shocking to the Vietnamese student and hard for them to accept. The absence of honorific terms in the English language compounds the problem and makes the Vietnamese student feel uneasy and uncomfortable when talking with their teachers. They are reluctant to ask questions in class because such behavior seems to them aggressive and disrespectful. Their confusion is increased when, to their surprise, their teachers reward such behavior in class.

Since they are not accustomed to talking in front of the class, they are shy and uncomfortable when asked to do so in the American classroom. They do not volunteer answers because they have been taught to be modest. If they need help, they probably will not ask for it.

Because the Vietnamese student does not know the limitations of the new freedom observed in the American classroom, the child may become a discipline problem. The inability to perceive the freedom limitations that exist on the playground or in the classroom is the cause for some of the misconduct or misbehavior attributed to the Vietnamese students. The students might be too quiet and be forgotten or labeled uncooperative, or they might be too loud, talk out of turn, and be judged a discipline problem. This lack of understanding is complicated and aggravated by the language barrier.

The language barrier. The language problem can be very acute when there is only one or very few Vietnamese students in the school. The lack of communication or understanding between the child and the school authority can cause a small misunderstanding to grow into a large emotional or discipline problem. The author was asked by a woman principal if a little boy in a kindergarten class knew Kung Fu because of his uncontrollable strength. Being the only Vietnamese in the school, he was totally confused and bewildered with no one to turn to for help. His tension had built to an explosive limit. Once explanations were given to him in Vietnamese, he was a changed child.

The language barrier also limits the child's social contacts with American peers. A high school teacher was concerned when a Vietnamese boy changed from being friendly and cooperative to being anti-social. A talk with the boy revealed that he did not know enough English to communicate with his peers, and as a result, he was slowly withdrawing from them. He was frustrated because he could not say "maybe later" or "not at this time" when he was asked to join in an activity. His abrupt responses seemed rude to his classmates, further frustrating him, and in effect, discouraging other social interaction.

Many of the directions and explanations in the American classroom are verbal. So one can imagine the tremendous amount of self-control that non-English speaking children maintain and confusion they feel if they can rely only on visual cues. These cues are not always dependable and mean that the child will always be one step behind the others. This causes social reactions and behavior to be out of place.

A child that appears to speak good English also can have problems. It is easy to be misled by good pronunciation of English and to assume that such a child has a good command of English. A child can appear to answer correctly by simply imitating others, not fully understanding what is being said. It is not easy to determine the extent of English that a child knows. The child could be silent and nonresponsive because English is not known or because English is known but the child is reacting to differences in the classroom atmosphere.

The conflicts discussed in this section are mentioned in an attempt to offer some insight into the unique situation of the Vietnamese refugee child. These problems should not be generalized or stereotyped and related to the entire Vietnamese population. Individual differences, as well as individual circumstances, still are the most important considerations in any case, for Vietnamese and Americans alike.

Case Studies

The following case studies and incidents are examples of some of the cross-cultural conflicts and emotional difficulties that Vietnamese refugee students have experienced in their adjustment to American schools.[1] These cases are presented with the modest goal of sharing experiences and concerns with other teachers and school personnel who are involved with the education of Vietnamese children.

Coeducational Experiences

Case 1: In a science class at a high school in the Midwest, a Vietnamese girl was paired with an American boy for lab work. The pair did not work well together and the girl, clearly needing help from her partner, never asked for help from the boy. Noticing the uneasiness between the two, the teacher split the pair. He found out later that the Vietnamese girl had rarely associated with boys before and had felt intense embarrassment at having to work closely with a boy for the first time.

Interpretation: Even though there was coeducation in Vietnam, boys and girls usually did not communicate or interact as frequently and as casually as in the United States. Although a mixed group did go out to have fun together, no definite pairing was involved. Single dating, as practiced in the United States was rare, and, where it is adopted by a boy and girl, usually means that they have reached the stage that, in the United States, would be called "going steady."

Case 2: A Vietnamese girl in the 10th grade in Missouri reportedly refused to go to her gym class. When asked for a valid reason by the gym teacher, she simply said she did not like gym. Only much later did the real reason appear. She revealed to a Vietnamese friend that she objected to being seen bare-legged, wearing gym shorts.

Interpretation: Coming from a region of Vietnam where old customs and traditions were still strong and where women, young and old, were never to be seen bare-legged, she confessed to an intense feeling of discomfort when the gym hour occurred.

To provide a sense of measure to this interesting case, however, we must add here the case of two Vietnamese high school girls, one in Georgia, and the other Maryland, who were drum majorettes for their respective high school bands last year. Not all young Vietnamese refugee girls were like the one in Missouri, or, to approach the issue from the other direction, not all of them were like the two drum majorettes.

Differences in Diet

Case 3: An eight-year-old Vietnamese child in an elementary school in Maryland complained of a stomach ache every day shortly after his lunch hour. His teacher was mystified because the same food and milk did not make any other child in the class sick. The cause was later identified to be the fresh milk, which was perfectly good, but to which the boy's digestive system was not accustomed.

Case 4: An American mother was surprised that her adopted Vietnamese son was still hungry even after eating two or three sandwiches for lunch. She did not realize that the Vietnamese do not eat much bread in Vietnam. As far as the little boy was concerned, a sandwich was more of a snack than a real meal.

Case 5: An American teacher shared her concern about the eating habits of her Vietnamese student with a colleague. The student had told her that he ate cold noodles for breakfast. A native Vietnamese resolved the situation when she eased the teacher's concern by explaining that the Vietnamese love to eat noodles. The *instant noodle* found in the American grocery store is very convenient and often preferred by the Vietnamese to bread and butter.

Interpretation: Food habits are different from one culture to the next. Rice is a staple in the Vietnamese diet while bread is a staple in the American diet. Pork is preferred to beef by most Vietnamese while the reverse is true in the United States. Fresh milk is likely to give some Vietnamese an upset stomach. They are used to boiled rather than homogenized milk and their bodies are said not to produce the type of enzyme necessary to digest fresh milk.

Climate and Clothing

Case 6: Two kindergarten teachers were discussing their experiences with Vietnamese students. The first teacher was concerned about a Vietnamese child who had cried the entire morning. In her class, all of the children had to remove their snow boots and put on regular shoes to wear in the classroom. She tried to explain this to the little boy as she took off his boots. The little boy cried, remained moody and unhappy, and did not participate in any of the class activities.

The kindergarten teacher next door had the same experience but used another approach. Noticing that her Vietnamese student kept looking at his boots, she realized that the boots were new and that wearing them was a different and new experience for him. She allowed him to wear the boots in the classroom. When it was time for physical education, the boy realized that the boots were too heavy for running so he took them off and joined the group.

Interpretation: Coming from a tropical country, Vietnamese refugee children are not used to the cold weather in the United States. Snow and winter clothes are a new experience for them. The sensitivity of the second teacher had resolved the problem of removing snow boots without causing emotional conflict for the child.

Treatment of Illness

Case 7: A Vietnamese boy was very sick with a high fever late one evening. His father used a form of acupuncture to try to lessen the fever. He scratched his son's back with a sharp piece of glass, dipped a piece of cotton in alcohol, lit it inside an empty cup, and quickly put the cup on certain places on the son's back. This treatment is called "cupping." The result was a messy back with bloody spots and red marks.[2] Despite all of the father's attempts, his son died that night. The sponsoring family panicked; to them the marks on the boy's body looked like child abuse. The police were called and the father was taken to jail for questioning the next day. That night the father took his own life by hanging himself.

Interpretation: A Vietnamese interpreter came the next day, revealing, too late, that the father had been in a desperate mental state. The rest of the family had been left behind in Vietnam. His son's death, complicated by his inability to explain the type of treatment that he had given him, caused him to despair and take his life. The method of treatment that the father had used is very common in Vietnam, especially in the countryside where medication is not readily available.

This incident illustrates that different types of health treatment, illness, and infection are common in other countries. A Vietnamese mother tends to treat diarrhea with less concern than an American mother. In contrast, a Vietnamese child, not accustomed to cold weather, is more susceptible to colds and to respiratory infections than the American child. Teachers should also be aware that Vietnamese mothers who are not familiar with cold weather conditions will tend to overdress or, at times, underdress their children. The frequent colds that the child may contract often result in fatigue and conductive hearing problems that can affect the child's learning ability.

Learning Problems

Case 8: A concerned teacher was worried about a Vietnamese high school boy who seemed to forget almost everything he learned in class. A mental deficiency was thought to be the cause. Later it was learned that he was totally confused by his current situation. His parents had given him to an American family to adopt, for they had seven children and were unable to take care of them all. This boy thought that he had only been sent away to school. He waited for his parents to come; he wrote them many letters; but he did not know how and where to contact them. He was unable to communicate his feelings and worries to his adopted parents because he spoke little English. He was wrapped up in his worries and had no desire to learn.

Interpretation: The adoption procedures in Vietnam and in the United States are very different. In the United States, when a child is adopted by another family, communication between the real parents and the child is legally discouraged and avoided. In Vietnam, this adoptive act tends to be less official. It is not unusual for a richer relative or friend to help by adopting a child of a less fortunate relative. The child will stay with the adoptive parents, whom he or she might call uncle and aunt, but will always remain the child of the biological parents.

Case 9: A teacher thought that his Vietnamese student had an auditory discrimination problem. He found out later that there are sounds in the English language that do not exist in the Vietnamese language. The student simply could not hear them, thus could not pronounce them correctly.

Case 10: Another teacher complained about the lack of retention by her Vietnamese student. She attempted to teach him two or three new vocabulary words each day, and he could not remember them. An observer noted that the words were given at random; they were not related to a unit or a subject. The student could not remember them because he had no reference upon which to organize his thought processes in order to retain what he had learned.

Case 11: A teacher was surprised to see a Vietnamese child color pictures of eggs *brown* and cows *yellow*. The surprise turned into laughter when a Vietnamese friend told her that Vietnamese eggs are brown in color and that there are more yellow cows in Vietnam than black or brown cows as in the United States.

Case 12: This case is about a Laotian boy, but it is reported here because many Vietnamese children have the same problem. The boy was a top scholar in the twelfth grade in his home country. In the United States, he repeated twelfth grade as a refugee teenager in an American high school. He received three successive warning notices for poor work in biology. In a short period of time, he had turned from a brilliant scholar to a pathetic near flunker, all due to his inability to speak English. The biology teacher graded his papers just like any other paper, without any consideration for his serious language handicap.

Interpretation: The language problem is still a major handicap for students. It is further complicated by the cultural trait of *face saving*, which affects the pride and self-esteem of the Vietnamese and causes them frustration and a loss in learning motivation. It is important that American teachers understand the consequence of failure for these students.

In summary, eating noodles for breakfast or calling a teacher "sir" are some incidents that initially may appear strange to American teachers. However, it is hoped that the above case studies will help teachers become sensitive to the unique needs of the Vietnamese and other refugee children as well as aware of the differences and difficulties that these refugee children face. The following section describes some of the administrative considerations and presents a protocol for evaluation of children suspected of having a learning problem.

Administrative Considerations

School Records

The Vietnamese name. When Vietnamese refugee students first entered American schools, there was a lot of confusion as to how to file their names in the school records. Vietnamese names are written in the opposite order of American names. The Vietnamese usually have three names, e.g., Nguyen Hy Vinh or Hoang Thi Thanh. The first name is the family name while the last name is the given name. Vietnamese use the given name for identification.

Vietnamese ages and birthdates. Certain confusion might arise from a different concept of age. Usually a Vietnamese has two ages, one related to chronological age and the other to *Tet* or the Lunar New Year. A person who is born prior to the Lunar New Year will be a year old on *Tet* regardless of whether he or she was born a few days prior to *Tet* or a whole year prior.

Since the date of *Tet* changes according to the Lunar calendar, this can be even more confusing to Americans. If *Tet* is on January 30, and a child is born on January 2, the child will be considered a year old, entering the second year after *Tet* (or after January 30). Some Vietnamese parents have given the *Tet* age to school administrators while others have adopted the American custom and have given their child's chronological age.

The determination of birthdates is complicated further when administrators are not aware of the Vietnamese custom of writing dates. As in many other countries, the date is written so that the day is first, then the month, and lastly the year. For example, in the United States, dates are commonly written in the following order: month-day-year—e.g., 6/7/79 = June 7, 1979, whereas, in Vietnam they are written day-month-year—e.g., 6/7/79 = July 6, 1979.

In order to avoid problems, it is suggested that school administrators ask for the child's birthdate by specifically requesting the month, day, and year of birth. If there is some doubt as to accuracy, a comparison can be made with records of the child's other siblings to see if the child's age appears to be accurate.

Grade and Special Service Placement

The next concern of the school administrator is the grade placement of the Vietnamese refugee students. Before the actual placement can be made, the child's previous school experience needs to be determined. Academic ability and emotional maturity must also be assessed. The first step should be to gather as much information on the child's past school experience as possible. This is an important factor in determining the appropriate grade placement of the child since the child's age level alone could be misleading. This is especially true in the case of Vietnamese children who lived in Vietnam during the war or who have been in refugee camps for long periods. Taking into account the child's past experience can prevent the placement of a student in the sixth grade because of age when the child actually has completed only third grade.

In summary, administrators should inquire as to the number of years of schooling, the grade level, and the type of school that the child attended. The educational background of the parents also should be investigated since this could have a positive or negative effect on the child's adjustment to school.

Speech and Language Considerations

Professionals working with Vietnamese children should be aware of the phonological and syntactical problems Vietnamese children may have as a result of the differences between their first and second language. A brief summary of the characteristics of the Vietnamese language will be presented along with possible confusions a child may experience when learning English. Further information on the role of interference and variables such as age and motivation regarding second language learning can be found in many sources such as Brown (1980).

The Vietnamese language is monosyllabic. There are no morpheme endings to mark tenses, plurals, or possessives. It is also a tonal language. Thus, meaning is indicated through the use of various tones for a particular monosyllabic utterance. Six different tones, marked by accents on the printed word, indicate six different meanings. The spelling of the word does not change, only the accent mark. Since English is characterized by intonation patterns in larger units, Vietnamese students must learn these patterns.

Phoneme discrimination and production may be affected due to the differences between the two language systems. For example, the Vietnamese child learning English may confuse the following words:

/ɛ/	as in bet	with	/æ/	as in bat
/ɪ/	as in bin	with	/i/	as in beet
/ʊ/	as in book	with	/u/	as in boot

Consonant patterns also differ in that Vietnamese has no consonant clusters and relatively few consonants occur in the final position. Voicing differences may exist such as confusing /g/ with /k/, /b/ with /p/, or /d/ with /t/. In addition, phonemes such as the voiced and voiceless *th* which do not occur in Vietnamese may present a problem for the child acquiring the English phonological system.

There are also other morphosyntactic differences between Vietnamese and English that may affect language learning. These include the use of suffixes, articles, question forms, negatives, and *be* forms. (For a further description *see A Manual for Indochinese Education*, 1976, or Phap, 1981.) In summary, it is important that the professionals working with a Vietnamese refugee child be sensitive to the language learning problems the child may have and how this may influence test results.

The Evaluation Process

As a school psychologist who is also Vietnamese, the author finds there are no test instruments available at this time that are completely culture free. The use of a standardized IQ test is not advisable for Vietnamese children due to the cultural content of such tests, and the results obtained are not a reliable indication of the child's true mental ability.

While a detailed review of the assessment of bilingual or non-English speaking children is not within the scope of this chapter, some thoughts on unbiased assessment should be included. The concern for providing culturally and linguistically relevant assessment procedures for minority children has provoked the development of various alternatives to traditional testing.

Laosa (1977) and Samuda (1975) summarize various testing alternatives and evaluate their appropriateness. Attempts to develop culture-free or culture-specific tests, to translate tests, or to use criterion referenced tests create as many problems as they attempt to solve. A modification of Tucker's model (1977) seems the most appropriate for assessing the bilingual bicultural child. The following categories of information should be included in the diagnostic-intervention process:

1. data available from observation in various settings
2. cumulative and medical records data
3. language dominance data
4. language competence data
5. educational achievement data
6. sensory-motor assessment data
7. adaptive behavior data
8. medical and developmental data
9. personality assessment data
10. intellectual and learning potential data

For many years the author has used this type of approach to assess Vietnamese refugee children. In order to clarify how this model can be applied, a summary of the author's day of work at a school may be of some practical use for coworkers in the field. This does not purport to be a model nor a process for complete evaluation. It is simply a sharing of experience and ideas.

1. Before going to school, the author has gathered background information from teachers regarding their specific concerns. Health information about the child also has been obtained.

2. A quick visit is made to the teachers and school administrators to check any possible change in the student's behavior or performance (negative or positive) since the referral date.

3. The student is followed throughout the school day. An attempt is made to observe the child in as many types of classroom activity as possible. These activities should include some academic work (math, reading, and class discussion), some physical activities (P.E., recess, art), and special classes (speech, language development, library). Not only are physical education and recess appropriate times to assess the child's motor coordination, but also they are good opportunities to observe the child's interaction with the peer group. Special classes are observed in order to evaluate the types of services that the local schools provide in order to coordinate any future services the child may need. In short, notes are taken on concrete observed behaviors, performance, the child's reactions, the peer group relationship, the teacher's attitude towards the child, and the child's self-perception.

   The specific concerns of the teachers are kept in mind during the observations. For example, if there is a question of emotional problems, the child's reaction to the peer group, the teacher, and the classroom atmosphere is specifically noted. If it is a question of learning difficulty, the child's academic work is assessed by asking questions such as:

   What can this child do in the class? How much was gained from the various lessons presented? Is it a language problem or a learning problem?

4. Noontime is spent with the parents either in their home or at school in order to learn about the child's background. The possible grade placement of the child also is discussed with the parents at this time.

5. Some time in the afternoon is spent with the child individually. Informal assessments are performed by having the child do the following: read passages in Vietnamese and English; compute basic math operations; do free drawing; or just talk, so the child's ability,

expressive language skills, and reactions to new school experiences may be learned.

6. A short period is allowed for a class visit to talk to the group. The goal of such a visit is to bring cultural understanding and awareness of the special needs of the child to the peer group.

7. Findings are then compiled, trying to answer such questions as:
   What is the student's capability and actual performance?
   What are the current skills that the student is performing?
   What skills are lacking?
   What are the problems that the child is possibly having?
   What parts of the lessons presented did the child understand, benefit from, and respond to?
   What parts were meaningless?
   An attempt is made to evaluate what the child can and cannot do, to see beyond the child's immediate reactions for possible underlying causes that may be related to cultural aspects as well as physical, emotional, or academic needs.

8. A preliminary school meeting is held with the child's present and previous teachers to exchange, compare, and discuss the information obtained.

9. A staff conference per P.L. 94–142 guidelines is then held to discuss the findings and to explore possible services and placement. This conference includes all persons involved with the child's education and the family's welfare. Usually there are local school administrators (principal, counselors), school district administrators (superintendent, director of special education services), teachers (of regular and special classes), tutors, parents, representatives of the family's sponsoring agencies (church members, individuals), and, if possible, community service personnel.

The Placement Decision

In determining the actual placement of the child, all aspects of the child's development are taken into consideration, and attempts are made to find the best available solution for the child's needs. Specialized educational professionals such as teachers in bilingual education, English as a Second Language (ESL), learning disabilities, and speech-language therapy, and trained tutors and aides are considered for providing help in cognitive and academic development of the child. Services of the counselor, community agencies, peer group, and buddy system are services that can be provided for emotional needs. The local YMCA is a possible outlet for the excess physical energy that a Vietnamese child might need. Final decisions are made by all of those involved including the parents.

Finding an appropriate placement for non-English speaking students with special emotional needs, as is the case of many Vietnamese refugee students, is a complex task involving much thought and consideration. The school and psychologist's role is often that of a facilitator or coordinator of school staff members rather than that of an evaluator and assessor.

Summary

Bilingual/bicultural assessment and educational planning for a non-English speaking Vietnamese student is a challenging task. It calls for insight, understanding, and acceptance of the child's cultural background in order to evaluate reactions and behaviors. It demands flexible use of existing evaluation measures and an attempt to make use of test data and information for educational programing rather than for labeling purposes. The evaluation process should be a continuous process to allow flexibility and changes in the placement as needed.

It should also be a team effort between teachers, administrators, other professionals, and parents. With a Vietnamese refugee child, parent's inclusion in the decision making of the child placement is a delicate and important factor. In most Asian cultures, the general attitude toward special education is often one of mistrust since special education classes are almost nonexistent in these countries. A *special child* is often cared for at home by the family, or extended family. It is very important that the parents be aware and be involved in all the steps of the educational planning and decision making for the child, especially in special education placement.

Professionals who have the responsibility for determining whether or not a Vietnamese child is adjusting to the new environment or is in need of special services must be aware of historical and current cultural and linguistic factors. Refugee children are a unique challenge for professionals, not only because they can be misdiagnosed, misclassified, or misunderstood, but because they may not receive appropriate services when they indeed have handicapping conditions.

Notes

[1]Some of the cases are adapted from *A Manual for Indochinese Refugee Education* (1976).

[2]A similar, frequent treatment is the application of a very hot coin to the afflicted person's skin (Ed. note).

[3]Vietnamese names are listed by Western convention.

References

Brown, H.D.:   *Principles of Language Learning and Teaching.* Englewood Cliffs, Prentice-Hall, 1980.

Laosa, L.:   Nonbiased assessment of children's abilities: Historical antecedents and current issues. In Oakland, T. (Ed.): *Psychological and Educational Assessment of Minority Children.* New York, Brunner and Mazel, 1977.

A Manual for Indochinese Refugee Education 1976-1977. Arlington, Virginia: National Indochinese Clearinghouse, Center for Applied Linguistics, 1976.

Phap, D.T.:   *A Contrastive Approach for Teaching English as a Second Language to Indochinese Students.* Intercultural Development Research Association, San Antonio, 1981.

Samuda, R.:   *Psychological Testing of American Minorities: Issues and Consequences.* New York, Harper and Row, 1975.

Tucker, J.:   Operationalizing the diagnostic-intervention process. In Oakland, T. (Ed.): *Psychological and Educational Assessment of Minority Children.* New York, Brunner and Mazel, 1977.

Vuong, T.:   *Getting to Know the Vietnamese and Their Culture.* New York, Frederick Ungar, 1976.

Wei, T.:   *Vietnamese Refugee Students.* Cambridge, National Assessment of Dissemination Center for Bilingual/Bicultural Education, 1980.

NOTE: Much of the information in this chapter has been summarized or reproduced in publications available from the Illinois Office of Education, State Board of Education and the Evaluation, Dissemination, and Assessment Center of Lesley College, Cambridge, Massachusetts, 1980. Quotes and information have been used with permission.

12

Learning Disability: The Case of the Bilingual Child

Effie Bozinou-Doukas

The history of *learning disability* in children as an area of scientific inquiry and a psychoeducational diagnostic category has been confusing and controversial. Disputes have focused on definitions and the concomitant implications for diagnosis and educational planning. Definitions make assumptions about the etiology of learning disability phenomena; therefore, there is no consensus on "just what causes learning difficulties in children." There is even doubt as to whether or not there is such a condition at all (Downing and Brown, 1967; Franklyn, 1962). Many terms have periodically been employed to describe learning disability: developmental aphasia (Johnson and Myklebust, 1967); dyslexia (Benton, 1975; Benton and Pearl, 1978; Critchley, 1970); minimal brain dysfunction or hyperactive child syndrome (Strauss and Lehtinen, 1947; Anderson, 1963; Burks, 1957); perceptual handicap (Birch, 1964; Kephart, 1960, 1968; Frostig and Maslow, 1973); strephosymbolia (Orton, 1925); and word-blindness (Hinshelwood, 1896, 1917). The terminology describing the youngster with learning disability varies from state to state, as Cruickshank (1967) noted:

If a child happens to live in the State of Michigan, educators refer to him as a perceptually disabled child. If the child is a resident of California, his education may be provided if he is classified as an educationally handicapped or neurologically handicapped child. In Bucks County, Pennsylvania, he will be placed in a class for children with language disorders. If he moves from California to

New York State, he will change from an educationally handicapped child to a brain-injured child. On the other hand, if he
moves from Michigan to Montgomery County, Maryland, he will
stop being a perceptually disabled child and become a child with
specific learning disability. (p. 2)

Federal Regulations

With the passing of the Education of All Handicapped Children Act, P.L.
94-142, the United States Congress has given legal entity to the term
learning disability. Thus, a maximum percentage of children are permitted
to be counted in the category of learning disabled. States are allowed to
designate 12% of all children age 5-17 as handicapped in general. Of the total
handicapped population, 2% may be included as learning disabled.

The unofficial *count* of learning disabled youngsters is much higher than the
government's figures of 2%. For example, Eisenberg (1966) estimated that
28% of the sixth graders in a large metropolitan area were reading two or more
years below grade level. He considers these pupils as learning disabled.
Myklebust and Boshes (1969), in a four-year study of third and fourth graders
in Chicago suburbs, estimated 7.5% to 15% learning disabled youngsters. The
official 2% estimate was based on a 1970 survey of 2,000 public school
principals by the National Center for Educational Statistics (Minskoff, 1973).
The large discrepancies between the various reported estimates of the prevalence of learning disability are the result of differences in the criteria each survey
has used to designate a child as learning disabled. The conservative estimate by
school officials was a result of using the government's definition as a guide.
That definition excludes many youngsters with reading difficulties, as the
criteria for entering the category are quite stringent. The other surveys were
based on broader definitions of learning disability namely such as significant
failure in reading performance.

The government's criteria, having appeared in the Federal Register in
1976 and again in 1977, establish rules and regulations as guidelines for
identification of children with learning disabilities. A formula is provided
for estimating the severity of underachievement, which is a measure of the
difference between IQ scores and achievement scores. This formula for
estimating the *extent* of underachievement is to be used as a working guide
for educators, while a team of evaluators are to determine the *cause* of
underachievement. The government's definition of learning disability
reflects the theoretical basis of its view in this area as well as views from a
large number of disciplines such as medicine, psychology, speech/language
pathology, and education. This definition has generated considerable controversy among professionals, particularly educators, and added to the
existing confusion surrounding identification of the children. The federal
criteria reads:

Those children who have a disorder in one or more of the basic psychological processes involved in understanding or in using language, spoken or written, which disorder may manifest itself in imperfect ability to listen, think, speak, read, write, spell, or do mathematical calculations. Such disorders include such conditions as perceptual handicaps, brain injury, minimal brain dysfunction, dyslexia, and developmental aphasia. Such term does not include children who have learning problems which are primarily the result of visual, hearing, or motor handicaps, or mental retardation, or emotional disturbance, or environmental, cultural, or economic disadvantage.[1]

Objections to the definition were voiced on many levels. For example, Lloyd, Sabatino, Miller, and Miller (1977) regarded the requirements for inclusion of a youngster in the category of learning disability as too strict. The exclusion of culturally disadvantaged youngsters in need of remedial help was criticized. The difficulty in identifying *disorders in the psychological processes* (Lloyd et al., 1977) with accuracy is the concern of others as well, e.g., Sulzbacher and Kenowitz (1977). Furthermore, because it is a definition by exclusion, there is general dissatisfaction as it is subject to misinterpretation without precise understanding of its terms, e.g., Benton, 1975; Rutter, 1978. In the government's definition of learning disability, terms like *mental retardation, economic and cultural disadvantage,* and *psychological processes* need to be better understood.

Using IQ/achievement discrepancy to measure the severity of learning disability has been questioned. The arguments focus on the validity of the IQ score, especially when applied to the economically and culturally disadvantaged (*see* Watson, Omark, Grouell, and Heller, 1980). Thus, the goverment definition's formula is viewed as prone to subjective and unreliable estimates of learning difficulty. The concern with the validity of a formula-based classification of youngsters is not a new one. Our experience in this country with tests quantifying abilities has been mixed at best. The objections to a numerical estimate of a child's learning disability reflects our society's emotional investment in the quantification of abilities in general (*see* Danielson and Bauer, 1978; Lloyd et al., 1977, for reviews).

It is not the purpose of this chapter to exhaust the controversies that surround the concept of learning disability. They are referred to here as compass points in the subsequent discussion of the learning disabled bilingual youngster. Bilingual educators are concerned that the federal guidelines' emphasis on IQ/achievement discrepancy may exclude bilingual youngsters from the category of learning disability or, even worse, misdiagnose underachievement in linguistic skills as disability in either psycholinguistic processes or intellectual functioning (Gonzales and Ortiz, 1977). The same authors refer to bilingual youngsters in the Southwest misplaced in special education classes as a result of achievement and/or IQ scores.

The errors of the past need not be repeated. The intent of P.L. 94-142, the Education of All Handicapped Children Act, is to make education available to *all* children, bilingual and monolingual alike. The challenge for educators in the 1980s is to implement the law by developing tools for accurate diagnosis of diabilities, designing appropriate learning programs, and training personnel.

Given the poorly understood nature of *learning disability* in general, and the lack of available diagnostic instruments in languages other than English, the problem of identifying learning disability in bilingual youngsters is especially difficult. Suggestions on diagnosis will be presented later in this chapter.

Bilingualism and Learning Disabilities

It appears that, aside from the difficulties a practitioner faces in identifying learning disabilities in youngsters, the relationship between bilingualism and learning disability needs to be addressed. Not long ago, and sometimes even still, bilingualism was thought of as *burdening the memory processes*, thus weakening the mind (Manuel and Wright, 1929; Smith, 1939). Extensive research in recent years has provided convincing evidence that far from being a cognitive deterrant, bilingualism is a cognitive asset that leads to a more flexible, resourceful, and creative intellect (Balkan, 1970; Landry, 1974; Pearl and Lambert, 1967). It is of vital importance when discussing bilingual children to separate bilingualism from learning disability.

A number of studies in the 1920s and 1930s reported lower IQ scores for bilingual children than for their monolingual peers. Low scores were reported on verbal tests of intelligence in particular (Manuel and Wright, 1929; Rigg, 1928; Smith, 1939). The differences were attributed to an "overload" on the memory due to the additional language, that, in turn, caused intellectual fatigue. However, when the father's occupation was introduced as a factor determining test score variation, the reported IQ differences tended to diminish (Jones, 1966). In addition, a number of studies reported educational attainment for bilingual school-age pupils, particularly in reading and spelling (Brazeau, 1958; Eckert and Marshal, 1939; Smith, 1939). Strong objections to such conclusions were heard even in those early years. Several studies reported no adverse affects of bilingualism on intellectual functioning (Arsenian, 1937; Carrow, 1957; Sanchez, 1934; Stark, 1940). No educational handicap was found in bilingual children when socioeconomic differences in the sample were controlled. Furthermore, bilingualism was viewed as an educational and cognitive asset (Carrow, 1957; Tireman, 1955; Totten, 1960).

In addition to concerns about the effects of bilingualism on intellectual and learning abilities in general, several studies have reported its effects on specific cognitive skills. Thus, Leopold (1949) reported that his daughter began to show flexibility in naming objects and a general tendency to be creative in her choice of words; because she was experiencing two phonetic forms for each object, phonetic form and meaning were not so rigidly identified. Recently, Janco-Worrall (1972) confirmed Leopold's findings, reporting that Afrikaan-English bilinguals tend to interpret meanings more frequently semantically than phonetically as did monolinguals.

Additional investigations on creativity have reported higher scores on measures of intelligence for bilingual children than for their monolingual peers. For example, Pearl and Lambert (1961) gave a battery of tests to 10-year-old bilingual and monolingual children in a school system of Montreal, Canada, and found that bilinguals scored higher on measures of intelligence, both verbal and nonverbal. In addition, a factor analysis of thirty-one variables indicated that the bilingual group possessed a more diversified set of mental traits than did the monolingual group. Therefore, Pearl and Lambert speculated that since the bilingual child has two symbols for every object, the child must conceptualize environmental events in terms of their general properties without reliance on linguistic symbols. Consequently, bilinguals become more skilled than monolinguals in learning abstract concepts and relations. Landry (1974) found that sixth grade bilingual children performed significantly better than monolingual children on a test of divergent thinking ability. Balkan (1970) found that bilingual 11-17-year-olds demonstrated greater cognitive flexibility than did their monolingual counterparts in a series of tests with socioeconomic class and intelligence levels controlled.

Despite the substantial evidence of the positive effects bilingualism has on creative abilities, it is still asked whether bilingualism affects children's linguistic skills, in particular. There is some evidence that certain linguistic skills may develop differently in bilingual children whose English skills were tested. Such differences are usually attributed to unfamiliarity with the English language. Bilingual children experience frustrations in the classroom because of general difficulties in understanding the language of instruction. Macnamara (1967, and Kellaghan and Macnamara, 1967) cited evidence indicating that bilingual children may understand the components of a problem yet be unable to solve it when the information is provided in their weaker language. In addition, a bilingual child can experience difficulties in the classroom because of ignorance of certain words, idioms, or grammatical structures. Thus bilingualism, far from being dismissed as a factor in learning, needs to be considered in planning pupils' education.

In a recent study (Bozinou, 1978) comparing English monolingual and Greek/English bilingual kindergarten children's scores on a task requiring verbal production and comprehension of the past and present progressive tenses, the bilingual children were deficient not in the comprehension of morphemes but in their production. Although similar patterns were present in the performance of monolingual controls, the differences in the performance of the bilingual population was pronounced. These findings were attributed to a more uneven acquisition of various linguistic abilities by bilingual children. It was concluded that expression of linguistic rules underestimates the bilingual child's competence in a second language.

Similarly, Rainstad and Potter (1974), in a study of Native American children's use of vocabulary and syntax, reported a general deficit in both areas. When compared with Anglo children of the same age, Native American children's receptive vocabulary measured much lower than their receptive syntax. No such intra-subject differences were found in the Anglo population. The Native American children's differences in vocabulary and syntax was viewed as an indication of uneven growth in language acquisition. Such findings point to the need for specific types of English as a Second Language (ESL) instruction rather than to permanent deficits in the bilingual child's linguistic abilities.

Yet the concern for the possible adverse effects of bilingualism is strong. The numerous studies of interference of bilingual person's first language with acquisition of a second language represent that concern. The research is theoretically related to notions of habit strength in the first language (L_1) interfering with newly acquired habits in the second language (L_2). Such conflicting habit strengths may, the theory postulates, impede learning (Haugen, 1953, 1956; Weinreich, 1953). Presence of interference has been reported by numerous authors (Lado, 1964; Oller and Richards, 1973; Richards, 1971; Schumann and Stenson, 1975; Svartvik, 1973). However, analysis of errors in second language learners indicates that, although some interlanguage interference is present, children usually acquire the second language in much the same way as they acquire the first, namely by abstracting rules and strategies, and in turn applying them to the linguistic code they are acquiring. Therefore, one observes similar generalizations, oversimplifications, and substitutions frequently reported during first language learning (Corder, 1967, 1975; Ervin-Tripp, 1973, 1974; Milon, 1974). Dulay and Burt (1972) analyzed data from observations of Spanish-speaking children learning English and found that what appeared to be interference errors could just as well reflect overgeneralizations that are present in the speech of monolingual children learning their first language.

In subsequent research, Dulay and Burt (1974) did an error analysis of English language samples of Spanish-, Chinese-, Japanese-, and Norwegian-speaking children learning English as a second language. They found that the types of mistakes made by the children were strikingly similar. In as much as the L_1 of the subjects was different, the similarities of the error patterns in L_2 could only be attributed to their ability to abstract general strategies for L_2 learning independent of L_1. The authors argued that children are able to construct rules for the speech they hear guided by general cognitive strategies as they formulate hypotheses about the language system being acquired. The same process was reported for children learning a first language (e.g., Ervin-Tripp, 1973). From this perspective there seems to be no need to postulate different processes in L_1 and L_2 learning.

Case studies literature, e.g., Leopold (1949), provides very little evidence of interference between languages, especially when L2 learning is supported by the child's social milieu. An imbalance in the amount of exposure and use of either L1 or L2 may create interference from the most frequently used language (Leopold, 1948; Rivers, 1964; Stern, 1970). A significant factor in avoiding interference, a balanced maintenance of linguistic skills in both L1 and L2, has been the basis for bilingual education.

A neglected area of study is the effect of differences in linguistic codes for language learners. Evans (1974) tested bilingual Spanish and monolingual English children on tasks of word-pair discrimination and single word imitation in both English and Spanish. Both groups made fewer errors in imitating words in the Spanish language. This finding may be attributed to a greater facility in the phonological configuration of the Spanish language. The bilingual children attained higher scores in imitating words in both languages, thus suggesting better skills in this area than the monolinguals.

From the preceding review of studies on the effects of bilingualism on cognitive and linguistic skills, it is apparent that there is no basis for fear that bilingualism may create "learning disability type" phenomena in children. On the contrary, bilingualism is found to be a cognitive asset enhancing creativity and increasing facility in phonological productions of different linguistic codes. Weakness in the acquisition of grammatical rules and in learning certain idiosyncracies of a given language, e.g., idioms and cliches, were reported for bilingual children. Such reports indicate the need for better instruction in both first and second languages but cannot be used as evidence of cognitive or linguistic deficits resulting from bilingualism.

Interference of the stronger language with the weaker is more likely if the levels of competence in the two languages are unequal. However, in acquiring a second language, the usual procedure is to apply broad cognitive strategies the same way as when learning a first language. The existing evidence does not support that L1 interference when acquiring L2 can create linguistic deficits.

Etiology

Let us now return to the cumbersome issue of identifying bilingual children with learning disabilities. Comments about the diversity of views on the nature of learning disorders have already been made. At this point the major perspectives will be reviewed and the clinical picture of learning disabled children will be reconstructed.

The volume of information available is enormous and begins at least with the work of Hinshelwood in the nineteenth century (Hinshelwood, 1896). Despite controversy, it is striking that clinical descriptions of learning disabled youngsters are very much alike. Invariably, academic retardation in the presence of normal intellectual abilities is reported, with linguistic skills—reading in particular—especially affected. Reading behavior of children with learning disabilities presents peculiarities that are not always seen in poor readers in general. Some of those are frequent reversals, substitutions, mirror writing, inconsistencies within the spectra of reading skills, i.e., excellent comprehension and very poor decoding skills, and almost always poor spelling. Other academic areas, such as arithmetic, may or may not be affected (Benton, 1975; Benton and Pearl, 1978; Myers and Hammill, 1969). The developmental history of these children may be within normal limits, although frequently delays in language acquisition (Mason, 1976; Rabinovitch, 1959) and in perceptual-motor skills (Kephart, 1960; Rutter, 1978) are mentioned.

Hyperactivity and a generally impulsive learning style is present in the majority of children with learning disabilities, but not all cases (Keogh, 1971; Strauss and Lehtinen, 1947; Virkkunen and Nuutila, 1976). Poor body concept, spatial disorientation, and laterality confusion are also described as being part of the syndrome (Cruickshank, 1967). Recent work in the information-processing abilities of learning disabled children has revealed a generally slower tempo in their retrieval mechanisms, especially of verbal materials (Vellutino, 1978). There is also agreement that the prevalence of the condition is much higher in boys than girls.

An apparent consensus about the cause of learning disability is that it is related to some sort of constitutional or biological failure (Rutter, 1978). The consensus, however, stops there and the literature is loaded with theories and paradigms attempting to identify the specific *constitutional failure* in question. A simple way to classify the various viewpoints is along the single- versus multiple-factor dimension (Benton, 1975). The medical organic deficit models are good examples of single-factor theories. In general, they attribute learning disability to neurological impairments in a specific area of the central nervous system. Thus, Hinshelwood (1896, 1917) attributed the reading and memory difficulties of the subjects he studied to lesions in the angular gyrus, the area he thought responsible for the functioning of the visual-spatial system.

Orton (1925) was the first to attribute learning disability to an imbalance between the function of the left and right hemispheres. He believed that association skills were present only in the left hemisphere while the right hemisphere contained mirrored images of the information in the left, minus associative skills. Where there is brain injury that results in imbalance of the delicate relationship between the two hemispheres, the right hemisphere may distort information in the left and present a mirrored image of it. He concluded it is the right hemisphere that is primary in processing verbal information for the learning disabled youngster.

Although visual-spatial deficits are frequently referred to as causative factors in learning disability, the hemispheric imbalance hypothesis constitutes a very active research area at present. For example, Guyer and

Friedman (1975) tested poor and normal readers on verbal and spatial tasks and found no differences between the two groups on the spatial tasks, but the poor readers failed on the verbal ones. It is suggested that learning disabled children may attempt to use a nonverbal information processing mode, i.e., in the right hemisphere, to deal with verbal information, resulting in failure to perform on verbal tasks. Such an explanation for the failure of poor readers relates very well to Orton's.

Perhaps the most promising investigations in this area are the studies of amplitude asymmetry of the alpha rhythym, although they associate hand preference with cerebral dominance, which has yet to be well established (Rutter, 1978). Subirana (1969) assessed the organization of the alpha rhythm and found that right-handed persons were best organized, while poorly lateralized children were the worst. Inasmuch as poor lateralization is one of the symptoms of dyslexia, the implications of these studies are, to some extent, applicable. Subsequently, Subirana and co-workers (Oller-Daurella and Maso-Subirana, 1965) reported increased asymmetry of the alpha rhythm in ambidexterous subjects and dyslexics. Other than the above-mentioned studies on alpha rhythm asymmetry (Hughes, 1978), the overwhelming majority of EEG studies, however, do not find differences in the neurological patterns of normals and dyslexics.

Muliple-factor theories generally implicate modality-specific deficits that represent distinct underlying causes of the disorder. Several authors make reference to different types of disability characterized by deficits in the auditory or visual sphere. The work of Myklebust (1971; Myklebust and Boshes, 1969) is representative of such thinking, as well as the diagnostic and remediation model of the Illinois Test of Psycholinguistic Abilities (Kirk and Kirk, 1975). In general, one or more of the following learning processes are usually considered impaired: visual or auditory perception, intersensory integration, verbal processing, or temporal sequence and recall. Impairment in the ability to integrate sensory experience, even when single modality processing is intact, has been proposed as well. Such impairments are the result of disruption in the perceptual/motor match of the experience and a subsequent failure to develop a dominance of perception over sensation (Birch, 1964; Kephart, 1960).

Within the context of multiple-factor theories, recent work in information-processing mechanisms is quite promising. Topics such as reaction time in retrieval and recall of verbal information, response speed, and flexibility with linguistic code utilization are subjects of a number of recent studies. Liberman, Shankweiler, Fischer, and Carter (1974) tested first grade children who had difficulty in learning to read on auditory discrimination and phonetic segmentation tasks. In the latter, children were to identify the number of syllables in a given word and to reconstruct the word orally. Although there was no difference in performance on the auditory discrimination task between poor and good readers, poor readers failed to perform at the same level as good readers on the phonetic segmentation task. Similar results are reported by Zifiak (1976) and Helfgott (1976). Such findings suggest a general insensitivity to the phonetic constituents of given words which may be necessary for establishing higher order relationships in code acquisition.

Vellutino and co-workers (Steger, Vellutino, and Meshaulam, 1972; Vellutino, Smith, Steger, and Kamin, 1975) found that on verbal learning tasks in general, dyslexic subjects were much less proficient than those with a history of reading difficulties. Poor readers consistently performed less adequately than normal readers on tests of both short-term and long-term memory of verbal materials. Such inadequacies were apparent specifically in the recall of linguistic units such as words and phrases.

Studies requesting poor and normal readers to name objects rapidly found that, in general, dyslexics were slower in vocalizing responses than normals (Denckla and Rudel, 1976; Perfetti and Hogaboam, 1975; Spring, 1976). In explaining such findings, it is suggested that learning disabled readers may be characterized by basic dysfunctions in word retrieval and/or motor encoding. A generally slower tempo of response to visual stimuli by dsylexic children has been also reported. When Stanley and Hall (1973) presented visual figures to both dyslexics and normal readers, a forty-second delay in recall was noted for the dyslexics; recall of letters in sequence was also delayed by fifteen seconds.

In reviewing the research on verbal-processing deficiencies, Vellutino (1978) suggests that learning disabled subjects lack implicit verbal coding devices that facilitate efficient storage and retrieval of stimulus imput. Such deficiencies may be the result of limited amounts of verbal information and/or inaccessability of such information. He further refers to the substitution and reversal errors commonly observed in the reading of dyslexic children as errors in information processing, or linguistic intrusions, rather than deficiencies in the perception of the visual or auditory symbols.

The lack of consensus in the literature on the type and number of psychological processes impaired in the learning disabled child suggests the possibility that we are not dealing with a single dimension, but rather multiple dimension disorders. What appears lacking in the literature are longitudinal studies of learning disabled children where changes in the manifestation of the disorder are studied. It is possible that a shift of symptoms indicative of perceptual deficit to those of linguistic deficit may take place over time. Symptoms generally considered as signs of learning disability may disappear after a certain age with only a lag in reading performance remaining.

Some recent studies have followed youngsters diagnosed as learning disabled. However, the available information is not adequate for definite conclusions. For example, Robinson and Schwartz (1973) followed forty-one children identified as having defects in visual perception and/or visual motor coordination at age 5–6 years. Three years later the children showed no more visual or motor difficulties than a matched control group without visual-spatial deficits. On the other hand, 30% of children with speech problems followed from kindergarten to second grade had reading problems as compared to only 5% of the controls (Mason, 1976).

A good example of developmental studies of perceptual abilities is the work of Koppitz (1963, 1975) who used the Bender-Gestalt test of Visual Motor Perception. Her data have established that *young* children produce defective protocols. However, they will be within normal limits when examined developmentally. If taken as absolute indicators of brain injury, errors on the Bender-Gestalt protocols of young children will misdiagnose learning disability in normal children.

In summarizing the recurrent themes present in the search for causes of learning disability, one can identify a preoccupation with cerebral functioning, specifically the significance of right hemisphere processing; frequent reference to signs of minimal brain dysfunction, such as perceptual deficits, laterality confusion, and hyperactivity; and, more recently, deficiencies in verbal information processing mechanisms. It is frequently asked whether or not the syndrome is developmental in nature and whether it may disappear after a certain age. There is a shift from the medical-organic model to studies of information-processing mechanisms without necessarily attempting to relate them to neurological referents.

Assessment

The assessment of learning disabled youngsters reflects the diversity of views presented. In general, the learning processes most frequently mentioned in the literature as impaired must continually be evaluated. At present there are batteries of tests available for assessing the extent of learning disability in English monolingual youngsters.[2] Because the scope of this chapter does not permit a detailed discussion of the assessment process, *see* Johnson and Myklebust (1967) and Kirk and Kirk (1975) for reviews on diagnosis and remediation.

In assessing bilingual youngsters' learning skills, certain factors must be considered. First of all, a decision has to be made about the language in which assessments are to be made. It is best to conduct the sessions bilingually and to utilize the dominant language whenever possible. Especially cumbersome is the evaluation of verbal skills, the primary indicators of the presence of verbal processing difficulties. Most instruments employed in the diagnosis of verbal abilities test such items as grammatical rules, phonetic segmentation, or sound blending.[2] A low score on such items in the case of bilingual youngsters is not necessarily an indicator of disability. It has been reported (Macnamara, 1967) that bilingual children do produce frequent grammatical errors, especially in the idiomatic expressions of the second language.

A bilingual child referred for learning disability evaluation must be assessed for language dominance and evaluations of the learning processes need to be conducted in both languages. Should consistent patterns of deficiencies be present in both languages, there is perhaps a sign of learning disability. Furthermore, given the controversy surrounding the identification of a bilingual child as learning disabled, no single indicator of deficit in any particular modality should be taken as a sign of learning disability. One needs to establish consistency in performance patterns in order to make a diagnosis.

Case Studies

The following two cases will attempt to illustrate the complexity involved in the diagnosis of learning disability in bilingual children and differences in the profiles of their abilities.

Andrea P., a 13-year-old Greek immigrant, was referred for evaluation of learning disability because, as her teacher put it, *she did not make the progress in school that other bilingual pupils in the school did*. Andrea participated in a battery of tests given bilingually. On the Automatic Level of the Illinois Test for Psycholinguistic Abilities, her performance was at the level of a six- or seven-year-old child. She made numerous errors in Grammatical Closure and Sound Blending. Yet, that information was not sufficient evidence to establish verbal processing problems.

The additional evidence was found in assessing verbal skills in her native language. It was striking that Andrea's writing sample in Greek included no accents. During several practice trials, it became apparent that Andrea was unable to integrate the auditory-sequential-spatial skill required in placing accents on words as required for correct spelling in Greek. One needs to hear the accent, syllabicate a word, and determine where in the visual-spatial sequence of the word the auditory-visual symbol of accent is to be placed. Subsequent testing on the Detroit Test of Learning Aptitude revealed a systematic difficulty in integrating experience across modalities. Tasks that required single modality performance gave her no difficulty. It must be noted that Andrea was Greek dominant and testing was done primarily in Greek.

Luis R., age 13, was a nonreader with a history of school failure and truancy. His Spanish oral language skills were far less developed than his English language skills. Assessment in Spanish was meaningless as he was far less proficient in Spanish than in English. Spanish was used only to establish a relationship with the examiner and the battery of tests was administered to him almost entirely in English. His profile indicated a very low score on the Bender-

Gestalt and on the Benton, a poorly developed body concept, and difficulties with spatial orientation. Psychiatric evaluations revealed hyperactivity related to minimal brain dysfunction. After a period taking Ritalin® (the medication often used with hyperactive children), Luis began to learn to read and to make significant progress in school.

His score on the Wechsler Intelligence Scale for Children-Revised (WISC-R) placed Luis in the bright normal category. A striking twenty-five point difference between the Verbal and Performance scales signaled very poor verbal skills as compared with nonverbal skills. He performed at the superior intellectual level on the nonverbal scale. (In contrast, Andrea had received a higher score on the Verbal scale than on the Performance; the difference was fourteen points.)

Luis' WISC-R scores were restructured according to the tripartiate grouping suggested by Bannatyne (1968, 1974) and revealed a pattern typical of what Bannatyne calls *genetic dyslexics*. He obtained the highest scaled score average on the *Spatial Category* (Block Design, Object Assembly, Picture Completion); an intermediate score on the *Conceptual Category* (Comprehension, Similarities, Vocabulary), and the lowest score on the *Sequential Category* (Digit Span, Coding, Picture Arrangement). (In contrast, the tripartiate division was not helpful in the case of Andrea, who received a higher score on the Sequential Category than on the Spatial.) Bannatyne (1968, 1974) maintained that genetic dyslexics obtain the lowest score on the sequential category, highest on spatial, and intermediate on conceptual. (Andrea, on the other hand, was very good in sequencing when one modality was involved, either auditory or visual. Her difficulty was apparent only when information from one modality needed to be sequentially interpreted through another.)

These two cases illustrate the complexity in identifying learning disabled bilingual children and the vastly different diagnostic profiles they present. One can almost select a different theoretical interpretation for each case. Andrea's difficulties with cross modality interpretation of perceptual information would most likely illustrate Kephart's (1960) and Birch's (1964) theories of perceptual organization attributing learning disability to deficiencies in the perceptual match of information across modalities. Luis' case illustrates the hyperactive child syndrome of Strauss and Lehtinen (1947).

Research on bilingual learning disabled children as a group is sparse; whatever is available indicates that their difficulties in learning resemble those reported for learning disabled youngsters in general. For example, Jorstad (1971) reported results on the Illinois Test of Psycholinguistic Abilities of twenty Mexican American elementary school-age youngsters in a rural school in Southern California. The mean scores for the learning disabled pupils were significantly below the cut-off score. The lowest scores were in the auditory areas, namely, Grammatic Closure, Auditory Association, Auditory Reception, Sound Blending, and Auditory Memory. It needs to be noted that comparisons were based on norms for the Mexican American student population of that school district.

Weakness in the auditory channel is not unique to the bilingual learning disabled (Kirk and Kirk, 1975). Whether or not this particular learning process is weak especially for this population of youngsters remains a question. Additional research is needed before any conclusion can be drawn. Furthermore, performance on items that employ grammatical rules should be viewed with caution because of possible unfamiliarity with the English language (*see* Chapters 2, 3, and 4). Future research should include testing on equivalent items in the native language as well. Items given only in English run the risk of confounding unfamiliarity with the language, resulting in process deficits.

A different issue facing a practitioner is which language to suggest for remediation of a bilingual youngster. In the two cases discussed above, Andrea was given remediation in her native language while Luis responded very well in English. Certainly the child's overall facility with a language is the determining factor. Acceptability of the language by the child's family and cultural milieu is another consideration that bilingual educators should take into account when deciding on the language of instruction (Engle, 1975).

Summary

In summary, available research at this time suggests no reason to believe that there is a relationship between bilingualism and learning disability. On the contrary, there is evidence that bilingualism contributes to the development of a more creative and flexible intellect. Deficits in learning need to be viewed separately from bilingualism and their presence in individual children must be carefully assessed. Youngsters must be evaluated bilingually when appropriate, in order to identify strengths and weaknesses in their learning processes. Misdiagnosing difficulty with a child's second language as a learning disability is entirely possible, especially since performance on linguistic rules constitutes a common procedure in assessing verbal skills.

What is especially needed from researchers are accurate reports on the numbers of bilingual children diagnosed as learning disabled and the methods used in assessing them. Research addressing the issues of how bilingual learning disabled children cope with disability, and how the resources of the educational system can be best employed to meet their needs would be most helpful to the practitioner.

Notes

[1]The definition of *learning disability* was first published in the Federal Register, Vol. 41, No. 230, November 26, 1976. Rules and regulations were published in the Federal Register on December 29, 1977.

[2]Clinicians vary on the tests they employ to assess learning disability. Here is a commonly used battery:

1. WISC-R to assess intellectual level and overall discrepancies in the various intellectual skills.
2. Bender-Gestalt; Benton Visual Retention Test; The Beery Burternica Developmental Test of Visual-Motor Integration (VMI): Any of these or a combination is used to assess visual perception skills.
3. A test of auditory discrimination such as the Wepman.
4. The Illinois Test of Psycholinguistic Abilities or the Detroit Test of Learning Aptitude. The former is used for elementary school-age children and the latter for junior high and high school pupils to assess a multitude of learning processes.
5. Informal tests of directionality; drawing of self for assessing body concept; informal writing samples.
6. The Slingerland Screening Tests or the Malcomesius Test of Specific Language Disability are used to assess reading and writing behaviors in particular.

It should be noted that many of these tests will be inappropriate for use with various minority populations (Watson, Grouell, Heller, and Omark, 1980).

References

Anderson, W.: The hyperkinetic child: A neurological appraisal. *Neurology, 13*:968–973, 1963.

Arsenian, S.: *Bilingualism and Mental Development.* New York, Columbia University, 1937.

Balkan, L.: *Les Effets Du Bilingualisme Sur Les Aptitudes Intellectuelles.* Brussels, 1970.

Bannatyne, A.: Diagnosing learning disabilities and writing remedial prescription. *J Learning Disabilities, 1*:242–249, 1968.

Bannatyne, A.: Diagnosis: A note on re-categorization of the WISC scaled scores. *J Learning Disabilities, 7*:272–273, 1974.

Benton, A.L.: Developmental dyslexia: Neurological aspects. In Friedlander, W.J. (Ed.): *Advances in Neurology.* New York, Raven, 1975.

Benton, A.L., and Pearl, D.: *Dyslexia: An Appraisal of Current Knowledge.* New York, Oxford University, 1978.

Birch, H.G. (Ed.): *Brain Damage in Children: The Biological and Social Aspects.* Baltimore, Williams and Wilkins, 1964.

Bozinou, E.:   *Comprehension and Production of Past Tense and Present Progressive among Monolingual and Bilingual Five Year Olds.* Paper presented at the annual meeting of the American Educational Research Association, Toronto, Canada, 1978.

Brazeau, E.J.:   Language differences and occupational experience. *Canadian J Economic and Political Science, 7:*279–290, 1958.

Burks, H.F.:   The effect on learning of brain pathology. *Exceptional Children, 24:*169–174, 1957.

Carrow, M.A.:   Linguistic functioning of bilingual and monolingual children. *J Speech and Hearing Disorders,22:*371–380, 1957.

Corder, S.P.:   The significance of learner's errors. *International Review of Applied Linguistics, 5:*161–170, 1967.

Corder, S.P.:   Error analysis, interlanguage and second language acquisition. *Language Teaching and Linguistics, 14:*201–218, 1975.

Critchley, M.:   *The Dyslexic Child.* Springfield, Thomas, 1970.

Cruickshank, W.M.:   *The Brain-Injured Child in Home, School, and Community.* Syracuse, Syracuse University, 1967.

Danielson, L.C., and Bauer, J.N.:   A formula based classification of learning disabled children: An examination of the issues. *J Learning Disabilities, 11:*50–64, 1978.

Denckla, M.B., and Rudel, R.:   Naming of object-drawings by dyslexic and other learning disabled children. *Brain and Language, 3:*1–15, 1976.

Downing, J. (Ed.):   *Comparative Reading.* New York, Macmillan, 1973.

Downing, J., and Brown, A.L. (Eds.):   *The Second International Reading Symposium.* London, Cassell, 1967.

Dulay, H.C., and Burt, M.K.:   Goofing: An indication of children's second language learning strategies. *Language Learning, 22:* 235–252, 1972.

Dulay, H.C., and Burt, M.D.:   Errors and strategies in child second language acquisition. *TESOL Quarterly, 8:*129–138, 1974.

Eckert, R.E., and Marshal, O.T.:   *When Youth Leave School.* New York, McGraw-Hill, 1938.

Eisenberg, L.:   The epidemiology of reading retardation and a program for preventive intervention. In Money, J. (Ed.): *The Disabled Reader: Education of the Dyslexic Child.* Baltimore, Johns Hopkins, 1966.

Engle, P.:   Language medium in early school years for minority language groups. *Review of Educational Research, 45:*283–325, 1975.

Ervin-Tripp, S.M.:   Some strategies for the first two years. In Moore, T.C. (Ed.): *Cognitive Development and the Acquisition of Language.* New York, Academic, 1973.

Ervin-Tripp, S.M.:   Is second language learning like the first? *TESOL Quarterly, 8:*111–127, 1974.

Evans, S.J.:   Word-pair discrimination and imitation abilities of preschool Spanish-speaking children. *J Learning Disabilities, 7:*49–56, 1974.

Franklyn, A.W. (Ed.): *Word Blindness or Specific Developmental Dyslexia.* London, Pitman, 1962.

Frostig, M., and Maslow, P.: *Learning Problems in the Classroom: Prevention and Remediation.* New York, Grune and Stratton, 1973.

Gonzalez, E., and Ortiz, L.: Social policy and education related to linguistically and culturally different groups. *J Learning Disabilities, 10*:11-17, 1977.

Guyer, B., and Friedman, M.: Hemispheric processing and cognitive style in learning disabled and normal children. *Child Development, 46*:658-668, 1975.

Haugen, E.: *The Norwegian Language in America.* Philadelphia, University of Pennsylvania, 1953.

Haugen, E.: *Bilingualism in the Americas.* Birmingham, University of Alabama, 1956.

Helfgott, J.: Phonemic segmentation and blending skills of kindergarten children: Implications for beginning reading acquisition. *Contemporary Educational Psychology, 1*:157-169, 1976.

Hinshelwood, J.: A case of dyslexia: A peculiar form of word-blindness. *Lancet, 2*:1451-1454, 1896.

Hinshelwood, J.: *Cogenital Word-Blindness.* London, Lewis, 1917.

Hughes, J.R.: Electroencephalographic and neurophysiological studies in dyslexia. In Benton, A., and Pearl, D. (Eds.): *Dyslexia.* New York, Oxford University, 1978.

Janco-Worrall, A.D.: Bilingualism and cognitive development. *Child Development, 43*:1390-1400, 1972.

Johnson, D.J., and Myklebust, H.R.: *Learning Disabilities.* New York, Grune and Stratton, 1967.

Jones, W.R.: *Bilingualism in Welsh Education.* Cardiff, University of Wales, 1966.

Jorstad, D.: Psycholinguistic Learning Disabilities in 20 Mexican-American students. *J Learning Disabilities, 4*:144-149, 1971.

Kellaghan, T., and Macnamara, J.: Reading in a second language. In Jenkinson, M.D. (Ed.): *Reading Instruction: An International Forum.* Newark, International Reading Assoc., 1967.

Keogh, B.: Hyperactivity and learning disorders: Review and speculation. *Exceptional Child, 38*:101-109, 1971.

Kephart, N.: *The Slow Learner in the Classroom.* Columbus, Merrill, 1960.

Kephart, N.: Let's not misunderstand dyslexia. *The Instructor, 78*:62-63, 1968.

Kirk, S.A., and Kirk, W.D.: *Psycholinguistic Learning Disabilities: Diagnosis and Remediation.* Urbana, University of Illinois, 1975.

Koppitz, E.M.: *The Bender-Gestalt Test for Young Children.* New York, Grune and Stratton, 1963.

Koppitz, E.M.: *The Bender-Gestalt Test for Young Children: Research and Application, 1963-1973*, Vol. II. New York, Grune and Stratton, 1975.

Lado, R.: *Language Teaching: A Scientific Approach.* New York, McGraw-Hill, 1964.

Landry, R.G.: A comparison of second language learners and monolinguals on divergent thinking tasks at the elementary school level. *Modern Language J, 58*:10-15, 1974.

Leopold, W.F.: *Speech Development of a Bilingual Child: A Linguist's Record.* (4 vols.) Evanston, Northwestern University, 1949.

Leopold, W.F.: Semantic learning in infant language. *Word, 4*:173-180, 1948.

Liberman, I.Y., Shankweiler, D., Fischer, F.W., and Carter, B.: Explicit syllable and phoneme segmentation in the young child. *J Experimental Child Psychology, 18*:201-212, 1974.

Lloyd, J., Sabatino, D., Miller, T., and Miller, S.: Proposed guidelines: Some open questions. *J Learning Disabilities, 10*:69-72, 1977.

Manuel, H.T., and Wright, C.E.: The language difficulties of Mexican children. *J Genetic Psychology, 36*:458-466, 1929.

Mason, A.W.: Specific (developmental) dyslexia. *Developmental Medicine and Child Neurology, 9*:183-190, 1976.

Mcnamara, J.: The effect of instruction in a weaker language. *J Social Issues, 23*:121-135, 1967.

Milon, J.P.: The development of negation in English by a second language learner. *TESOL Quarterly, 8*:137-143, 1974.

Minskoff, J.G.: Differential approaches to prevalence estimates of learning disabilities. In De la Cruz (Ed.): *Minimal Brain Dysfunction.* New York, New York Academy of Sciences, 1973.

Myers, P.I., and Hammill, D.D.: *Methods for Learning Disorders.* New York, John Wiley, 1969.

Myklebust, H.R. (Ed.): *Progress in Learning Disabilities*, Vol. II. New York, Grune and Stratton, 1971.

Myklebust, H.R., and Boshes, B.: *Final Report: Minimal Brain Damage in Children.* Washington, D.C., Department of Health, Education, and Welfare, 1969.

Oller-Daurella, L., and Maso-Subirana, E.: Semiologia clinica y EEG de la lateralidad preferencial. Libro de ponencias, VIII. *Congreso Nacional de Neuro-Psiquiatra,* Madrid, 1965.

Oller, J., and Richard, J. (Eds.): *Focus on the Learner: Pragmatic Perspectives for the Language Teacher.* Rowley, Newbury House, 1973.

Orton, S.T.: Word-blindness in school children. *Archives of Neurology and Psychiatry, 14*:582-615, 1925.

Owen, W.F.: Dyslexia: Genetic aspects. In Benton, A., and Pearl, D. (Eds.): *Dyslexia.* New York, Oxford University, 1978.

Pearl, E., and Lambert, W.E.: The relation of bilingualism to intelligence. *Psychological Monographs, 27:*Whole No. 546, 1967.

Perfetti, C.A., and Hogaboam, T.: The relationship between single word decoding and reading comprehension skill. *J Educational Psychology, 67:*461–469, 1975.

Rabinovitch, R.D.: Reading and learning disabilities. In Arieti, S. (Ed.): *American Handbook of Psychiatry.* New York, Basic Books, 1959.

Rainstad, V., and Potter, R.: Differences in vocabulary and syntax usage between Nez Perce Indians and white kindergarten children. *J Learning Disabilities, 7:*35–41, 1974.

Richards, J.: Error analysis and second language strategies. *Language Sciences, 17:*12–22, 1971.

Rigg, M.: Some further data on the language handicap. *J Educational Psychology, 19:*256, 1928.

Rivers, W.: *The Psychologist and the Foreign Language Teacher.* Chicago, University of Chicago, 1964.

Robinson, M.E., and Schwartz, L.B.: Visuo-motor skills and reading ability: A longitudinal study. *Developmental Medicine and Child Neurology, 15:*281–286, 1973.

Rutter, M.: Prevalence and types of dyslexia. In Benton, A.L., and Pearl, D. (Eds.): *Dyslexia: An Appraisal of Current Knowledge.* New York, Oxford University, 1978.

Sanchez, G.I.: Bilingualism and mental measures. *J Applied Psychology, 18:*765–772, 1934.

Schumann, J., and Stenson, N. (Eds.): *New Frontiers in Language Learning.* Rowley, Newbury House, 1975.

Smith, M.E.: Some light on the problem of bilingualism as found from a study of the progress in mastery of English amoung preschool children of non-American ancestry in Hawaii. *Genetic Psychology Monographs, 21:*121–284, 1939.

Spring, C.: Encoding speech and memory span in dyslexic children. *J Special Education, 10:*35–40, 1976.

Stanley, G., and Hall, R.: Short term visual information processing in dyslexics. *Child Development, 44:*841–844, 1973.

Stanley, G., and Hall, R.: A comparison of dyslexics and normals in recalling letter arrays after brief presentations. *British J Educational Psychology, 43:*301–304, 1973.

Stark, W.A.: The effect of bilingualism on general intelligence: An investigation carried out in certain Dublin primary schools. *British J Educational Psychology, 10:*78–79, 1940.

Steger, J.A., Vellutino, F.R., and Meshaulam, U.: Visual-tactile and tactile-tactile paired associate learning in normal and poor readers. *Perceptual and Motor Skills, 35:*263–266, 1972.

Stern, H.H.: *Perspectives on Second-language Teaching.* Toronto, Ontario Institute for Studies in Education, 1970.

Strauss, A., and Lehtinen, L.S.:   *Psychopathology and Education of the Brain-injured Child*. New York, Grune and Stratton, 1947.

Subirana, A.:   Handedness and cerebral dominance. In Vinken, P.J., and Bruyn, G.W. (Eds.): *Handbook of Clinical Neurology*, vol. 4. Amsterdam, North Holland, 1969.

Sulzbacher, S., and Kenowitz, L.A.:   At last a definition of learning disabilities we can live with? *J Learning Disabilities, 10*:8–12, 1977.

Svartvik, J.:   *Errata: Papers in error analysis*. Lund, Gleerup, 1973.

Tireman, L.S.:   The bilingual child and his reading vocabulary. *Elementary English, 32*:33–35, 1955.

Totten, G.O.:   Bringing up children bilingually. *American Scandinavian Review, 48*:42–50, 1960.

Vellutino, F.R., Smith, H., Steger, J.A., and Kamin, M.:   Reading disability: Age differences and the perceptual deficit hypothesis. *Child Development, 46*:487–493, 1975.

Vellutino, F.R.:   Toward an understanding of dyslexia: Psychological factors in specific reading disability. In Benton, R.L., and Pearl, D. (Eds.): *Dyslexia: An Appraisal of Current Knowledge*. New York, Oxford University, 1978.

Virkkunen, M., and Nuutila, A.:   Specific reading retardation, hyperactive child syndrome, and juvenile delinquency. *Acta Psychiatrica Scandinavia, 54*:25–28, 1976.

Watson, D.L., Omark, D.R., Grouell, S.L., and Heller, B.:   *Nondiscriminatory Assessment: Practitioner's Handbook*, vol. 1. Sacramento, California State Department of Education, 1980.

Watson, D.L., Grouell, S.L., Heller, B., and Omark, D.R.:   *Nondiscriminatory Assessment: Text Matrix*, vol. 2. Sacramento, California State Department of Education, 1980.

Weinreich, U.:   *Languages in Contact*. Hague, Mouton, 1953.

Zifiak, M.:   Phonological awareness and reading acquisition in first grade children. Unpublished doctoral dissertation, University of Connecticut, 1976.

13

Bilingual Mentally Retarded Children: Language Confusion or Real Deficits?

Richard Pacheco

This chapter will examine non-English and limited English-speaking children ultimately assigned to the special education classroom. Since the Hispanic or Spanish-speaking population is the most numerous among the public school students considered Limited English Proficient (LEP) or Limited English Speaking (LES), the focus will be on them. When these children register as students in the school system, they are not automatically enrolled in special education based on their limited English proficiency or Hispanic heritage. Instead, they are placed in special education after having been exposed to the formal education setting for a number of years and having gone through an assessment process. It would seem useful to trace the history and performance of this group and identify those factors that make them unique as students. In particular, this chapter will discuss the most obvious differences between *mainstream* children referred for psychological assessment and placement in a special education class and referrals of bilingual children who have had the dual language experience.

A History of Failure

The United States Commission on Civil Rights (1971) reported that Spanish-speaking children, the majority of whom are Mexican American,

have the highest rate of public school attrition before high school gradua-
tion of three major ethnic groups, Mexican American, Black, and American
Indian in the Southwest. Only 60% were still in school at the beginning of the
tenth grade. More recent figures (United States Bureau of the Census, 1980)
reports that only 45% of the Hispanic 25 years old and older completed high
school, and only 2% received college degrees. The central question that must
be asked is why would this particular group consistently do so poorly within
our public schools? The following three hypotheses are proposed:

Hypothesis 1. The Spanish bilingual population is born with a lower
ability to conceptualize and master the particular activities and skills necessary to succeed within the school
system.

Hypothesis 2. School systems have an ethnic bias toward these children
and do not want them to succeed and, therefore, deliberately frustrate them by placing academic obstacles in their
way or by placing them in special education classes.

Hypothesis 3. The bilingual children encounter the unique linguistic
phenomenon of a dual language experience, which can,
under certain circumstances, result in confusion in both
languages and thus impede the learning process.

In Response to Hypothesis One

Most educators believe that cognitive abilities are generally distributed
along the normal curve for all populations. The incidence of malnutrition,
drugs, poor pre- and post-natal care, and so forth may shift the percentages
slightly. There appear to be no studies where these factors have influenced
the general range of intelligence significantly among the Spanish bilingual
population as compared to the mainstream population. Therefore, let us
concede that the Spanish-speaking population's cognitive potential (or any
minority population's potential) is distributed in much the same manner as
the majority population (*see* Chapters 2 and 3).

In Response to Hypothesis Two

That school districts deliberately place bilingual children in special
education classes in order to repress their achievement merits a close look.
School systems, by design, were created to help nurture children through the
developmental stages, exposing them to experiences and educational tasks
that enable them to grow to be full-fledged, contributing members of
society—producers-consumers. These children should be literate, with
competencies in areas such as math, science, geography, history, and civics,

by the end of high school. When these assumptions are not realized, the public usually reacts with an uproar and demands competency exams for students as well as teachers. For a school system deliberately to place in operation a mechanism that would academically suppress any given population, is counter to the very task for which it was created.

That any school system would also choose to place these children in special education classrooms, adding to the cost of their education, seems inconsistent. However, these children have historically been placed in disproportionately higher numbers in special education classes. Why? In one Texas study, the number of Mexican Americans placed in special education classes was twice that of Anglos proportionate to their numbers (Meisgier, 1966). According to Mercer's research, conducted between 1953 and 1969, approximately 13% of the children attending public schools in California had Hispanic surnames but represent 26% of the special education class population (1977).

Recently there seems to be a reversal of this pattern of disproportionate representation, possibly because of P.L. 94–142. In one of California's largest districts, children from non-English-speaking homes currently constitute 15% of the communication-handicapped, special education enrollment, while they are only 18% of the general population (California State Department of Education, 1981). This turnabout will be discussed in more detail later. Even though the focus of this chapter is not on assessment but reasons for potential special education referral, it may be useful to examine some of the conflicts in the assessment procedure.

The United States District Court case in California of *Larry P*. v. *Riles* (1979) illustrates two perceptions of the equity of the assessment procedure. The issue was whether IQ tests were culturally biased and therefore invalid when applied to a nonmainstream student. The school system representatives claimed that IQ tests were only one way of evaluating children placed in educable mentally retarded (EMR) classes. However, the defendent's own studies showed that IQ scores were the main if not the only reason for placement. Judge Robert Peckham ruled that IQ tests were culturally and racially biased in the placing of a black child in an EMR classroom; the ruling also stated that the conduct of school authorities, in connection with the history of IQ testing and special education in California, reveals an unlawful intent to segregate. The *Diana* v. *California School Board* (1973) court case had more or less ruled similarly concerning a Mexican American child.

IQ tests still seem to be the major determinant for recommending and assigning children to classes for the mentally retarded (MR). Current practices (and P.L. 94–142) recommend that a committee of the referring teacher, the special education teacher, the superintendent in charge of special education or his or her representative, the school psychologist, and the school nurse confer prior to the placement of a child in special education. However, observations by the author, based on attendance at many of these meetings as a special education teacher, suggest that the child's academic performance in the mainstream classroom and the school pyschologist's IQ report are the determining factors in the decisions recommending special education.

Even though statistics show that the special education classroom population is disproportionately composed of bilingual children, it is hard to believe that school districts planned it this way. Actually, the academic performance of these children in the mainstream classroom appears to serve as the catalyst for it all. Contributing factors such as curriculum that minimizes any carryover of knowledge between the school environment and home environment, low expectations by the teaching staff, few successful role models, and little involvement by parents would naturally add to the failure rate of children. However, the bottom line is that bilingual children still perform significantly lower on academic tasks when compared to the mainstream population, and this initiates the mainstream teachers' referrals for psychological evaluation and consequent placement in mentally retarded classrooms.

The bilingualism or ethnicity of the child is not what school districts typically examine when they place children in special education. That is not to say a school system would not support *de facto* segregation or oppose busing, but these are political rather pedagogical considerations. These same school districts that have a disproportionate number of Hispanic bilingual representation in their special education classrooms would probably enthusiastically accept any number of middle or upper socioeconomic class children, who did not speak English, from any country in the world, including Mexico. In all probability, these children would not be placed in special education classes in any greater proportion than the mainstream child. The point is that the aspect of being non-English-speaking or limited English-speaking would not become the reason for placement in special education. Instead, low performance on academic tasks on a continuing basis is usually what motivates teachers to recommend children for evaluation.

In Response to Hypothesis Three

Hispanic bilingual children enrolled in the school system bring to that system many experiences in a language other than English may also have English language experiences and may suffer from language confusion. All of these factors may impede learning in the classroom. These children may perform academically similarly to mainstream (Anglo) children who are retarded. Not being able to succeed with these children, teachers may recommend they be evaluated. Mainstream teachers usually have approximately thirty students to nurture through the curriculum. When LEP students who have historically performed poorly, possibly affecting teachers' expectations, continue to (a) fail in learning the basic skills, (b) read two to four grade levels below their age level, and (c) do not respond to remediation, it is understandable why teachers may concede and refer them for evaluation.

The conflict we see between the school system and the language minority child is usually not one of racial or ethnic bias toward students with whom the school is not successful. As stated previously, school systems must also perform at an acceptable level or come into conflict with the public. If the public perceives that schools are not meeting their goals with reasonable success, the public will impose demands upon the schools. The current high school students' competency exams prior to granting the diploma and the outcry for teacher competency exams after graduating from teacher training institutions attest to the responsibility of the schools to society.

Schools often will accept reluctantly a student population perceived as having a low probability of yielding its fair share of *successful* students. Such students place the schools in the position of possibly not succeeding at a level acceptable to the public. Schools usually will accept the responsibility to educate these students only under court mandate. The refusal by Texas schools to accept children in the school system whose parents are not documented as legal is a good example of this sentiment.

The single outstanding characteristic of the Hispanic students that distinguishes them from the mainstream pedagogically, is the dual language experience. This bilingualism is probably the most misunderstood phenomenon in the school system today. Adding to the confusion are research reports in the journals that present diverse findings. There seems to be no consensus of what bilingualism is or whether its effects are positive or negative. The majority of the earlier studies (pre-1962) fairly consistently found bilingualism to affect negatively proficiency in both languages. Because later studies have shown the opposite, it would be useful to view both current and past research in this area.

Definitions of Bilingualism

There has been an assumption that bilingual children represent a homogenous population whose proficiency in both languages is equal to that of native monolingual speakers. It may well be that this assumption stems from Bloomfield, who was one of the early linguistic authorities on languages in the United States during the 1930s. Weinreich (1953) describes bilingualism as alternately using two languages and producing complete and meaningful utterances in each. Macnamara (1969) has used the term *bilingual* to denote persons who possess one of the following language skills: speaking, writing, listening, reading—even to a minimal degree—in a second language.

Other linguists such as MacKey suggest that bilingualism is more complex than just simply equal mastery of two languages:

To begin with, there are many types of bilinguals. There are those who are "at home" in two languages; those who speak a second language fluently with some of the features (sounds, structure, or vocabulary) of their native language, and those who speak both languages differently than the unilinguals in the same area. There are also those who have a mastery of the syntax and vocabulary of two languages and the pronunciation of both languages, but an incomplete or imperfect knowledge of the vocabulary and/or syntax of the second language; and those who have an equal but different vocabulary in both languages—those, for instance, who count in one language and pray in another. (1956, pp. 4–5)

Some linguists distinguish types of bilinguals in terms of the acquisition process of the two languages. Malherbe (1969) says that there is natural bilingualism acquired in a spontaneous and unplanned fashion and an artificial bilingualism that is the result of deliberate and systematic teaching. Similarly, O'Doherty (1958) differentiates between the bilingual who has mastered two languages and the pseudo-bilingual who has mastered one means of social intercourse proportional to the age and social group and who has, in addition, acquired some knowledge of another means of communication without mastering it.

Different descriptions or definitions of bilingualism seem dependent upon the authors of the definitions and their perception of the context. This point has been discussed by such scholars as Ferguson (1964), Gumperz (1964), and Fishman (1969, 1971), who have described the functional differentiation of the bilingual's two languages in terms of *diglossia*, a term referring to the situation specific or domain specific use of languages or dialects. In this context, both MacKey (1962) and Fishman (1971) argue that existence of bilingualism presupposes continuation of separate language communities, as occurs within many United States communities.

Effects of Bilingualism

Studies continue to show that the effects of bilingualism can be either positive or negative, depending upon the population studied and who authored the study. For the educator, this ambiguity in the research findings causes an uneasiness; the teacher does not really know whether developing a language other than English is harming the child. On the one hand, the tendency for the well-intentioned, concerned teacher could be toward the development of the language of the country, English. On the other hand, if the educator develops the child's home or first language, it may be because of intuition and blind faith that it is good for the child, rather than based on sound research.

Negative Findings

Research earlier in this century usually found negative effects of bilingualism. Bilingual children, compared with monolingual children, scored lower on measures of intelligence; they were over-age for their grade levels and educators felt that they generally were difficult to teach. When both verbal and nonverbal IQ tests were used (Altus, 1953; Barke, 1933; Carrow, 1957; Stark, 1940), the results seemed to suggest that bilingual children were at a disadvantage on verbal IQ tests but not always on the nonverbal tests. For example, Darcy (1946) investigated the effects of bilingualism on measured intelligence of 212 Italian American preschool children. It was found that the bilingual group scored significantly lower than the monolingual on the Stanford-Binet and so it was concluded that the bilinguals suffered from *language handicap*. Eisenson sums up the attitude quite well in a speech pathology book written in 1956:

> Bilingual influences, except possibly for the superior child, necessitate constant adjustments which make learning of one language a difficult task. The child must exert special effort to maintain himself in a given linguistic groove. If the effort becomes excessive, emotionality may result which is likely to interfere with further language learning.... Whenever possible, therefore, it is advised that the young child be exposed only to the influence of the language which will become his educational tool. (p. 89)

Reports of negative effects of bilingualism have continued to surface. A recent study by Tsushima and Hogan (1975) report that Japanese English bilinguals in grades four and five performed at a significantly lower level than did monolingual children on measures of verbal and academic skills. A study in Singapore (Torrance, Gowan, Wu, and Aliotti, 1970) reported that children in grades three, four, and five who were attending bilingual schools performed at a significantly lower level in fluency and flexibility.

Positive Findings

Since the presentation of the Peal and Lambert Study of 1962, most research has shown a reversal of the earlier findings. The earlier studies had failed to control for such variables as age, sex, and socioeconomic levels. In the Southwest the majority of studies were investigating children of migrant parents with no or little educational background and no stability or continuity of educational programs.

Cummins (1976) hypothesizes that the level of linguistic competence attained by a bilingual child may mediate the effects of the child's bilingual learning experience. He states, specifically, that there may be a *threshold* level of linguistic competence a child must attain in order to avoid cognitive deficits and to allow the potentially beneficial aspects of becoming bilingual to influence cognitive functioning. Mexican American children's learning experience may corroborate such a hypothesis; never having formally developed the first language, they cannot have reached the presumed threshold level of competence.

Lambert (1975) has suggested that studies reporting negative relationships, as opposed to the positive association between bilingualism and cognition, can be distinguished in terms of *additiveness* and *subtractiveness* of the students studied. Many of the early studies contained bilingual students from language minority groups whose second language was usually the dominant and more prestigious language. The bilingualism of these subjects is termed *subtractive* in that the bilinguals' competence in a second language at any time illustrated the concept of subtracting the first language and replacing it with the second language. This situation also reflects the present language situation of the Mexican American in the Southwest; Spanish is subtracted and replaced by English.

The most recent studies generally have reported positive cognitive consequences associated with bilingualism when comparisons are made with monolingual students. Bilinguals score higher on tasks involving divergent thinking (Carringer, 1974; Landry, 1974). Bilinguals showed greater skill at auditory reorganization of verbal material, were capable of more flexible manipulation of the linguistic code, and were more advanced in concrete operational thinking (Ben-Zeev, 1972; Ianco-Worrall, 1972).

Such studies have generally involved middle- and upper-class subjects whose first language is dominant, or at least prestigious, and in no danger of replacement by the second language. As Lambert (1975) suggests, these children are adding another language to their repertory of skills. The evidence from bilingual education programs in such *additive* settings indicate that, in general, children achieve high levels of second language competence at no cost to their first language (Cohen, 1975; Lambert and Tucker, 1972; Swain, 1974).

Generalization of findings in research studies must be done with extreme caution. Cummins (1976) states that the search for consistent research results is based on a false premise, i.e., that there is but one single phenomenon or state called bilingualism that ought to influence the mental lives of all bilinguals in much the same way. There is an enormous variety of bilingual learning situations, in which different combinations of cognitive, attitudinal, social, and educational factors are operative. Thus, the learning of two languages is going to affect cognition in different ways depending on the ages at which the languages are learned, separate or simultaneous learning, the opportunities for using both languages in the home, school, and wider community, and the prestige of each of the two languages.

We turn now to a study that parallels the language situation of the southwestern United States more closely than does any other in the literature. The findings of the Finnish National Commission Report to UNESCO (Skutnabb-Kangas and Toukomoaa, 1976) strongly supports the proposition of first language development. Sweden has a large Finnish working class migrant population with an estimated 30,000 children in public schools. Fewer Finns learn Swedish than any of the other immigrant nationality groups. This group is characterized by identity conflicts, lack of self-esteem, and shame about their own language and nationality (Skutnabb-Kangas and Toukomoaa, 1976). Paulston (1977) reports that the data on the Finnish children in Sweden are particularly significant because both the receiver country and the sender country are highly developed, industrialized modern societies with school achievement norms for children. In addition, Sweden is a quasi-socialist society where problems of health care, diet, and unemployment are not significant intervening variables. Such conditions are often cited as contributory factors in the lack of school achievement by minority group children in the United States.

In general, Skutnabb-Kangas and Toukomoaa (1976) found that the children's rate of improvement in Swedish was not as fast as regression in the mother tongue. Although ability factors influenced the learning of Swedish, it is very clear that the better a pupil has preserved the mother tongue, the better are the prerequisites for learning the second language. Overwhelmingly, the better a student knew Finnish (as a function of having attended school for several years in Finland), the better was the acquisition of Swedish.

An examination of language skills of siblings found that those who moved from Finland at an average age of ten had preserved an almost normal Finnish language level and they also approach the normal level in the Swedish language of Swedish pupils. Those who moved at the age of twelve also achieve language skills comparable to those of the Swedes although learning the language takes place more slowly. The children who moved under the age of six, or who were born in Sweden, do not do as well. Their Swedish language development often stopped at about age twelve, possibly because of their poor grounding in their first language (L_1). Worst off are the pupils who were seven or eight when they moved to Sweden. The evidence is perfectly clear that L_1 development facilitates the learning of the second language, and there are serious implications that without such development neither language may be learned well (Paulston, 1977).

Research on the Mexican American Population

Research on the Mexican American population in the Southwest (Carrow, 1955, 1971; Cornejo, 1969; Metcalf, 1973) indicates that the majority of Mexican American children are dominant English speakers with varying degrees of bilingual skills. Mace (1972) found that most Mexican American children enter school with all the English language structures normally controlled by monolingual Anglo English speakers of the same age. As Omark and Watson suggest in Chapter 2, intelligence tests primarily are language tests. Hence, these results are not surprising. The early study by Carrow (1955) of 50 third grade bilingual and monolingual children of similar socioeconomic status and intelligence reported no difference in oral English language functioning as measured by length of clause, number of words uttered per unit of time, index of subordination, and complexity of sentence structure.

A more recent study by Carrow (1971) compared the comprehension of English and Spanish in a group of preschool Mexican American children of lower socioeconomic status. Linguistically, the children varied widely in the extent to which they understood the two languages. The greater proportion of children at the age levels studied (ranging from three years, ten months to six years, nine months) understood English better than Spanish. Only 30% demonstrated sufficient comprehension of both languages to be considered functionally bilingual.

Working with nonmigrants in Harlingen, Austin, San Benito, and Del Valle, Texas, Cornejo (1969) found Mexican American children to be English dominant; they expressed themselves better in English than in Spanish and would switch to English automatically when asked questions in Spanish that they could not answer. However, in the reverse situation, they would remain silent or say that they did not know rather than switch to Spanish. In their investigations of Mexican Americans, Matluch and Mace (1973) state that their impression is that Mexican Americans in both northern and southern California are English dominant. It would seem that, on the surface, language is not the causal factor for school drop-out and low academic profiles for Mexican American children. Following from the Finnish-Swedish studies, however, the prediction would be that the Mexican American students should not be as proficient in English as Anglo students because their first language is not well developed.

In summation, the question continues to arise in all involved with bilingual programs in the United States: Why are the results of their programs consistently negative? This review of studies whose results were positive should have some significance for American programs. Because the positive findings in these later studies have usually been associated with balanced bilinguals does not necessarily mean they are not meaningful to the Mexican American and Spanish/English bilingual programs. A child may not have to be a balanced bilingual before anything positive can happen. It may be that the child may only have to reach a *threshold*.

The Language Confused Bilingual Child

Hispanic children who are ultimately referred for psychological testing by a teacher generally are performing poorly in the subject matter areas (reading, math, science, social studies, and language arts). In fact, this low performance is primarily the cause or reason for the referral. Usually by the time children are referred for testing they are in the fourth or fifth years in the school system and are two to four years behind. They probably also exhibit disruptive behavior, frustration, or apathy. Referral for testing would seem a natural avenue to be explored. The children's evident inability or unwillingness to perform or conform to expected norms can hardly be argued.

Low levels of academic performance are rarely so evident at initial entrance into the school system that they require attention. These minority children may have been a little slower in kindergarten or first grade than their peers and teachers may have felt that with a little individualized instruction and remediation the problems would go away. It is also possible that the children were shy, quiet, withdrawn, or sort of blended into the woodwork and did not really demand the attention of the teachers. Academic tasks at this stage are usually of a concrete nature and can be committed to memory. By the time children reach the fourth through sixth grade, when the tasks are more abstract, when the concrete aspects of language and learning must be applied in more abstract ways, the children's low performance becomes apparent. By this time, the children are frustrated, disruptive, and demand more of the teachers' attention.

This high level of frustration is not specific to the children only. The classroom teachers also become frustrated with their inability to succeed academically with these children. Teachers have certain expectations about the levels of performance and skills of the children who enter their classes at the beginning of the year, and there are expectations about the effects of their teaching on the children.

1. Children enrolling in class at the beginning of the year will come with an established set of social behaviors and a linguistic foundation upon which instruction can be based.
2. These behaviors and language foundation correlate positively with the developmental scale for specific grade and age levels.
3. The children are of reasonable intelligence and will respond positively to instruction, progressing at an accepted pace.
4. Any problems in the social or academic areas can be remediated with individualization and / or curriculum modification.

These expectations are fairly reasonable. When the expectations are not met, the teacher becomes frustrated and outside expertise is sought, usually in the form of psychological assessment.

At this point, let us examine the case of a mentally retarded, language-confused, bilingual child who has gone through just the type of experience previously discussed. Elizabeth was a child who was placed in a fourth through sixth grade bilingual EMR classroom taught by the author. Elizabeth was 10 years old when she came to the EMR class, reading at a 1.5 grade level, and her math skills were at a 2.1 grade level.

Following is a modification of the report submitted by the district psychologist upon the conclusion of a meeting of the assistant superintendent in charge of special programs, the school nurse, the principal, the recommending classroom teacher, and the special education teacher. They unanimously decided to place the child in an EMR class.

Name: Elizabeth   **Grade:** Fourth
Birth Date: 11-12-64   **Age:** 10 years   **Test Date:** 11-5-74

Brief Summary and Recommendations:

Elizabeth is a child of below average intelligence. WISC-R full scale IQ is 71. She is experiencing difficulty in school achievement and social adjustment. The principle causative factors for this difficulty include: low academic potential and developmental lags in those areas required for reading, writing, and math, distractability, and very poor memory skills. Additional individual remediation will be needed in the areas of reading, writing, and math. Medical, hearing, vision, and neurological examinations are indicated. Individual assistance with the English language is indicated; the ESL program would be helpful. Significant learning disabilities will require a specialized curriculum. *EMR class placement is recommended for consideration. Elizabeth is a marginal candidate for special class placement.*

Statement of Problem:

Elizabeth was referred for a general assessment of mental abilities, overall development level, and social adjustment. She has experienced difficulty in all areas of academic achievement and social growth. She requires considerable attention and is often disruptive in class.

Social, Economic, and Cultural Background:

Elizabeth lives with her mother and father. She has one brother, age 6, and three sisters, ages 6 and 1 year and 5 months. Interpersonal relationships between Elizabeth and her family are described as close to the mother but distant from the father. The mother and father are currently unemployed. The economic status of the family is described as poor. The family is presently being assisted by welfare. English and Spanish are spoken in the home.

As one can see, Elizabeth fits the classic pattern. She had been in the school district for four years before she was finally evaluated and placed in a class for the mentally retarded. Her communication was in English and Spanish. She was two to three years behind in her math and reading skills and had become disruptive in the classroom before finally being referred. Elizabeth was commuting between two cultures and because she had parents who mixed their languages, they did not provide the opportunity for her to develop either language separately nor efficiently. She had not developed vocabulary and concepts in either language that would allow her to make sense out of the academic tasks required. This problem was compounded by the possibility that the parents may have been illiterate or uneducated as well. Because of the low socioeconomic status indicated, she also had not had the necessary home experience that could have provided a foundation for learning the curricular tasks.

A Probable Cause

According to Cummins (1979), a child must reach a *threshold* of competence in the native language before a second language (L₂) can be mastered. Several investigators have drawn attention to bilingual children who have been exposed to both languages in an unsystematic fashion prior to school and come to school with less than nativelike command of the vocabulary and syntactic structures of both L₁ and L₂ (Gonzalez, 1979; Kaminsky, 1976). Gonzalez suggests that under these conditions children may switch codes because they do not know the label for a particular concept in the language they are speaking but have it readily available in the other language. Because the languages are not separated, each acts as a crutch for the other with the result that the children may fail to develop full proficiency in either language. Kaminsky has argued that these bilingual children may fail to develop fluent reading skills, since their knowledge of syntactic rules and vocabulary of each language may be insufficient to make accurate predications regarding the information in the text.

The content and activities in the traditional curriculum of an elementary school offers very little to motivate a child like Elizabeth. She could not identify with many of the experiences in her books and could find no experiences in her background enabling her to generalize to the tasks required. According to Bloom and Lahey (1978), if speech addressed to children does not make sense relative to what the child knows or is attending to, it would make no sense at all; such speech could not be a model for learning. The same thing might be said of the reading curriculum Elizabeth had been studying for four years. Bloom and Lahey also state that language disorder refers to any disruption in the learning of a native language. The use of English in an unsystematic fashion in the home with content unrelated to what she knew in the school system could quite possibly disrupt her learning of a native language that caused language disorders in both L₁ and L₂.

Language involves interactions among content, form, and use. Normal language development, according to Bloom and Lahey (1978), has been described as the successful interaction among the three. Content is the ideas expressed, *semantics*; form is the correct or incorrect arrangement of the words, *syntax*; and use is the functional expression of the ideas, *pragmatics*.

However, the different ways in which these components can interact with each other can result in disorders of form, content, or use. Disorder of form would mean that children's ideas about the world and abilities to communicate these ideas are more intact than their knowledge of the linguistic system for representing and communicating these ideas. For example, when Elizabeth would go to Mexicali, Mexico (Baja California), to visit her grandparents, she would come back to school able to relate detail and sequence of events that were quite sophisticated. The grandparents in Mexico could not speak English, so everything the child saw and did was in one language, Spanish. However, Elizabeth knew more than she could relate because of her limited proficiency in both languages.

In English, Elizabeth produced a disorder of use. According to Bloom and Lahey (1978), with these children, learning the system to encode ideas appears to be less of a problem than using the system for communication. During her four years in the public school, Elizabeth committed to memory many of the forms and content in English, but she would use them inconsistently or incorrectly. For example, names of cities, states, and countries were used interchangeably, the concept of direction was confused; sometimes north became south, east, or west; measurements of distance such as feet, inches, or miles were used in description with no consistency or correctness, e.g., a room could become four miles by five miles in length and width.

It became evident that Elizabeth needed to be given the opportunity to separate her languages more systematically. The school system had immersed her in English from the first day of kindergarten; however, the majority of her experiences, concepts, and vocabulary were in Spanish. The result was that she had become English dominant but with a language disorder. She mixed the two languages for certain uses, mostly for describing activities that related to her home and community. A conference with her parents revealed that they indeed did mix languages. Their language at home was syntactically and semantically Spanish, with significant borrowing of English lexicon.

Because the only pure language experiences the child had were in Mexico, it was decided to develop her Spanish systematically, using the language experience approach. Stories for her to read were developed about her grandmother's house, about Mexicali, about the town in which she lived, and about her games, friends, and dreams. During the morning hours, her class would work only in Spanish, and, in the afternoon, they would work only in English. Since the students in the classroom were entirely Mexican American, all of the children had similar problems and could benefit from this arrangement. This language experience approach also made it easier to structure content and language medium of instruction. The effects of Spanish development on Elizabeth's English were quite exciting. She began to ask about capitalization, periods, paragraphs—things she was never interested in before. Her descriptions became more precise and detailed toward the end of the year.

Following is a modified report of the psychological evaluation on the same child by the same psychologist after six months of developing her communication and academic skills in her native language.

Name: Elizabeth   **Grade:** 4 EMR
Birth Date: 11-12-64   **Test Date:** 5-22-75

Statement of Problem:

Elizabeth was referred for reassessment of mental abilities, developmental level, and personal adjustment. She was last tested 11-5-74. The special class teacher feels significant growth has occurred since her last placement, *and she may now qualify for regular class placement. Social growth has been outstanding.*

Brief Summary and Recommendations:

Elizabeth is a child of average intelligence. WISC-R full scale IQ is 80. The auditory attention span is moderately depressed, and auditory stimuli must be presented in short sequences. Individual remediation continues to be needed in the areas of reading, writing, and math. Reading instruction should be set at the 3.4 grade level and should employ appropriate age interest materials. Math instruction should be at the 3.4 grade level and should emphasize the development of basic skills. Individual assistance with English is indicated. A therapeutic supportive approach continues to be needed. She shows significant improvements in overcoming previous learning deficiencies. *Educationally Handicapped class placement continues to be a viable option at this time. Very careful monitoring of performance will be important.*

Educational History:

Elizabeth is currently assigned to the EMR program. Academic achievement has been outstanding in this program. School attendance has been good. The overall school adjustment is considered to be above average.

The question of whether or not Elizabeth would function at higher than an EMR range if she were exposed to only one language both in and out of school is meaningless. She *does* function at a low academic level, and there *are* two languages in her life. Her positive response to a bilingual special education program, however, is obvious.

There are many Elizabeths in our school districts who are functionally retarded with respect to their school performance. Elizabeth was not the only child in that class to show significant growth in English after having formally developed competencies, such as reading, in their first language.

An instructional approach that focuses on the experiences of the children and is presented in the language that has formed the base of their mental manipulations is, therefore, a viable approach to special education of bilingual developmentally delayed children.

Several questions can be raised regarding children like Elizabeth as well as other LEP children who may eventually be assigned to special education classrooms. Do evaluation instruments and evaluators take into account cultural and linguistic bias? Are these children erroneously categorized retarded and placed in special education classes? What factors help one predict whether teaching in L_1 or L_2 or both languages will best help the child, assuming the diagnosis of retardation to be correct? How appropriate are English as a Second Language classes for bilingual EMH children? These questions have haunted and will continue to haunt school districts. The complexity of the questions offer no simple solutions.

Current Problems

Because of lawsuits such as *Diana* v. *California State Board of Education* and *Larry P.* v. *Riles*, public school systems have become ultra-sensitive to the possibility of mislabeling, miscategorizing, and misplacing minority children in special education classes. Consequently, school districts may be going in the other direction by not identifying these children and, in effect, denying them the services needed and mandated by the Education of all Handicapped Children Act (P.L. 94–142).

The emergence of bilingual education programs for language minority children has further confused the issue. Many of these programs are either vague or inconsistent in their goals and objectives in reference to L_1 development. Because of federal, state, and local mandates, many of these programs emphasize the English curriculum too quickly, making the programs ineffective. Very little native language development occurs in any consistent manner. While there are some programs that have committed themselves to a good educational program with separation of the languages and an emphasis on native language development, the greater portion of these programs mix the languages, use a translation method and transition to an English curriculum and medium of instruction in too short a time. As illustrated above, the recent research emphasizes that a strong development in L_1 will foster a good acquisition of an L_2.

On the other hand, many teachers and principals, in good faith, hesitate to refer bilingual children for evaluation because they understand that if the children are placed in special education classrooms, the instruction and materials will be in English. There are currently very few bilingual special education teachers. Therefore, teachers and principals may opt to leave these children in bilingual classrooms where they at least understand the language. This approach places enormous responsibilities on bilingual classroom teachers. They not only have to instruct thirty other children in two languages, but they are not trained to teach language-confused children who exhibit poor memory skills, have developmental lags, or are socially disruptive.

Underreferral and sensitivity to possible misclassification has reduced the Hispanic special education population significantly, particularly in the areas of communicative handicap, learning disability, and mental retardation. The national incidence figures for special education is 12% for all conditions (Landurand, 1980). The Federal Bureau of Education for the Handicapped (Gallegos, 1980) states that the percentages of children identified as having speech/language handicaps, learning disabilities, and mental retardation are 3.5, 3.0, and 3.0, respectively. Using these figures, let us examine how Hispanic children are being served in special education in one state.

California has the largest Hispanic school population (953,295) in the United States (Commission for Teacher Preparation and Licensing, 1980). Therefore, these figures will be used as reported. According to the 12% national incidence figure reported, 114,395 students should be served by special education programs. However, only 24,778 Hispanic students were served during the 1979–80 school year. This figure includes communicatively handicapped, physically handicapped, learning handicapped, and severely handicapped children.

In an effort to refrain from classifying children as retarded, the above categories are the only ones allowed under the current California legislation (A.B. 1870). All districts are now submitting their *Master Plans,* as required under this bill, to eliminate the retarded category. Children who previously were labeled EMR are now placed in either the communicatively handicapped or the learning handicapped category. Districts that are still working on their Master Plans continue to report in the EMR category. The figures for communicatively handicapped, learning handicapped, and the remaining EMR children are as follows:

Communicatively Handicapped	5,764
Learning Handicapped	11,633
EMR	3,410
Total	20,807

Taking the expected incidence figures for these handicapped, i.e., 3.5, 3.0, 3.0 percent, there should be a minimum of 90,563 students in these categories. Far less than one-third of the expected population of this minority are being served. Presumably, the same phenomenon is occurring for the other minorities. The historical overrepresentation in special education classes has now become underrepresentation, at least in California. Bilingual children should not be overrepresented in mentally retarded classes or elsewhere because they are learning a new language. Children in need of special services should not be underrepresented because they are in bilingual classrooms. Children's individual needs have to be assessed and taught if bilingual education is to become a reality.

The obvious need is for bilingual special education teachers. However, until that need is met, special education personnel must work more closely with bilingual teachers (Pacheco and Omark, 1983). Techniques and materials from special education need to be made culturally and linguistically relevant for bilingual exceptional children. Such children are not being adequately served in either program alone.

An even more important issue is that school districts must continue to assess and identify those minority children with special needs. This means that tests and assessment procedures will have to be modified so that exceptional children can be identified in relationship to the cultural and language experiences to which they have been exposed. Without such identification, no one else can do anything.

References

Altus, G.T.:   W.I.S.C. patterns of a selective sample of bilingual school children. *J Genetic Psychology, 83*:241, 1953.

Barke, E.M.:   A study of the comparative intelligence of children in certain bilingual and monoglot schools in South Wales. *British J Educational Psychology, 237*, 1933.

Ben-Zeev, S.:   The influence of bilingualism on cognitive development and cognitive strategy. Unpublished Ph.D. dissertation, University of Chicago, 1972.

Bloom, L. and Lahey, M.:   *Language Development and Language Disorder.* New York, John Wiley, 1978.

California State Department of Education: *Special Education Pupil Count and Staff Data.* Sacramento, California State Department of Education, 1981.

Carringer, D.C.:   Creative thinking abilities of Mexican youth. *J Cross-cultural Psychology, 5*:200, 1974.

Carrow, M.A.:   A comparative study of the linguistic functioning of the bilingual Spanish-American children and monolingual Anglo children at the third grade level. Unpublished Ph.D. dissertation, Northwestern University, 1955.

Carrow, M.A.:   Linguistic functioning of bilingual and monolingual children. *J Speech and Hearing Disorders, 22*:371, 1957.

Carrow, E.:   Auditory comprehension of English by monolingual and bilingual preschool children. *Modern Language J, 55*:299, 1971.

Cohen, A.D.: *A Sociolinguistic Approach to Bilingual Education: Experiments in the American Southwest.* Rowley, Newbury House, 1975.

Commission for Teacher Preparation and Licensing: *Report on the Changing Population of California Schools.* Sacramento, State of California, 1980.

Cornejo, R.J.: Bilingualism: A study of the lexicon of five year old Spanish speaking children of Texas. Unpublished Ph.D. dissertation, University of Texas, 1969.

Cummins, J.: The influence of bilingualism on cognitive growth: A synthesis of research findings and explanatory hypothesis. ED 125311 (ERIC), 1976.

Cummins, J.: Linguistic interdependence and the educational development of bilingual children. *Review of Educational Research, 49*:227, 1979.

Darcy, N.T.: The effects of bilingualism upon the measurement of the intelligence of children of preschool age. *J Educational Psychology, 37*:21, 1946.

Eisenson, J.: *Speech Disorders: Principles and Practices of Therapy.* New York, Appleton-Century-Crofts, 1956.

Ferguson, C.A.: Diglossia. In Hymes, D. (Ed.): *Language in Culture and Society.* New York, Harper and Row, 1964.

Fishman, J.A.: The measurement and description of widespread and relatively stable bilingualism. *Modern Language J, 53*:153, 1969.

Fishman, J.A.: *Bilingualism in the Barrio.* New York, Yeshiva University, 1971.

Gallegos, R.: Bilingual bicultural education—Special education: An interface. ED 187081 (ERIC), 1980.

Gonzalez, G.: Teaching bilingual children. *Bilingual Education: Current Perspectives, 2*, Arlington Center for Applied Linguistics, 1979.

Gumperz, J.: Linguistic and social interaction in two communities. In Gumperz, J., and Hymes, D. (Eds.): *The Ethnology of Communication. American Anthropologist, 66*:137, 1964.

Ianco-Worrall, A.: Bilingualism and cognitive development. *Child Development, 43*:1390, 1972.

Kaminsky, S.: Bilingualism and learning to read. In Simoes, A. (Ed.): *The Bilingual Child.* New York, Academic, 1976.

Lambert, W.E.: *The Effects of Bilingualism in the Individual: Cognitive and Sociocultural Consequences.* Paper presented at a conference on Bilingualism, Plattsburgh, State University of New York, 1975.

Lambert, W.E., and Tucker, G.R.: *Bilingual Education of Children: The St. Lambert Experiment.* Rowley, Newbury House, 1972.

Landry, R.G.: A comparison of second language learners and monolinguals on divergent thinking tasks at the elementary school level. *Modern Language J, 58*:10, 1974.

Landurand, P.:   A promising practice. *Issues in Bilingual/Bicultural Special Education.* ED 189795 (ERIC), 1980.

Mace, G.J.:   *A Linguistic Profile of Children Entering Seattle Public School Kindergarten in September, 1972.* Austin, University of Texas, 1972.

MacKey, W.F.:   Toward a redefinition of bilingualism. *J Canadian Linguistic Association, 2*:4, 1956.

MacKey, W.F.:   The description of bilingualism. *Canadian J Linguistics, 7*:51, 1962.

Macnamara, J.:   Problems of bilingualism. In Kelly, L.G. (Ed.): *Description and Measurement of Bilingualism: An International Seminar, University of Moncton, June 6 to 14, 1967.* Toronto, University of Toronto, 1969.

Malherbe, E.G.:   Natural and artificial bilingualism. In Kelly, L.G. (Ed.): *Description and Measurement of Bilingualism: An International Seminar, University of Moncton, June 6 to 14, 1967.* Toronto, University of Toronto, 1969.

Matluch, J., and Mace, B.:   Language characteristics of Mexican American children: Implications for assessment. *J School Psychology, 11*: 68, 1973.

Meisgier, C.:   *The Doubly Disadvantaged.* Austin, University of Texas, 1966.

Mercer, J.:   Implications of current assessment procedures of Mexican American children. *Bilingual Education Paper Series.* Los Angeles, National Dissemination and Assessment Center, California State University, Los Angeles, 1977.

Metcalf, A.A.:   Mexican American English in southern California. *Western Review, 9*:12, 1973.

O'Doherty, E.F.:   Bilingualism: Educational aspects. *The Advancement of Science, 14*:282, 1958.

Pacheco, R., and Omark, D.R.:   *Special Education and Bilingual Education: Working Together.* San Diego, College-Hill, 1983.

Paulston, L.B.:   Research. *Bilingual Education: Current Perspectives—Linguistics.* Arlington, Center for Applied Linguistics, 1977.

Peal, E., and Lambert, W.:   The relation of bilingualism to intelligence. *Psychological Monographs, 2*:1962.

Skutnabb-Kangas, T., and Toukomoaa, P.:   *Teaching Migrant Children's Mother-Tongue and Learning the Language of the Host Country in the Context of the Sociocultural Situation of the Migrant Family.* Helsinki, The Finnish National Commission for UNESCO, 1976.

Stark, W.A.:   The effect of bilingualism on general intelligence: An investigation carried out in certain Dublin schools. *British J Educational Psychology,* 1940.

Swain, M.:   French immersion programs across Canada. *Canadian Modern Language Review, 31*:117, 1974.

Torrance, E.P., Gowan, J.C., Wu, J.M., and Aliotti, N.C.: Creative functioning of monolingual and bilingual children in Singapore. *J Educational Psychology, 11*:72, 1970.

Tsushima, W.T., and Hogan, T.P.: Verbal ability and school achievement of bilingual and monolingual children of different ages. *J Educational Research, 68*:349, 1975.

United States Bureau of the Census: *Census Reports.* Washington, D.C., U.S. Government Printing Office, 1980.

United States Commission on Civil Rights: *Report II, Mexican American Educational Series.* Washington, D.C., U.S. Government Printing Office, 1971.

Weinreich, U.: *Languages in Contact.* New York, Mouton, 1953.

14

Emotional and Behavioral Disorders in Bilingual Children

Richard R. DeBlassie

A great deal of information relative to children labeled as "emotionally disturbed," "emotionally disordered," or "behaviorally disordered" can be found in the literature. There is, however, a paucity of information available on the child who is both bilingual and emotionally or behaviorally disordered. The purpose of this chapter, therefore, is to provide a treatise on the bilingual emotionally or behaviorally disordered child. Examples will be drawn from the author's experience with the "minimally acculturated" Mexican American (or Chicano or Hispanic child of Mexican or Spanish-Mexican heritage) bilingual child, but the principles may be generalized to similar ethnic groups.

The Culturally Different Child

Many bilingual children, e.g., Mexican American, Native American, Puerto Rican, Cuban, particularly those living in the "culture of poverty" who live in urban ghettos or barrios or on reservations, or in poverty stricken rural areas, can usually be ascribed the term "culturally different." In this context, these children are somewhat disadvantaged in that they tend to have difficulty merging into the dominant culture of middle-class America. This is not to imply that such children are "culturally deprived" since they have a viable culture of their own, a well developed language, as well as traditions, customs, and mores.

The point is that because they come from a different culture, which is sometimes regarded as "inferior" by many who belong to the middle-class American mainstream, they have a tendency to have difficulty adjusting to a "new" or unfamiliar culture. Many of these difficulties in adjustment to the mainstream can be attributed to both extrinsic and intrinsic factors, some of which will be discussed in a later section.

The Culturally Different Bilingual Child

Johnson (1970) lists several characteristics, shared in varying degrees by culturally different children, that are consistent with this author's observations of culturally different bilingual children, especially Mexican American youth and other ethnic minorities. Some of the characteristics are an experiential background that does not fit the expectations of a middle-class oriented curriculum—a rural background (although a large percentage of such children are found in urban barrios), economic impoverishment, including self-perpetuating spiritual, moral, aspirational, and economic poverty; and a feeling of rejection by the dominant society. Other characteristics of these children are a relatively poor self-concept, aggressiveness, nonadherence to the values of the dominant culture, a poor attention span, and a conceptual development that does not fit the expectations of middle-class-oriented teachers. In addition, they are frequently linguistically handicapped. Often they live in a negative environment that could be described as ugly and disorderly. The consequences of poverty influence most of these characteristics and they would be expected to be the same in lower-class Anglo communities.

Although this list of characteristics of culturally different bilingual children seems to be heavily weighted with *negatives*, there are a number of writers (e.g., DeBlassie, 1976; Gordon, 1968; and Riessman, 1964) who suggest that many strengths possessed by culturally different children are overlooked. The following represent a synthesis of observations by such authors: a belief in collective group values, a more genuine egalitarianism, an ability to learn concrete concepts, a feeling of security coming from many family members (especially the extended family), a resourcefulness, an ability to cope, a use of complex language and behavioral patterns within their environment, a freedom from self-blame, an enjoyment of other family members without competition, and an adherence to the importance of Christianity in their lives, especially Catholicism.

Influence of Ethnicity/Race and Socioeconomic Status

One can be reasonably sure that many people subscribe to the idea that culturally different bilingual youth are so different from children of the dominant culture that they need diverse approaches in terms of classroom strategies or methodologies. A major assumption inherent in this belief is that these children are different because they are Mexican American, Native American, Cuban, Puerto Rican, and bilingual, and therefore happen to possess different values, mores, or traditions that consequently require different teaching styles. Rather, it can be argued that *differences* among minority group and majority group children are more a function of the strata to which they belong, as opposed to their belonging to a particular ethnic or racial group. More specifically, many of the characteristics attributed to culturally different bilingual children characterize low socioeconomic class children, regardless of race or ethnicity. Middle- and upper-class bilingual, Mexican American children, for example, cannot be ascribed the aforementioned characteristics since they have become acculturated or assimilated into the dominant culture primarily due to their higher socioeconomic circumstances.

A major thesis in this chapter is that the success that bilingual children enjoy or do not enjoy is heavily influenced by the socioeconomic status (SES) of the family. If the SES of the Mexican American or Native American family is middle-class or higher, there is a higher probability of success in the schools and in society. If, on the other hand, bilingual children are of a lower SES, there is a high probability that they are not part of the dominant culture or mainstream and are, therefore, culturally different. Many children who are classified as culturally different and/or bilingual have the added burden of being emotionally disturbed or behaviorally disordered.

Emotionally Disturbed/Behaviorally Disordered Children

Definition

Personnel, including classroom teachers, counselors, administrators, and other special school personnel, e.g., nurses, social workers, school psychologists, working with students whose problems revolve around relatively profound "emotional problems" should be versed in a variety of ways of understanding these problems (Rhodes, 1970). Emotional disturbance is so complex that a vast repertoire of knowledge and skills are required of those working with emotionally disturbed or behaviorally disordered (ED/BD) children. The terms *emotionally disturbed* and *behaviorally disordered* are used synonymously in this chapter since both terms enjoy equal usage in the literature.

The incidence of ED/BD children in the school population is not fully known. Some authorities estimate that 2–7% of school-age children can be classified as ED/BD. Assuming that this is an acceptable estimate, let us proceed to characterize the typical ED/BD child even though "there is little agreement and great variability among the most widely accepted definitions and classifications of emotional disturbance" (Rhodes, 1970, p. 2).

Characteristics of the Emotionally Disturbed/Behaviorally Disordered

Within the educational setting, the emotionally disturbed/behaviorally disordered child is one whose behavior may be discordant in his or her relationship with others and/or whose academic achievement may be impaired due to inability to learn given the presented teaching techniques. The child's current behavior manifests either an extreme or a persistent failure to adapt and function intellectually, emotionally, and socially at a level commensurate with his or her chronological age.

One or more of the following possible referral characteristics may be acutely or persistently observed:[1]

Behavioral referral characteristics
1. Inability to learn when all other factors appear to be normal.
2. Inability to form and maintain satisfactory peer and teacher relationships.
3. Presence of physical complaints without accompanying physical condition.
4. Pervasive moods of unhappiness or depression.
5. Immature and inappropriate types of behavior or feelings under normal conditions.
6. Behavior that is disruptive in the regular educational program.

Physical referral characteristics
1. Gross or fine motor skills within the average range for the chronological age level.

Developmental speech and language referral characteristics
1. Language structure and vocabulary usually within the average range, although there may be accompanying organic or anatomical defects, marked delay in language development, an absence of language, or language behavior highly inappropriate to the environment.

Intellectual ability and school achievement referral characteristics
1. Intellectual level tends to be normally distributed; however, may score lower on an individual intelligence test than would be expected from general observation of the child.
2. Varying academic achievement.

Other school achievement referral characteristics have been suggested in a study by the California State Department of Education (1961). The conclusions of that study indicated ED/BD children as compared to normal children were (a) seriously below average in school achievement, (b) sent to the vice-principal more often for disciplinary action, (c) more often dropped from school or left school, (d) more often absent from school without excuses, (e) more frequently sent to the health department for illness, need of rest, or discomfort, (f) more often served by school counselors, (g) more often the subject of home calls by child welfare workers and attendance officers, (h) subject to more contacts with police, (i) more likely to be on probation, (j) found more frequently to commit penal and vehicle code violations, and (k) more frequently referred to local guidance clinics.

Problems of Emotionally Disturbed/Behaviorally Disordered Culturally Different Bilingual Mexican American Youth

Many of the problems of ED/BD culturally different, bilingual Mexican American children are probably representative of those of other ethnic minority bilingual children. Since Mexican American children come within the expertise of this author, the discussion will focus on bilingual Mexican American youth with the expectation that the reader can generalize to other ethnic minorities. Two major facets will be discussed: *social problems*—assimilation/acculturation to mainstream, language/communication skills, and discrimination—and *individual reactions*—hostile aggression and negativism, disruptiveness, high anxiety, withdrawal and regressive tendencies, depression and apathy, interpersonal problems, and fantasy. Each of these will be discussed separately.

Social Problems

There are some people who hold to the theory that many of the problems displayed by Mexican American ED/BD culturally different children could be resolved or minimized if the concept of cultural pluralism were followed and adhered to by our society and the school system (DeBlassie, 1976). Cultural pluralism assumes that individuals will not be expected to forgo their own cultural heritage or identity in order to exist and develop within the context of the broad American social system. Havighurst (1974) defines cultural pluralism as mutual appreciation and understanding of the various cultures in our society; cooperation of the various groups in the civic and economic institutions of society; peaceful coexistence of diverse life-styles, folkways, manners, language patterns, religious beliefs, and family structures; and autonomy for each group to work out its own social future as long as it does not interfere with the same right of other groups.

Inherent in the phenomenon of cultural pluralism, however, is the problem of acculturation or assimilation into the dominant culture. Acculturation (herein used synonymously with the term "assimilation") is usually defined as the relative degree to which individuals have moved towards adopting as their own the values and world view of the dominant society. A major problem in this regard is the dilemma faced by many culturally different Mexican American bilingual youth who are, in effect, torn between two worlds. The realities of life may force the bicultural bilingual youth to seriously consider the necessity to assimilate the dominant middle-class culture. Accompanying this stress is the pressure to conform to their own cultural values and mores. Rios and Ofman (1972) speak of this dilemma in terms of the Mexican American student:

> If the Chicano becomes like the Anglo he may become successful in "that" world, but the consequences are a shame of and loss of connectedness with his family. If he "sticks" with his rootedness, he becomes an alien in school and in the larger community. He becomes "caught" on the point between the idea of cultural pluralism and the press of the melting pot. (p. 254)

This ambivalence, brought about by intraethnic pressures, is complemented many times over by influences stemming from the dominant group members. More specifically, due to a number of barriers, including prejudice, discrimination, cultural distance, poverty, and disease, that limit to varying degrees the Mexican American's upward mobility, Mexican Americans have managed to attain different degrees of socioeconomic status and related degrees of acculturation. The lack of ability to assimilate based on both interethnic and intraethnic reasons has relegated a large number of Mexican American families to the culture of poverty. This frequently gives rise to feelings of hostility, disruptiveness, anxiety, withdrawal, depression, apathy, interpersonal relationship strains, and fantasy. These are individual reactions to being rejected, in general, by the dominant society.

Language problems and a lack of the communication skills necessary in attempting to function in the dominant culture present another series of problems for the culturally different Mexican American child. In this regard, Pollack and Menacker (1971) make the following observation:

> The Spanish spoken by Puerto Ricans and Mexican American students in this country is not afforded very much respect by most school personnel who work with them....The policy in most schools in the continental United States has been to exclude, wherever possible, the native language spoken by its students. There are still some schools where Puerto Rican and Mexican American children are punished for speaking Spanish. In many schools of the Southwest, there has been a long history of punitive measures taken to prevent Spanish from being spoken. (p. 43)

Nava (1970) indicates that the teaching of English in public schools has certain social and psychological consequences that many instructors and administrators may not fully realize. He states:

> The net effect of English language instruction is often destructive of the self-image and very ego of many Spanish-speaking children ....Efforts to suppress certain ethnic backgrounds cause long-lasting wounds and these result in social maladjustment and under-achievement. These outward manifestations frustrate teachers. Moreover, these negative results cause the loss to society of many thousands of potentially highly productive individuals.... A sophisticated person would say that public schools damage the self-image they bring to school. (p. 126)

The implications of the language barrier for the Mexican American youth are attested to by Browning and McLemore (1964):

> Many Spanish-surname children are put at a major disadvantage in their schooling because they literally have no real command of any language. Even their knowledge of Spanish often is limited to the spoken word, for they are not taught by their parents either to read or write it. The children generally have only a rudimentary knowledge of English, the language of instruction in the public school ....As a consequence, it is no wonder that their performance in school often is poor and retarded from the very beginning. Further, as a consequence, their sense of inferiority with respect to their Anglo classmates tends to widen rather than diminish over time. (p. 64)

It would seem quite obvious that language problems and a lack of communication skills could become real obstacles in culturally different bilingual youth functioning with a minimal degree of proficiency in a curriculum that is based on the needs of the dominant culture rather than on the needs of these youth. Again, the frustrations accompanying the detriments in language skills result in many individual behavior reactions.

The discrimination suffered by culturally different bilingual Mexican American youth, which results in specific behavior reactions, seems to be well documented. Burma (1970), for example, indicates that many Mexican Americans have been subjected to personal prejudice in social situations and to stereotyping and to discrimination in occupations, housing, education, and political activity. He lists, furthermore, a number of responses (negative, positive, or neutral) to prejudice and discrimination by Mexican Americans, many made by youth. Some of the more negative responses exhibited by Mexican Americans are: (a) withdraw deep into the Chicano community and avoid all possible contacts with Anglos, (b) use discrimination as an excuse for not trying to achieve, (c) demonstrate nonviolent physical reactions as in "sit-ins" or participate in boycotts, riots, looting, selective vandalism, or personal physical violence, or (d) hold prejudice against the Mexican American group (self-hatred), or against Anglos, Jews, Blacks, or any other minority.

The United States Commission on Civil Rights (1970) issued a report on the treatment of Mexican Americans in terms of law enforcement. A prevalence of complaints was found about the use of excessive and discriminating force by law officers dealing with Mexican Americans in various parts of the Southwest. Many complaints alleged discriminatory treatment of Mexican American juveniles by law enforcement officers. Even today, the news media are replete with reports documenting such behavior on the part of some law enforcement agencies toward Mexican American youth.

Stoddard (1973) highlights the type of discrimination that Mexican Americans have suffered in terms of ethnicity. In the past, negative status has been bestowed upon Mexican Americans by the dominant Anglo Americans based on the ethnocentric idea that Caucasian Americans are superior to non-Caucasian Americans. To rid themselves of the inferior status accorded by Anglos, Mexican Americans tend to reject either their ethnic ancestry or the dominant society. In recent years, Stoddard argues, the latter alternative has become increasingly popular.

Mexican American youth are affected not only by the negative status accorded by many Anglos, but by skin color as well (Stoddard, 1973). An important implication here for Mexican American ED/BD children is that once the idea that light skin is more desirable than dark skin is internalized, a negative attitude begins to develop toward the self, an intense self-hatred that produces feelings of inadequacy and inferiority.

Individual Reactions

One can surmise only that the *social problems* (acculturation, communication skills, and discrimination) referred to above naturally lead to various individual reactions, many of which fit the characteristics of the ED/BD Mexican American child. One effect of social problems is that many bilingual, culturally different Mexican American children do become emotionally disturbed or behaviorally disordered. One type of individual reaction that has developed in ED/BD Mexican American children is hostile aggression and/or negativism. This type of reaction is evidenced in negative behavior directed toward teachers (especially non-Mexican American teachers), classmates, and authority figures. Hostile aggression is typically expressed as anger and frustration, fighting, and other destructive behaviors. ED/BD children also bully their peers and gang up against teachers, coaches, administrators, and others, to run rampant if high enough in numbers to feel confident enough to be destructive.

Disruptiveness is a second type of behavior engaged in by ED/BD Mexican American children. The most easily identified ED/BD students are the disruptive ones. These students do not follow directions, do not pursue a task long enough to complete it, and seem to be unable to cooperate with either peers or adults. Children displaying these behaviors are difficult to ignore in a classroom; therefore, they are very likely to be referred for counseling and related services.

Although anxiety is a normal part of life, *high* anxiety is often a symptom of ED/BD Mexican American children. Despert (1970) uses the term *neurotic anxiety* to describe the magnitude of this anxiety. Highly anxious children sometimes attempt to deal with this anxiety by seeking repeated exposures to dangerous situations, either in actuality or in fantasy. ED/BD Mexican American children may jump from extremely high places, attempt to cross streets in heavily congested traffic, or engage in "macho" types of superfeats.

The Mexican American ED/BD child's inability to cope may also be manifested in varying degrees of depression and apathy. Such children exhibit depression by remaining generally unhappy or downtrodden even in situations most other children enjoy. For example, when they are encouraged to attend school celebrations for sports victories, they would not be capable of sharing in the good feeling of being victorious. Apathetic behavior involves a type of lethargic reaction seemingly conveying a lack of interest or concern or displaying little or no feeling or emotion.

Withdrawal and regressive behaviors constitute another type of individual reaction of ED/BD children. Withdrawal behaviors may range from physical/social isolation to autistic behavior in which the child is noncommunicative, detached from reality, and pathologically impaired. Regressive behavior is a type of reaction in which the child engages in behaviors more appropriate to earlier stages of development. These include thumbsucking, crying, whining, infantile speech, and bedwetting. These behaviors, not acceptable to many Mexican American parents, are sometimes physically punished. Peers frequently tease and make fun of children manifesting these behaviors. These children may have extreme difficulty in forming relationships. Even less severely disabled students often have difficulty establishing or maintaining satisfactory interpersonal relationships with their teachers or peers. This can lead to children's indulgence in fantasy to meet their social needs. Withdrawal into fantasy typically involves daydreaming on the part of the child in an attempt to escape from the world of reality and gratifies desires in fantasy achievements.

Gearheart and Weishahn (1976) discuss this phenomenon under the category of *withdrawal into fantasy*: "The isolate in the class, the one who shuns involvement with peers or teachers, is sometimes far more troubled and in greater need of assistance than the aggressive child. This child does not express antagonism toward authority and therefore may be ignored as the teacher exerts every effort toward finding help for the aggressive child" (p. 146).

The various individual reactions can be expected in various degrees in almost all children. It is, however, the unusual frequency or intensity that signals that the child needs help (Gearheart and Weishahn, 1976). Reinert (1976) suggests these behaviors are exhibited "in the wrong places, at the wrong time, in the presence of the wrong people, and to an inappropriate degree" (p. 44).

Intervention and Therapeutic Strategies

Various strategies have been suggested and used by teachers and therapists in working with emotionally disturbed/ behavior disordered children. There is, however, a dearth of information in the research literature on virtually all culturally different ED/ BD bilingual children, and specifically on the Mexican American ED/ BD bilingual child. This writer has searched the literature for such information and has failed to find any studies in this area. The following intervention and therapeutic strategies represent, therefore, a distillate of the writer's own experiences, discussions with personnel who work with ED/ BD children, and literature on strategies for ED/ BD children that can be used with Mexican American children and perhaps generalized and adapted for other bilingual bicultural children with similar backgrounds.

The Relationship Model

Relationship counseling, as the label implies, leans heavily on the establishment of a good interpersonal relationship between the teacher, or counselor, and the ED/ BD child. According to DeBlassie and Lebsock (1979), it also presupposes that (a) ED/ BD children are worthy of dignity and respect; (b) with the help of the counselor, or teacher, ED/ BD children are capable of solving their problems and accepting responsibility for future behavior within the limitations of their physical and/ or emotional attributes; (c) the helper provides a set of core conditions including empathy, unconditional positive regard, acceptance, congruence (an authentic or genuine personal image), and openness, which will enable the ED/ BD child to experience personal growth, insight, and behavioral changes leading to a more content, well adjusted life; (d) ED/ BD children are able to communicate and/ or interact verbally, or through play media, with the counselor, or teacher, in such a way that positive behavioral changes can occur; and (e) the helper and the counselor establish an environment of mutual respect, open and honest communication, permissiveness with limits placed on physical violence, confidentiality, nonjudgment, and sensitive relationships characterized by flexible interaction. Some counselors or teachers might find this type of counseling ineffective with ED/ BD children, especially bilingual children who need a more directive, counselor-lead, tangible type of counseling.

Experience has proven that relationship counseling can be very effective, especially with ED/ BD children. It is felt that one of the things that can be accomplished through relationship counseling is the establishing of trust on the part of children who are starving in the area of interpersonal skills. ED/BD Mexican American children can especially benefit from this approach which focuses on helping children feel worthwhile, important, and capable of achieving some degree of academic and interpersonal success.

Behavior Modification

Behavior modification as a technique in teaching and counseling has also been found to be effective in working with ED/BD children. In this approach to teaching or counseling, instead of asking "why" children behave as they do or attempting to relate their problems to "how" the central nervous system is functioning, the teacher or counselor asks simply "what" behaviors the children exhibit that interfere with learning or functioning. For instance, this strategy considers the interfering behaviors the ED/ BD child exhibits in the classroom as *learned* behaviors. The teacher or counselor using this strategy is also more concerned with the disadvantages and negative consequences inherent in allowing the child to maintain maladaptive behavior rather than in the long-standing controversy over whether symptom removal constitutes a cure or a mere masking of the real problem (Hewett, 1968).

Harshman (1974) presents a few elementary steps based on behavior modification techniques which are effective for changing behavior. These steps, intended primarily for the classroom teacher, are readily applicable to counseling situations involving ED/ BD Mexican American children: (a) what behaviors are undesirable for each time and place must be ascertained, (b) what behavior the teacher wishes the child to substitute for the self-defeating response should be established, (c) the task should then be cut into small increments of gain so that the child can build upon successes rather than be set in motion in a series of failures, (d) the teacher should know the child well enough to have some idea of what constitutes rewards. To do this will require extensive observation of the child in a variety of settings and at different times of day, and (e) the child should be reinforced immediately when the desired task has been performed.

What is really happening in this five-fold process, according to Harshman, is that the child is learning new behaviors that the teacher deems crucial to satisfy social, academic, and personal requirements. The child at the same time is unlearning certain behaviors the teacher finds undesirable and the child has found to lead to unpleasant consequences. The end result turns out to be a modification of the child's behavior patterns. It is important to stress that these steps work so well with ED/BD children that such procedures are effective both in individual and group teaching or counseling situations. Finally, it should be realized that behavior modification techniques are characterized by at least two elements: the focus on overt, observable behavior and the application of concepts drawn from learning theory.

It is often apparent that rational decisions are sometimes not made by ED/BD children because they may not have the appropriate verbal or reflective abilities necessary. If the counseling situation is limited to verbal expression, the behavior change may not result. A behavioral approach to teaching or counseling may help the teacher or counselor accomplish the desired behavioral changes in the child. The children are rewarded for what they actually do, not for verbalizing their behaviors. The behaviors to be reinforced must be specifically defined. When this approach is taken, the child is less likely to meet with failure in the classroom situation and the teacher is less likely to think the child is lacking in readiness. When using this approach, teachers must think of themselves as behavior engineers, not only as feeling reflectors. This method works best when counselors or their trainees can continue the reward system outside the classroom situation.

The Ecological Model

The latest trends in personality theory research stress the interdependence of the individual and environment. Rhodes (1970) says that "The fact of reciprocity between environment and either growth and development or behavior strongly suggests a newly emerging approach to emotional disturbance which should be discussed.... This is the ecological approach...the ecological approach suggests a bridge of conceptions and actions between the more established models" (p. 41). According to Rhodes, the following are the major elements of the ecological model: (a) modifying the child's environment to ensure a change in behavior, (b) emotional disturbance arising in interaction of the individual with various significant others, (c) problem of emotional disturbance lying in the capacity of "strange," different, or custom-violating characteristics that release collective agitation in the surrounding environmental "field" or microcommunity. Rhodes concludes his discussion of using the ecological model with emotionally disturbed children by suggesting four types of interventions: (a) crisis intervention, (b) community liaison, (c) group dynamic approach, and (d) curricular adaptation.

The three models mentioned above each has its unique merits when used with ED/BD children. Experience has lead the writer to favor the ecological model for working with bilingual ED/BD Mexican American children and, probably, other bilingual children. Several reasons are offered for this opinion. If the thesis that culturally different bilingual ED/BD children are a product of their environment, a major causal effect, it would seem logical that the environment warrants being modified as a means of enhancing positive growth on the part of these children.

Secondly, if "strange," different, or custom-violating characteristics have the capacity of releasing collective agitation in the surrounding environment, it would seem that the ecological model attempts to minimize such factors and to modify the environment in such a way that ED/BD children are not violated in terms of their customs, traditions, language, or mores.

Lastly, the ecological model seems to stress the idea that emotional disturbance lies in the interaction between the individual and various significant others in the environmental settings. "Significant others" play a major role in influencing the ED/BD bilingual child's life. Factors such as respect for authority, the highly knit nuclear family, and the strong extended family that can be capitalized by school personnel working with ED/BD children within the context of the family, the home, and the neighborhood.

Notes

[1]From *A Plan for the Delivery of Special Education Services in New Mexico—Part III: Special Education Regulations—1975* and used with permission of Eli S. Gutierrez, Director, Division of Special Education, Department of Education, Santa Fe, New Mexico. This list is representative of those in other sources.

References

Browning, H.L., and McLemore, S.O.: *A Statistical Profile of the Spanish-surname Population of Texas.* Austin, Bureau of Business Research, 1964.

Burma, J.: *Mexican-Americans in the United States: A Reader.* Cambridge, Schenkman, 1970.

California State Department of Education: *The Education of Emotionally Handicapped Children.* Sacramento, State Department of Education, 1961.

DeBlassie, R.R.: *Counseling with Mexican American Youth: Preconceptions and Processes.* Austin, Learning Concepts, 1976.

DeBlassie, R.R., and Lebsock, M.J.: Counseling with handicapped children. *Elementary School Guidance and Counseling,* 1979.

Despert, J.: *The Emotionally Disturbed Child.* Garden City, Anchor, 1970.

Gearheart, B.R., and Weishahn, M.W.: *The Handicapped Child in the Regular Classroom*. St. Louis, C.V. Mosby, 1976.

Gordon, J.E.: Counseling the disadvantaged youth. In Ames, W.E., and Grambs, J.D. (Eds.): *Counseling the Disadvantaged Youth*. Englewood Cliffs, Prentice-Hall, 1968.

Harshman, H.W.: Behavior modification with emotionally disturbed children. In Saunders, T. (Ed.): *Approaches with Emotionally Disturbed Children*. Hickesville, Exposition, 1974.

Havighurst, R.J.: The American Indian: From assimilation to cultural pluralism. *Educational Leadership, 31*:585–589, 1974.

Hewett, F.M. (Ed.): *The Emotionally Disturbed Child in the Classroom*. Boston, Allyn and Bacon, 1968.

Johnson, K.R.: *Teaching the Culturally Disadvantaged: A Rationale Approach*. Chicago, Science Research Associates, 1970.

Nava, J.: Cultural background and barriers that affect learning by Spanish-speaking children. In Burma, J.H. (Ed.): *Mexican-Americans in the United States: A Reader*. Cambridge, Schenkman, 1970.

Pollack, E.W., and Menacker, J.: *Spanish-speaking Students and Guidance*. New York, Houghton Mifflin, 1971.

Reinert, H.R.: *Children in Conflict: Educational Strategies*. St. Louis, C.V. Mosby, 1976.

Riessman, F.: The overlooked positives of disadvantaged groups. *J Negro Education, 16*:225–231, 1964.

Rhodes, W.C.: *The Emotionally Disturbed Student and Guidance*. New York, Houghton Mifflin, 1970.

Rios, R., and Ofman, W.: The Chicano, counseling, and reality. In Brown, D., and Srebalus, D.J. (Eds.): *Contemporary Guidance Concepts and Practices*. Dubuque, William C. Brown, 1972.

Stoddard, E.: *Mexican Americans*. New York, Random, 1973.

United States Commission on Civil Rights: *Teachers and Students: Differences in Teacher Interaction with Mexican American and Anglo Students*. Washington, D.C., U.S. Government Printing Office, 1970.

15

Educating the Talented Child in a Pluralistic Society

Philip A. Perrone
Narciso Alemán

Contemporary definitions of exceptional intellect, creativity, and talent among children and adolescents stem from strongly stated opinions, hypothetical constructs or theories, and statistical studies. At the Guidance Institute for Talented Students at the University of Wisconsin, over 20 years of observation and analysis of talented children and adolescents into their adult years, supplemented by parent and teacher observations, have led to the identification of four general talent areas. Inherent in the definition of talent is that an individual be compared to his or her peers both within a community and on a national scale. The following are the four talent areas:

1. Rapid accumulation and assimilation of existing knowledge, with variations according to various fields of study.
2. Effective leadership, which includes observation, planning, organization, and implementation of a plan.
3. Interpersonal sensitivity, sometimes referred to as empathy, requiring the understanding of both verbal and nonverbal communication of others.
4. Performance in the arts, music, drama, and athletics.

Individuals may be talented in more than one area and in more than one field within any of these four areas. An individual may demonstrate varying degrees of originality or creativity depending upon environmental support, opportunity, and diversity of stimuli. Although some people are more efficient and effective in their ability to receive, process, and communicate, a supportive environment is considered critical for any talent to be realized. Neither contemporary research nor historical analysis demonstrates direct relationship between eminence and social class or heritability.

Historical analyses of eminent persons from 500 BC through 1900 AD by Simonton (1975) suggest that certain patterns, trends, and circumstances are related to attaining eminence in various fields. Using path-analysis and factor analysis, Simonton identified two major types of eminent creators: *discursive* (including fields such as science, philosophy, literature, and music) and *presentational* (including fields like painting, sculpture, and architecture). Eminent philosophers and artists were found to have grown up and been most productive in relatively stable social systems or social eras that accommodated many different points of view. Futhermore, there is an absence of powerful role models in the development of eminent philosophers and artists, although lesser thinkers and musicians seemingly produce better if they have mentors.

Another noteworthy finding from historical and contemporary analyses is that sensitivity, integration, and creation are integral elements in achieving eminence or mastery in the arts. Philosophy, literature, and the arts flourish where diversity of thought exists, although these areas require a relatively stable government or social system in order to maximize individual accomplishments. Education is related to creative eminence up to a point; however, high levels of education seemingly stifle creativity. This curvilinear relationship is similar to the relationship found between tested intelligence and measures of creativity reported by Wallach and Kogan (1965). Amount of education was found to be unrelated to leadership, although leaders were found to be knowledgeable and versatile.

Historical analysis of Nobel Prize winners and nominees indicates that creative and productive eminence does not adhere to geographical or linguistic boundaries. Eminence in literature and the promotion of peace are truly international. The Nobel Prizes awarded in the sciences, however, suggest that the concentration of a country's resources on selected fields can lead to an increased attainment of Nobel Prizes. For example, Russia and the United States have become dominant in producing discoveries in physics and medicine. Increasingly, scientific mastery requires a longer incubation period prior to any productive or creative effort.

Historical analyses have not been made of ethnic and cultural characteristics of such eminent people as Hammurabi, Tlacaelel I, Atahualpa, Simon Bolivar, Don Benito Juarez, and Don Pedro Albizu Campos. Cursory knowledge of the accomplishments of such individuals readily attests to the monumental impact of their acts upon the course of human life and history. What factors formed their development, perspective, or their mission? Each of these people, as have other prominent figures, faced and met the challenge of a recognized social need. Where does one find those individuals with the potential to become artists, leaders, and scientists? Do these individuals just emerge as a result of sheer drive and raw talent, or can society create environments where thousands of persons capable of making contributions to the health and welfare of society will emerge on the scene?

In working with those ethnic and cultural groups in the United States that have been largely denied access to education and employment opportunities, one becomes aware that these groups have been able to survive through the creation and development of semiisolated alternative cultures. Even though attempts have begun to offset cultural isolation, many of the values, practices, and customs of these groups still remain. It is these values, traditions, and practices that are the essence of cultural identity but in turn, must be translated to eventually merge with the dominant culture if all members of society are to benefit from a true melding and build upon cultural diversity.

In the quest to merge the ethnic and cultural groups, the United States has largely ignored and wasted the values, traditions, and customs of these minorities. Yet it is these same qualities that can now help the United States overcome a massive waste of both natural and human resources. Where is the diversity of ideas, opinions, perspectives, and values that will forge a philosophy of survival, unity, brotherhood, and cooperation? It may be largely in the people who have been relegated to the performance of menial tasks and who have become scapegoats to explain the crises that American society faces.

It seems more reasonable that the United States, and other pluralistic societies with one predominant culture, present a variety of challenges in defining and nurturing the talented among all subcultures. The Guidance Institute for Talented Students has begun to confront the issues involved in understanding multicultural giftedness. This chapter is an attempt to share some of what has been learned.

Issues in the Study of Multicultural Giftedness

Where does one begin? As in any struggle, one begins with the first step. There is a paucity of research in the area of multicultural giftedness; thus, intuitive knowledge and experience become the initial guides. Accumulated experience can provide a growing body of knowledge that will eventually be quantifiable and verifiable.

The Institute initially relied on intuition for the identification and selection of talented students from several ethnic and cultural groups. Currently, it is seeking to document and communicate to educators the talents identified that should be enhanced. Various identification procedures are being tried, adapted, reevaluated, and retested. Individual case studies, continual parental involvement, and the guidance of community support committees for each minority group all provide counsel for planning and implementation. These resources help formulate the proper questions and point to the proper direction for inquiry. At this time it is not possible for the Institute to operate from an advanced, highly developed, and sophisticated model, but rather it attempts to catch up on years of neglect and generations of failing to focus on multicultural giftedness.

Several complex questions have presented themselves during the initial efforts of the Institute. Some deal with direction, rapidity, degree of assimilation, and acculturation of the students identified. Other concerns have to do with economic and home environment of the children identified. These concerns become important in view of the support, encouragement, and understanding these children need at home.

> There is the case of two talented Hispanic children whose mother works as a subprofessional and has the opportunity to become professional by completing her academic degree. The father, a tannery worker, who may or may not be literate, senses, on the one hand, the reliance of the children upon the mother for support and assistance on school work yet, on the other hand, feels excluded and threatened by this situation, an especially acute problem in view of the traditional role of the father in Mexican culture. At issue for the educator is how to continue working with the children and the mother while dealing effectively with the concerns of the father.

Another overriding problem affecting the Institute's ethnic and cultural projects is the lack of direction and substance in bilingual education. There is confusion regarding what is bicultural or bilingual and what educational efforts should be implemented in these areas. The Institute does not have the resources to address these complex problems. Yet these problems must be addressed because they affect the project objectives of identifying and educating talented children in a pluralistic society. Definitions of multilingualism and multiculturalism are important when planning discussions with community representatives of each ethnic and cultural group, as well as when the programing phase of the project begins. For example, development of curricula, instructional materials, and methods, becomes a salient issue related to the complex problems inherent in defining bilingual education.

Another issue to be addressed is academic achievement orientation among pupils from different subcultures. Banks, McQuater, and Hubbard (1978) have critiqued and summarized research regarding divergent patterns of achievement among Anglos and Blacks. Similar analyses have not been conducted regarding Mexican American, Puerto Rican, and Native American populations' achievement, but the conclusions of Banks et al. seem applicable for any child who is not a middle-class Anglo. For example, it is noted that individuals whose early experiences have occurred within a distinct subculture are likely to develop patterns of interest and activities different from interests and favored activities of the larger culture. Children from subcultures must learn the interests and values of the dominant culture, which the schools promote, as well as those of their primary reference group. Moreover, minority children must learn how to ameliorate the differences or cope with the stress that arises from living in an environment with conflicting interests and values.

Research has demonstrated that children from minority cultures judge their ability and effort as less important than luck in explaining their scholastic success. Females are more likely than males to attribute failure to their inability and attribute their success to luck (Nichols, 1975). These findings suggest minority students, females in particular, may perform in the classroom below their abilities because they believe success is beyond their control or because they lack the ability to succeed.

An additional problem area is the need for educators to share the culture of the minority children they teach. The research in this area is equivocal, but the issue still warrants consideration. For example, in controlled experiments Banks et al. (1978) showed that "approval" by Black experimenters affected performance of Black pupils more favorably than "approval" by Anglo experimenters. Furthermore, Banks, Stitl, Curtis, and McQuater (1977) suggest that when a Black child's initial interest toward a task is positive, the support of an Anglo teacher can evoke low interest in achievement. Conversely, Black students receiving support from Black teachers were found to maintain their level of achievement interest. Apparently children from the Black subculture and possibly from other minority subcultures have learned not to trust Anglos who are supportive—"it's a trick." On the other hand, the minority child's hostility or apathy may be expected by the teacher and may even serve to reinforce the child's achievement motivation, so that the child may learn in spite of, or to spite, the Anglo teacher.

The Talented Child in a Pluralistic Society

At the Institute, it has been observed that gifted children from minority cultures possess talents valued and nurtured within their own culture, but these talents frequently go unrecognized in school. In the home, the child's behavior may be valued, nurtured, and rewarded; in the school, the child may be ignored or treated as a misfit. Being ignored and rejected creates the groundwork for eventual segregation from the educational, economic, and political opportunities of the majority culture. In addressing these problems, the Foundation for Exceptional Children in 1974 hosted a conference entitled *Talent Delayed—Talent Denied: The Culturally Different Gifted Child* (Gallagher, 1974). The conferees agreed that the definition of gifted was too narrow and that there were a host of other barriers to action for culturally different gifted children. These consensual barriers included various aspects of the curriculum, system procedures, and, most important, the attitudes and values of decision-makers.

As a first step in broadening the definition of giftedness, staff at the Institute conferred with educational leaders, spiritual leaders, family members, and students representing four cultures: Native Americans, Mexican Americans, Puerto Ricans, and a Bilialian religious group of Afro-Americans with a great commitment to their own educational system. A three-day meeting was held separately with each of these cultural groups for the purpose of delineating the valued and exceptional behaviors within each culture. The following reports represent concerns of specific members within each minority culture and do not necessarily represent the concerns or values of any minority culture in general.

Questions may arise concerning the need to have two separate approaches for the Spanish-speaking populations, i.e., one approach for Mexican American students and another for Puerto Rican students. This division of the two Hispanic groups was done because the concerns and values of the cultural representatives clearly supported the need to differentiate between Mexican American and Puerto Rican giftedness. In this first year, the Institute's attempt to substantiate or modify these general guidelines has been based upon further data obtained from the children, their families, and teachers. A synthesis of the reported values as they relate to a definition of giftedness within each culture follows.

Puerto Rican

Some values that are an integral part of the Puerto Rican culture include respect for the land, the culture, and the elders. Before the 1950s, life was tied to survival. This preoccupation with survival, related to the land and its crops, was altered for youth after the 1950s and immigration to the mainland. Curriculum materials should make note of the various conditions that reflect present socioeconomic reality, such as single parent families, economic needs, and unemployment. Puerto Rican children in the United States must be prepared for the harshness of life, such as discrimination, substance abuse, and crime.

The following are additional contradictions between the Puerto Rican culture and the dominant middle-class Anglo culture: a child's talent or giftedness may not be readily evident because individualism, assertiveness, and competition are not valued. Being respectful and behaving properly is valued as much if not more than acting knowledgeably. In Spanish, there are formal and informal pronouns and verb conjugations used to address elders or strangers. Difficulty in making the English transition when addressing teachers may cause the child to be hesitant or unconfident. Competition within the family, or with one's peers, is not valued; thus, achievement at the expense of others will most likely be avoided. There may also be a differentiation of responsibilities at home based on sex roles incompatible with responsibilities and expectations at school, again causing hesitancy or conflict that will further mask a child's talent. Lastly, children have learned to think and decide by seeking counsel of their family rather than acting independently. For the Puerto Rican child, the teacher must be sensitive to how all the above will influence and effect manifestation of the child's talent.

Mexican American

Mexican Americans find themselves in a complex dilemma because they are caught between two dominant cultures; the United States consumerism and the traditional Mexican culture of their forefathers which stresses cooperation and conservation. Mexican people are related more closely to the American Indian culture and value cooperativeness more than individualism. *[handwritten: NOT TRUE! Note that, anglos make much better soldiers - aunt following orders]*
Mexican families develop respect for elders, the law, and authority. While these traits are beneficial within the cultural context of the Mexican community and the extended family, they present a vulnerability when submerged in American culture. Moreover, such attitudes lend themselves to manipulation by others in the school system. The traits of respect for elders, law, and authority place the Mexican American child in a position of expectant cooperation, obedience, and group-direction, rather than one of *[handwritten: or one of selfish ego-mania]* individual initiative, self-direction, or self-indulgence. In contrast, the design of the school system values individual competition and, within limits, encourages and rewards self-initiative. This presents a contradiction for the Mexican American child, who is expected, in one environment (the home), to be patient, unobtrusive, cooperative, and await direction or instructions *[handwritten: or stab friends in the back]* and, in the other (the school), is expected to compete, even against his or her own friends, and have self-initiative.

Giftedness among these children is most easily identifiable in language manipulation. Mexican American children who speak both Spanish and English may demonstrate a facility to manipulate both languages in order to convey more subtle and finer meanings in their expressions. A specific characteristic of this linguistic talent is the use of *calo*, a street language spoken by young people. *Calo* may be interspersed with Anglicized Spanish words or vice versa. Another talent may be the creation of entirely new words using both languages in new combinations. Although children who ask a great many questions are sometimes considered gifted, questions are usually discouraged by overworked parents, especially as it becomes increasingly difficult to answer them.

Bilalian Gifted (Afro-American)

A definition of giftedness within the Bilalian culture is closely related to religious values. The Basic Cardinal Virtues taught by Imam Wallace D.

Muhammad are faith, prudence, temperance, and fortitude. In addition, Brother Muhammad states that one's attitude is comprised of knowing, feeling, and behaving. Other teachings include the notion of four motivating factors of development that constitute the environment: culture, business, economics, and education. Parents are the ones who teach the children their relationship to authority. Therefore, the conditions of rearing have a basically important effect upon how children view legitimate authority and authority figures.

The primary goal of the program for children from a Bilalian culture is to develop more effective means and strategies in order to create a better environment for learning and bringing together the parent, the student, and the teacher. The term *trust* is more important than *gifted* or *talented* in that these students have trusts from Almighty God, Allah; each child is entrusted with some talent or gift. The Institute's task is to identify these entrustments, provide means for their development, and generalize from these results for the benefit of all children.

Native Americans

Native Americans also find themselves caught between the school's value of independence and the home and community value of interdependence of all living things and natural matter. The American society forces upon the Native American a belief in independence. Schools reinforce the importance of independence in many ways, including classroom seating arrangements. Pupils are seated behind each other so that all one sees is the back of one's peers, and the only face is that of the teacher. Such a seating arrangement reinforces independence from peers and dependence on the teacher. In contrast, according to American Indian values, everyone would be seated in a circle so that each other's face could be seen and interdependence encouraged.

Another basic value is collective decision-making. The American Indian has for thousands of years decided matters collectively and through discussion. In the United States, through representative government, there has been a negation of the traditional value of discussing matters until everyone has voiced an opinion and there is no more discussion.

The Menominee, Ojibwa, Oneida, Chippewa, and other tribes make up the Woodland Tribes indigenous to Wisconsin. The expansion of commercial interests of corporations and population settlements has limited and, in many instances, curtailed the lands which once were designated as reservations for these tribes. The lack of jobs, future, and opportunity has forced many of these Indians to migrate to the urban areas of Wisconsin. Many of these tribal members return to the reservation to maintain their tribal status, but these trips become more and more infrequent for the young Indian who has grown up and lived in the urban area. Economic conditions also affect familial relationships, tribal traditions, and customs. In addition, the youth are bombarded by the mass culture of the United States consumerist society.

The loss of language is one of the major problems faced by the adults and, consequently, the youth. Yet, the manifestation of talent, creativity, and leadership, in the traditional sense of the Indian, is via language. As part of the value of language skills, many tribes interviewed place a high value on a sense of humor. One does not expect a sense of humor to be valued by the American Indian stereotype immortalized by the cinematography industry.

Other Native American values are in relationship to nature. They have Earth, the best teacher, as their instructor. It is necessary to have a personal relationship with Earth Mother. High value is placed on one's attitude toward the environment. If one accepts Earth as Mother and walks upon her, then it follows that one must do so with a great deal of care and caution.

Red Power is the sum of all things and interactions. Red Power does not mean only Indian power. Red Power is Love. Red Power is for all peoples. The blood of all people is red. The love of all people is red. Love is the basis for all interaction and therefore of teaching.

Guidelines for Identification and Educational Programing of Talented Students

Identifying students for gifted and talented programs is a difficult and complex task. Paradoxically, many schools begin gifted programs by attempting identification before seriously considering program objectives. However, once selection occurs, many program goals are necessarily predetermined. After consulting with over 100 school systems that have established gifted programs during the past 20 years, failure to establish program goals before identifying pupils was found to be the single greatest obstacle to implementing a successful program. Some critical issues include the relationship of identification criteria and program objectives, selection procedures, and involvement. Following is a two-phase guideline for developing a program for talented students.

Phase I
1. Identify a coordinator.
2. Appoint a Parent Advisory Committee and a Professional Steering Committee.
3. Develop philosophy, goals, and objectives.
4. Design a program with differentiated content, techniques, materials, and learning environments consistent with philosophy, goals, and objectives.

5. Begin workshops and in-service meetings with administrators, teachers, and other school personnel.
6. Identify teachers of the gifted and talented.
7. Design assessment schedule and identify procedures to be used.
8. Begin regular staff meetings.
9. Orient parents and students to program goals and student needs.
10. Collect and develop relevant curricular materials.
11. Plan pre- and postevaluation materials for the program.

Phase II

1. Organize a Community Resource (person-experiences) Catalogue.
2. Designate resource centers and a resource person at each school.
3. Develop case conference materials and procedures so students can be identified and programmed according to their educational needs.
4. Continue regular public dissemination of information.
5. Meet regularly with parents of the gifted and talented students.
6. Continue screening new arrivals in the district.
7. Prepare a written curriculum (to be done by the curriculum personnel and teachers of gifted and talented classes).

The establishment of goals and objectives for ethnic and cultural talent projects does not appear to be a major problem; the need is so great that any direction, effort, or suggestion is an improvement over the present void. Thus, it is not a question of direction, but a question of which void does one try to fill first? How many resources are available to accomplish the task? What is the substance that will be used to fill these voids? How does one positively encourage and facilitate learning among children being identified? How does one program for these students, while keeping them with their peers so they may serve as an example? Which materials need to be developed first? What will be the best documenting process that can be made accessible to others? How can an educational system, which has denied the validity of these people, be changed in a way that will not be threatening?

In an attempt to begin somewhere, the Institute has identified reading skills as basic to accomplishment in all other subjects. Math and science are secondary subjects that need attention. These reading programs need to be cultural, historical, economical, and social in content, so that the participating students, teachers, parents, and counselors can learn from the process.

Defining Program Objectives

There are three major issues that must be resolved when objectives are set and students identified: (a) what can be done, (b) for how many students, and (c) how long will it take? Programing is likely to be directed at enrichment, balance of skill areas, psychological needs, or some combination of these. It should be decided whether to program for overlapping needs of many students or to set goals based on the needs of individual students. A program oriented toward in-depth individual assessment and individualized programing will be capable of serving fewer students than one with a broader orientation.

The question of how long it will take to meet program objectives for a particular student must take into consideration at what point the initial intervention occurs and the criteria used to determine when objectives have been achieved. The age of students at the time of selection should be a function of program objectives and availability of resources. It is also important to consider the extent of commitment to those selected as they progress through the higher levels of education. For example, if the decision has been made to begin by selecting children in kindergarten through third grades, will the commitment end in third grade? Will next year's gifted kindergarten children be included? Should children participate for varying lengths of time?

Defining Selection Criteria

Probably the most difficult and controversial task is defining the criteria for the selection of students. In essence, determining selection criteria is the same as defining *giftedness*, because those selected will be known as gifted. There is not one, or even ten, universally accepted definitions of giftedness. Nonetheless, all subjective and intuitive hunches people have, and the differing biases of what kinds of behavior constitute giftedness, must be reduced to a set of observable and measurable traits by which students will be selected.

The selection process is further complicated because usually more students seem to fit the definition than can be served. Criteria must therefore be narrowed or specified sufficiently in order to be useful in finally rendering only the number of students the program has been designed to serve. There is no foolproof method by which the best possible selection can be made or criteria defined. A schema is needed for weighing factors relative to one another.

Whatever tools are used for selection, one rule of thumb is applied. Do not include procedures than cannot be readily observed or measured with some degree of reliability. While it has been noted that it is desirable to include many different kinds of data, there is also the risk of having too much data. Without such a schema it can be very difficult to make sense of large amounts of information. It is advisable to determine the relative importance of data before any information about students is gathered. One way of doing this is to construct tiers or hierarchies of data to be used in successive rounds for eliminating candidates. Such an approach can also aid in developing a plan for using data before student information is obtained. These procedures will serve as a restraint against gathering data that cannot be used.

Individualized Assessment

How are educators to determine, for each student, what strengths require encouragement, additional stimuli, and positive reinforcement, and what weaknesses may demand supplemental practice? If the goal is to facilitate development that uses as much potential as possible and considers the total person, e.g., affective as well as cognitive, personal as well as social, process as well as product development, then educators must be willing to recognize diversity of needs between and within individuals in order to program adequately. This suggests a need for comprehensive assessment activities. A case study approach seems essential in assessing talented students. Clearly there are a great many variables that are important to understand regarding each student's strengths and weaknesses, interests, and learning style. Educators need to be aware of what a student does or produces as well as *how* a student processes information.

In addition to knowing something about each student's behavior, cognitive style, and affective style, educators must also be concerned about forces that influence these factors, historically, currently, and futuristically (anticipated occurrences). In a very broad sense, these influences can be broken down into internal and external. Perceptions, characteristic emotional responses, and associations that occur inside a person are internal forces that help determine "what one is." The culture in which one grows, the emotional climate of one's family, birth order, and the classroom environment are all examples of external variables that impinge upon the student and help shape behavior, cognition, and affect.

The Institute concentrates its elementary level assessment in seven areas: the arts, physical skills, reading, mathematics, science, creativity, and social relations. There is also a need to focus on the sources of reinforcement and the attribution of desirable outcomes to oneself or others. At the elementary school level, the assessment is more inclusive because both attitudes and skills may require special attention. Also, it is apparent that a more coordinated effort across school levels could greatly enhance each district's ability to meet the needs of talented pupils:

Small numbers of elementary pupils can benefit from acceleration/enrichment in math, reading, and the arts, preferably in small, ungraded groups, taught by teachers or community members knowledgeable in particular fields. Secondary school teachers in math, science, English, and foreign languages would be a natural for teaching classes (possibly meeting twice a week). These teachers could serve as curriculum consultants to elementary teachers and also help select and train their own top students to teach talented elementary school pupils. As these pupils move into higher grades the subject matter teacher would become an advisor or learning coordinator in the subject matter field. Another approach might involve arranging for and helping students with correspondence courses or college courses taken for credit.

Although it is unusual to have high school teachers take responsibility for teaching elementary school pupils, if the necessary arrangements (assignments) can be made, talented pupils could benefit greatly. The central thrust of any program, and the example presented in particular, represents the *full* utilization of existing resources.

The program in grades seven and eight is oriented toward helping students maintain or develop positive attitudes toward self and school. Included are overall talent descriptions obtained from students, parents, and teachers; measures of general achievement and creativity orientation; recommendations for individual and group counseling; and suggestions to students, parents, and teachers regarding ways to facilitate student development. The eighth grade assessment focuses more on preparation for making immediate, e.g., high school curricula choices, and longer term educational plans.

At the secondary level, the Institute focuses attention on the career guidance needs of talented students. It should be noted that as part of this process there are continuous efforts to help students understand their learning styles, personal development, and psychosocial needs. Student assessment and parent, student, teacher, and counselor interview procedures are used to develop career guidance and career education recommendations for talented students. After years of testing the usefulness of various instruments, questionnaires, learning experiences, and report forms, the Institute has developed a program that provides students, parents, and counselors a programmatic approach to career planning and decision making. Institute staff members consult with school counselors regarding recommendations and, when possible, suggest or design materials and programs to help better meet the career guidance needs of talented high school students.

In order to further self-understanding, students are asked to complete instruments designed to assess responsibility, achievement motivation, job knowledge, creativity, and career related values. This information is summarized and interpretations discussed with students, parents, and counselors. A written report encompassing all the information, subject to student review, is sent to both the school and family. In subsequent years, increased emphasis is placed on educational and vocational planning and decision making.

Teaching Survival Skills

One further focus of the Guidance Institute is to help culturally different gifted children develop survival skills in the classroom. One must identify stereotypical behaviors that become barriers to acceptance and recognition of minority students and then develop the means to overcome these barriers. The initial emphasis of the Institute has been on the students themselves. Minority students are sensitive to stereotypes, even if they cannot fully comprehend or verbalize their negative effect in their relationship with teachers. Cartledge and Milburn (1978) refer to these factors as "The 'Hidden' Curriculum."

The basic approach in developing survival skills is to first identify the classroom behaviors that correlate with achievement and then teach students how to develop successful or useful classroom behaviors and then control inappropriate behaviors. Some of the following behaviors have been found to relate positively to success in American schools: smiling, answering questions, maintaining eye contact, seeking out the teacher for assistance, and volunteering. Behaviors perceived as negative by teachers include frowning, looking out the window, talking with classmates, slumping in the seat, and looking around. These survival skills assist children to achieve better in school until such time teachers operate from a more open or encompassing value system.

If students master the survival skills, develop basic learning skills, and develop positive attitudes towards themselves and school, then scholastic achievement should improve. Also, the aspirations and eventual accomplishments of gifted and nongifted minority children should increase.

The Institute provides materials and consultation services to interested educators at cost. Further information can be obtained by writing either author at the following address:

> Guidance Institute for Talented Students
> Room 349 Education Building
> University of Wisconsin
> Madison, WI 53706

References

Banks, W.C., Stitl, K. R., Curtis, H.A., and McQuater, G.V.: Perceived-objectivity and the effect of evaluative reinforcement upon compliance and self-evaluation of Blacks. *J Experimental Social Psychology, 13*: 452–462, 1977.

Banks, W.C., McQuater, G.V., and Hubbard, J.L.: Toward a reconceptualization of the social-cognitive bases of achievement orientations in Blacks. *Review of Educational Research, 3*:381–397, 1978.

Cartledge, G.G., and Milburn, J.F.: The case for teaching social skills in the classroom: A review. *Review of Educational Research, 1*:133–156, 1978.

Gallagher, J.J.: *Talent Delayed—Talent Denied: The Culturally Different Gifted Child: A Conference Report.* Reston, The Foundation for Exceptional Children, 1974.

Nichols, J.G.: Causal attribution and other achievement-related cognitions: Effects of task outcomes, attainment values and sex. *J Personality and Social Psychology, 31*:379–389, 1975.

Simonton, D.K.: Interdisciplinary creativity over historical time: A correlational analysis of general fluctuations. *Social Behavior and Personality, 3*:181–188, 1975.

Wallach, M., and Kogan, N.: *Modes of Thinking in Young Children: A Study of the Creativity-Intelligence Distinction.* New York, Holt, Rinehart, and Winston, 1965.

16

Genetic Counseling for Families of Chicano Children with Birth Defects

Marion D. Meyerson

A child with a birth defect can bring both joys and problems to a family. Questions are raised and must be answered. Treatment procedures need to be considered and evaluated. Genetic counseling often provides the starting point for the family who has a child with a birth defect. It is necessary to view each family as a unique unit, considering both group and individual concerns and responses. Family attitudes towards counseling, treatment, and genetic disorders must be considered. Successful genetic counseling must be based on accurate information regarding birth defects, their etiology, and treatment. Equally significant is the need for empathic understanding of the individuals who seek this counseling. If the families represent one or more of the many ethnic minorities in the United States, cultural attitudes figure powerfully in the counselees' initial and long-term responses.

In many California cities, more than one-fourth of the population is Chicano/Mexican American. These labels are controversial. Some feel the term *Chicano* is derogatory and others object to the hyphenation of *Mexican-American*. Because the author met and learned about Americans of Mexican descent on a college campus where the word *Chicano* was preferred, it will be used throughout this chapter.

Most Chicano families are bicultural; many are bilingual. Chicano values and beliefs are diverse and, although all ideas are not shared by all members of the community, there are many attitudes that remain strongly ingrained in this ethnic group. Little information has been published concerning Chicano attitudes toward birth defects. Most of the information in this chapter was obtained from clinical experience, from interviews with Chicano professionals and parents, and from genetic counselors who work with Chicano families.[1]

This chapter represents an overview of general genetic concerns followed by a discussion of genetic counseling and specific related cultural values held by many Chicano families. The overwhelming consensus of the professionals who contributed to this chapter was that Chicano cultural values were very positive influences in the care and acceptance of children with birth defects.

Etiology of Birth Defects

The causes of birth defects can be grouped in several categories. Birth defects can be caused by chromosomal abnormalities, defective genes, multifactorial inheritance, teratogenic drugs or infectious agents that damage the fetus, and factors that are yet unknown. A discussion of the various causes follows.

Chromosomal Abnormalities

Chromosomes carry hereditary material and are present in every body cell. Each normal individual has 46 chromosomes, half of which are inherited from the mother and the other half from the father. Forty-four of these chromosomes (or 22 pairs) are called autosomes, and the remaining two are sex chromosomes (two X chromosomes for a female, an X and Y chromosome for a male). The chromosomes can be obtained from a blood or tissue sample. These samples are then cultured in a laboratory and examined visually under a microscope during cell division so they can be organized into a graphic display called a karyotype. Through this process, abnormalities in the chromosomal makeup of an individual can be identified.

Abnormal karyotypes might occur if some chromosomal material is missing or if there is an extra chromosome. Down's syndrome (Figure 16-1) is the most common birth defect resulting from a chromosomal abnormality. Because of an extra chromosome at pair number 21, a number of characteristics including mental retardation are demonstrated by the affected child (*see* Figure 16-2). Although women of any age can have a child with Down's syndrome, the risk increases with increased maternal age. In other words, a woman over 45 has a greater risk of bearing a child with Down's syndrome than does a 25-year-old woman. However, because of the higher birth rate among younger women, most Down's syndrome babies are born to younger mothers.

FIGURE 16-1
Mother and Down's Syndrome Child

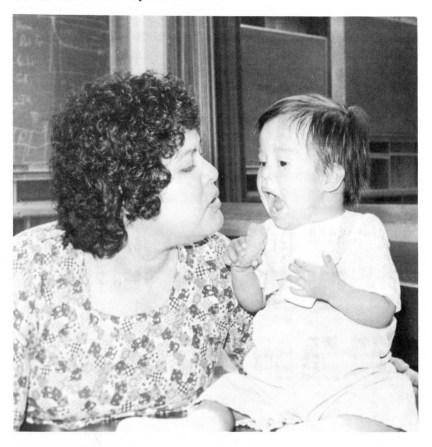

Defective Genes

Genes are located on the chromosomes and are inherited from each parent. In addition to the genetic material that determines eye and hair color, body type, and other features that tend to make us look like other members of our families, we each carry some genes that could produce a birth defective child.

Autosomal dominant inheritance. One kind of genetic disease is caused by autosomal dominant transmission. In this type, the gene produces some effect, however variable, in every individual who inherits it. Every affected individual has an affected parent, unless the defect is a new mutation in an individual. In other words, the disease may already be present in the family or it may arise spontaneously in an individual. In any event, each affected

FIGURE 16-2

In this representation of a karyotype, the paired chromosomes are organized in order of decreasing length and are then assigned numbers. An extra 21st chromosome can be seen alongside the 21st pair; hence the diagnosis of Trisomy 21 or the Down's syndrome.

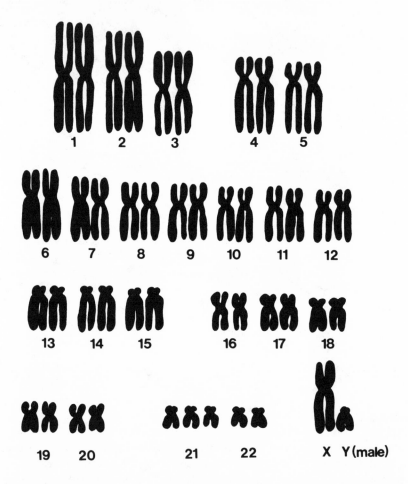

person who mates with an unaffected spouse runs a 50-50 chance of bearing a child who will inherit the condition. Unaffected family members will probably not have affected offspring.

An example of an autosomal dominant problem is the Treacher Collins syndrome, also called mandibulofacial dysostosis. Individuals affected by the Treacher Collins syndrome are born with facial malformations including underdevelopment of the jaw, cheekbones, and external ears. Those affected with the Treacher Collins syndrome are generally of normal intelligence.

Autosomal recessive inheritance. In autosomal recessive inheritance, the parents of an affected child appear normal, but both are carriers of the same altered gene. It is unusual for two individuals to carry the same gene. However, if they do, each of their children has one chance in four of being affected and two chances in four of being carriers like the parents. There is also one chance in four of the child being completely normal and a non-carrier of the particular gene in question. In autosomal recessive inheritance there is an increased likelihood that consanguinity may have occurred in the family; in other words, the parents are related by blood and both might have inherited the gene from a common ancestor.

Among the most commonly carried autosomal recessive gene is the one of cystic fibrosis, a disease affecting respiration and digestion. The altered gene for cystic fibrosis is carried by one out of every 25 individuals.

X-linked inheritance. The X-linked inherited diseases occur when a mother carries a defective gene on one of her X (sex) chromosomes. Because she has a normal X chromosome in addition to the altered one, she will probably not manifest any signs of the problem. Each of her sons has a 50-50 chance of inheriting the mutant gene. Since males have only one X chromosome (and one Y chromosome), if a son inherits one that is abnormal, he will have the condition. Of her daughters, 50% run the risk of being carriers, who can then transmit the gene to half of their sons. Duchenne muscular dystrophy, a progressive muscle wasting disease, is an example of an X-linked inheritance.

Multifactorial Inheritance

Multifactorial inheritance is not as clearly understood as chromosomal and genetic transmission. Multifactorial disorders result from the interaction of genetic and nongenetic factors. A marginal genetic susceptability that would otherwise go unrecognized might combine with an agent in the fetal environment to produce a disorder. Risk figures used in counseling parents who have given birth to a child with a multifactorial disorder are called empiric risk figures. These risk figures are probabilities derived from observations of large numbers of affected families. If a family has one child with a condition such as spina bifida or cleft lip or palate, there is a 3 to 6% chance of having a second child with a similar defect.

Teratogenic Drugs and Infectious Agents

Teratogens deform the fetus after conception. They can be classified into categories including infectious agents and drugs. The rubella virus is a teratogen. If a woman contracts rubella during the first trimester of pregnancy, her offspring has a significant chance of having serious congenital defects including deafness, vision impairment, heart defects, mental retardation, motor problems, and growth deficiency. It is hoped that mass immunization with the effective rubella vaccine will reduce this risk in women contracting the disease.

Drugs ingested by the mother during pregnancy may also affect the fetus. Most of us are familiar with the serious limb deformities resulting from the ingestion of a seemingly innocent drug called thalidomide. We are now aware that many other drugs, including some anticoagulants, anticonvulsants, hormones, and alcohol, may have serious effects on the developing fetus. Recent recognition of the occurrence of mental retardation and physical abnormalities resulting from fetal alcohol syndrome has focused attention on the serious risk taken by pregnant women who are chronic alcoholics.

Syndromes of Unknown Origin

There are thousands of syndromes that have been identified and named. The largest group of these (rather than fitting into the categories of chromosomal, genetic, multifactorial, or teratogenic abnormalities) are classed as syndromes of unknown origin. An example of a birth defect of unknown etiology is the Moebius syndrome, which involves facial paralysis and limb defects. As research and dissemination of findings continue, more of the syndromes in the unknown category are being reclassified in one of the known categories.

Other Factors Relating to Birth Defects

Prenatal Detection of Birth Defects

The purpose of genetic counseling is to provide information regarding birth defects and their risk of recurrence. It is apparent, however, that many who seek genetic counseling have already experienced a personal disappointment or tragedy because of the loss of a baby or the birth of an individual with a syndrome in the family. Some seek counseling because of advanced maternal age. There is much that can currently be offered by counseling and through prenatal detection of birth defects. The information derived from the various methods described below may assist the family in making decisions.

In a fetal detection procedure called amniocentesis, a small amount of amniotic fluid can be drawn from a woman in the fifteenth to eighteenth week of pregnancy. The fluid can reveal much about the fetus including the presence of a chromosomal abnormality, a neural tube defect, and at least 80 genetic disorders. If the fetus is found to have a defect, the parents are given the option of terminating the pregnancy. For those defects which can be helped with prenatal or perinatal medical intervention, treatment may be suggested. Other prenatal detection methods include ultrasound and fetoscopy, both of which help to visualize the fetus so that missing limbs or other gross malformations can be noted.

Carrier detection tests are now possible for over 60 biochemical diseases. If a child with one of these diseases is born to a family, all members can be tested to determine the risk of recurrence within the family. Continued research is directed at improvement of both prenatal and carrier detection so that information and alternatives for the family can be maximized.

Ethnic Differences in the Incidence of Birth Defects

Genetic differences exist among various ethnic groups. The frequency of certain diseases appears to be higher within specific groups, especially in those individuals whose parents did not marry outside their ethnic circles. Although many genetically inherited diseases have been reported to be significantly increased among members of other ethnic and/or racial groups (McKusick, 1975), there have been no such reports for Chicanos. There have been, however, as yet unproven suspicions of greater numbers of cleft lip and palate and of neural tube defects among Chicanos in California. These birth defects are multifactorially inherited, which means the transmission and risk factors are less categorical. Among the many factors speculated to be contributing to this suspected increase in frequency is exposure to pesticides among migrant farm workers, many of whom are Chicanos.

The ethnic variations in the incidence of the aforementioned multifactorial defects warrant vigorous investigation, documentation, and action. Certainly poor nutrition, fatigue, inadequate health care, as well as chemical exposure on farms and in packing houses would present a risk to the unborn (Diaz, 1974). These factors, however, are probably related more to low socioeconomic status than to ethnicity, and the number of affected infants will hopefully decrease as the economic status of Chicanos improves.

Genetic Counseling

General Principles

The functions of genetic counseling are many and varied. Perhaps the most critical is the formulation of an accurate diagnosis of the affected child or adult. Without a diagnosis, little useful information regarding treatment, prognosis, or recurrence risks for family members can be offered. With an accurate diagnosis, the family can be presented with information that will allow alternatives in the decision-making process concerning treatment modalities and future pregnancies.

A detailed family history, including a pedigree that can show patterns of inheritance, is the first step in diagnosis. Analysis of the medical records of the affected child plus a physical examination by the physician working with the genetic team generally follow. Laboratory tests for the child and possibly for other family members may be required. Sometimes a set of character-istics may not fit the pattern of any known syndrome and may baffle even the most knowledgeable genetics team. However, most individuals can antici-pate an accurate diagnosis plus up-to-date information of the course the problem will take and the risk of recurrence for the affected individuals and other members of the family.

In other words, a family who brings a child for evaluation by a genetics team can expect information on a number of factors. The nature of the child's birth defect can be described. The kinds of physical and/or mental problems that can be anticipated may be clarified. There may be a discussion of the probability of success with medical treatment and educational training, the degree of progression of the disease, and the life span of other affected individuals. The likelihood of the affected child reproducing a similarly affected baby and the risk carried by the parents and siblings of having other children with the defect can also be determined and discussed.

Cultural Attitudes Toward Etiology

Whatever the training and orientation of the genetic counselor, the ultimate success of the counseling interaction is dependent upon the way in which information is integrated by the counselee. The degree and pattern of integration will be significantly affected by the cultural attitudes of the families.

Ethnic and socioeconomic groups have variant belief systems that affect their attitudes toward the etiology of birth defects. Individuals within these groups also vary. The counseling literature indicates that mainstream individuals may persist in idiosyncratic beliefs, e.g., not going to church or having sexual relations during pregnancy, regarding their child's deformity in spite of intellectual acknowledgement of genetic information.[2] The following discussion about how cultural attitudes and beliefs affect genetic counseling of Chicanos in California is meant to sensitize the reader to the importance of recognizing cultural beliefs. The author does not intend to suggest that all members of this group share the same belief system nor that one value system is better than another.

Chicanos in California represent a wide variety of length of residence in the United States. Some families have been in the Southwest for several hundred years. Many are newly arrived. This continued immigration and the proximity of Mexico to the United States may well be responsible for the preservation of traditional values. Folklore and folk medicine infuse the health concepts of many Chicanos. Pregnancy, for example, is said to be fraught with hazards related to the moon, to thunder, and to eclipses (Newman, 1969). Such natural forces are thought to have the power to cause fetal damage (Madsen, 1964). Clark (1970) reported that individuals in a California barrio attributed cleft palate to the mother's exposure to an eclipse during pregnancy. A local colleague recounted that, in one Chicano family with whom he worked, a child's hydrocephaly was said to be caused by a precious stone in his head. Current success with shunt surgery has helped reduce this etiological explanation (Prattes, 1979).

Other prenatal influences are thought to cause birth defects. *Susto*, for example, is a frightful or stressful situation causing the loss of soul. It appears when stress is felt (Rubel, 1964) and is among the emotional upsets that are thought to affect the development of the fetus. *Mal puesto* (witchcraft) and *mal ojo* (evil eye) are also believed to cause birth defects and other illnesses. Some professionals reported that attributing causality to these external factors often frees the family from guilt. Without guilt feelings, coping with reality in a constructive way becomes easier. Other Chicanos frequently refer to punishment for sins as a causal factor. One mother reported she was being punished for having been a rebellious child. Another mother thought she was being punished because she felt envy. Some parents describe the occurrence as "my cross to bear."

When external natural forces or the emotional fright of *susto* affect the pregnant woman, several cultural techniques can be employed to counteract the negative effects. The woman will probably consult with a neighbor or relative and use protective devices, such as hanging keys from her waist, sweeping the *susto* out with a broom, or placing a broken egg under a bed. If the healing devices of neighbors are thought to be inadequate, the woman may consult a *curandero* (folk-healer). Rubel (1966) described *curanderos* as deriving their powers from God. Local Chicanos varied in their opinions concerning the prevalence of *curanderos* in central California. One Chicano professional said that although *curanderos* are discussed, there are few of them locally, and they are rarely consulted. Others indicated that they frequently work with *curanderos* on behalf of a client or patient.

A number of external and internal factors are suspected by many Chicanos as causal agents of birth defects. A study by Baca (1975) of Mexican American and Anglo parents of institutionalized retarded children noted much greater adherence to religious explanations by the Mexican Americans, greater reliance on folk-healing, and stronger influence of the extended family in the decision-making process. Other aspects of coping and adjustment behaviors appeared to be the same for both groups.

When an Anglo professional describes the cause in terms of medical genetics, the Chicano family may quietly reject the explanation, accept it without question, or combine the genetic and folk analyses. One genetic counselor recalled giving an explanation of a chromosomal abnormality to a family with a Down's syndrome child. She took care to use the language of the family, spoke slowly and at length, and encouraged frequent questions. When she was at the point where she felt the family truly understood the nature of the problem, the father concluded the meeting by telling her that the word *chromosome* in Spanish is *eclipse*.

Cultural Responses to Treatment Procedures

Professionals working with parents of birth defective children often stress similarities in the responses of both Chicano and Anglo families. A number of differences have also been reported, that may be related to ethnic values. Chicanos demonstrate a positive acceptance of life and a willingness to "take the good with the bad." A primary feature is the recognition of the condition coupled with the affection for the child. Mentally retarded youngsters, for example, are called *enfermitos*, a term that connotes both responsibility for caring for the *sick one*, and a sense of love, shown by the use of the diminutive. The acceptance of reality may be part of the philosophy of fatalism, which is often maligned by sociologists. It is apparent, however, that acceptance can be a very positive feature in avoiding "cureshopping" and getting down to the business of living with a handicapped child. Field sources note that *fatalismo* is easy to work through when the child makes observable gains through training. Families appear eager to incorporate into their lives small practical tasks that can help the child.

The extended family structure among Chicanos easily absorbs the very young and the very old. This structure allows also for a variety of caretakers and, when coupled with the reluctance to send a handicapped child away, minimizes the number of Chicano youngsters who are institutionalized. A recent report of ethnic characteristics of patients in a state mental hospital in California appeared to suggest a proportional underrepresentation of Mexican Americans. In contrast, special day classes for the retarded in a California city recorded a higher percentage of Spanish-surnamed children than would be expected. Chicano families generally keep their children at home and enroll them in special classes in the public schools rather than send them to residential institutions. An exception to this rule might be children of migrant workers. The harsh and mobile existence with inadequate facilities and the enlisting of all children in the work process may preclude keeping a seriously handicapped child with the family.

Family ties may remain strong, but urban living and the search for better jobs spread the extended unit into different neighborhoods. Because more mothers and grandmothers are working outside of the home, family care for handicapped children may become more difficult. If this trend continues, Chicano children might in the future be institutionalized with the same frequency as their Anglo counterparts. Although initially suspicious of the bureaucratic nature of most agencies, Chicano families appear to overcome this response and are appreciative of the services provided. Professionals report that Chicano families are less likely than Anglos to feel that services "are coming to them." Some families are so nondemanding that an unobservant professional might forget about them.

Along with the sense of responsibility for the child and the affection manifested, many Chicano families feel that handicapped children "suffer enough," and should not be subject to extensive discipline. Several professionals reported that oversolicitousness impedes the development of a handicapped child's independent behavior. Others indicated that permissiveness was no more prevalent in the Chicano clients than in their non-Chicano families. In any event, an understanding of the possible existence of this permissive attitude might make it easier to approach the family and demonstrate that the children are actually happier with some behavior training.

Curanderos may be sought by the family of a birth defective child for advice on treatment. Kiev (1968) noted that *curanderos* maintain the family's confidence by never being in doubt about the diagnosis and treatment. Rather than focus on laboratory methods, the *curandero* turns to religious forces that are more meaningful to the people. Rubel (1966) stated that many Chicanos maximize the credibility of folk-healers in order to defend traditional values from mockery by Anglos.

Views Regarding Recurrence Risks and Prenatal Intervention

Genetic counselors have long been aware of disparate reactions to risk figures. One individual sees a 25% risk of having a child affected with an autosomal recessive problem such as cystic fibrosis as very high; another views the 75% chance of having a normal child as good odds. A number of counselors have reported that Chicanos, on the whole, do not perceive risks as highly negative. One counselor observed that the families with whom she has worked expect problems in what was considered a "tougher life." They were not as shocked by the occurrence of a birth defect as Anglos might be.

In part because of a long Catholic tradition, Chicanos are generally against abortion. Therefore, some of the prenatal detection methods such as amniocentesis, which lead to an option for abortion, are not accepted. It was indicated that many priests in the community neither condemn nor condone abortion to their parishioners and, therefore, allow a degree of individual determination.

Several spoke of an intense fear of needles as a deterrent to acceptance of prenatal diagnosis. Younger generations with Anglo educations and Anglo value systems may regard abortion as a more favorable option when prenatal detection methods reveal a fetus affected with a chromosomal or neural tube defect. Sex may also determine one's attitude toward abortion, as was indicated in a study by Naranjo and Lockhart (1978). Young, middle-class Mexican Americans and Anglos responded to a number of genetic counseling cases by giving their preferences for pregnancy intervention. The females of both groups tended to approve more of abortion; the males were for no intervention.

Implications for Counseling

Folk medicine remains a strong force for many Chicanos. Some are reluctant to discuss it because of derision by non-Chicanos. Others are able to combine folk explanations and folk-healing methods with mainstream medical practices in an attempt to "cover all bases." Gomez and Cook (1978) noted the cultural conflict that might result from the effort to integrate the "Mexican" and "American" cultures. Nall and Speilberg (1967) found no impact of folk beliefs on the acceptance or rejection of medical treatment by individual Mexican Americans.

Certainly, a counselor advising a family about the diagnosis and prognosis for a child with a birth defect must recognize any dual orientation and avoid belittling the acceptance of traditional values. Even when a counselor privately rejects the curative value of herbs or massage, if the parents are still seeking standard treatment procedures in schools and clinics, the faith in the herbal cure should not upset the remedial applecart. The child may even become the recipient of added attention and encouragement, which are generally positive features.

A frequent complaint from Chicano families is that professionals focus only on the *bad* or *undesirable* behavioral aspects. Some of the families resisted continued visits until the counselor began emphasizing the positive qualities in the child and the family and demonstrated respect for cultural values. A lack of response to a letter does not mean lack of family interest in the welfare of a handicapped child. Professionals must reach out on a one-to-one basis in order to gain the confidence of the families. Initial failure to keep appointments must also be understood in a cultural context. DeBlassie (1976) noted that, to a Chicano, an appointment is "very white." Personal reminders and patient explanations will usually work. Family members must be included in counseling because of strong extended family ties. If a translator must be used in counseling the family, great care should be taken that the translator is trained so that erroneous information is not transmitted (Watson et al., 1980). A case should be made to increase the number of trained genetic counselors that are fluent in Spanish!

Chicano families have been reported to appear less concerned about the future of a mentally or physically handicapped child. Rather than view this as uncaring or simplistic, the positive features that undergird this faith should be understood. Certainly, the tradition of extended-family-care relieves the burden of wondering "who will care for this child when I'm gone." The societal structure in a barrio community assigns roles to people, instead of stressing individual accomplishments. Therefore, an individual with a mental or physical handicap may still have status in the social system.

Respect for the beliefs and values of the Chicano family is imperative in establishing the trust needed for successful counseling. If an individual maintains that *susto* caused a birth defect, it would not be helpful to continue insisting on a genetic cause. If the guilt involved in sending a severely afflicted child to a residential institution would be too difficult for parents to accept, they must be supported in their decision to keep the child at home. Baca (1969) observed that when professionals reject Chicano values, the families may appear to politely accept counsel, but will understandably not follow through. Trust will be lost, and the family may have to relinquish the support and advocacy of the counselor.

Martinez and Martin (1966) described evidence of the widespread belief in folk-healing among urban Chicanos that does *not* preclude visits to physicians or standard medical treatment. If medical care is to be patient oriented, a clearer understanding of *curanderismo* is warranted.

Certainly, the professionals to whom this book is addressed—the teachers, speech/language pathologists, audiologists, psychologists, counselors, and students—need to increase their knowledge about the causes and treatment procedures for exceptional children and, at the same time, heighten their sensitivity to differences in cultural attitudes. Many of the cultural values specific to Chicano and other minority families can yield long-term positive gains for the child with a birth defect.

Notes

[1] I am grateful to the following people for their advice and insights: Alysia Andrade, John Carey, Kathy Carillo, Wallace Carroll, Paul Chacon, Ben Cuellar, Cynthia Curry, Tony de la Torre, Fred Escalante, Corinne Florez, Urbano Gonzales, Gil Guerrero, Mary Lou Hickman, Marian Karian, Jesus Luna, Theresa Perez, Nancy Ramey, Alex Saragoza, and Lea Ybarra-Soriano.

[2] Indeed, so-called Third World medical systems have many strengths, not the least of which is the inclusion of family and community in the treatment procedure so that pain and guilt can be shared (Henderson and Primeaux, 1981).

References

Baca, G.M.:   Forty families: A comparative study of Mexican-American and Anglo parents of an institutionalized retarded child. *Dissertation Abstracts International, 36*:3128-A, 1975.

Baca, J.E.:   Some health beliefs of the Spanish-speaking. *American J Nursing, 69*:2172–2176, 1969.

Clark, M.:   *Health in the Mexican-American Culture.* Berkeley, University of California, 1970.

DeBlassie, R.R.:   *Counseling with Mexican-American Youth.* Austin, Learning Concepts, 1976.

Diaz, M.N.:   The infant in Mexican-American culture. In *Birth Defects: Original Article Series.* New York, The National Foundation March of Dimes, *10,* 1974.

Gomez, E., and Cook, K.:   *Chicano Culture and Mental Health.* San Antonio, Our Lady of the Lake University, 1978.

Henderson, G., and Primeaux, M.:   The importance of folk medicine. In Henderson, G., and Primeaux, M. (Eds.): *Transcultural Health Care.* Menlo Park, Addison-Wesley, 1981.

Kiev, A.:   *Curanderismo: Mexican-American Folk Psychiatry.* New York, Free Press, 1968.

Madsen, W.:   *The Mexican-Americans of South Texas.* New York, Holt, Rinehart, and Winston, 1964.

Martinez, C., and Martin, H.W.:   Folk diseases among urban Mexican-Americans. *JAMA, 196*:147–150, 1966.

McKusick, V.A.:   *Mendelian Inheritance in Man.* Baltimore, Johns Hopkins University, 1975.

Nall, F.C., and Speilberg, J.:   Social and cultural factors in the responses of Mexican-Americans to medical treatment. *J Health and Social Behavior, 8*:299–308, 1967.

Naranjo, M.S.F., and Lockhart, L.H.:   *Quantitative Analysis and Discussion of Mexican and Anglo Americans' Responses to Intervention in Genetic Disease.* Paper presented at Birth Defects Conference, San Francisco, 1978.

Newman, L.F.:   Folklore of pregnancy: Wives' tales in Contra Costa County, California. *Western Folklore, 28*:112–135, 1969.

Prattes, O.P.:   Beliefs of the Mexican-American family. In Hymovich, D.P., and Barnard, M.U. (Eds.): *Family Health Care: Vol. 1, General Perspectives.* New York, McGraw-Hill, 1979.

Press, I.:   Urban folk medicine: A fictional overview. *American Anthropologist, 80*:71–83, 1978.

Rubel, A.J.:   The epidemiology of a folk illness: Susto in Hispanic America. *Ethnology, 3*:268–283, 1964.

Rubel, A.J.:   *Across the Tracks: Mexican-Americans in a Texas City.* Austin, University of Texas, 1966.

Watson, D.L., Omark, D.R., Grouell, S., and Heller, B.:   *Nondiscriminatory Assessment: A Practitioner's Guide*, Vol. I. Sacramento, California Department of Education, 1980.

National Issues and
Model Programs

17

Educational Issues, Ideology, and the Role of National Organizations

Njeri Nuru

> The true impediment to cultural pluralism is that we have had culturally deficient educators attempting to teach culturally different children. ....Our sins are sins of omission rather than comission. We can't teach within a context where cultural differences are extant if we don't know what the cultural differences are. Therein lies our dilemma. We can't teach what we don't know. (Aragon, 1973, p. 78)

The purpose of this chapter is to provoke critical reflection on the concrete problems national organizations, training programs, and we as a society confront in the process of bilingual/bicultural education in a pluralistic society. Three assumptions form the basis of this chapter: that language is both a product and a conveyor of one's culture; that culture is the "expression in particular and specific forms of...the relationships linking man(kind) to his or her environment" (Toure, 1969, p. 13); and that the society in which we live is one of cultural pluralism, and, in order to survive as a nation worthy of its people, there must be cultural coexistence without hegemony.

Bilingual/biculturalism is a pedagogical problem, i.e., a problem of equal education opportunity for all students. According to Friere (1978), pedagogical problems are both political and ideological. Schools, therefore, like "national culture in general cannot be separated from economics and politics" (Lenin and Stalin, 1970, p. 10). Bilingual/bicultural education is a political issue. Realizing that local education agencies are governed by publically elected trustees, it should be no surprise that most instituted educational changes are politically based rather than professionally based (Valverde, 1978).

Bilingual/bicultural education must be viewed as a subsystem within a larger system—a pole or moment within a total unity. The role of the subsystem is to bring practical concreteness to the larger system, that larger system being *equal educational opportunity*. National organizations and training institutions as vehicles for such a reality must be in concert with the ideology of that larger system.

Representative of that larger system, federal policy and court decisions have attempted to clarify the legal responsibility of school districts for limited English and non-English speaking children. Title VI, Section 601 of the Civil Rights Act of 1964 states that "No person in the United States shall, on the ground of race, color, or national origin, be excluded from participation in, or be subjected to discrimination under any program or activity receiving federal financial assistance." In 1970, the United States Department of Health, Education, and Welfare, Office of Civil Rights, issued a memorandum of clarification of these 1964 requirements. The memorandum indicated that where inability of national origin minority group children to speak and understand the English language excludes them from effective participation in an educational program, the school district must take steps to rectify their language deficiency in order to open its instructional program to them. The Bilingual Education Act (Elementary and Secondary Education Act, Title VII) of 1978 that provided governmental legitimacy to bilingual education recognized the political feasibility of offering basic instruction in a language other than Standard American English, and institutionalized the concept of educational opportunity as being synonymous with equal education.

The goals of national organizations and training institutions must struggle toward the concrete reality of the larger system; be that system formalized and existent, e.g., federal legislation, a progressive new mentality, or revolutionary new society in formation. Questions national organizations and training institutions should ask in regard to bilingual/ bicultural education must be theoretical and practical, not merely intellectual abstractions. Organizations should explore their dynamic relationships to each other and their role in the larger reality, by analyzing their identity, purpose, and direction (kwa Salaam, 1981).

Identity: The identifying characteristics of an organization can be true or false, imposed or self-determined. *True or false*: Does the identity of the organization correspond to reality—to what is? *Imposed*: Is the identity of the organization thrust upon it without regard to its individual needs? Is the organization merely reflecting the images and instructions of some other institution or individual? *Self-determined*: Does the organization create, define, and control itself?

Purpose: An organization reflects its self-defined long-range and short-range goals. The following are key questions: (a) *What to know* in order to develop programatic content and its organization? (b) *What is for or against what or whom?* Examples: Knowledge and understanding of Black English benefits Black children (*who*) and their Black culture (*what*). Knowledge of the inequitable social, economic, educational, and health care practices in

South Africa benefits South African Blacks (*who*) and is against the heinous apartheid system (*what*) of South Africa (Cole, 1980b). Political clarity and ideology are absolutely essential in establishing the purpose of organizational goals.

Direction: Given true identity and self-determined purpose, direction will follow. Direction is the organization's plan for the achievement of its goals; simply, knowing *how* to achieve *what*, and *why* to achieve it. For example, a plan (*how*) for the development of a classless educational model for free public higher education (*what*) in order to meet the educational needs of the masses of children in this society (*why*).

Education and Socialization

Education has many roles with respect to socialization. Education is the key to economic well-being, moral development, and access to and participation in the political process, the center of preparation for life, a dimension of social practice, a political/pedagogical training, a major source of acculturation in the country in which any people live, and a social process that involves *reading* the world. To put this sociocultural act, education, into a revolutionary perspective is essential.

That education is a source or tool of acculturation is an understatement. Schools exist for the culture, not vice versa. Schools, whether primary, secondary, collegiate, or vocational, are cultural products established and organized to socialize students towards societal norms that preserve and strengthen the *status quo* and maintain and advance a cultural way of life (Carnoy, 1974). This goal is achieved in part by schools that profess equal opportunity, but, in practice, perpetuate inequality in society by differentially socializing students on the basis of race, sex, and social class. Therefore, the relationship between schools at any level and local, state, and national agencies and organizations is important in achieving the objective of relating school experiences to life, the community, and the neighborhood.

If race, sex, and class inequality are fostered in schools that are charged with the preparation of our future world-makers (artists, economists, educators, historians, law enforcers, lawyers, linguists, physicians, politicians, sociologists, and most importantly, laborers), what kind of world can we expect in the future? Surely the same kind of world we have today—one in which discrimination is perpetuated on the basis of race, sex, class, age, and disability. One need look only at percentage representation statistics for higher education, employment, institutionalization, and incarceration for obvious examples of how discrimination is perpetuated today.

This problem was recognized by the United States Commissioner of Education whose first report to the country and Congress on the condition of bilingual education in the nation urged changes in legislation so that children in bilingual/bicultural projects would not have their civil rights violated (U.S. Commission of Education, 1976). Despite this recommendation, state education agencies still show disproportionate misplacement of handicapped ethnic minority children (Nuru, and Coppock, 1979).

The Importance of Culture

Culture and national identity constitute one of the most important areas of life study. Far more than realized, we, as individuals, are products of our specific cultures. Unfortunately, America is an unfinished nation of cultural confusion that is a fetter to cultural pluralism.

If we would want to understand people, we would study and understand culture on an international scale. It is within the context of a culture that we dream, formulate questions, shape our ideals, stage our rebellions, and discipline our minds. For example, we dream the dreams that culture suggests—be they from our own indigenous culture or from the society in which we live, function, and assimilate to varying degrees. For instance, if mass media, one of the most powerful propaganda tools of a culture, promotes such things as straight hair swinging in the wind, narrow noses, unaffordable cars, homes, and designer jeans, then these are the things of which the masses will dream and to which the masses will aspire. For example, many American women did not aspire to wearing the traditional braided hairstyles of women from various African tribes in response to serious Afro-American women wearing the same. They did, however, respond to this cultural tradition when it was popularized out of its cultural context as a *creation* of the white fashion industry and attributed to white women.

Only few critically examine such behavior within the context of their own indigenous culture. Therefore, the danger exists, especially for our children and our future, of becoming suffused by the beliefs, customs, and culture of the society in which they live to the point that they believe any diversity is perverse, substandard, unacceptable, or wrong. The game by any other name is still the same, the *good guys* have white skins, wear white hats, speak Standard American English, and never lose a fight! It follows, then, that it is the critical understanding of culture that is essential to any and all education.

Children need the cultural end of education in order to function in American society without loss of individual cultural identity. Skills without cultural education will not allow this. Further, the psychological impact of our schools on culturally different children may be personal conflict severe enough to affect their ability to function effectively, not only within the larger society, but also within their own community. Schools, as presently established, do not form a continuous link with ghetto and Black culture and are essentially foreign establishments as far as many Black students are concerned (Wilson, 1978). So, too, is the case with many Hispanic students of barrio and Hispanic culture.

In the United States, the pressure by the public school system to assimilate minorities has been continuous. It is impossible, however, to provide the best possible educational opportunity without being aware of and responsive to cultural pluralism and ethnic diversity. This must be done on a national scale with leadership from the national level in national organizations and in our training institutions.

There is a great disparity between American rhetoric on equality and the objective reality of experiences in the schools. It is said that America is a melting pot. One is only restricted as far as *who* melts, and *how much* melting is to be done *where* and *when*. Traditionally, during assimilation minorities "give themselves to the culture and to the dominant language" (Friere, 1970), thus forming a *uni*culture. In contrast, in most colonial countries, the vast majority of the peasant population escapes the more destructive power of the colonizers and survives. By becoming *bi*cultural, they preserve significant aspects of their culture.

The position espoused here is neither assimilation/integrationist nor separatist. It is one of cultural pluralism, coexistence, and parity in a common society (Sizemore, 1973). It is internationalism—where different social groups are independent as well as interdependent, where the tension between similarity and difference is lifted, and where "no single set of values and standards is sufficient to inspire the full range of human possibilities" (Sizemore, p. 50). In preparation for this reality, the culturally different should not give themselves to the dominant culture and language. Rather, they should assume the necessary aspects of the dominant culture and master the dominant language in order to survive and create a climate in which equal economic, political, social, and educational opportunities are possible. At the same time, the culturally different should resist being transformed and retain with fervor their independent culture and cultural identity. Only then will the culturally different be fully equipped to forge the necessary struggle for cultural pluralism.

Programs' and educators' behaviors frequently are based on cultural chauvinism and designed to divest the culturally different from their cultural identity, rather than to encourage bicultural presence. Biculturalism, however, can only be a threat to those who embrace a *master race* ethic and unicultural perspective.

Cultural education is essential. Also essential is the bilingual or bidialectal aspect. Language, as a practical consciousness, is a concrete representation of a cultural milieu, serving not only a communication function but also an identity function. National organizations and training programs active in the area of bilingual/biculturalism recognize and support the importance of language for cultural communication and identity.

Benign Neglect

While serving as Director of a minority program in a major professional organization, the author tried unsuccessfully to obtain administrative approval for a project on recruitment and career-ladder education for Native Americans. At that time, this national association claimed less than 10 American Indians out of 30,000 members. Although the project was thought to have merit, it was felt, in effect, that the problems of Native Americans were not of enough concern to focus on it at the national level. It was stressed that the association should focus on things that were of major concern to the membership, which could be interpreted as "the Anglos." At that time, middle ear disease was the major nonfatal health problem and primary cause of hearing impairment among the grossly underserved population of Native Americans, yet this made no difference (*see* Chapter 10).

Although the project was not supported by this national speech and hearing association, the Sensory Disabilities Program of the Indian Health Service (IHS) provided financial support for the author's fact-finding mission to several Indian reservations. Subsequently, the IHS agreed to support the planning of one of its conferences to be held at the University of New Mexico, to have the problem addressed at the national level. Once again, the national association refused to support this effort or to cooperate with the IHS in co-sponsoring or providing financial support for this conference. This type of insensitivity is probably not unique among predominantly Anglo national organizations. However, it does illustrate the struggle that exists: on the one hand, the bureaucracy, in order to educate the educators, follows the leaders (who are predominantly Anglo); on the other hand, the real need is for the educators to reach the public, including those almost exclusively the non-Anglo, who are unserved, underrepresented, and underserved populations.

Will it take a major coup on the part of groups such as Blacks, Hispanics, Native Americans, and the handicapped to gain their human and constitutional rights? Even then, there still exists the problem of past injustices that bind minorities with emotional shackles. One cannot put an individual in an athletic event, remove his or her shackles, and expect that individual to keep pace with everyone else. Those centuries of shackles have caused handicapping wounds that may require decades to heal and overcome. National organizations and training institutions, therefore, must show leadership in moving beyond mere acceptance to placate racial and ethnic groups, to recognition and encouragement of the right to existence and self-determination of these different cultures.

Educational institutions and organizations must be dedicated to the cultural enrichment of all children through affirmation and preservation of cultural variations and alternatives. Is America anything other than the personification of cultural diversity? In reality, America is a nation of immigrants, refugees, and former slaves, all having brought across the waters their cultures and ethnic and national customs. All of these people have struggled in a new environment, many with a new curriculum and a new language; all enriching each other through association. Indeed, America has long been a country whose uniqueness and vitality resulted from its human diversity (Stent, Hazard, and Rivlin, 1973).

Attitudes and beliefs of a nation's inhabitants, especially its youth, are shaped by its educational institutions. That shaping is not accidental. It is both strategically and systematically implemented on a national scale and can be either beneficial or extremely dangerous. Our national leaders and national organizations, schools, colleges, and training programs should be committed to the development at all levels of the educational process to the tenets that individual worth and dignity are fundamental and that people of various social and ethnic backgrounds can learn freely from one another, understand who they are, and where they are going. Otherwise, we are a nation in serious trouble. Evidence of such commitment would be the existence of faculty, staff, and student bodies that reflect proportionately the culturally diverse nature of our society.

Language and Culture[1]

All children have a right to develop linguistic abilities consonant with their highest aspirations. Unfortunately, the societal attitudes attached to socially stigmatized varieties of English transcend the linguistic competence of such dialects and affect the child's aspirations. The reality for the child is that these attitudes may serve later as a basis for and impact upon academic placement, education, and employment.

The imposition of the language of the ruler or majority culture on the ruled or minority culture is a fundamental condition of domination. It is not by chance that *the rulers* speak of their own language as *language* and the language of the ruled as *dialect*; the *superiority* and *richness* of the former placed over and against the *poverty* and *inferiority* of the latter.

In 1979, parents of eleven Black students living in Ann Arbor's Green Road Housing Project filed federal suit in Michigan's Eastern District Court accusing school officials at Martin Luther King, Jr. High School of insensitivity to the indigenous speech of these students. Parents demanded that school authorities *recognize* Black English as a formal and distinct dialect with a cultural/historical basis and its own grammatical structure. In what has become known as the Ann Arbor Decision, the judge ruled that the school district must recognize Black English, the language the students speak at home, and develop a program for helping teachers to recognize this language and take it into account when teaching Standard American English to speakers whose indigenous language is Black English.

The judge summarized, however, that Black dialect is not "a language that is...an acceptable method of communication in the educational world, in the commercial community, in the community of arts and sciences, or among professionals (Joiner, 1979). The validity of an alternative system from which to draw as needed on a day-to-day basis therefore exists on a social basis alone. However, it is no longer a question of the legitimacy of Black English, but what to do about it and the many other variations of English encountered in the Schools.

Fanon (1967) stressed that to take on a language is to take on a culture. How then must Blacks, Hispanics, Asians, and other ethnic communities take on this language, this self-proclaimed standard, without sacrifice to their own indigenous cultures? After all, any other language/dialect would have done just as well.

What is suggested is that the learning of Standard American English as a *second* language is sufficient to function adequately within the mainstream of American society. As Wilson (1978) suggested, the learning of a new language for the *primary* purpose of assimilation is the first step toward alienation and can throw the child into the midst of a personal crisis. Essentially, what is needed is to become bilingual/bidialectal/bicultural; acquiring Standard American English as a second language, or according to Dillard (1972) a *quasi-foreign language*, and becoming knowledgeable of Anglo American culture.

It is both a challenge and a responsibility to assist children who speak various dialects in becoming fluent in the alternative system of Standard American English without sacrifice to their culture, positive self-image, and chances to learn. For example, Black dialect is not a problem, it is a difference; one that is rooted in slavery as well as in rich heritage, learned from and spoken in many Black homes and communities. Although Black dialect is spoken by only some of the people some of the time, "it is and has been used at some time by eighty percent of the Black people in this country" (Joiner, 1979). It is a reality that most Black children, as well as the large number of children in other ethnic communities, still grow up in environments where "White English" is the exception rather than the rule.

The problem in schools is whether a linguistic feature is a legitimate difference or indicative of a speech and/or language disorder. If a feature is characteristic of the speech of the child's peers and community, i.e., the speaker's indigenous norms, it is a legitimate linguistic as well as cultural difference and should be approached accordingly. If the linguistic feature is peculiar to a single child, a disorder should be suspected and further evaluation by a speech-language pathologist, preferably one fluent in the language/dialect of the child, should be obtained. Left unidentified, a genuine speech or language disorder may seriously affect a child's cognitive skills, growth, and development.

Teacher Attitudes

Physical desegregation can be legislated, but attitudes cannot. Attitudes on the part of teachers and national organizations are extremely important in progressing toward the free society this country professes. In addition to skills and knowledge, teacher attitudes must be a major focus and, in many cases, will need to be reshaped for the positive education of the bilingual/bicultural child. The fact that early programs were established with negative connotations of *disadvantaged* and *cultually deprived* suggests the reality of prejudicial attitudes.

Educational research has shown that teachers' attitudes affect students behavior and that many teachers' attitudes are negative regarding human differences, especially cultural differences (Ramirez and Ramirez, 1974). This phenomenon results in painful psychological problems for a child. For example, rejection of Spanish dialect, Black dialect, or of anything in the cultural life of the child is essentially a rejection of the child. Language, once again, serves not only a communicative function, but also an identity function.

Addressing a Leadership Training Institute on Multicultural Education, Geneva Gay, in discussing teacher attitudes, made quite clear that introspection is a prerequisite for change. She indicated that it is of primary importance that teachers become:

> consciously aware of their own racial and ethnic attitudes, values, beliefs, and behaviors. They need to recognize and clarify their own ethnic heritages and cultural identities, and understand how these influence their behaviors and perceptions of reality. This means satisfying their need to be secure in knowing who they are and what they believe. Once they understand their own ethnic heritage and needs to discover feelings of personal worth, and become familiar with how these processes work, they are more likely to appreciate, respect, and better facilitate needs and processes in students. (1976, p. 5)

Policy Statements, Resolutions, and Action

In order to identify efforts of national organizations in the area of bilingual/biculturalism, the author conducted a survey of 52 organizations in 1979. The return rate was 33%. The content of the survey questionnaire was aimed at determining (a) whether or not each organization had an official position on bilingual/biculturalism, and, if so, what that position was; (b) if the organization had a specific program (special or within the organizational structure) or persons responsible for concerns in the area of bilingual/ biculturalism; (c) what the organization's goals and objectives were in the areas of bilingual/ biculturalism; and (d) what specific activities had been conducted or were planned to address the problems of bilingual/ biculturalism.

Among the 17 organizations responding, several had official positions, resolutions, or special projects. Only a few, the Center for Applied Linguistics, National Education Association, and Association for Supervision and Curriculum Development, had organizational units or staffed projects whose primary responsibility was in the area of bilingual/ biculturalism. More commonly, organizations indicated that the area of bilingual/ biculturalism was an *expanded* role of an existing program. The expanded role model was implemented often in lieu of a separate organizational unit, to maximize the use of existing human resources. It is an understatement that there appears to be a gap between theory and practice. Only the productive activities on the part of the national organizations can attest to whether deployment of personnel was the case, or whether a token effort to placate minority membership advocacy or to alleviate federal pressures was the impetus for policy development and implementation.

Survey results indicate national organizations are at various stages in addressing concerns in the area of bilingual/ biculturalism. Most organizations are at the level of policy statement, there being a large gap between policy statement and committed action. Organizations that are serious in their policy statements will proceed to fill this gap.

The following organizations were found to be active in the area of bilingual/ biculturalism.

American Association of School Administrators (AASA)

The AASA does not have a specific program in bilingual/ biculturalism. However, the AASA formalized a position in its 1979 Platform and Resolutions. In essence, the resolution recognizes bilingual instruction as a useful educational strategy for students whose home language is other than English, the intent of which is transitional in nature. The resolution also indicates that a local education agency should be responsible for carrying out *only* those guidelines as published in the *Federal Register* (AASA, 1979).

American Association of Community and Junior Colleges (AACJC)

AACJC holds as one of its goals the development and assistance of community colleges in providing bilingual/ bicultural programs and services. AACJC has no formal program, but its Board of Directors has formally endorsed the principle of equal educational opportunity for all citizens and sponsored bilingual educational workshops and conferences. One project toward this goal has focused on the development of services for Spanish-speaking students in community colleges and was supported by a grant from the W.K. Kellogg Foundation. AACJC also has affiliated itself with other organizations in an attempt to mobilize toward this goal. El Congresso Nacional de Asantos Colegiales is a council affiliated with AACJC and the International/Intercultural Consortium is a group of approximately 40 colleges supporting special services at AACJC.

Association for Supervision and Curriculum Development (ASCD)

ASCD has a well-staffed Latino Project on Bilingual Education. ASCD has passed three resolutions related to bilingualism and has been responsible for several published articles and one booklet in the area of bilingual education. Existing plans are for an annual conference activity on bilingual education and for publication of a handbook titled *English as a Second Language for the Hispanic Child*.

Center for Applied Linguistics (CAL)

The Center for Applied Linguistics is probably one of the most active organizations in the area of bilingual/bicultural education. This internationally recognized leader in bilingual and multicultural education has as its aim the application of linguistic science to the resolution of social and educational problems. In 1974, CAL assisted the San Francisco Unified School District in development of the Master Plan for Bilingual/Bicultural Education. CAL also has prepared the *Guidelines for the Preparation and Certification of Teachers of Bilingual/Bicultural Education*.

The Center's main emphasis is pragmatic: classroom teaching. In the area of teacher education, CAL stresses the inclusion of linguistic information and preservice and inservice training. CAL has developed criteria for adequate training and skills in the areas of language proficiency, the nature and function of language in society, instructional methods, curriculum development, assessment, and evaluation.

Information dissemination is a major role of this research and service organization. Dissemination vehicles have included workshops, training, and publications. Since 1975, CAL has housed the National Indochinese Clearinghouse and Technical Assistance Center, which has published over 50 specialized bulletins and guides for teachers and sponsors of refugee children and adults.

National Association of State Boards of Education (NASBE)

Bilingual/biculturalism was one of the major issues singled out at the 1979 convention of NASBE, specifically the cultural and linguistic diversity presently found in schools, and projections for the future. A group of Hispanic state board members has been focusing its efforts on the concerns of bilingual/bicultural children and their cultural diversity. The development of a position paper on bilingual/bicultural education and policy implications for state board members has been assigned.

In 1979, NASBE adopted an official position on bilingual/bicultural education which is included in its document on *Standing Resolutions and Position Statements* (NASBE, 1979). Its position addresses the availability of transitional programs that teach subject matter in both English and the primary language of the pupil to assure the continued educational development of such students. It also encourages parents "to learn and to help their children learn and use English as their primary language." This position contrasts with comments in the previous Language and Culture section of this chapter.

NASBE's concern with the needs of special populations led to the adoption of two resolutions that include the cultural as well as the linguistic aspects of the student population. The first such resolution addresses the needs of Native American children; the second refers to the migrant population (NASBE, 1979):

1. Educational programs for Native Americans should acknowledge the diversity of their culture and traditions. Native Americans should be involved in the development and administration of such programs. Training for teachers of Native American students should include education in the history, culture, traditions, customs, and values of Native Americans.
2. Cooperative efforts should be developed to assure identification and education of all migrant children.

The goal of NASBE as an agency is to facilitate informed decision making by State Board Members by providing training and technical assistance. Its background paper developed on the topic of bilingual/bicultural education will serve the purpose of generating additional areas of interests as identified by members. NASBE, in turn, will respond to these at the state, regional, and national levels.

Its second goal, related to government affairs, is to keep members informed on congressional activity and legislative matters affecting education in the states. NASBE has monitored closely the legislative mandates that have a direct impact on bilingual education, such as the Bilingual Education Act of 1968, Title I of the Elementary and Secondary Education Act, and the Emergency School Aid Act.

National Education Association (NEA)

NEA activities include publications, training, and legislative monitoring in response to its primary goals and objectives for bilingual/bicultural education. The activities include legislative support, awareness training, and dissemination of information.

NEA believes that the bilingual education process uses a student's primary language as the principle medium of instruction, while teaching the language of the predominant culture in an organized program encompassing a multicultural curriculum. It urges that bilingual/multicultural programs include as a goal functional proficiency in English, with emphasis on the development of those basic reading skills essential to the successful pursuit of other disciplines. NEA also believes that legislation must provide funds to expand current multicultural and bilingual language programs, including those programs for teacher preparation necessary to provide equal opportunity to all students in the public schools. Accordingly, appropriate federal legislation is supported and NEA affiliates are urged to seek state legislation that requires bilingual/multicultural education according to educational need.

Student National Education Association (SNEA)

The SNEA has adopted two very specific resolutions on bilingual/multicultural education and human relations in the schools:

R-2. Bilingual-Multicultural Education

The Student National Education Association supports appropriate legislation that requires bilingual-multicultural education according to educational need. The Association believes that educational materials and processes should accurately portray cultural diversity and the contributions of ethnic minority groups. Ethnic minority teachers must be involved in selecting educational materials and preparing teachers for their use.

R-6. Human Relations in the School

The Student National Education Association believes that improved human relations is essential to the school environment. To improve human relations in schools, the Association supports:

a. School recruitment policies that will ensure culturally diverse certified and support staff.
b. The reduction of class size.
c. Research and development of means to reduce prejudiced behavior.

In addition to publication of a *Human Relations Training in Teacher Education Handbook* which advocates teacher training in bilingual/multicultural education, SNEA has periodically conducted bilingual/multicultural workshops for its members and is presently developing a multiethnic awareness packet. Their major activity in this area of bilingual/multicultural education deals with the education and preparation of future teachers and, as such, endeavors to have an impact upon teacher education curricula at colleges and universities across the country.

Speech Communication Association (SCA)

Responsibilities in the area of bilingual/biculturalism are a part of the duties of the SCA Director of Educational Services. A Subcommittee on Educational Program Development exists as a part of this program. Although formal goals and objectives in the area of bilingual/biculturalism are still in the development process, bilingual/bicultural program standards and test criteria have been developed. A national conference on assessment and testing of oral communication competence is forthcoming.

Among SCA criteria for evaluating instruments and procedures of assessing speaking and listening are two which have impact on the assessment of the bilingual/bicultural client:

1. Assessment should test skills that are important for various communication settings rather than be limited to one setting. Assessment should permit a range of *acceptable* response, where such a range is appropriate.
2. The SCA, in conjunction with the American Speech-Language-Hearing Association, prepared *Basic Assumptions of Standards for Effective Oral Communication Programs.* Among those assumptions are included: (a) there is a wide range of communication competence among speakers of the same language; and (b) communication competence is not dependent upon use of a particular form of language. (SCA, 1979, p. 2)

What We Can Do

The February 1981 Convention of the Council for Exceptional Children (CEC) in New Orleans is one example of what can be done. Half of the four day conference was dedicated to the bilingual exceptional child while the other half addressed the needs of the Black child. Problems and issues were raised and addressed, including the application of therapy approaches, programs, and other educational innovations. Special interest groups further exchanged ideas, shared research, and developed consultant rosters. Some of the same participants continued their discussions in the Bilingual/ Bicultural Special Interest Groups meeting in Los Angeles at the May 1981 convention of the National Black Association of Speech, Language, and Hearing, where specific recommendations were made for the national organization to consider. CEC continued its efforts for bilingual children with another national conference in Phoenix in October, 1982.

In its policy position on multicultural education, the American Federation of Teachers outlines four major thrusts as an integral part of the educational process: (a) the teaching of values that support cultural diversity and individual uniqueness, (b) the encouragement of the qualitative expansions of existing ethnic cultures and their incorporation into the mainstream of American socioeconomic and political life, (c) the support of exploration of alternative and emerging lifestyles, and (d) the encouragement of multiculturalism, multilingualism, and multidialectism (Shanker, 1978). When accepting these as a basis for development, there are several worthy areas in which activity should be initiated, in some cases increased, or in yet other cases continued. These areas encompass testing, credentialing, certification, inservice training, research, funding, evaluation, and model program development.

Testing

The role of national organizations and training programs in test development, clarification, guidance, and their use and misuse can be positive and powerful or negative and dangerous. Tests must be developed for cultural/ethnic groups: not as a means of changing standards criteria but as a vehicle for making criteria applicable, appropriate, and valid for cultural/ethnic groups. In addition, innovative ways are needed to administer both existing and new tests. Examples of such innovations are the System of Multicultural Pluralistic Assessment (SOMPA System) developed by Mercer (1979) and the Inventory of Social Dialect Features developed by Cole (1980a, 1980b). Other useful tests may be found in *A Resource Guide to Multicultural Tests and Materials* (Cole and Snope, 1981) and *Nondiscriminatory Assessment: Vol. I, A Practioner's Guide and Vol. II, A Test Matrix* (Watson, Omark, Grouell, and Heller, 1980).

Although test results do provide evidence of learning and are helpful when viewed in their proper context, their importance frequently is exaggerated, and their results are misused. An example of such misuse is the labeling or *mislabeling* of children with high aptitude and poor test performance. While the abolition of standardized tests is not advocated, there should be a national effort in both teacher and public education to investigate their strengths and weaknesses, proper uses, and definite limitations. Further, the roles of education and training extend to and have impact on publisher requirements in terms of dissemination of materials. Lobbying by national organizations for federal and state legislation for publisher requirements for test materials is recommended.

Credentials and Certification

Certification and licensure of bilingual personnel must be promoted and encouraged on a national scale and at the national level. Such licensure/certification should include requirements in substantive instructional areas, especially mathematics, art, science, and elementary education, as well as in the areas of bilingual education and language skills. Teacher credentials in the area of fluency are of fundamental concern. True bilingualism assumes equal competence and fluency in the English language as well as another. It has been observed that many teachers considered to be bilingual are not, and speak English poorly (Shanker, 1978). Others have been found to speak only English.

State Boards of Education, national organizations, and training programs can be instrumental in changing state teacher certification requirements. An example of such a needed change is the expansion of national accreditation standards to include human relations training for all teachers (SNEA, 1976). State funded contracts could extend this reality to the local level.

Research and Funding

National organizations and training programs must encourage, promote, and serve as catalysts for increases in the quantity and quality of research in the area of bilingual/biculturalism. Accordingly, national organizations must take aggressive leadership roles in seeking increased general funding as well as new program funding. The emphasis should be on pragmatic and meaningful research designed to meet the dialectical needs of the classroom teacher. Special focus also should be on support for programs that can be maintained at the local level following termination of outside funding.

Inservice Training

Inservice training, research, and programs will depend in large part on funding. Inservice training must not be limited to new personnel but also be considered primary for the training and retaining of existing personnel, especially in cases of new bilingual program development. In some areas, children still are being placed in bilingual education programs on the basis of surname or ethnic background. Only demonstrated deficiency in English proficiency should be used as the placement criterion (Ward and Maldonado, 1979). Therefore, dissemination of information and implementation must be *en masse*, with a multiplier effect that filters to the local level in increasing numbers.

Evaluation

Essential to all training must be evaluation to assure that appropriate skills and understanding have been achieved (*see* Chapter 20). Program evaluation illustrates that too many bilingual education programs are not effective and/or have deviated from the intent of the supporting federal program. Regulations designed to implement the Bilingual Education Act are therefore important.

To end the abuse and ineffectiveness of some bilingual programs, accountability measures must be strengthened. Evaluation therefore must be a critical moment in the event of bilingual/bicultural education. Viewed appropriately, it will serve as an ultimate link in the search for new forms of action. It is appropriate to look at one's own practice as a problem—the critical moment of evaluation, critical reflection. Between the concrete context of praxis and the theoretical context of critical reflection there must be a dialectical relationship. Critical reflection should be an indispensable component of daily praxis in order to develop a new theory that will in turn illumine new practice.

Model Program

Traditional bilingual eduation programs are transitional in nature for the purpose of placing children in regular school programs as soon as possible. However, all do not function as transitional programs; a study by the American Institutes for Research for the United States Office of Education found that "in the programs examined less than one-third of the students in the bilingual programs were there because of limited English speaking ability and that students with language deficiencies have been retained in bilingual programs after having achieved competency in English" (Ward and Maldonado, 1979, p. 9).

The model bilingual education program would be one in which there is an English language program for non-English speakers, a specific foreign langue program for English-speaking students, and instruction in curriculum areas in both languages. Such a program would meet the needs of non-English speaking and limited English-speaking children by providing basic skills (regular curriculum) instruction in a language in which the students are fluent and can effectively participate (their dominant language), as well as intensive English language instruction. Although the development of such programs is possible, until more money is available, they will be impossible on a national scale.

Conclusion

The struggle for cultural pluralism is before us, and it is an international one. The internal social revolution in the United States and the social and political revolution throughout the world today will test United States national policy and attitudes toward human differences and human rights. To provide for the needs of the bilingual/bicultural child, conditions must be established under which equal education, social, economic, and political opportunities are possible, we must bridge the gap between theory and practice.

National organizations and training programs must have true self-determined identity and a politically and ideologically clear purpose. That identity and purpose must be directed by committed initiative, creativity, and action toward filling the sociocultural needs of limited English-speaking and non-English speaking children and children who speak socially stigmatized dialects. Only when we achieve social, cultural, educational, economic, and political parity will we as a nation be worthy of our peoples and our tomorrows.

Note

[1]The section titled "Language and Culture" is from Nuru, U.: Black English: Who Be a Winner? *Black Child Journal, 1* (3), 1980. Courtesy of *Black Child Journal,* Chicago, Illinois.

References

AASA: American Association of School Administrators 1979 Platform and Resolutions. Article 54. *Bilingual Education.* Arlington, American Association of School Administrators, 1979.

Aragon, J.:   An impediment to cultural pluralism: Culturally deficient teachers attempting to teach culturally different children. In Stent, M., Hazard, W., and Rivlin, H.N. (Eds.): *Cultural Pluralism in Education: A Mandate for Change.* New York, Appleton-Century-Crofts, 1973.

Carnoy, M.:   *Education as Cultural Imperialism.* New York, David McKay, 1974.

Cole, L.T.: *Comments of the American Speech-Language-Hearing Association Concerning the Effects of the Apartheid System in South Africa on Service Delivery and Training in Speech Pathology and Audiology.* Rockville, American Speech-Language-Hearing Association, 1980a.

Cole, L.T.: *The Developmental Analysis of Social Dialect Features in the Spontaneous Language of Pre-School Black Children.* Dissertation, Northwestern University, 1980b.

Cole, L.T., and Snope, T.: A resource guide to multicultural tests and materials. *ASHA, 23,* 1981.

Dillard, J.L.: *Black English: Its History and Usage in the United States.* New York, Random House, 1972.

Fanon, F.: *Black Skin, White Masks.* New York, Grove, 1967.

Friere, P.: *Pedagogy of the Oppressed.* New York, Seaburg, 1970.

Friere, P.: *Pedagogy in Process.* New York, Seaburg, 1978.

Gay, G.: *Curriculum for Multicultural Teacher Education.* Presented at the Leadership Training Institute on Multicultural Education in Teacher Education, American Association of Colleges for Teacher Education and the U.S. Office of Education, Washington, D.C., April, 1976.

Joiner, C.W.: *Memorandum Opinion and Order: Martin Luther King Junior Elementary School Children, et al. v. Ann Arbor School District Board* (Civil Action No. 7-71861). United States District Court. Eastern District of Michigan, Southern Division. Detroit, July 12, 1979.

kwa Salaam, T.: *Working Together We Can Make a Change.* New Orleans, Nkombo, 1981.

Lenin, V.I., and Stalin, J.V.: *Selections from V.I. Lenin and J.V. Stalin on the National Colonial Question.* Calcutta, Calcutta Book House, 1970.

Mercer, J.: *System of Multicultural Pluralistic Assessment.* New York, Psychological Corp, 1979.

NASBE: *Standing Resolutions and Position Statements.* Washington, D.C., National Association of State Boards of Education, 1979.

Nuru, N., and Coppock, B.: *General State Supervision of Services to All Handicapped Children.* Washington, D.C., Council of Chief State School Officers, 1979.

Nuru, N.: Black English: Who be a winner? *Black Child J, 1,* 1980.

Ramirez, M., III, and Ramirez, C.: *Cultural Democracy, Bicognitive Development in Education.* New York, Academic, 1974.

SCH: *Resources for Assessment in Communication.* Falls Church, Speech Communication Association, 1979.

Shanker, A.: AFT position and policy in regard to multicultural education and in regard to ethnic groups and their related educational problems. *Educational Issues,* March, 1978.

Shanker, A.: Where we stand. Bilingual education must be expanded. *New York Times,* May 28, 1978.

Sizemore, B.:   Making the schools a vehicle for cultural pluralism. In Stent, M., Hazard, W.R., and Rivlin, H.N. (Eds.): *Cultural Pluralism in Education: A Mandate for Change*. New York, Appleton-Century-Crofts, 1973.

Student National Education Association: *Human Relations Training in Teacher Education Handbook*. Washington, D.C., Student National Education Association, 1976.

Stent, M., Hazard, W.R., and Rivlin, H.N. (Eds.):   *Cultural Pluralism in Education: A Mandate for Change*. New York, Appleton-Century-Crofts, 1973.

Toure, S.:   A dialectical approach to culture. *The Black Scholar, November*, 1969.

United States Commission of Education: *First Report of the U.S. Commissioner of Education to the U.S. and Congress on the Condition of Bilingual Education in the Nation*. Fall River, National Assessment and Dissemination Center, 1976.

Valverde, L.A. (Ed.):   *Bilingual Education for Latinos*. Washington, D.C., Association for Supervision and Curriculum Development, 1978.

Ward, J.G., and Maldonado, D.:   *Language and Children: The Issues of Bilingual Education*. Washington, D.C., American Federation of Teachers, 1979.

Watson, D.L., Omark, D.R., Grouell, S., and Heller, B.:   *Nondiscriminatory Assessment: Vol. I, Practitioner's Handbook and Vol. II, A Test Matrix*. Sacramento, California State Department of Education, 1980.

Wilson, A.N.:   *Developmental Psychology of the Black Child*. New York, Africana Research Publications, 1978.

Federal Legislation

Civil Rights Act of 1964, Title VI, Section 601.

Memorandum of Clarification, Department of Health, Education, and Welfare, U.S. Office of Civil Rights, 1970.

Elementary and Secondary Education Act, Title I and Title VII. Bilingual Education Act, 1978.

18

Model Preschool Programs for Handicapped Bilingual Children

Joyce Evans

When children are 6 years of age or older, the responsibility for educational programing is reasonably clear; it rests with public schools. For younger children the responsibility is less clearly defined, and a variety of agencies as well as professions may be responsible. Federal or state support of programs and services for preschoolers and their families is reflected through local services provided by various agencies such as day care or Head Start programs as well as public school programs. The handicapped, bilingual preschooler represents a subset of the children served by a variety of agencies and professionals. In this chapter, *bilingual* refers to speakers who are non-English proficient (NEP), limited English proficient (LEP), or bilingual.

Public child care programs, such as those supported by Title XX of the Social Security Act or Head Start funding, provide services for income-eligible preschoolers, some of whom are bilingual and some of whom are also handicapped. Public schools in many states provide special education programs for young handicapped children, some of whom are bilingual. Often, these programs are supported by or initiated with federal funding from the Office of Special Education (formerly the Bureau of Education for the Handicapped). To meet the needs of the handicapped preschooler in nonpublic school as well as public school settings, the Office of Special Education (OSE) has funded a number of First Chance model projects that provide direct service to children and serve as a demonstration model. All of the children in these programs are handicapped; some are also bilingual. Thus, in contrast to programs for elementary and secondary level students, responsibility for the young bilingual child who is also handicapped does not rest exclusively with the public schools.

Litigation and legislation related to bilingual education and special education have been discussed in previous chapters. However, it is important to note that, in spite of the enactment of P.L. 94–142, the Education for All Handicapped Children Act, in many states programing for preschool handicapped children remains permissive, not mandatory. Issues of language, identification, and assessment have been discussed in earlier chapters. These issues are even more potent when applied to the younger child. Assessment is a difficult as well as controversial issue for all young children and becomes even more complex when the factors of culture and native language must be considered.

A distinction should be made here between bilingual programs and English as a Second Language (ESL) programs. Since the passage of the Bilingual Education Act, the trend has been toward the use of the child's native language as a medium of instruction. Often all programs using this approach are erroneously called bilingual programs. A true bilingual program is one in which emphasis is on increasing the child's proficiency in the first language and using this language for instructional purposes, as well as instructing the child in the development of English language skills. More often, programs are actually transfer or transitional programs, focusing on teaching English and using the child's first language as a means of communication only until mastery of English is sufficient for future academic progress. These transitional programs are more accurately referred to as ESL Programs. In a bilingual program, ESL is an instructional component of the total curriculum, but equal emphasis is on development of basic knowledge in the child's first language.

For the handicapped preschooler, this distinction is particularly important. In an ESL program, where the emphasis is on learning English, children may fall behind in learning basic information or concepts because there is no instruction in their first language. On the other hand, because many handicapped children have difficulty in both understanding what they hear and in speaking either language, the question arises as to whether they should be required to learn two languages, or in some cases, three languages. For example, should a child with a severe hearing impairment learn Spanish, English, and Signing? The question of instructional language is unresolved and needs to be addressed by future research.

The needs of non-English-speaking preschoolers who are also handicapped have received limited attention, and available written information is limited. Traditional approaches of reviewing the literature, including computer searches, were of little assistance in preparing this chapter. Even programs currently in operation have produced few articles. Funding is often so tenuous that program directors focus on seeking funds for continuing their programs rather than preparing journal articles or resource documents for information retrieval centers such as ERIC.

In order to identify model programs for the bilingual handicapped, the Office of Special Education provided a list of all First Chance projects which assist bilingual children and Resource Access Projects supported by the Administration for Children, Youth, and Families. Information on Head Start programs that serve the target group was supplied. Other programs were identified through a literature search and by personal experience.

Program Descriptions

Several types of programs serving the bilingual handicapped preschooler are briefly described in the following sections, including both home-based and center- or class-based programs. Few of these programs are limited to bilingual or non-English speakers, although only programs that have at least one-third enrollment of bilingual children are included. Many Head Start and day care programs provide services for bilingual preschoolers, including some who are also handicapped. However, only those programs that have clearly identifiable services for the handicapped bilingual are described below.

The various programs described in this chapter have many basic similarities as well as some differences and unique characteristics. A more comprehensive description of the individual programs is available through ERIC (Evans, 1980). Additional information about a specific program may be obtained by writing each one.

All of the programs were initiated with some type of federal funding as a special or model program. Many of the programs continue to receive federal or state funding, and a few are now supported by local public schools. Nearly all of the project directors interviewed consider the stability and adequacy of funding a major problem.

All of the persons interviewed stated that their programs focus on the specific needs of the individual child, and individualized plans are developed with input from various professionals. The number and types of professionals participating in the development of individual plans vary. A few programs have a variety of specialists on staff, e.g., speech/language pathologists and physical therapists. Other programs employ specialists on a half-day or part-time basis and some programs employ outside consultants as needed. In turn, the use of local resources varies. Programs with few on-staff specialists utilize community resources to a greater extent.

In all of the programs, instruction of the child focuses on development of basic skills, such as self-help and language, rather than academic instruction. The extent to which instruction focuses on development of the child's primary language varies. Some programs include instruction in both languages, while others are ESL programs using the home language to develop English language skills.

Parents are involved in all of the programs, although the extent of involvement varies. Several programs, particularly those serving children under the age of 3, are home-based rather than center- or classroom-based. In the home-based programs training or instruction is usually directed towards parents or other family members rather than the child. However, some of the center-based programs also instruct parents on ways of working with their children. The importance of parents is definitely recognized, and in many cases the desire for increased parental involvement was stated.

Paraprofessionals or teacher aides play an important role in all programs but the extent of direct responsibility varies. In home-based programs the paraprofessional often serves as the home instructor or visitor for the child and family, with direct instructional responsibility. In public school classroom-based programs, the paraprofessional usually assists the teacher, has less direct instructional responsibility, and has less contact with parents. In several programs, the paraprofessional is the only bilingual staff person; however, in a few programs all staff are bilingual.

The most obvious differences among programs relate to the target group of children served. Programs funded specifically to serve handicapped children, such as the First Chance and public school programs, do not include nonhandicapped children. In contrast, programs funded by the Administration of Children, Youth, and Families (Head Start, and Indian, and Migrant Program Development) serve handicapped children within a larger group of nonhandicapped children. Another major difference is that some programs serve children beginning at birth and other programs serve older preschoolers.

These differences and similarities reflect the underlying philosophies and approaches to meeting local needs in working with bilingual handicapped children and their families. Also reflected are very practical aspects such as funding. More money means more staff, more specialists, and the ability to provide family assistance as well as direct child instruction.

Program Summaries

The following program summaries were obtained through written questionnaires and telephone interviews, usually with the program director. To obtain information about model programs for handicapped bilingual children, more than 250 letters were written and more than 50 telephone calls were made. In addition, several personal interviews were conducted. Questions asked were related to the following topics: (a) site setting and funding, (b) number, types, and ages of handicapped children, (c) identification and selection procedures, (d) staffing, (e) parent involvement, (f) program focus, (g) instructional language, and (h) major problems encountered.

All of the information provided could not be included in the following summaries. Therefore, the name and address of the contact person follows each program title for those who wish to obtain more detailed information. The program summaries are ordered chronologically according to the ages of the children served.

Infant/Parent Education Program and Drew State Preschool Program

>Vivian Weinstein
>Charles R. Drew Medical School
>12021 Wilmington
>Los Angeles, CA 90059

Handicapped children from birth through 5 years are served through a combination of the Infant/Parent Education Program, the Drew State Preschool Program, and the Los Angeles County Schools Program. These programs are located in or near the area of the Martin Luther King, Jr. Hospital in the Watts Community of Los Angeles.

In the Infant/Parent Education Program approximately half of the 27 children are Mexican American, and of this group 90% of the parents are Spanish-speakers, recent immigrants from Mexico. The Community Health Worker works with parents and acts as a translator. When the children are 6 to 9 months old, a center-based, 1-day-a-week program is initiated.

The Drew State Preschool Program serves thirty-two 3-to-5-year-old children, 15 of whom are handicapped. Of the total group, approximately 25% are Mexican American, and one-half of these are from monolingual Spanish-speaking homes. In this integrated program, center-based classes are conducted for three and one-half hours each day, and a hot lunch is served. Handicapped children are transported to the center and nonhandicapped children are from the immediate area. One of the greatest strengths of this integrated program is the learning that occurs when the handicapped and nonhandicapped children are placed together.

The Los Angeles County Schools Program serves approximately 32 children from 18 months through 3 years, including children referred from the Infant/Parent Education Program. Approximately one-third of these children are from Spanish-speaking homes. Center-based classes meet daily for four hours, and home visits are conducted periodically.

One of the major problems is the extreme poverty of the families in this area. Parents are often overwhelmed by lack of basic necessities, overcrowding, health problems, and other poverty-related problems. Often more than one child in a family has a handicapping condition. The enormity of the problem was underestimated initially, necessitating increased emphasis on helping parents learn how to cope with the system in matters such as obtaining food stamps or health services or interacting with the school.

Handicapped Early Childhood Assistance Program

Mary Cavazos, Director
940 E. Washington
Brownsville, TX 78520

This project serves approximately 40 handicapped Mexican Americans under the age of 3 years; 80% are monolingual Spanish-speakers; and Spanish is the primary language for the remaining 20%. The project staff serves the children in a home-based program with consultant assistance from Pan American University, Brownsville, TX, which also provides staff training. Relevancy of lesson plans and parent involvement activities to the language and culture of the families is essential, as many families are recent arrivals from Mexico.

Lori Ann Infant Center

Ann Benninghove, Coordinator
651 B Street
Fresno, CA 93760

An average of 40 children under 3 years of age who have been identified to have developmental delay or who are at risk because of prenatal or birth trauma are served by the Lori Ann Center. Begun by a small group of parents, financial assistance was provided initially by a variety of private and public sources. Today the greatly expanded program is supported by state special education funds. The Lori Ann Center serves Black, Anglo, and Mexican American children through a home program for children under 18 months of age and a center program for older children.

Parent involvement is an integral part of both the home and center programs. Monthly parent meetings are social as well as educational, and parents of children attending the center are asked to visit and observe in the classroom whenever possible. Although formal follow-up studies have not been conducted, yearly reports are made to the California State Department of Education regarding change in the children's performance and referrals to other public and private preschool programs. In general, children leaving the program have been placed in classes for the physically handicapped, trainable mentally retarded, visually handicapped, or in the Development Center for Children with Multiple Handicaps.

Sunshine Cottage/Trinity University Parent-Infant Program

June Grant
Trinity University
715 Stadium Drive
San Antonio, TX 78284

Hearing-impaired Mexican American children under the age of 3 years, many of whom are multi-handicapped, are served in this program (*see* Chapter 19). An average of 17 children and their parents attend the home demonstration center each week, and a bilingual staff member works with each parent and child in the home on a weekly basis. At age 3, the children move into public school classes for the hearing-impaired or into regular preschool programs.

Infant-Parent Training Program

Madeline Sutherland
Mental Health-Mental Retardation Center
3804 Cherrywood
Austin, TX 78722

Approximately 100 handicapped children under age 3, 35% of whom are Mexican American, are served in this program. Many of the aides and parent volunteers are bilingual, although this is not a major problem since few families are non-English-speaking. A unique feature of this program is the provision of child care services for working mothers. At age 3, most of the children enter public school classes for the handicapped, although some of the children are able to enter regular nursery school programs.

Transportation has been a major problem, as the Infant/Parent Center serves primarily a poverty-level population. Because the children served are so very young, they tire easily, and the length of instruction time is limited. Written reports of this program were completed as a part of First Chance reporting, and a number of products have been produced, including: *Parents and Children, Activities and Environments for Infants and Toddlers* and *Developmental Roles and Anchor Goals in Infant Education*, by Drezek. These are available upon request from the Infant-Parent Training Program.

Comprehensive Infant Intervention Program

Isaura Barrera
Project CIIP, Cardenas Center
3300 Ruiz Street
San Antonio, TX 78228

Mexican American children are served through flexible combinations of home- and center-based programs from birth until eligible for public school early childhood programs for the handicapped at age 3. Children with all types of handicapping conditions are included, and many of the children are multiply handicapped.

A unique feature of this program is the use of Total Communication (verbal and nonverbal) as well as English and Spanish for instructional purposes. The children are taught in the language to which they are most responsive and the language in which the greatest progress can be made. A second language is introduced as appropriate based on (a) the child's ability to handle two languages, (b) the parents' preference, and (c) potential placement as an adult.

Birth Through Two for the Visually Handicapped

Pat Adkins
6138 Aztec
El Paso, TX 79925

Visually impaired children under the age of 3 years are served in this experimental program of the Region XIX Education Service Center in El Paso. Located in a cottage setting, children and parents learn together in living room, bedroom, and kitchen "classrooms" with closed circuit television used for observation and micro-teaching with parents. Spanish is the primary instructional language since many of the parents speak only Spanish. Community support is excellent, and the program rapidly achieved visiblity and acceptance because of a previous project for older preschoolers (*see* El Paso Early Childhood Education as described in this chapter).

A major problem faced in starting this program was the lack of teachers trained to work with the visually handicapped. Staff development including visits to other centers and extension courses on the visually impaired conducted by Texas Tech University (Lubbock, TX) has resulted in certification of several teachers who now work in the public schools as well as in this program.

El Paso Early Childhood Education Programs

Janet Rasmussen
El Paso Independent School District
6101 Hughey
El Paso, TX 79925

Of the two hundred and fifty 3-to-5-year-old preschool handicapped children served by the El Paso Independent School District, approximately half are Spanish speakers. The program was initiated and operated for six years by the Region XIX Education Service Center before being incorporated into the public schools. Most classes serve all types of handicapped children, but a few classes are provided specifically for the visually impaired, the emotionally disturbed, and the orthopedically handicapped. In addition, a regional day school for the deaf serves the severely hearing-impaired child. Mexican American children are integrated into the early childhood classes for the handicapped in which either the aide or the teacher is a Spanish speaker.

Many of the children have delayed language in Spanish as well as English, and some are simply nonverbal children. A critical feature of placement meetings is parental input regarding the classroom instructional language for their child.

Through the years, parent participation has decreased. When the First Chance project was initiated as a federally-funded model, parents were required to participate at least 2½ hours each week, but this requirement could not be maintained after the program became a part of the public school system. The children's progress was more rapid and there was more carryover to the home when parents were actually involved in the program.

Infant-Family Project and CSULA-Aztec Head Start Early Training Project

Annette Tessler   Pat Simmons

Department of Special Education
California State University
5151 State University Drive
Los Angeles, CA 90032

Two separate programs serve young handicapped children on the California State University campus at Los Angeles (CSULA). The directors of both programs are in the Department of Special Education, so draw upon many of the same resources and integrate the information of the two programs. The Infant Family Project serves 32 handicapped children under age 3, 90% of whom are from Spanish-speaking families. The CSULA-Aztec Head Start Training Project serves both handicapped and nonhandicapped children from 18 months through 36 months of age.

A unique feature of the Infant-Family Project is the focus on helping parents to become more self-confident as individuals, more competent as parents, and better able to find and use community resources. A Home-School Coordinator hired from the local community is available on a 24 hour basis in order to meet family needs whenever they may arise.

Employing staff from the local community has been one of the features that strengthen this program. Each staff person is very carefully selected on the basis of previous experience working with young children and sensitivity to the cultural needs of the population served. Staff training in child development and special education is provided, and staff members often pursue college course work.

The CSULA-Aztec program has the dual focus of providing direct services to children and training other Head Start personnel. Of the children receiving services, 40% are handicapped and all but two are from Mexican American families. One of the most successful aspects of this project has been the integration of handicapped and nonhandicapped children. The handicapped children have gained through the social interaction, language, and behavior modeling of the nonhandicapped children; and the nonhandicapped children have gained by learning to socialize and accept individual differences. Parents also have benefited from this integrated approach because it has helped them to focus on the positive ways in which children interact and develop.

Careful study, understanding, and sensitivity to the many variables of the *local* community, e.g., social, religious, political, economic, and family relations are stressed. Many parents in this area are in awe or fearful of authority figures and are reluctant to express their needs and concerns. Employment of staff from the community has been a critical factor in alleviating this problem.

Early Stimulation Program

> Carmen Arroyo, Director
> Parent Child Center
> Box 8
> Grand View, WA 98944

Through a combination of home- and center-based programs, the Early Stimulation Program serves all types of handicapped children. This program enrolls an average of 16 children from birth to 4 years, 95% of whom are Mexican American. All of the staff are bilingual, and most of the instruction is in Spanish and English with emphasis placed on the particular cultural needs of the target population.

In the center-based program, which includes the nonhandicapped as well as the handicapped, children are served in three classrooms of approximately eight children for three hours each day. Other children receive one to two hours of home instruction each week from the Home Teacher who works with the parent and child. Parents are actively involved in all aspects of the program, and other community resources are utilized for services such as speech and hearing assistance.

Navajo Special Education Early Childhood Development Program

Eugene Gorman, Director
Box 1267
Shiprock, NM 87420

Thirty-two young Navajo children from birth through 8 years of age with multiple handicapping conditions are served in this project administered by the Navajo tribe. A center-based program is provided for children who live no more than a one hour round trip from school and children who are too young to attend school or who live too far away to participate in a home-based program. Instructional language for the children is based primarily on the parents' preference, which is usually Navajo and/or English. Language development in Navajo is particularly important as about half the children live with monolingual parents and/or grandparents.

A unique feature is the help of the local CETA and Foster Grandparent program which add to the program staff. Finding bilingual professionals in the area of special education and early childhood development on the Navajo reservation is difficult. To address this problem, paraprofessional staff are pursuing Child Development associate certifications through a local branch of the Navajo Community College.

Arlington Child Development Center

Lillian E. Brown, Director
Arlington Community Action Program, Inc.
2410 Columbia Pike
Arlington, VA 22204

A Head Start program serving an average of 150 children between the ages of 2 and 5 years, the Arlington Child Development Center includes Black, Anglo, Vietnamese, Iranian, Cambodian, and Hispanic children. Approximately 10% of the enrolled children are also handicapped, primarily in the areas of hearing, vision, or speech/language. Two of the nine aides and one teacher, as well as some of the volunteers who assist in the classroom, are bilingual. This center-based program operates on an 8-hour daily basis with Spanish and English used for instructional purposes.

Integrated Model for Handicapped Early Childhood Development

Miriam Sour, Director
1877 Jerome Avenue
Bronx, NY 10452

A total of 140 children, 20% of whom are handicapped, are enrolled in this program, which is located in two public schools in the district. Three- and 4-year-olds are the primary focus, although a few 5-year-olds who function at a younger level are also included. Children included represent the district's population, which is primarily Black and Hispanic. All the children live in economically depressed inner city areas, and 90% of their families receive funds from Aid to Dependent Children.

In order to serve many children with limited space and staff, the children do not attend school on a traditional 5-day per week schedule. Small groups, e.g., 10 children, attend classes twice a week for 2½ hours, and larger groups, 15 children, attend classes four times a week for 2½ hours. The fifth day of each week is reserved for parent-child workshops.

A unique feature of this program is the provision for a parent room at each site that is staffed by a full-time family assistant. The parent room is open to entire families on a continuous basis and the family assistant helps parents in obtaining information about local services such as welfare, Aid for Dependent Children, and food stamps. Through the weekly parent-child workshops, instruction also is provided on topics of particular interest to the parents.

Written information on the project is available from the project director and the chapter titled "Parent Involvement" in *Early Education in Spanish Speaking Communities* (Trohanis, 1978) gives details on parental involvement in this program. In addition, a 16mm film, "Step by Step," has been produced, available in English or Spanish.

Advancing Individual Development

Cornelia Hanna, Project Director
San Felipe-Del Rio Consolidated Independent School District
Box 1229
300 West Martin
Del Rio, TX 78840

Flexibility in scheduling of classroom- or home-based instruction to meet the specific needs of each child and family characterizes this program, which serves approximately 34 children with all types of handicapping conditions. Of the total group, 65% are Mexican American and many are monolingual Spanish speakers.

The unique arrangement of regular preschool classes, bilingual classes, and special education classes in the same building permits various alternatives for serving the handicapped child in classroom programs. In this school district, all kindergarten and pre-kindergarten children are bused to one of six campuses. One campus includes 10 kindergarten classes for nonhandicapped children, one class for nonhandicapped bilingual children, and two self-contained classes for preschool handicapped children, one serving the severely involved child and the other serving the moderately involved child. With this arrangement, plus the availability of a resource room teacher, it is possible to include some handicapped children within regular preschool classes for varying amounts of time. In addition, there is a home-based program for the very young or severely involved child.

The overall goal of the program is to maximize the probability that the child will be able to function successfully in the regular school program by first grade, or sooner. For some handicapped children, this means a home-based program before age 3 until they can move into the classroom program. Others start in the special program for 3-year-olds and spend part of the day in the regular bilingual program by the time they are 4 years old. All teachers and aides in the special education classes are bilingual, and the language of instruction depends on the needs of the child.

The dedication of the staff and their flexibility in scheduling home visits were cited by the project director as the primary features which have made this program successful. Written materials developed as a part of this project include the *Del Rio Language Screening Tests* (Toronto et al., 1975); *Primary Acquisition of Language; Things That Work for Us: a Handbook of Instructional Methods and Techniques for Young Children;* and *First Chance Outreach*. Copies of these materials or information on availability may be obtained from the Project Director.

Special Needs Early Childhood Program

Peg Fraher, Early Childhood Program Specialist
City of Boston Public Schools
26 Court Street
Boston, MA 02108

An average of fourteen 3-to-5-year-old bilingual children with various special needs are served in this program for non-English-speakers. All forms of media (print, radio, and television) are used to communicate information about this service citywide to parents and agencies. Flyers printed in seven languages are also distributed to all kindergarten and elementary school children to take home.

The child's first language is the primary language of instruction, with English taught as a second language according to the child's proficiency. Parents have the option to have their children attend a non-English-speaking program or an English-speaking program. Another unique feature is an eight week summer camp program supported by the City of Boston Parks and Recreation Department.

Texas Migrant Council Head Start Program

John Gonzales, Director
Box 917
Laredo, TX 78041

More than eighteen hundred 3-to-5-year-old migrant children, including nearly 200 identified handicapped children, were served by the Texas Migrant Council (TMC) with a projected enrollment of 3,400 by 1980 and a proportionate increase in the number of handicapped children served. In contrast to other programs that serve a localized area, the TMC includes multiple centers in three home-based areas of Texas: The Valley Area, located in south Texas; the Wintergarten Area, centered around Laredo in southwest Texas; and the Panhandle Area, centered around the Lubbock area. Enrollment is limited to children of migrant workers and all families are Spanish-speaking.

The geographical distance between centers in Texas is extremely great—more than 800 miles from centers in Lubbock to centers in Brownsville. This distance factor creates some unique problems in meeting the needs of the handicapped children in the various centers. A handicap coordinator for TMC is based in Laredo, and a handicap services specialist located in each area seeks local resources for meeting specialized needs. In each area Vista volunteers with special education training supplement the services of a speech/language pathologist who also provides inservice training. However, special services are basically a matter of finding local resources to meet the specialized needs of each child. The types of agencies and services vary greatly, and services in small towns are quite limited.

The unique feature of this program is that, for four to five months each year, the staff and the centers migrate to other states. However, staff from the TMC centers do not necessarily move to the same location as the children with whom they work during the winter months. One of the major problems is locating services and qualifying children for services in other states. Often families and children have moved to another migrant area by the time arrangements for testing or special services have been made. The migrant workers follow the crops, often changing destinations while en route or staying in an area for only a few days or weeks.

Because the handicapped children are integrated with nonhandicapped children, all teachers and assistants are responsible for working with the handicapped. Staff turnover is sometimes as high as 50% per year because of low salaries and the four to six months of travel; consequently, staff training is a continuous necessity. Many of the teaching staff are working toward or have completed Child Development associate training. In addition to training provided by the TMC staff, staff-training opportunities from other federally funded projects, such as the Portage Project in Wisconsin and Alternatives for Paraprofessional Training at Southwest Educational Development Laboratory in Austin, TX, are also utilized.

Although not a model program in the sense of other programs described, TMC represents one way of helping the handicapped child by drawing upon the resources of other agencies such as the Department of Health, Commission for the Blind, Mental Health and Mental Retardation Centers, the Department of Human Resources, and other community agencies in Texas. Similar agencies in other states provide services during the months TMC is out of Texas. This program also represents a unique approach to serving the needs of a population by molding the program to the target population, rather than suggesting the population should be molded into a traditional delivery-of-services approach.

Illinois Department of Children and Family Services

Elena de los Santos Mycue, Director
Illinois Migrant Head Start Project, Office of Child Development
Illinois Department of Children and Family Services
#1 North Old State Capitol Plaza
Springfield, IL 62706

Each year over 600 migrant children are received into the Illinois Migrant Head Start Project. Of this number nearly 10% have one or more handicapping conditions. The children are served by 12 community agencies under contract with the Illinois Migrant Head Start Project, which is part of the Illinois Department of Children and Family Services. All types of handicapping conditions, ranging from mild to severe problems, are served within the context of the regular migrant program, and nearly all the children are Spanish speakers.

Of these 12 agencies, only four are open on a year-round basis. The others are seasonal centers, receiving children who have migrated from home bases in Texas and Florida. One of the major problems is that, although the seasonal centers are open from March through November, the migrant families and their children are not present for the entire nine months.

Depending on the crops and job availability, families may remain in an area for only a few weeks. When handicapped children are identified, local resources are utilized whenever possible. However, locating bilingual resource persons is also a problem. In other instances, parents leave their handicapped children to stay with other family members at their home base during the migration season, so these children may or may not receive services during those months.

Parent involvement is recognized as a critical element of the child's program. Bilingual parent-involvement personnel are employed at the state and local level. Yet, the very nature of the migrant work in this area presents unique problems. Parents work very long hours, and children are in the centers from 7:00 a.m. to 6:00 p.m. During peak times, parents often work extra shift hours. Of necessity, work with parents is on an individual basis only.

Other Program Resources

Other programs have also contributed information and approaches for working with young bilingual children who are handicapped. Although some of these are no longer operational, the materials developed and their program descriptions may prove helpful.

The Responsive Environment Program for Spanish American Children in Clovis, New Mexico, was initiated in the early 1970s as a federally funded First Chance project. However, in New Mexico the public schools do not include programs for preschool handicapped children, and this model program was disbanded at the end of its Outreach year. One of the interesting features of the program was a mobile Learning Resource Center serving children in isolated areas. A catalogue of materials (*see* Askins, n.d., and *Responsive Environment Project* in references), many of which are written in Spanish, is available from Ted Olmos, Clovis Municipal Schools, Clovis, NM 88101.

Project LATON (Louisiana, Arkansas, Texas, Oklahoma, New Mexico) was designed for parents of handicapped children in the Head Start program, including Mexican American parents. Program materials for parents and parent groups are available in both Spanish and English. For more information on these materials and others, contact Dr. Mary Tom Riley, College of Home Economics, Texas Tech University, Lubbock, TX 79401.

The Southwest Educational Development Laboratory in Austin, Texas, has also developed material for teachers and parents of preschool bilingual handicapped children; these are listed in the reference section of this chapter. Abstracts of these materials and project reports are available from

Dr. Joyce Evans, Southwest Educational Development Laboratory, 211 East 7th Street, Austin, TX 78701.

During the winter of 1977, the Technical Assistance Development System held a conference in San Diego, California, on Practices for Preschool Handicapped Children in Spanish Speaking Communities. Reports from this conference are summarized in the book, *Early Education in Spanish-Speaking Communities* (Trohanis, 1978). Of particular interest are sections dealing with parent involvement and community awareness and an annotated listing of materials for use with young bilingual children.

Summary and Suggestions

Developing bilingual programs for preschool handicapped children requires time, effort, patience, and the ability to solve problems. Project directors interviewed for this chapter described a number of similar problems and offered the following suggestions for others interested in initiating similar programs.

It takes time. Hiring staff and developing a cooperating working relationship takes at least a year or more. This is particularly true when the staff represents different disciplines such as special education, child development, and speech therapy. Learning to talk the same professional language and recognizing how the various disciplines can work together requires openness and communication between staff members. Awareness and sensitivity to cultural differences between staff members is another critical factor. Allowing time for staff members to develop communication and cooperative work-relationships is critical.

Community support is important. Identifying children's needs, establishing relationships with other community professionals, and establishing the value of the program requires good public relations as well as time. Contacts with physicians, nurses, social workers, and other agencies must be actively cultivated. A clear understanding of the community's culture is also critical. A minimum of one to two years was described as necessary for developing program credibility and good community relations for a program at the beginning.

Parents must be involved. Parents were repeatedly cited as an essential element of the various programs. Responsibility for the child is often shared with others in the extended Mexican American family and all family members should be included. It is extremely important for the project staff to be aware of the social and cultural values of the group with whom they are working. The ability to speak the children's first language or their second language is not enough. Several directors cited the importance of having some staff from the community. Many parents, particularly those who are very poor and those who have recently immigrated, often are fearful of anyone in authority. They communicate more freely with someone from the community.

Be alert to "burn out." Working with young handicapped children, particularly in self-contained classes for the severe and profoundly handicapped, is tiring. Teachers and aides often "burn out" after two or three years. Moving them into another class with less involved or nonhandicapped children for a year or two has been helpful in reducing staff turnover. This was not mentioned as a problem at sites which serve the nonhandicapped and handicapped together, however.

Recognize the "mother factor." Teachers and aides who are also parents have a background of day-to-day experience that is helpful in working with young handicapped children. They are also more realistic in their expectations of what parents can do at home to help their children. Sometimes there are concerns about male staff members making home visits alone; it therefore is best to have a female staff member accompany him. However, men are effective in working with young children in the classroom because many children come from fatherless homes so that male-female staffs provide a balance for the children.

Language is a sensitive issue. Several points were identified related to language. Misidentification of a child as language-handicapped because the child does not speak English did not appear to be a problem in the programs described. Project directors were quite sensitive to this issue, and, as stated previously, children are identified as language-handicapped only when they are nonverbal or have problems in their first language.

The Spanish spoken within and between communities often varies. Simply "speaking Spanish" may not be sufficient. Formal training in Spanish may not be adequate for full communication with parents in the local community, as many nuances can be missed by not understanding the variations in Spanish. Several directors cited the importance of having persons from the local Spanish-speaking community on the staff, in addition to others who speak Spanish.

In several instances parents are not enthusiastic about their children receiving instruction in Spanish, even though the children may speak Spanish in the home. Parents perceive schools and centers as places where the child is to learn English. Bilingual instruction may be seen as holding the child back rather than as a means of developing the child's basic concepts while also learning English. Several directors stated that the parents' desires are followed to the extent that instruction in Spanish is available. This is decided on an individual basis rather than a programmatic one.

Review other programs. The project directors concurred as to the importance of collecting and reviewing all possible information from other programs and adapting materials when possible (e.g., Bluma, Sherer, Frohman, Hilliard, 1976). Each child, parent, and community has unique characteristics, and materials that work well in one area rarely can be transported completely to a different area. Individualization and local adaptation are usually necessary.

In conducting the survey of model programs, several important issues came to light. In some cases, programs identified initially were found to be no longer in existence. After an initial period of federal funding, local support was not available, so the program closed. In a sense, this is not too surprising. Parental support and community pressure are key factors in obtaining local support. When parents have difficulty communicating and are burdened with their own financial and personal problems, they have little energy left to press for continuation of a local preschool program. Also, parental support for preschool programs is fleeting; when children enter the public school system, their parents' interest in the preschool program decreases. Parental interest must be continually recruited by the programs.

Finally, there is very little written information on preschool programs for bilingual handicapped children. As future programs are developed, funding should include provisions for publishing and disseminating reports on their success and failure and problems encountered as well as written materials that others could use in teaching young bilingual handicapped children.

References

Askins, B.E.: *Responsive Environment Program for Spanish American Children (REPSAC)*, Final Evaluation Report. Clovis, Clovis Public School (EDC 96086), no date.

Bluma, S., Sherer, M., Frohman, A., and Hilliard, J.: *The Portage Project*. Portage, Cooperative Educational Service Agency, 1976.

Drezek, W.: *Developmental Roles and Anchor Goals in Infant Education*. Unpublished paper, Austin, Infant-Parent Training Program, no date.

Drezek, W.: *Parents and Children, Activities and Environments for Infants and Toddlers*. Unpublished paper, Austin, Infant-Parent Training Program, no date.

First Chance—Outreach and San Felipe-Del Rio Consolidated Independent School District: *Things That Work for Us: A Handbook of Instructional Methods and Techniques for Young Children*. Del Rio, no date.

Primary Acquisition of Language (PAL): Oral Language Dominance Measure, K-3. Austin, Texas Education Agency, Publications Distribution Section, 1975.

The Responsive Environment Program for Spanish American Children (REPSAC) Catalogue of Instructional Materials from Learning Resource Center. Clovis, Clovis Public Schools, no date.

Southwest Educational Development Laboratory: *How To Fill Your Toy Shelves Without Emptying Your Pocketbook/ Como Llenar sus Estantes con Jugetes sin Gastar Mucho Dinero*. Reston, Council for Exceptional Children, 1976.

Southwest Educational Development Laboratory: *Spanish/English Language Performance Screening (S/ELPS)*. Monterey, CTB/McGraw-Hill, 1978.

Southwest Educational Development Laboratory: *Working with Parents of Handicapped Children/ Trabajando con los Padres de Niños con Impedimentos*. Reston, Council for Exceptional Children, 1976.

Toronto, A., Leverman, D., Hanna, C., Rosenzweig, P., and Maldonado, A.: *Del Rio Language Screening Test*. Austin, National Educational Laboratory Publishers, 1975.

Trohanis, P.L. (Ed.): *Early Education in Spanish-Speaking Communities*. New York, Walker and Company, 1978.

19

The Bilingual Hearing Impaired: Teaching Children and Preparing Teachers

June Grant

Current Status of Bilingual Programs for Hearing-Impaired Children

When one investigates the status of bilingual education for hearing-impaired children, one is immediately impressed with the paucity of programs and the dearth of literature. Although hearing impairment of all degrees from mild to profound is a low incidence handicap (Ross, 1977), the actual number of hearing-impaired children is sizeable. Among this handicapped group there appears to be very little research concerning the hearing-impaired child from a bilingual or non-English-speaking home. For example, a computer search using the descriptors *hearing-impaired* and *bilingual education* revealed only six citations relevant.

An operational definition of the term *hearing-impaired* is necessary because its use has different meanings in different contexts. Hearing loss is not an all-or-none condition, but rather represents a broad continuum from mild impairment to moderate, severe, profound hearing loss, or total deafness. A detailed classification of hearing levels and their consequences will not appear in this chapter. Children with mild and moderate hearing impairments acquire language, but not without deficiencies and problems (Goetzinger, 1962), and are generally referred to as hard-of-hearing. Children with severe and profound losses who are sometimes referred to as deaf will not acquire language without intervention, and the proficiency level reached is dependent upon many factors (Davis and Silverman, 1978;

Greenstein and McConville, 1976). Therefore, the term *hearing-impaired* will be used to refer to the broad spectrum of disability, with various modifiers used to specify degree of impairment.

The impact of federal mandates requiring services for children of bilingual/bicultural backgrounds and those requiring services for all handicapped children have stimulated awareness of the inadequacies of existing services and have served as catalysts for the implementation of a few programs throughout the nation. An examination of the situation in Texas may serve as a case in point. According to *Priorities of the State Board of Education*, two of seven priorities in the area of direct instruction are bilingual multicultural education and education for the handicapped. The State Education Agency (SEA) responded promptly to this mandate. By the 1975 deadline, the SEA had defined standards and developed course descriptions for these areas. It subsequently trained half the required number of teachers within two years and the other half during the third year. It also adopted and provided appropriate textbooks and materials, provided technical assistance to school districts, and promoted the concept of the confluence of cultures and the recognition of the need for bilingual/multicultural education.

The priority for the education of the handicapped states that, in order to achieve the goal of full services by 1980 for all handicapped children, the SEA would need to implement a comprehensive special education program in all districts and make special education services an essential element in its 20 regional service centers. In addition, the SEA would need to develop further the statewide comprehensive plan for the deaf consisting of the Regional Day School Program and The Texas School for the Deaf, revise and/or develop new certification standards, design and implement inservice opportunities for teachers in regular programs, and integrate education of the handicapped with other educational programs.

One would assume that a program would resolve the problems faced by hearing-impaired children from limited English or non-English-speaking homes at two levels: ameliorating their problems as hearing-impaired children, and assisting them in attaining their educational goals through their home language and through English. Unfortunately, such is generally not the case. Moreover, most of these children carry the burden of a third educationally handicapping condition—poverty. Of the 109 children enrolled on one campus of the Regional Day School for the Deaf in San Antonio during the 1978–79 academic year, 72% of them qualify for free breakfast and lunch programs, signifying that their family incomes are considered at the poverty level. Since poverty is a culture with its own sanctions and prohibitions (DeBlassie, 1976; *see* Chapter 14), it is clear that these children have multiple obstacles to overcome on their road to academic achievement.

These problems have not gone unnoticed in Texas, and the *Statewide Design for Education of the Deaf in Texas* (1974) "recognizes the goals of bilingual education for Texas public school students as significant goals for bilingual deaf students" (p. 10). the *Design* repeats the primary goal of bilingual education as successful achievement of the goals of the educational process using two languages, developing proficiency in both, but assuring the mastery of English by all students.

Despite this commitment to bilingual education for the hearing handicapped in Texas, there are only two bilingual programs for hearing-impaired children, both of which are in the San Antonio area. In contrast, the Rio Grande Valley area on the United States/Mexico border, where concentration of Mexican Americans is even greater than in the San Antonio area, has no bilingual programs. An examination of the enrollment of the Regional Day School for the Deaf on the border in Brownsville, Texas, reveals that of the 78 children enrolled, approximately 98% have Spanish surnames. It is estimated that the language of the home in 75% of these families is predominantly Spanish, with little or no English used in ordinary family discourse.

It appears that the handicap of hearing impairment supersedes all other educational problems to the extent that the entire focus of remedial measures is on the hearing impairment, as if two priorities cannot be dealt with simultaneously. It is clear that, while the priorities have been stated and plans to implement programs have been designed, integrating bilingual programs and programs for hearing-impaired children has seldom been achieved or even initiated to any significant extent.

The exceptions to the above statement are the two programs in San Antonio mentioned above. The Edgewood Independent School District, whose population is 93% Spanish-surnamed, maintains a highly developed bilingual/bicultural program. In addition to the bilingual/bicultural program in the elementary and secondary grades, the José Cardenas Handicapped Children's Center provides services for handicapped children from birth through elementary school. Within the program the dual needs of the non-English-speaking handicapped children are served. It should be added that a large percentage of the students in this district qualify for free lunches, indicating pervasive poverty, the third obstacle to academic achievement.

The second program in San Antonio providing specific services for hearing-impaired children from non-English-speaking homes is the Sunshine Cottage/Trinity University Parent/Infant Program. The unique feature of this program is that the infants and parents are served both in their homes and in the home demonstration center on the Sunshine Cottage campus. In this program, the language used for interchange may be Spanish, English, or both, depending upon family practice and preference. The teacher/counselor at the home demonstration center is bilingual and bilingual graduate students serve the parent and infants in their home (*see* Chapter 18).

It appears that in Texas there is some awareness of the multiple problems confronting hearing-impaired students from non-English-speaking, lower socioeconomic level homes, because there are programs that address each of these handicapping conditions separately. Very little headway, however, is being made to integrate the remedial and compensatory measures that can mitigate all the difficulties these children experience.

Efforts to ascertain the extent of services in other states have not been very fruitful. Correspondence to directors of programs for hearing-impaired children has proved to be nonproductive and traditional methods of reviewing literature have yielded very little useful information. Even the volume, *Bilingual/Bicultural Education: Titles and Abstracts of Doctoral Dissertations* (1977) contains only two titles concerned with bilingualism and special education, and both these studies involved children who were mentally retarded, not hearing-impaired.

Definite strides in program development, however, are being made in some geographic areas. For example, CREED VII is a major project addressing the problem of educating Hispanic hearing-impaired children in the New York city area (Cortez, 1979). This project's research revealed that: more than half the population in schools for the deaf were Hispanic; the Hispanic students' achievement was lower than the non-Hispanic students; Spanish was the language in about 90% of the homes; and the Hispanic students from poverty level homes achieved less academically than the Hispanic students from middle-class homes. Again, the element of poverty plays a significant role.

Recognizing that some of the children's problems have roots in the home, a program involving both classroom activities and family services has been implemented in New York city. The general principles of bilingual/bicultural education have been introduced into the classroom. Families have been attracted to school activities and provided with counseling by Hispanic professionals, a service not formerly effective when offered by non-Hispanic professionals (Cortez, 1979).

In sum, there are numerous bilingual programs for students from non-English-speaking homes. There are programs for handicapped children, of which many address the special needs of these children. However, there seems to be a decided scarcity of programs designed specifically for bilingual hearing-impaired children.

Special Problems in the Education of Hearing-Impaired Children

As the problems of hearing impairment are examined, some possible explanations for so little attention to the issue of bilingualism come to light. First of all, the most handicapping aspect of hearing impairment is the concomitant language deficit (Kretschmer and Kretschmer, 1978). The literature is replete with studies showing that deaf children's language performance is significantly inferior to that of normal-hearing children of the same chronological age (Blackwell, 1978; Kohl, 1964; Lee, 1966; McNeill, 1966; Rosenstein and McGinitie, 1969). Furthermore, evidence shows that the level of spoken language attained by hearing-impaired children is related to the degree of hearing loss (Kretschmer and Kretschmer, 1978; Ling, 1976).

In addition to the problems that many normal-hearing children from non-English speaking homes have in translating or switching from their home language to English, the hearing-impaired child is struggling to acquire *a* language, be it English, Spanish, or Sign Language. The language deficit most hearing-impaired children and adults in a monolingual environment experience is so severe that it is rare that a deaf adult reads at a fifth grade level or better (Moores, 1978). For hearing-impaired children, the difficulty of acquiring adequate linguistic competence for communication and cognition, let alone creative expression, far overrides the question of bilingual education versus English as a Second Language (ESL).

There are several explanations that can account for the differences in language abilities between normal-hearing and hearing-impaired children. Two factors become paramount if the additional problem of bilingualism/biculturalism for hearing-impaired children is to be managed in a positive fashion: First, linguistic stimulation is imperative during the critical or resonant period of language acquisition, and second, appropriate amplification must be initiated early in life.

In regard to the resonant period for language acquisition, the abundant literature on the language acquisition process (Bloom, 1970; Braine, 1963; Brown, 1973, Lenneberg, 1966; McNeill, 1970) indicates that very young children can become quite proficient language users. The literature also indicates that children follow the same sequential pattern in acquiring this skill, although at different rates; that they accomplish the bulk of the task in a short period of time, usually less than two years; and that they are virtually finished by the time they are 30 to 36 months of age (Ling and Ling, 1978). The implications of these findings are far-reaching for all hearing-impaired children, but are especially damaging to the hearing-impaired child whose home language is not that of the dominant culture. The overriding implication is that many hearing-impaired children are not identified as such until after they have passed through the greater part of the resonant period (Grant, 1975), thereby losing the tremendous natural advantage of neurological "ripeness" (Lenneberg, 1966). Hearing-impaired children from non-English-speaking homes often miss language stimulation during the critical period. When they are finally identified and start in remedial programs that include hearing amplification, they are more often than not exposed to English in the program and Spanish at home, a condition not conducive to optimum language and concept development (*A Resource Manual*, 1971).

The keystone to language acquisition for hearing-impaired children ideally is abundant linguistic stimulation during the resonant period through the normal channel, namely audition (Simmons-Martin, 1975). There are investigators whose work has shown that, with the appropriate education approach (Collins-Ahlgren, 1974), hearing-impaired children can acquire language in a manner very similar to normal-hearing children. Teacher/counselors instruct parents in techniques for supplying the appropriate linguistic data for young hearing-impaired children to match their actions, thoughts, desires, and feelings. This input needs to be in the language of the home—the language in which the parents and siblings are most comfortable (Grant, 1973). It needs to be copious, and it needs to occur during the critical period for language acquisition if hearing-impaired children are to approximate the language usage abilities of normal-hearing children.

The other highly significant factor in the language acquisition process of hearing-impaired children is the extent of the impairment, or more important, the extent to which the residual hearing can be amplified and thereby utilized for linguistic stimulation (*see* Chapter 8). The principal sensory modality involved in the acquisition of language is audition (Ling, 1976; Ling and Ling, 1978; Sanders, 1971; Wilson, Ross, and Calvert, 1974), although gestures, facial expressions, and body language undoubtedly play important roles (Kess, 1976). However, if children's residual hearing can be amplified to the extent that they can receive linguistic input auditorially, and if they can be taught to process these linguistic data so as to internalize the grammatical rules of the language, then they stand the chance of acquiring language comparable to that of normal-hearing children (Kretschmer and Kretschmer, 1978). In other words, as a general rule, the more language hearing-impaired children can process auditorially, the more closely their language output will approximate that of normal-hearing children.

The importance for hearing-impaired children of these two factors, linguistic stimulation and amplification to promote the use of residual hearing during the critical period for language acquisition, takes on special significance in the education of hearing-impaired children from non-English-speaking homes. Identification and assessment of these children is often later than the ideal first 6 months of life or even the first year. Possible causes for this late identification may be: (a) poor medical attention, a concomitant of poverty, that ubiquitous handicapper, (b) the wish of parents to protect a handicapped child from the hardships of the outside world, (c) heritage that accepts the fate of parenting a handicapped child without complaining or seeking professional help, a common characteristic of the Mexican American culture (*A Resource Manual*, 1971), or (d) naiveté regarding early remediation of a handicapped condition as imperative.

With the advent of Child Find[1] and other public information efforts in Spanish as well as English, there has been a slight trend—in San Antonio at least—for parents of young children to seek professional assistance when they suspect a handicapping condition. The second factor, the delay in amplification of residual hearing, is, of course, a consequence of late identification.

The English-speaking professionals provide another complicating factor when working with non-English-speaking hearing-impaired children and their families, especially when the handicap is first identified. While some communities, San Antonio among them, have a cadre of Spanish-surnamed pediatricians (14 listed in the 1978 San Antonio telephone directory) and family practice specialists (37), there are generally few, if any, Spanish-speaking otologists and audiologists. Therefore, even if the parents may or may not have a professional who can advise them in their native language at the primary care-giving level, they must begin to function in a second language when they are referred to other specialists. The trauma of ascertaining that one's child is seriously handicapped is in itself a shocking experience, and much has been written to describe the state of shock, guilt, and sorrow that parents suffer (Moores, 1978; Moses, 1977; Schlesinger and Meadow, 1972). Many non-English-speaking parents must come to grips with the reality of this situation without the benefit of professional counseling, or with "translated" explanations and suggestions—not a very satisfactory compromise (Grant, 1973; *see also* Chapter 16)

A Rationale for Bilingual Programs for Hearing-Impaired Children

A rationale for bilingual education programs for hearing-impaired children assumes a solid premise for such programs for hearing children. However, most normal-hearing children enter public school programs at 5 or 6 years of age, having already acquired substantial command of their native language. This is too late for hearing-impaired children from monolingual homes. The solution for them is bilingual programs that start with their parents at that very first pediatric/audiologic encounter. The psychological and emotional support that parents need during the identification period should be provided in the parents' language by a member of their culture (Grant, 1973). Once the parents have conquered their emotions and have accepted their child's hearing impairment, they can embark on a rehabilitation program.

Such a program will instruct the parents in techniques of using everyday home experiences to promote language acquisition by providing their child with an abundance of linguistic stimulation appropriate to the infant's activities (Simmons-Martin, 1975; 1978). It is highly improbable that the parents can become immediately fluent and comfortable enough in English to provide adequate linguistic data for the child to infer the syntactic structure of the language. The term *hearing impairment* is particularly appropriate in this context, in that precise audiological evaluation of very young infants is improbable, and expectations are often biased by the label attached to a handicapping condition (Wilson, Ross, and Calvert, 1974).

One of the basic tenets of bilingual programs is that the best medium for children's learning, especially during the early school years, is their native language. Another basic tenet is that reading and writing in the first language should precede literacy in the second (Andersson and Boyer, 1970; Saville-Troike, 1973; *A Resource Manual*, 1971).

Yet this sequence is not the typical one for most hearing-impaired children from non-English-speaking homes, for they are usually placed in English-speaking classrooms for the hearing-impaired. The scarcity of specialized bilingual programs further demonstrates this point. How unrealistic to expect linguistic accomplishments of hearing-impaired children that have been recognized as improbable for normal-hearing children. The practice of instructing children initially in their native language instead of plunging them immediately into English language programs will expedite, not impede, their acquiring competency in English (Andersson and Boyer, 1970).

Educators and parents who view the command of English as a prerequisite to economic and social mobility need to be assured that bilingual programs contain as one of their objectives the use of English as well as the children's native language (Gaarder, 1967). Fluency in English is a goal whether a program is truly bilingual, i.e., instruction in both languages throughout the curriculum, or is a transitional or an ESL program, i.e., the use of two languages only until the children achieve enough proficiency in English to proceed academically.

Another benefit of bilingualism is the introduction of an additional channel for symbolic representation, an important aspect of cognitive ability. This additional symbol system can stimulate metalinguistic awareness, the ability of an individual to think about language itself. When children first begin to talk, they do not separate the linguistic labels they use from the objects or actions they represent (Bever, 1970; Cazden, 1972). In other words, the word *mama* is part and parcel of the person to the young child. According to Bloom (1973), these young children when learning to talk use linguistic labels coincidentally as they are structuring their cognitive activities. As their language and cognitive activities become more sophisticated, they can begin to function more symbolically, and language plays an important role in their cognitive development (Bruner, Oliver, and Greenfield, 1966; *see also* Chapter 20).

For a child attaching two symbols to the same object or concept is a step toward metalinguistic awareness and cognitive development (Cazden, 1972). Such an ability could be highly beneficial to hearing-impaired children struggling to acquire proficiency in language usage. The realization that every creature, every object, every activity in their lives can be represented symbolically, not in one set of symbols, but in two, promotes the concept of the function of language. It is often a very difficult concept for hearing-impaired children to acquire and yet a prerequisite to language facility.

It is interesting to note that many of the suggestions for good pedagogical proceedings in bilingual programs (Andersson and Boyer, 1970; Saville-Troike, 1973; *A Resource Manual*, 1971) are standard practices in the education of the hearing-impaired. For example, it is recommended that experiences be provided as a basis for many activities. The importance of firsthand experiences, as opposed to vicarious ones, has long been a cornerstone of language development for the hearing-impaired (Grant, 1979).

Another admonition in the literature for bilingual education is to teach new vocabulary in a realistic context, not in isolation. Teachers of hearing-impaired children have always had to abide by this principle in order to achieve any vocabulary growth in their pupils (Simmons-Martin, 1975, 1978). The strategy of developing new concepts using familiar words and objects and developing new vocabulary through familiar concepts is not new to educators of hearing-impaired children. These suggestions are good pedagogical practices in any setting, but many children can learn easily in spite of less than optimal conditions and practices. However, special children, hearing-impaired, and children from non-English-speaking homes require special considerations and techniques. They learn because of the teachers and teaching methods, not in spite of them. Directors of bilingual programs for hearing-impaired children or administrators contemplating the implementation of such programs should be completely conversant with the special needs and parameters of bilingual programs. They should also infuse into their curricula accommodating measures necessary for the hearing-impaired children to achieve academically.

The practice of teaching hearing-impaired children English at school while all members of their families speak only Spanish at home makes pariahs of the children, no matter how loving and caring the home environment may be. There are areas of San Antonio, as there are in many higly concentrated Mexican American communities, where the dominant language is Spanish, not English. Street names and signs are in Spanish, merchandise advertisements and signs are in Spanish, the showings at the movie theatres are in Spanish, church services are in Spanish, radio and television broadcasts are in Spanish. The child to whom this environment is alien is an outcast at home.

The Preparation of Personnel for Bilingual Hearing-Impaired Children

Being cognizant of the distinct needs of hearing-impaired children and the equally distinct needs of Mexican American children, the Bureau of Education for the Handicapped funded a workshop whose task it was to delineate the considerations that must be incorporated into personnel preparation programs for birth to 4-year-old hearing-impaired infants (Grant, 1973). The principles developed during the workshop have served as guidelines in the design of the preparation program initiated at Trinity University in 1974. With modifications to suit local conditions, they may serve as guideposts for other personnel preparation programs.

The competencies can be clustered into five basic areas:

1. Early childhood development, which includes topics such as patterns of sensori-motor, social, personality, language, cognitive, and creative development in children.
2. In teaching in the home, students investigate family structures, parent/child relationships, sibling and peer relationships, and behavior modification techniques.
3. Under the rubric of society and culture, the students study the implications of bilingualism/biculturalism on family life and structure, the effects of socioeconomic status on families and their relationships to the community, the impact of religion on the family, and health practices of the family.
4. The study of bilingualism and linguistics includes knowledge of the acquisition and development of language, the implications of linguistic theory, the competency/performance distinction, and sociolinguistics.
5. In the study of hearing impairment, students acquire knowledge of the implications of hearing impairment on language acquisition, cognition, and adaptive behavior, the basic concepts of the speech and hearing mechanisms and their functions, techniques of stimulation and utilization of residual hearing, and methods and techniques of developing language for hearing-impaired children.

In addition to academic course work, the bilingual graduate students in the teacher/counselor preparation program provide services to the parents in their homes. They also serve as advocates for the parents and infants. The activities can involve making appointments with other professionals (audiologists, otologists, psychologists, and those at social agencies) and serving as interpreters during those sessions. In addition, they instruct and guide the parents in techniques for promoting language acquisition by their handicapped children. Through course work, seminars, field experiences, and practicum experiences in the homes of the hearing-impaired infants, the students acquire the required knowledge and skills.

Sunshine Cottage/Trinity University Parent/Infant Program initiated in 1978 is supported by the combined resources of Sunshine Cottage School for Deaf Children and the teacher preparation program at Trinity University. It is an integral part of the teacher/counselor preparation program. There is a simulated home on the Sunshine Cottage campus and parents and their infants visit there once weekly with the bilingual professional teacher/counselor. During this session the parents are instructed in various techniques for utilizing the natural home environment to the greatest extent for the development of the infant in all areas: motor, cognitive, language, affect, and creative. The parents can discuss and receive counsel on any problems they are encountering with their handicapped child. In addition, the parents are visited once weekly in their home by the graduate student who helps them implement the activities and interactions that were performed at the demonstration home. The student has observed this family in the demonstration home, and therefore knows what objectives the teacher and parents have agreed upon for that week.

The students attend the monthly parent meetings at the demonstration home. Each student plans at least one meeting with the assistance and guidance of a parent or family. It is up to the student to inspire as much parental planning and participation as possible. The students must ascertain the subjects the parents want to discuss. These meetings are a valuable experience for both students and parents. The students become privy to the parents' concerns and anxieties, and the parents garner strength and enthusiasm from one another.

There are currently very few university programs designed particularly to prepare personnel to serve infants below 3 years of age. However, some states are now mandating services for hearing-impaired and other handicapped children from birth through 21 years of age. As such services are implemented, the demand for qualified personnel will be critical.

The Hard-of-Hearing Child

Up to this point, this chapter has been concerned with non-English-speaking hearing-impaired children in general, referring to the entire spectrum of hearing impairment as defined previously. While each child is unique, and all of the child's educational, psychosocial, affective, and motor needs should be considered on an individual basis, there is a group of hearing-impaired children whose overall needs have received little more than lip service in the past. These are children with mild to moderate impairments who are traditionally described as *hard-of-hearing*.

The problem of demarcating areas of hearing loss into categories labeled deaf and *hard-of-hearing* is troublesome, and researchers in the field do not all agree about how to resolve this problem. Boothroyd, Erber and Levitt (reported in Stark, 1974) feel there are decided changes in speech reception and/or production around the 90 to 95 dB level, and these experts would draw the line there. Ross (1977) would increase the level to the 95 to 100 dB hearing level under favorable conditions. In contrast to this low threshold dividing line, Davis and Silverman (1978) would differentiate between hard-of-hearing and deaf children at 70 dB, the level generally considered the division between moderate and severe hearing impairments.

The question of precisely defining the extent of hearing impairment of hard-of-hearing children is extremely difficult, since so many factors can influence the use a hard-of-hearing child makes of any residual hearing. The most important influence is, naturally, the extent of the hearing impairment or to put it more positively, the amount of residual hearing as measured audiologically (*see* Chapter 7). However, as precise as an audiogram may appear, there are still ambiguities in interpretation, and "dividing" lines cannot be drawn unequivocally. Children with highly similar audiograms or matching *average* hearing levels can function quite differently due to factors other than actual hearing thresholds. Some of these factors are the age at which the child's impairment was identified and amplification was initiated (in other words, the child's listening age as opposed to his or her chronological age), the quantity and appropriateness of the linguistic input the child received during the critical period of language acquisition, the quality and suitability of the rehabilitation program itself, the parents' attitude toward the child's hearing impairment, parental expectations for the child, parental support, the child's intelligence, and the presence or absence of other handicapping conditions. It is obvious that such labeling can be very ambiguous with different connotations for different people.

It is necessary also to consider how small a hearing loss a child must sustain in order to be considered hard-of-hearing. *Normal* thresholds are described as an approximate 20 dB band (Davis and Silverman, 1978). Yet children with mild hearing impairments, 30 to 45 dB, have been reported to demonstrate difficulty in articulation and auditory discrimination (Goetzinger, 1962). Quigley and Thomure (1968) reported academic retardation among children with as little as 14 dB hearing losses. The adverse consequences of even mild hearing impairments becomes magnified when the complications of a non-English-speaking home environment and possible poverty are added.

As with severe and profound hearing impairments, it is appropriate to examine first the problems accompanying the identification of mild to moderate impairments. In contrast to the former group, the hard-of-hearing child can acquire language with or perhaps without noticeable deviations. Parents are justifiably not alerted when children under 5 years of age have not mastered all the phonemes and syntax of the language. Unlike the severe or profoundly hearing-impaired children, the hard-of-hearing child *does* hear and respond to the environmental noises and auditory cues in the home: the phone is heard, as is the ring of the doorbell, the dog's bark, the drone of the vacuum cleaner, and the swish of the washing machine.

To complicate matters even further, many mild and moderate hearing impairments are caused by otitis media (*see* Chapter 10) and are thus transitory. The parents may suspect a hearing impairment one week but have all their fears allayed the next when the infection has cleared. However, such intermittent lapses take their toll on language acquisition especially if they occur frequently and during the critical period for language acquisition (White, 1979). Children from poverty level homes, whose medical care is often substandard, show a high incidence of middle ear disease. Their middle ear infections frequently go untreated for prolonged periods of time exacerbating the hearing impairment and increasing the chance of complications (Davis and Silverman, 1978) and permanent hearing impairment.

It is apparent that the identification of mild to moderate hearing impairments can be difficult. Any teacher of hearing-impaired children can name at least several children who have been assigned to classes for mentally retarded children because poor language performance and academic achievement were assumed to be the result of mental retardation, while the possibility of hearing impairment was not explored. The number of hard-of-hearing children in regular classrooms is estimated at 5% of the total population; most of this group require special considerations to some degree (Davis and Silverman, 1978).

The above discussion has concerned any hard-of-hearing child, but the hard-of-hearing child from a bilingual background or a monolingual non-English background requires very special consideration. It has been suggested that the optimum educational setting for children with mild and moderate hearing impairments is the *mainstream* classroom (Barton, 1977). However, such children require preferential seating in all classroom situations and special instructional services such as auditory training (including the use of hearing aids), speech reading, speech therapy, and academic tutoring, if necessary (Davis and Silverman, 1978). If hard-of-hearing children from non-English-speaking homes are fortunate enough to have the hearing handicap identified, they are placed in an educational program for hearing-impaired children. In many programs, children are grouped with regard to their levels of hearing, and instruction is provided at different paces from that for the severely and profoundly hearing-impaired. However, there are virtually no programs that address themselves to the dual problems of hearing impairment and bilingualism.

The educational plight of hard-of-hearing children from the non-English-speaking home can be more damaging than that of severely or profoundly hearing-impaired children. These children with mild or moderate hearing impairments are acquiring some language in their homes, but it is not the language of instruction at school. According to Ling and Ling (1978), the ideal resolution to their problems is to promote the development of the home language under 3 years of age and introduce the second language through tutoring in play situations in nursery schools where the children can profit from the model of normally speaking peers (cf., Erickson and Omark, 1981). This solution is seldom the case in Texas or apparently most other states. In a conversation with the director of the Regional Day School for the Deaf in Brownsville, Texas, this dilemma was emphasized.

It was stated that the confusion these children experience, with English language instruction at school and the use of Spanish in all their other encounters, is extreme. It seems that the hardship is greater for the hard-of-hearing children than for the profoundly deaf. Yet the director is helpless in alleviating the situation without a staff of teachers with specific skills and knowledge in bilingual education, in addition to training for work with hearing-impaired children.

The mainstreaming process of any handicapped child is a complicated process, but the hearing-impaired child with bilingual needs presents exceptional difficulties. In addition to the support system outlined above, these children's needs must be met by classroom teachers who have positive attitudes toward both handicapping conditions and bilingualism/biculturalism (Grant, 1973). Additionally, there must be open communication between administration, the classroom, and support services. Such requirements are not easy to fulfill, but, in a democracy where the objective is for the greatest possible development of all its citizens, these goals should be within grasp.

Summary

In the United States there are numerous bilingual programs for hearing-impaired children (*American Annals of the Deaf*, 1978), and numerous bilingual programs for hearing children (U.S. Commission of Civil Rights, 1971), but very few programs for hearing-impaired children from bilingual or non-English-speaking homes. The difficulties encountered by these children are well-known to their teachers and to administrative personnel. In some instances, efforts to ameliorate the problems are in operation, and, in some cases, programs are in the planning stage. Language deficit, being the most pervasive aspect of hearing impairment, compounds the problems of bilingualism, a manifestation of language function.

Understanding the educational consequences of hearing impairment or understanding the problems of bilingualism does not give one adequate insight into the problems faced by the hearing-impaired child from a bilingual or non-English-speaking home. To provide completely appropriate programs for these children there needs to be specially prepared personnel. There are very few institutions engaged in such programs.

The problems of the mildly to moderately hearing-impaired bilingual child are not identical to those of the severely or profoundly hearing-impaired child. The former group is possibly even more disadvantaged than the latter and deserves programs especially designed to meet its needs.

The status of education for hearing-impaired bilingual children in the United States is seriously inadequate at present. The education profession and the public are currently receptive to the needs of these two minority groups: the hearing-impaired child and the bilingual child. It is hoped that in the future, attention and resources can be turned to the children who suffer from this dual handicapping condition.

Note

[1]Child Find was a multimedia attempt to make the public aware of the services available to handicapped children. Readers, viewers, and listeners in Texas were urged to contact their Regional Service Centers for information and to report the handicapped children not being served.

References

American Annals of the Deaf directory of programs and services. *American Annals of the Deaf, 123*, 1978.

Andersson, T., and Boyer, M.: *Bilingual Schooling in the United States*, vol. 1. Washington, D.C., U.S. Government Printing Office, 1970.

Barton, S.: The educational environment. In Davis, J. (Ed.): *Our Forgotten Children: Hard-of-Hearing Pupils in the Schools*. Minneapolis, The University of Minnesota, 1977.

Bever, T.G.: The cognitive basis for linguistic structures. In Hayes, J.R. (Ed.): *Cognition and the Development of Language*. New York, Wiley, 1970.

Bilingual/Bicultural Education: Titles and Abstracts of Doctoral Dissertations. Los Angeles, National Dissemination and Assessment Center, 1977.

Blackwell, P.M.: *Sentences and Other Systems*. Washington, D.C., A.G. Bell Association for the Deaf, 1978.

Bloom, L.: *Language Development: Form and Function in Emerging Grammars*. Cambridge, M.I.T., 1970.

Bloom, L.: *One Word at a Time: The Use of Single-Word Utterances before Syntax*. Hague, Mouton, 1973.

Braine, M.: The ontogeny of English phrase structure: The first phase. *Language, 39*:1–14, 1963.

Brown, R.A.: *A First Language: The Early Stages*. Cambridge, Harvard University, 1973.

Bruner, J.S., Oliver, R.R., and Greenfield, P.M.: *Studies in Cognitive Growth*. New York, Wiley, 1966.

Cazden, C.B.: *Child Language and Education*. New York, Holt, Rinehart, and Winston, 1972.

Collins-Ahlgren, M.: Teaching English as a second language to young deaf children. *J Speech and Hearing Disorders, 39*:486–500, 1974.

Cortez, E.L.:   Meeting the needs of Hispanic deaf children. *Audiology and Hearing Education,* 5:24, 1979.

Davis, H., and Silverman, S.R.:   *Hearing and Deafness.* New York, Holt, Rinehart, and Winston, 1978.

DeBlassie, R.R.:   *Counseling with Mexican American Youth: Preconceptions and Processes.* Austin, Learning Concepts, 1976.

Erickson, J.G., and Omark, D.R.:   Social relationships and communicative interactions of mainstreamed communication handicapped preschool children. *Instructional Science,* 9:253–268, 1980.

Gaarder, A.B.:   *Paper presented to Senator Yarborough's special subcommittee on bilingual education.* United States Ninetieth Congress, First Session, May 18, 1967.

Goetzinger, C.P.:   Effects of small perceptive losses on language and on speech discrimination. *Volta Review,* 64:408–414, 1962.

Grant, J.M.:   *Proceedings of a Workshop on the Preparation of Personnel in Education of Bilingual Hearing-Impaired Children.* San Antonio, Trinity University, 1973.

Grant, J.M.:   *A study of the development of eight hearing-impaired preschool children from Spanish-speaking homes.* Unpublished doctoral dissertation, University of Texas, 1975.

Grant, J.M.:   Experience: The foundation for language acquisition. In Simmons-Martin, A., and Calvert, D. (Eds.): *Parent-Infant Intervention: Communication Disorders.* New York, Grune & Stratton, 1979.

Greenstein, J.M., and McConville, B.B.:   *Mother-Infant Communication and Language Acquisition in Deaf Infants.* New York, Altro Work Shops, 1976.

Kess, J.F.:   *Psycholinguistics: Introductory Perspectives.* New York, Academic, 1976

Kohl, H.R.:   *Language and Education of the Deaf.* New York, Center for Urban Education, 1964.

Kretschmer, R.R., and Kretschmer, L.W.:   *Language Development and Intervention with the Hearing-Impaired.* Baltimore, University Park, 1978.

Lee, L.L.:   Developmental sentence types: A method for comparing normal and deviant syntactic development. *J Speech and Hearing Disorders,* 31:311–321, 1966.

Lenneberg, E.H.:   The natural history of language. In Smith, K., and Miller, G.A. (Eds.): *The Genesis of Language.* Cambridge, M.I.T., 1966.

Ling, D.:   *Speech and the Hearing-Impaired Child.* Washington, D.C., A.G. Bell Association for the Deaf, 1976.

Ling, D., and Ling, A.H.:   *Aural Rehabilitation.* Washington, D.C., A.G. Bell Association for the Deaf, 1978.

McNeill, D.:   The capacity for language acquisition. *Volta Review,* 68: 17–33, 1966.

McNeill, D.:   *The Acquisition of Language: The Study of Developmental Linguistics.* New York, Harper and Row, 1970.

Mexican American Education Study, United States Commission on Civil Rights, 1971.

Moores, D.F.:   *Educating the Deaf: Psychology, Principles, and Practices.* Boston, Houghton Mifflin, 1978.

Moses, K.:   Parenting a hearing-impaired child. *Volta Review, 81*:73–80, 1979.

Quigley, S.P., and Thomure, F.E.:   *Some Effects of Hearing Impairment upon School Performance.* Springfield, Illinois Office of Education, 1968.

A Resourse Manual for Implementing Bilingual Education Programs. Austin, Texas Education Agency, 1971.

Rosenstein, J., and MacGinitie, W.H.:   *Verbal Behavior of the Deaf Child.* New York, Teachers College Press, 1969.

Ross, M.:   Definitions and descriptions. In Davis, J. (Ed.): *Our Forgotten Children: Hard-of-Hearing Pupils in the Schools.* Minneapolis, University of Minnesota, 1977.

Sanders, D.A.:   *Aural Rehabilitation.* Englewood Cliffs, Prentice-Hall, 1971.

Saville-Troike, M.:   *Bilingual Children.* Arlington, Center for Applied Linguistics, 1973.

Schlesinger, H.S., and Meadow, K.P.:   Emotional support to parents: How, when, and by whom. In Lillie, D. (Ed.): *Parent Programs in Child Development Centers.* Chapel Hill, Technical Assistance Development System, 1972.

Simmons-Martin, A.:   *Chats with Johnny's Parents.* Washington, D.C., A.G. Bell Association for the Deaf, 1975.

Simmons-Martin, A.:   Early management procedures for the hearing-impaired child. In Martin, F. (Ed.): *Pediatrics Audiology.* Englewood Cliffs, Prentice-Hall, 1978.

Stark, R.E.:   *Sensory Capabilities of Hearing-Impaired Children.* Baltimore, University Park Press, 1974.

Statewide Design for Education of the Deaf in Texas. Austin, Texas Education Agency, Department of Special Education and Special Schools, 1974.

U.S. Commission of Civil Rights: *Mexican-American Education Study.* Washington, D.C., U.S. Government Printing Office, 1971.

White, B.:   The special importance of hearing ability for the development of infants and toddlers. In Simmons-Martin, A., and Calvert, D. (Eds.): *Parent-Infant Intervention: Communication Disorders.* New York, Grune & Stratton, 1979.

Wilson, G.B., Ross, M., and Calvert, D.:   An experimental study of the semantics of deafness. *Volta Review, 76*:408–414, 1974.

20

Bilingual Special Education: A Challenge to Evaluation Practices[1]

Barbara L. Tymitz

Bilingual education programs and special education programs share several important dimensions. Each area has suffered from far too much unsubstantiated criticism and far too little meaningful or well conceived evaluation. Each field can also be characterized as controversial where the attending emotionalism of respective advocacy groups have sought redress from documented inequities, directly from educational institutions as well as from the courts. Both types of programs are exceedingly complex and call into question certain social and educational values that other kinds of instructional program areas simply do not provoke.

In the field of bilingual education the issues of maintenance and assimilation, coupled with cultural pluralism and the equal protection of the law, are often in conflict with pedagogical strategies, adding to the confusion as to what an ideal bilingual education program should be or do. No single criterion is sufficient to define or describe the programs that have developed, nor has any clearly defined standard emerged against which to evaluate the effectiveness, adequacy, or success of bilingual education in general.

The evaluation of special education programs is no less complicated. Issues related to identification of handicapping conditions, classification procedures, nondiscriminatory testing, case conferences, mainstreaming, due process, and parental involvement all add to the difficulty of accurately assessing program impact and effectiveness. The enactment as well as the implementation of P.L. 94–142, the Education for All Handicapped Children Act, with its specification of individualized education programing for each handicapped child, has created considerable pressure for educators to develop evaluation strategies that not only make sense instructionally, but also facilitate statutory compliance.

While the fields of special education and bilingual education are each of sufficient complexity to create methodological challenges, the evaluation of bilingual special education programs presents even more demanding complications. As Wolf (1978) discusses in an essay on the policy implications of bilingual special education, many of the advocates of each specialized area are actually demanding opposed policy resolutions. The conflict that currently besets the field of bilingual special education is exacerbated by evaluation efforts, particularly when those efforts rely on traditional quantitative approaches that in the past have not served either field well.

The subtle kind of interaction that occurs between and among program participants is multidimensional and must be carefully documented and understood within any programmatic evaluation strategy. For example, little is known, or at least documented in the professional literature, regarding ethnic group attitudes toward handicapped members of that group. What social and cultural norms apply to the handicapped across diverse nationalities has important implications for the kinds of special education services that will be desirable or even acceptable (*see* Chapter 15). Evaluation studies that fail to examine the contextual factors of bilingual special programs are doomed to failure from the outset, despite technical soundness or methodological insight.

In essence, programmatic issues and strategy problems have affected the direction and outcome of past evaluation studies in both special and bilingual education programs. Because bilingual special programs operate as more than the sum of two educational fields joined together, it is likely that these same concerns will affect bilingual special education with even more intensity. This chapter will briefly review issues and problems but, more significantly, it will point to new directions in evaluation conceptualization practice that can respond to the complexity inherent in providing education programs for bilingual exceptional children.

Programmatic Issues Affecting Evaluation in Bilingual Special Education

Bilingual education arose in response to the political and social pressures of ethnic groups (Mead, 1978). Yet it also arose in response to the needs of regular educators who mislabeled limited English-proficient (LEP) children as retarded. Programs also arose in response to special educators who found the LEP children placed in their classes to be far more responsive to education and instruction than could be expected of a retarded child.

Educators became aware that, for many of these children, learning ability was not impaired: knowledge of English was the missing ability that would enable LEP children to succeed (Blanco, 1977).

Bilingual/bicultural programs were designed to provide access to education and the opportunity to succeed for children with limited English-speaking ability. Many children did succeed in acquiring sufficient proficiency in English to become successful in regular classrooms. However, during this process, teachers found other problems among those failing to learn English in a reasonable time. Some of these children demonstrated that they had learning problems that interfered with the acquisition of English and with retention of skills or content material. No categorical placements fit the children with this double set of needs (Cortes, 1977).

The need for educational programs for LEP children who also demonstrated handicapping conditions that interfered with successful learning in a regular classroom was identified. Such a program would provide an individualized program for each child. English would be taught as the second language, with content area instruction in the home or dominant language of the child. Those planning the program would provide for the needs of the students in the native or home language of each student as well as in English, to the degree that each student would respond to English as a means of instruction (Abbott and Peterson, 1975).

As children were placed in such programs, their individual differences could not be put aside. Children brought their unique language abilities in addition to their single and multiple handicaps. Two realizations emerged: (a) it was probable that the use of the native language would be necessary for a longer period of time for handicapped LEP children since the handicap (other than orthopedic) precluded rapid progress in second language acquisition and (b) for many children, the first language would not be intact to a sufficient degree to serve all learning and communication needs.

Neither bilingual education teachers nor special education teachers were adequately prepared in the skills required to teach these handicapped children (Carrasquillo, 1977; Illinois Board of Higher Education, 1974). Bilingual education teachers often were chosen on the basis of their skill in the first language; they were not trained in the skills and techniques of special education. On the other hand, the special educator lacked the ability to speak the child's first language and, in many cases, lacked familiarity with the second language acquisition process. It was difficult (often impossible) for either teacher to communicate with the students or to provide the necessary explanations for learning activities.

To those not involved in the bilingual program or to those who were uninformed about it, bilingual classroom teachers became "resource teachers" who removed children from regular classes for mysterious reasons much like the special educators. The educational roles of the bilingual teacher and the special education teacher became confused and increasingly ill-defined. With diminished clarity in roles, their success in meeting program objectives was challenged. The effectiveness of transition and mainstreaming efforts could not be assured. Programs presenting these problems were particularly vulnerable when evaluated since many evaluation studies utilized a discrepancy model that compared original program objectives with actual outcomes. Programs were judged to be ineffective although it was clear that the program objectives were sometimes beyond the scope of the most well-intentioned human endeavor.

In many instances, gaps between program needs and program implementation created additional evaluation concerns:

1. Groups of individuals seeking to implement new programs designed those programs with little guidance from personnel experienced in program operation.
2. Programs were often implemented before sufficient planning and public relations procedures had been developed (Troike, 1977).
3. Programs assumed fairly amorphous conditions (Iiams, 1978). Evaluation could not be completed in terms of standard program models nor could one program be readily compared to another.
4. Completed program evaluations, both internal and external, were largely unavailable or difficult to locate.

It was apparent that requirements for Title VII proposals included an evaluation component, but not specific guidelines for what should be evaluated or how the evaluation should be managed. State guidelines for programs in special education were not always congruent with Title VII requirements. The design of the evaluations attempting to satisfy either set of requirements did not allow for the development of a body of information about success factors or growth expectations. When program research was planned, the research resources went to the universities, while the implementation resources went to the district programs for direct services to students. The result was a lack of solid research behind the implementations as well as a lack of implementation for the research findings. Evaluation plans and outcomes suffered from both.

Both federal and state evaluation plans tended to require specific information about students as acquired from standardized tests. Test data were inappropriately used to compare effectiveness of dissimilar programs (Mullen, 1973; Cronbach, 1975). Further, there was little or no information on which particular aspects of the educational program led to certain test results. Local programs needed diagnostic information to plan the general program and the program for each student. Processes and instruments for acquiring this information were not yet developed (Garza, 1976). In essence, federal and state evaluation plans did not provide the program staff with the information they wanted to know.

Most unfortunate is that the evaluation of these programs at times projected bad faith and further discouraged those involved (Troika, 1978), especially when impressions of external critics were presented as fact, and accusations were based on limited information. Political and cultural groups with their own aims rejected valid educational processes in favor of group power or status within a community. Consequently, bilingual programs often became insular and protective of narrow interests (Epstein, 1977).

Programmatic issues such as the degree of language difficulty, nature of individual handicaps, teacher skills, completeness of program design, or requirements for achievement testing rarely function in isolation. A cursory approach may fail to uncover interrelationships. All of these issues, however, serve to influence program evaluation in both process and outcome descriptions. At best, past evaluation efforts have only partially considered these complexities. Moreover, evaluation studies have not fully addressed critical issues in methodological design as they apply to the field of bilingual special education.

Methodological Issues in Past Program Evaluations

In examining existing evaluation studies, two competing practices can be identified. First, one might well draw the conclusion that evaluation is synonymous with assessment (Eisner, 1977; Guba, 1969; House, 1976). Recent designs continue to increase in statistical complexity and elaboration in assessing performance of children in bilingual or bilingual special programs. This focus on child achievement assessment data holds constant even when the object of the study is described as *program evaluation.*

Consider how a large number of programs include participation of community agencies, parents, and other family members, yet few evaluation efforts have addressed these activities with in-depth systematic approaches (Etherson, Moesser, and Sancho, 1977; Mullen, 1973; Nason, 1980). Occasionally, feedback from these groups may be solicited via questionnaires, but such instruments typically employ structured, closed-response items whose data are presented ultimately in concise quantitative form. Like the assessment of children, we simply learn this: How many can, how many cannot, how many do, how many do not. Information that clarifies the whys and hows goes unsolicited and unrecorded.

A second practice addresses the multiple purposes of the direction of special programs for bilingual handicapped children (Sanua, 1975; Board of Education, City of Detroit, 1976). Essentially there are three prevailing concerns:

1. How would we like children to feel—about themselves, their culture, and other cultures?
2. What knowledge would we like children to acquire?

like children to be able to do academically, physically,

not separate from each other, nor are they confined to
...ance. Program evaluation that artificially separates or
...r program concern is at best incomplete and poorly
...ment studies are unlikely to capture a true picture of
...entation and effectiveness. Similarly, evaluation based on
negative critique or unclear, sometimes erroneous, assumptions do little to
inform about the best practices possible. All of these practices, however,
have contributed to methodological weaknesses in past studies.

Evaluation as Testing

The utilization of testing procedures as the sole criterion for judging the
worth of programs needs to be challenged for several reasons. To begin with,
administering tests to handicapped bilingual children presents serious
problems related to the validity and reliability in the use and the meaning
attached to the results of such testing procedures for any one child (DeAvila
and Duncan, 1978; *see also* Chapter 4 and 6). While bilingual test development is currently underway (Locks, Pletcher, and Reynolds, 1978), the use
of adapted instruments that contain numerous modifications that weaken
test construction is often unsatisfactory (Shutt and Hannon, 1973). Even
when the test has been translated into the first language of the child,
significant communication problems can occur.

Efforts to use test vocabulary and patterns common to the various
dialects of the language and understandable to *all* who speak the language
are essential for nondiscriminatory testing (cf., Chapter 2). However, the
search for general forms known to all creates still another problem: the level
of language created is far above the level used by speakers of the language.
Thus, it cannot be expected that the language will be understood by those at
lower stages of development or by those never instructed in the more formal
aspects of the language. Similarly, subtleties of style variations complicate
test modifications and translations. The applicability of the revised instrument to handicapped bilingual children is challenged in much the same way
as are the modified standardized instruments used to test achievement of
native-born English-speaking handicapped children.

Inadequacies in the design of test batteries have further diminished the
utility of assessment data. Language profiles of bilingual handicapped
children require the measurement of concept development in both languages. Test procedures necessitate ways to discover proficiency levels
attained in each language as well as the relationship between the languages

as input and output processes for cognition (*see* Chapter 12). When one considers the receptive and expressive skills of each language, it becomes obvious that the assessment should include eight separate measures of language skill, e.g., listening, speaking, reading, and writing in both languages (Silverman, Noa, and Russell, 1978). Past evaluation studies present few examples of comprehensive batteries including these areas of assessment.

The practice of using total scores, standard deviations, or summative criterion reference data fails to provide information on the cognitive processes the child employs (McClelland, 1977). A child's *incorrect* answer may result because the tester and child share different interpretations of a phenomenon (Kamii, 1975; Magoon, 1977; Tymitz, 1977). It is possible for children to be performing the cognitive operations being tested but still to provide an answer judged to be incorrect (as in the following example):

> The teacher asked Amy to draw as many round things as she could think of. Amy then drew a lampshade, a water faucet, and a garbage can. Ninety-three of the 100 teachers viewing the drawing stated that Amy did not understand the concept of round and was thus unable to generate examples of round objects. In actuality, Amy had indeed produced three very identifiable objects whose perimeter all shared the characteristic of roundness. (Tymitz, 1977, p. 141)

Attending to the differing cognitive style, structures, and strategies children employ to achieve a response is a vital key to understanding performance (Messick, 1975; Riegel, 1972; Tymitz, 1977). To accept that summative low test scores are indicative of the child's inability or, on a broader level, indicative of program ineffectiveness is both erroneous and unfair (Cazden, 1970; Cicourel, Jennings, Jennings, Leiter, MacKay, Mehan, and Roth, 1974; McClellan, 1977).

In addition to the problems in test construction, administration, and interpretation when testing handicapped bilingual children, there is the dilemma of not being able to measure some of the more desirable qualities for which programs implicitly and explicitly strive (Magoon, 1977; Wilson, 1977). There are currently no tests that appropriately measure qualities such as curiosity, thoughtfulness, sense of wonder, commitment, or persistence; yet these attitudes and behaviors have special significance for programs and people who concern themselves with the education of bilingual handicapped children.

To judge the success or failure of programs on the basis of children's test performance does not do justice to those programs, and all who are involved in or affected by them, nor does it lead to a meaningful understanding of those programs (or of the child). Evaluation includes identifying areas of strength and weakness (Lesser, 1975). Test results alone tell us very little about children and very little about their programs.

Evaluation as Criticism

While the practice of using performance assessment to conduct program evaluation tends to result in program termination, shake-ups, or general dismay among program personnel, equally common is the trend of using evaluation to negatively critique a program. The skill of critiquing suffers in evaluation: consequently, programs suffer. Connotatively, to critique is "to consider the merits and demerits and judge accordingly" (Webster, 1976). However, in evaluation, critiquing has become a predominantly negative function. Evaluators often assume an approach that disproportionately emphasizes what is wrong with a program, what goals are unreached, and what the children are not receiving or not doing. Of course, one can find evaluation studies that begin with a customary "pat on the back," but the overwhelming content of most reports is generally unsupportive. This is not to say that there may be some programs deserving strong negative evaluative comment, yet even these and future programs can benefit from more than a barrage of blame. Fault-finding comes easy, and virtually everyone can do it.

Neophyte evaluators are especially prone to this negative stance. The fault-finding is as much a consequence of evaluation methodology as it is an evaluative posture (Cohen and Bruck, 1975; Sjoberg, 1975). By design, experimental, psychometric, and behavioristic models do not afford information that helps to explain or understand a program. Aspects of a large program that are valuable become obscured or diminished in importance when placed in the context of accumulated negative information. Descriptions that might help to guide decisions are unavailable. If one views the purpose of evaluation as an aid to decision making, there is little latitude in different directions to pursue when one is presented with evaluative data that concentrates on identifying the negative factors in a program's operation or its effects.

Unclear Evaluation

Evaluation studies that neglect to clarify operational definitions have diminished utility. In this regard, studies have typically grouped children under incorrect categories of language ability. For example, CHESS and Associates (1978) argued that the American Institutes for Research (AIR) study (1977) treated limited English-speaking ability students as if they were monolingual Spanish-speaking. The often used focus of measuring bilingual student growth in relation to their peers fails to acknowledge that students who truly belong in transitional bilingual programs have no peers in the regular classroom (Educational Testing Service, 1976). The profiles the latter present are truly unique.

Past studies have failed to state the assumptions that underlie the methodological design, the data categorization, and, ultimately, the data analysis. It is common to see measures of *attitudes toward school* as an indicator of program effectiveness. A child is judged as having more positive feeling toward school if there is an increase in that child's attendance or participation in extra-curricular activities. The operational assumption goes something like this: the child who acquires more language facility and develops a stronger self-concept will demonstrate this by joining monolingual peers in social activities; therefore, the program's effectiveness may be assessed on this variable. However, circumstances within a context; i.e., availability of transportation or family constraints, can preclude the child's participation in extra-curricular events even though the child is progressing toward the desired program goals.

Psychometric evaluation designs do not allow for these qualifications (Messick, 1975). More importantly, the validity of the assumption itself might well be questioned. Does language facility correlate with frequency of extra-curricular activity? Is this correlation a useful indicator of program effectiveness? Whether or not agreement can be reached on this or any assumption, the absense of clearly stated operational assumptions challenges the intent of the evaluation, while also weakening the credibility of inferences derived from the data.

What then, do these observations suggest in terms of *future* evaluation studies?

First, given that program goals involve both process and product outcomes, the design of evaluation strategies to collect and assess data must become more *congruent* with the phenomena under study. It is critical that study designs have the capacity to evaluate the many different ways children learn and develop and that studies are able to capture and portray the perceptions, attitudes, and beliefs of all program participants. Methodologies must provide for both quantitative and qualitative measures of change, with the data presented in ways that have meaning and *provide guidance* to the various audiences of the evaluation.

Second, rather than a preoccupation with fault-finding, evaluations must engage in the far more difficult task of understanding and describing program effects in their entirety. Evaluations must be directed to include more challenging questions: What works in the program? Why is it working? What is not working? How can those who implement the program make it work? Because such questions counter undue emphasis on performance, they require the use of evaluation strategies that are responsive to the complexities of individual children, individual programs, and individual contexts.

Third, as bilingual special education continues to develop, evaluation designs must attend to the philosophical, applied research, and legal issues that confront practitioners. Under these conditions evaluators become more than test technicians geared toward performance assessment and statistical survey. Instead, the evaluation is guided by an informed knowledge of definitions, assumptions, and issues understood by those in the field. It is important to recognize that an informed evaluation is no less objective. Ultimately, however, it offers greater utility since inferences and recommendations are more closely tied to a data base that has validity in its conceptualization.

The Naturalistic Approach to Program Evaluation

An evaluation appoach employing naturalistic inquiry strategies (Stake, 1967; Wolf, 1979; Wolf and Tymitz, 1977a, b, c) is highly appropriate to evaluation efforts in bilingual special education, for it embodies assumptions and methods far more congruent with variables under study in such programs. Naturalistic evaluation *responds* to the complexities of contexts, participants' multiple perceptions, and varying interpretations of program process and outcomes. According to Stake (1972), evaluation is responsive "if it orients more directly to program activities than to program intents, if it responds to audience requirements for information, and if the different value-perspectives present are referred to in reporting the success of the program" (p. 1). Naturalistic inquiry strategies attempt to present documentation through natural language representing as closely as possible how people feel, what they know, and how they know it and identifying their concerns, beliefs, perceptions, and understandings.

When designing a naturalistic evaluation plan, the emphasis on achievement data is not of primary importance. What becomes of primary importance is useful description to promote understanding of and reflection on the program for the many persons involved in it—children, parents, teachers, and other staff. The evaluation proceeds with frequent ongoing input by program participants.

The salient feature of effective naturalistic evaluation is its utility for these audiences. Utility to other audiences, such as a funding agency, is a simultaneous, but secondary, intent (House, 1976). Naturalistic evaluation techniques can provide a data base for systematic decision making and program development tailored to the context under study (Cronbach, 1975; Guba, 1978; Partlett and Hamilton, 1976; Wolf and Tymitz, 1976, 1977b).

The evaluation design develops throughout the process of the study. In other words, the evaluator does not begin with an immutable design, tightly controlled variables, or assigned experimental groups. The evaluator instead begins by determining, with the help of various audiences, what information will be of value. The information is then gathered systematically from a range of program participants and other relevant informants.

It is important to note that while assessment data do not usurp the primary evaluation focus, their inclusion is quite appropriate. Tests and test scores *do* have a place, and that place is secure as long as tests are used by evaluators to add information to the total profile of the child or of the program. In responsive evaluation, sources of information are varied. Together they lend increased potential for diagnostic accuracy and usefulness (Mercer and Lewis, 1978), with the guidelines for nondiscriminatory testing more readily satisfied (Federal Register, 1977).

The testing of children's ability and achievement should begin with an assessment of the means available by which they can express their knowledge and abilities. Language assessment becomes the prelude to ability and achievement testing. Bilingual special education program evaluation must include measurement of the receptive and expressive skills of the first language, accompanied by an evaluation of the receptive and expressive skills of the second language (usually English). Measures should include proficiency in each language and a determination of which language is more useful to the child for certain purposes. These assessment data are interpreted in the context of descriptive data collected (Erickson and Omark, 1981). A range of tentative explanations are presented to better understand the significance of test scores, particularly in terms of program decisions. Naturalistic evaluation does *not* sacrifice quantitative data to qualitative data. Rather, the approach has the capability and flexibility to include both, with its desired ideal being that each set of data will be better understood and explained by the other.

Naturalistic evaluation does not simply mean the evaluator will consider only what the program directors or clients wish. The evaluator must be skillful in identifying and pursuing addditional lines of inquiry that seem relevant and useful to the study. While program personnel may not suggest such informants as state education department personnel or siblings, the evaluator must consider all potential data sources and, if necessary, negotiate for their participation in the study.

The naturalistic evaluation approach relies on a variety of informal but systematic data collection strategies. These include interviews, observations, shadow studies, and artifact study. Each will be briefly described:

Interviews

Data from interviews using naturalistic inquiry methods form a substantial portion of the evaluation information base. The interview process is developmental and interactive. Each interview (and each question) builds upon information that has preceded it. Interviews using a naturalistic approach are unlike those conducted in numerous past evaluations that employed questionnaire formats with preconceived questions that forced structures on the studies that were often illogical, irrelevant, or insensitive to the actualities that existed.

Naturalistic strategies are aimed at gathering answers to questions judged to be valid and important to those persons seen as the objects of study. The evaluator starts with an initial framework for asking questions. The framework is based on the evaluator's study of existing theory related to the inquiry and extant political, educational, economic, and legal matters that might impinge on the study and program in question. Program participants as respondents permit the framework to be reworked or redesigned for their informational needs, as well as the informational needs of other audiences.

Interviews are conducted across many levels of participants and program beneficiaries, *including the children who are daily involved in the program.* Respondents are typically interviewed several times so that cross-checking, validation, and clarification are enhanced.

Basic interviewing skills include listening, question asking, flexibility, coping with ambiguity, and resiliency. Other skills more difficult to describe involve the ability to think spontaneously, to analyze and synthesize data *in situ* so as to eliminate or illuminate inferences, to avoid moral pigeonholing, to understand self-prejudices, to take useful notes and accurately summarize information, to become facile in conversing with people, and to learn how to move through natural settings with ease (Wolf and Tymitz, 1977a).

Observations

Insights gained from frequent, but spaced, observations enrich the contextual data of a study. The evaluator must be a sensitive, curious, and skilled onlooker so as to maximize careful interpretation of this kind of data. Structured, rigid checklists are inappropriate. Instead, observers function with a set of issues or concerns around which to cluster observations.

Shadow Studies

The purpose of shadow studies is to inform the evaluator of the direct and indirect consequence of the program as they are experienced by the participants. Shadow studies require that the evaluator select a child or group of children to focus on for an extended, but uninterrupted, time period. Opportunity to follow program participants through their activities provides contextual data different from observational data. In essence, the evaluator gains a sense of how and what program parts work together. What happens, for example, when the mainstreamed bilingual child moves in a daily routine from the special education classroom to the regular classroom and back again? What occurs when the child or group of children play together, lunch together, seat themselves on the bus, or make transitions between any of these events? Shadow studies become "slice of life" episodes that allow a description of possible program effects from a contextually bound interrelated perspective.

Artifact Study

This strategy requires the analysis of various existing information resources:

documented program goals and objectives	curriculum guides
newsletters	program brochures
parent correspondence	special events/calendars
student workbooks and other program materials	parent information packets (including due process guidelines)
completed student worksheets, artwork, projects	audiotapes (student performance; special programs)
in-service program guides	attendance records
relevant fiscal information sheets	documented media coverage (newspaper, radio, television)
teacher anecdotal records	cumulative records (including case conference proceedings)
relevant school board policy statements	

It is critical that the evaluator recognize and adhere to the confidentiality restrictions of artifacts such as Individualized Education Programs. In such instances samples of blank forms may be useful. For example, it may be possible to verify whether or not the language on the forms is clear to parents, teachers, or other staff.

Artifact analysis provides in-depth information about program components. From these, data on specific program elements that are possibly related are placed within the macroview yielded through observation and shadow studies.

Naturalistic strategies are interrelated; therefore, function somewhat simultaneously. It is likely that the evaluator will attempt to corroborate interview data through shadow study or that observations will be cross-checked though interviews. The process is developmental. At times, one strategy will take precedence over another, such as, during the initiation of the study, when a partial artifact analysis can serve to inform the evaluator about given contextual variables. Of greatest importance is the recognition that, regardless of the form any particular study has assumed, it is incumbent upon the evaluator to support all inferences, conclusions, and recommendations through a data base that is congruent with the statements being offered.

Undertaking an evaluation employing naturalistic strategies requires rigorous application. Using naturalistic strategies does not infer an unscientific approach. Researchers operating within the naturalistic framework engage in conceptual stages important to the inquiry process: immersion, investigation, transaction, narration, and consideration. Operational stages include entré, negotiation, mapping the territory, value delineation, exposition of biases, trust-building, credibility, timing, toleration, and visibility (Wolf, 1979). While there may be fewer numbers in the substance of the report, there tends to be greater meaning and utility in the descriptions and analysis provided through in-depth study of program participants. Other primary concerns regarding the necessary skills and application of the approach are reflected in the following questions:

When Should Naturalistic Evaluation Be Used?

Both formative and summative evaluation can be provided through this approach. The strategies are uniquely sensitive to the complexities in evaluating the particular nature of each program and the children in these programs. Use of techniques is most appropriate when program personnel seek in-depth information from a range of respondents on program development, implementation, and impact.

Who Can/Should Do Naturalistic Evaluation?

Any evaluation should be conducted by one who has training and experience in the methods to be employed. All who are involved in naturalistic evaluation must recognize that the techniques go well beyond "doing what comes naturally." Rigor in design and implementation of the evaluation is essential. Skill in interpreting both quantitative and qualitative data is required. The evaluator must be able to present data to a variety of audiences with a range of informational needs. If the evaluation is to be completed by program personnel, that must become a major responsibility of the evaluation team. It is unlikely that an evaluation study relegated as an additional program personnel staff activity will yield the depth of data that can inform program decisions.

The credentials of *internal* and *external* persons should be considered for any evaluation. Established expertise of the evaluator typically creates greater acceptance of study results and recommendations.

How Long Should the Evaluation Extend?

Each study must be designed to answer the informational needs of the evaluation audience. Some evaluation requests are more in-depth than others and obviously require additional time to complete. However, any use of naturalistic strategies presents similar characteristics that affect the duration of the study. The approach involves numerous contacts with the program staff and participants: observations should be collected at varied time intervals; data and inferences must be cross-checked and validated. The length of each study is likewise affected by the number of program participants and the extensiveness of evaluation staff. Program personnel should be able to identify these characteristics in a well-executed evaluation using naturalistic strategies.

How Is the Evaluation Report Presented to the Various Audiences?

Typically, the report is presented in final form to the primary evaluation audience, i.e., program director or funding agency. The report includes all quantitative data, a readable narrative that presents the qualitative data, and a detailed discussion of the interpretations and implications of both sets of data; what they mean separately and what they mean as they operate together in the program. Supporting documents, i.e., test scores, program outlines, curricula, are included for the reader's reference. While some audiences will have an expressed interest in certain portions of the report, each reader should be advised of the availability of the report in its entirety.

Closely following the completion of the report, an opportunity for evaluation audiences to discuss it should be arranged. Such interactions should be conducted with the evaluation team to clarify questions about the report. The dialogue that ensues frequently provides the program personnel with a common understanding of the evaluation as well as future directions to pursue.

Conclusion

The naturalistic approach to evaluation is an alternative (not a substitute) to the traditional psychometric design, which focuses on test performance and assessment. Use of the naturalistic methods allows for the collection of data from a variety of sources. Descriptions, inferences, and any recommendations are derived from an integration of these data sources. It is from this integration, enhanced by careful questioning, frequent observations, and cross-validation, that a true picture of the program will emerge.

It would not be unfair to say that the history of program evaluation in bilingual education has been clouded and that the utility of evaluation to *any* of the audiences has been obfuscated. Those who conduct evaluations of bilingual special education programs can, at this time, view the contextual and methodological problems in past studies from a perspective that guards against repetition of the use of inadequate designs and inappropriate methodologies. Evaluation need not be negative; nor should evaluation be placating. It should be informing and useful. The unique nature of bilingual programs and the individual profiles of handicapped bilingual children illustrate the necessity of evaluation studies that respond to these basic criteria.

Note

[1]The author wishes to acknowledge the contributions of Anne Kiefer, Assistant Director for Administrative Training Title VII Bilingual Education, State of Illinois.

References

Abbott, R., and Peterson, J.:   *Learning disabilities—They're all around you.* 1975. (ED 128 529).

American Institutes for Research, Bilingual Studies Center: *Evaluation of the Impact of ESEA Title VII Spanish/English Bilingual Education Program.* Palo Alto, February, 1977. (ED 138 091).

Blanco, G.:   *The Educational Perspective, Bilingual Education, Current Perspectives: Education.* Arlington, Center for Applied Linguistics, 1977.

The Board of Education of the City of Detroit: *Guide to the Implementation of Bilingual-Bicultural Education.* Detroit, 1976.

Carrasquillo, A.:   *New directions for special education through a bilingual bicultural approach.* Paper presented at the Annual International Convention, Council for Exceptional Children, Atlanta, April, 1977. (ED 139 173)

Cazden, C.:   The neglected situation in child language research and education. In Williams, F. (Ed.): *Language and Poverty: Perspectives on a Theme.* Chicago, Martham, 1970.

CHESS and Associates: *Summary of the AIR Report on Bilingual Education.* Costa Mesa, 1978.

Cicourel, A.V., Jennings, K.H., Jennings, S.H.M., Leiter, K.C.W., MacKay, R., Mehan, H., and Roth, D.R.:   *Language Use and School Performance.* New York, Academic, 1974.

Cohen, A., and Bruck, M.:   *Evaluation of the Illinois Downstate Bilingual Program, 1975-1976.* Center for Applied Linguistics, Arlington, 1975.

Cortes, L.A.:   *Student's reaction to bilingual special education.* Paper presented at the Annual International Convention, Council for Exceptional Children, Atlanta, April, 1977. (ED 139 174).

Cronbach, L.J.:   Beyond the two disciplines of scientific psychology. *American Psychologist, 30:*115-127, 1975.

DeAvila, E., and Duncan, S.: *A Few Thoughts About Language Assessment: The Lau Decision Reconsidered.* National Dissemination and Assessment Center. California State University, Los Angeles, *1*:8, March, 1978.

Educational Testing Service, Bilingual Education. *Focus, 2,* 1976

Eisner, E.W.: On the uses of educational connoisseurship and criticism for evaluating classroom life. *Teachers College Record, 78*:345-358, 1977.

Epstein, N.: *Language, Ethnicity and the Schools: Policy Alternatives for Bilingual-Bicultural Education.* Washington, D.C., George Washington University Institute for Educational Leadership, 1977.

Erickson, J.G., and Omark, D.R.: *Communication Assessment of the Bilingual, Bicultural Child: Issues and Guidelines.* Baltimore, University Park, 1981.

Etherson, E., Moesser, A., and Sancho, A.: *The CHESS Guide to Project Evaluation.* CHESS and Associates, Inc., Costa Mesa, 1977.

Federal Register, 42:163, August 23, 1977.

Garza, S.: *Language assessment identifying LESA's.* October, 1976. (ED 144 415)

Guba, E.G.: The failure of educational evaluation. *Educational Technology, 9(5)*:29-38, 1969.

Guba, E.G.: Toward a Metholodogy of Naturalistic Inquiry in Educational Evaluation. *CSS Monograph Series in Evaluation, 8,* Los Angeles, UCLA, 1978.

House, E.R.: Justice in evaluation. In Glass, G.V. (Ed.): *Evaluation Studies Review Annual, 1,* Beverly Hills, Sage, 1976.

Iiams, T.: The gathering storm over bilingual education. *Phi Delta Kappan, 59(4)*:226-230, 1978.

Illinois Board of Higher Education: *Bilingual Teacher Preparation Conference Report.* December, 1974.

Kamii, C.: One intelligence indivisible. *Young Children, 30*:228-238, 1975.

Lesser, S.: *Improving Bilingual Instruction and Services in Special Schools. New York City Board of Education.* Brooklyn, Office of Education Evaluation, June, 1975. (ED 139 893)

Locks, N., Pletcher, B., and Reynolds, D.: *Language Assessment Instruments for Limited-English-Speaking Students: A Needs Analysis.* U.S. Department of Health, Education, and Welfare, Washington, D.C., National Institute of Education, October, 1978.

Magoon, A.J.: Constructivist research. *Review of Education, 49*:651, 1977.

McClelland, D.C.: Testing for competence rather than for "intelligence." *American Psychologist, 28*:1-14, 1977.

Mead, M.: The conversation of insight: Educational understanding of bilingualism. *Teachers College Record, 49(4)*:207-221, 1978.

Mercer, J., and Lewis, J.:   *Introduction to System of Multicultural Pluralistic Assessment.* New York, Psychological Corporation, 1978.

Messick, S.:   The standard problem: Meaning and values in measurement and evaluation. *American Psychologist, 30*:955–966, 1975.

Mullen, F.:   *Psychological services to Spanish speaking children in the schools of Chicago.* April, 1973. (ED 091 451)

Nason, F. de O.C. de: *Final Evaluation Report: Project Build.* November, 1980. (ED 199 371)

Parlett, M., and Hamilton, D.:   Evaluation as illumination: A new approach to the study of innovative programs. In Glass, G.V. (Ed.): *Evaluation Studies Review Annual, 1,* Beverly Hills, Sage, 1976.

Riegel, K.F.:   Influence of economic and political ideologies on the development of developmental psychology. *Psychological Bulletin, 78*:129–141, 1972.

Sanua, V.:   *Bilingual Program for Physically Handicapped Children; School Year, 1974–1975.* New York City Board of Education, Brooklyn, Office of Educational Evaluation, 1975. (ED 137 448)

Shutt, D., and Hannon, T.:   *The Psychological Evaluation of Bilingual Pupils Utilizing the Hiskey-Nebraska Test of Learning Aptitudes.* A validation study. April, 1973. (ED 109 215)

Silverman, R., Noa, J., and Russell, R.:   *Oral Language Tests for Bilingual Students.* Portland, NREL, 1978.

Sjoberg, G.:   Politics, ethics, and evaluation research. In Guttentag, M., and Struening, E.L. (Eds.): *Handbook of Evaluation Research, 2.* Beverly Hills, Sage, 1975.

Stake, R.:   The countenance of educational evaluation. *Teachers College Record, 68(7)*:523–540, 1967.

Stake, R.E.:   *Responsive Evaluation.* Urbana, Center for Instructional Research and Curriculum Evaluation, University of Illinois, December, 1972.

Troike, C.:   *Introduction, Bilingual Education: Current Perspectives.* Arlington, Center for Applied Linguistics, 1977.

Troike, C.:   *Research Evidence for the Effectiveness of Bilingual Education.* Arlington, Center for Applied Linguistics, 1978.

Tymitz, B.:   *The Relationship of Differentiated Teaching Learning Interactions on Teachers' Frame of Reference in Understanding Cognitions and Behaviors of a Learning Disabled Child.* Unpublished doctoral dissertation. University of Illinois, 1977.

Webster's New Collegiate Dictionary. Springfield, Merriam, 1976.

Wilson, S.:   The use of ethnographic techniques in educational research. *Review of Educational Research, 47*:245–265, 1977.

Wolf, R.L.:   *Policy Implications of Bilingual Special Education.* Occasional Paper Series, Indiana Center for Evaluation, Indiana University, December, 1978.

Wolf, R.L.: *Some Conceptual and Operational Considerations of Naturalistic Evaluation Methodology.* Occasional Paper Series, Indiana Center for Evaluation, Indiana University, 1979.

Wolf, R., and Tymitz, B.: Ethnography and reading: Matching inquiry mode to process. *Reading Research Quarterly, 12(1):* 1976.

Wolf, R., and Tymitz, B.: *An Investigator's Guide to Naturalistic/Judicial Inquiry* (with R.L. Wolf) NERO and Associates, Roselyn, 1977a.

Wolf, R., and Tymitz, B.: *Enhancing Policy Formulation Through Naturalistic/Judicial Procedures: A Study of the Impact of P.L. 94-142.* Final report. Bureau of Education for the Handicapped, September, 1977b.

Wolf, R., and Tymitz, B.: Toward more natural inquiry in education. *CEDR Quarterly, Phi Delta Kappan*, October, 1977c.

21

Training Paraprofessionals for Identification and Intervention with Communicatively Disordered Bilinguals

Gloria Toliver-Weddington
Marion D. Meyerson

In 1970, the Commission on Supportive Personnel of the American Speech and Hearing Association (ASHA) published *Guidelines for Supportive Personnel in Speech Pathology and Audiology* and recognized the category of "Communicative Aides." The move came in response to a desire for regulation of the use of paraprofessionals who were already assigned to a plethora of programs. Among the settings where the use of communication aides appeared most beneficial were those in which there were significant numbers of bilingual/bicultural children. Minority speech and hearing professionals were and are few and far between, and trained aides were utilized in the hopes of bridging the cultural and linguistic gap between the clinician and the clients and their families.

Before and since this ASHA policy statement, a number of projects and programs have been described in the literature (Alpiner, Ogden, and Wiggins, 1970; Berman, 1976; Braunstein, 1972; Carrier, 1970; Costello and Schoen, 1978; Dopheide and Dallinger, 1976; Frith and Teller, 1982; Galloway and Blue, 1975; Jelinek, 1976; Lynch, 1972; Pickering and Dopheide, 1976; Sommers et al., 1976). These projects and programs reflect a diversity in background, training, and utilization of aides and give rise to some common features and promising trends. This chapter will review information and explore pertinent areas regarding paraprofessionals. If paraprofessionals are to be assigned to work with the communicatively handicapped bilingual child, one should consider the following questions: who are the paraprofessionals, why are they needed, what are their roles, and how should they be trained?

Who Are the Paraprofessionals?

The terms *aides* and *paraprofessionals* are used interchangeably to include both salaried workers and volunteers. Their professional and life roles vary and represent different age levels, sexes, educational levels, socioeconomic status, ethnic groups, languages and dialects spoken, and experience. They include students, teachers, nurses, occupational and physical therapists, trained paraprofessionals, and children's peers.

Students

The students who assist the speech/language clinician are commonly graduate students majoring in speech/language pathology and audiology at a local college or university, although students from other disciplines also have assumed this role. The abilities and knowledge of students can vary, ranging from a total lack of theoretical and practical background to competency. The student paraprofessionals are generally enthusiastic and excited about their duties and anticipate having total responsibility for clients. Coursework should help students perform duties as paraprofessionals. The experience they receive as paraprofessionals can be valuable in increasing the relevancy of the course content and making learning more meaningful. A program at a major university that used students majoring in communicative disorders as paraprofessionals indicated that they showed increased self-confidence in clinical practice following the experience (Hall and Knutson, 1978). The differences between clinical practice and paraprofessional activity are considerable in that the paraprofessional is not permitted to plan or evaluate therapy, or carry out diagnostic procedures without the direct and constant supervision of the speech/language clinician, while these activities are part of the process of clinical practice.

Example:
A senior in a college communicative disorders program is serving as an aide while doing preclinical coursework. She works with severely communicatively handicapped children in a developmental center and is currently assisting in controlling drooling and in encouraging visual tracking of objects (*see* Figure 21–1).

FIGURE 21-1
Preclinical speech-language pathology student assisting professional in therapy program.

Teachers

The teacher serving in the role of paraprofessional does not necessarily perform the same duties as other paraprofessionals who work directly with the speech/language clinician. However, the teacher can provide significant help to the communicatively handicapped child in the development of new communicative behaviors within the classroom setting. The teacher may frequently be asked to observe, record, and reinforce certain communicative behaviors. In addition, the teacher may be encouraged to modify teaching techniques used with small or large groups in order to help the child with a communicative disorder.

Example:
A first grade teacher modifies pronunciation of bilingual children while teaching phonics during a reading lesson.

Parents

Because parents spend a significant amount of time with their children, they are in a unique position to help their own children and others as well. P.L. 94-142 requires that the parents and the speech/language clinician agree on the goals and objectives developed for each child receiving services. This mandate gives the parents an opportunity to meet with the speech/language clinician to discuss the children's program and progress. The parents may be asked to help in the development of their child's communicative skills at home or to assist their child and other children at school. By working as a paraprofessional with the speech/language clinician, the parent has a chance to observe the process involved in speech and language therapy, and to participate in the therapeutic process. The trained parent can also work with other parents as a liaison between the school and the community.

Example:
A Mexican American mother is serving as an aide in the local kindergarten. She is assisting the speech/language clinician in recording, translating, and analyzing spontaneous language samples obtained in the classroom and on the playground.

Allied Health Professionals

Nurses often work with communicatively handicapped individuals whom they can assist in the development of communicative skills. The speech/language clinician can suggest ways in which the nurse can work on the patient's speech while engaged in nursing care.

Since many communicatively handicapped individuals often need other types of therapies, it is possible for the occupational and physical therapists to assist in the development of communication (Cromwell, 1974). Because these paraprofessionals work closely with their patients, they can perform assignments prepared by the speech/language clinician.

Example:
A nurse at a state institution has been trained to name body parts while delivering nursing care to residents.

Peer Teaching

Using clients' peers to assist in the training of handicapped individuals can be effective in working with the mentally retarded, learning disabled, laryngectomees, and aphasics. Peer assistance has become one of the most useful methods that the speech/language clinician has for helping the communicatively handicapped client to achieve maximum skills as rapidly as possible. Groher (1976) reported improved articulation skills among children who were trained by older children who also had articulation errors. The older child can become a role model for the younger child and, at the same time, heighten self-esteem. A study described by Cloward (1976)

FIGURE 21-2

Peer tutor working with young LEP child under supervision of speech-language pathologist.

indicated that even when the tutor was a low achieving student, the tutor's own reading skills greatly improved while tutoring a younger child.

Example:
Fourth grade bilingual children are helping Spanish monolingual first graders increase their English vocabulary. (*see* Figure 21-2).

Salaried Paraprofessionals

The paraprofessional who is hired as an aide has a different role and responsibility from the paraprofessionals described above. These aides have been trained to do a specific job for a salary. They work directly with the speech/language clinician in an effort to improve program effectiveness. They also assume certain responsibilities in order to free the clinician from relatively simple, routine activities. This released time allows the speech/language clinician to focus on planning and implementing instructional programs and providing more intensive therapy for the more severe cases. A salary does not of itself add to the competence of paraprofessionals, but often the seriousness of the role and continuity of the program is boosted by providing salaries, rather than relying on volunteers' time.

When paraprofessionals are hired, training is generally provided by the employer. Such training does not usually involve formal coursework, but is done through on-the-job training in which the speech/language clinician describes the duties the aides are expected to perform and demonstrates specific activities. Such training is not necessarily transferable to other situations nor to other clients.

Example:
A salaried communication aide in a predominantly Chicano school is working with children with multiple articulation errors on carryover of target phonemes.

In summary, there are many types of paraprofessionals or aides who can assist in the rehabilitation of communicatively handicapped individuals. Although their ages and lifestyles vary, their primary function is basically the same—enhancing the effectiveness of speech/language therapy.

Why Are They Needed?

The need for bilingual/bicultural paraprofessionals in speech/language pathology is obvious, but relatively little attention has been given to their training or their duties. In this country, approximately 16% of the population speak languages other than English as a first language (Pickering, 1976). Although bilingual paraprofessionals have been employed in medical facilities as intake personnel and have assisted physicians in communicating with patients, as well as in schools as resource personnel, this practice has not been carried over into the field of communicative disorders. If the speech/language clinician is to truly understand the disorders of non-English proficient (NEP) and limited-English proficient (LEP) students, the clinician must examine their native languages rather than the language of the school.

In the schools, for example, bilingual paraprofessionals are a necessary part of the schools' attempts to encourage cultural pluralism. Partly because of the paucity of bilingual classroom teachers, bilingual paraprofessionals have been employed to assist the monolingual English teacher in bilingual classrooms. School personnel who live in the children's community and speak the same language are role models who can encourage positive self-identification and feelings of self-worth among these children. Bilingual paraprofessionals can also assist in motivating the children to achieve in school and to improve their communicative skills (Davies, 1977).

The Head Start program has been employing paraprofessionals since 1965. Head Start, serving a multicultural, multilingual group from low income communities, employs paraprofessionals to bridge the gap between the children and their teachers. That is, paraprofessionals are capable of interpreting the characteristics of each group to the other since they usually share the cultural and linguistic experiences of both. These paraprofessionals are selected from the community and thus understand the community lifestyle and perspectives. In addition, the paraprofessionals, having worked in the professional world, are knowledgeable about professional perspectives and goals.

A summary of functions ascribed to bilingual paraprofessionals have been noted by Goodwin (1977). Although these functions are discussed in relationship to classroom paraprofessionals, one can see the relevancy to bilingual/bicultural communication aides. The following roles are indicated:

Translator. The bilingual paraprofessional has the responsibility to provide the child with information that is generated in the class and to transmit information from the child to the teacher and other members of the class. The translator not only translates what is happening in the class, but actually teaches new information and concepts in the child's dominant language.

Reinforcer. The bilingual paraprofessional reinforces the child's correct responses, provides stimulation and encouragement, and monitors the child's feelings. This paraprofessional also counsels children with academic or emotional difficulties.

Model. The bilingual paraprofessional becomes a model for the children as one who successfully engages in the behaviors of two cultures and speaks both languages. The children have someone to emulate and to approach.

Monitor. The paraprofessional also assists the teacher in the classroom, on the playground, at the bus stop, and in the cafeteria by monitoring and disciplining the children's behavior. In this capacity, the paraprofessional has an opportunity to demonstrate leadership abilities and to teach classroom material, games, and activities.

Advocate. In cases of conflict between the child and the school, the bilingual paraprofessional becomes an advocate for the child and the family by explaining their legal rights and the responsibilities of the school to provide an appropriate education for all exceptional children. This can be done in a language that is familiar to the family. The paraprofessional serves as a spokesperson for the family in the meetings that determine the placement of the child in special education programs.

In summary, the general roles of paraprofessionals in the schools have been clearly established. These classroom aides have been supplementing the work of teachers for many years and more recently bilingual aides have been employed to support the educational process.

What Are Their Roles?

The guidelines developed by the American Speech/Language and Hearing Association require that paraprofessionals be directly supervised by ASHA certified clinicians. Speech/language clinicians assign the duties to the paraprofessionals, define and maintain specific lines of responsibility and authority, assure that the paraprofessional is responsible only to the clinician in all client-related activities, and continually evaluate the paraprofessional's performance. The paraprofessional should not be responsible for making decisions regarding diagnosis, management, or future disposition of clients (ASHA, 1970).

The duties of the paraprofessionals vary from one setting to another. They are expected to assist the clinician with clients by working with them directly as well as in supportive activities. Contact with clients might involve drilling on specific sounds or linguistic patterns. The paraprofessional follows a lesson plan developed by the speech/language clinician.

Within the guidelines of the American Speech/Language and Hearing Association, paraprofessionals perform many functions. Alpiner, Ogden, and Wiggins (1970) and Scalero and Eskenazi (1976) have utilized them in the following ways: (a) assisting in articulation, language, hearing, and stuttering therapy; (b) conducting clerical work; (c) facilitating professional-family contact; (d) assisting in preparing instructional material; and (e) enforcing required safety and disciplinary rules with students enrolled in therapy.

Bilingual/Bicultural Paraprofessionals

Except for a statement regarding the ability of the paraprofessional "to understand and to sympathize with the cultural and linguistic heritages of the areas from which the clients come" (Commission on Supportive Personnel, 1970, p. 79), ASHA guidelines offer no specific roles or responsibilities for bilingual/bicultural paraprofessionals. This issue has not been specifically addressed by the Committee on Supportive Personnel nor by the Legislative Council.

Bilingual paraprofessionals are in a unique position to provide services in the schools, hospitals, and community agencies, and also receive and utilize specialized training in a rapidly growing profession. They can intervene in situations in which a monolingual English-speaking speech/language clinician can never be effective, especially in situations in which two languages, or a language other than English, is necessary.

Among the duties the bilingual/bicultural paraprofessionals in communicative disorders might perform are the following:

1. The bilingual/bicultural paraprofessional could assist the speech/language clinician in the screening and assessment of speech, language, and hearing of clients. P.L. 94–142 and P.L. 95–561 and other regulations require the testing of children in the schools must be done in their native language. This approach would require either the employment of bilingual/bicultural speech/language clinicians or the

use of bilingual/bicultural paraprofessionals. The latter appears to be the most practical solution at this time since bilingual/bicultural speech/language clinicians are few in numbers.

The monolingual English speech/language clinician *cannot adequately assess* the communicative abilities of individuals who speak languages other than English. A translator is generally of limited assistance because of unfamiliarity with methods of describing language, assessment procedures, language development, or the use of terminology. Therefore, a trained bilingual/bicultural paraprofessional is not only able to translate, but can also interpret stimuli and responses between the client and the speech/language clinician, and administer assessment procedures directly to the client in the native language.

2. The bilingual/bicultural paraprofessional can provide direct intervention with the clients by implementing an instructional program planned by the speech/language clinician. The bilingual/bicultural paraprofessional can also assist the client in developing communicative behaviors in the native language utilizing culturally and linguistically relevant materials and activities for the sessions.

3. The bilingual/bicultural paraprofessional may work directly with group members who are progressing at a slower pace in therapy. Individual assistance can be provided to those who are having difficulty keeping pace with their peers.

4. The bilingual/bicultural paraprofessional can serve as translator and interpreter for the client and the client's family. On occasion, direct translation is all that is necessary for the speech/language clinician, the client, and the family to understand each other. However, at other times, it may be necessary for the bilingual/bicultural paraprofessional to interpret or explain concepts to the client and/or the family. For this reason it is important that the bilingual/bicultural paraprofessional have some specific training in speech pathology about necessary clinical information so that the paraprofessional can provide this service competently. An untrained paraprofessional or translator cannot meet this need adequately.

5. The bilingual/bicultural paraprofessional may work as a liaison between the speech/language clinician and community agencies involved with social, medical, psychological, and rehabilitative services. The bilingual/bicultural paraprofessional is selected from the bilingual community and thus can become aware of agencies and personnel more readily than the speech/language clinician who does not represent the community. Such communication with community agencies can be very important to the speech/language clinician and the clients when making referrals and providing cooperative services.

6. The bilingual/bicultural paraprofessional may assist in counseling the client and the family by explaining the findings of diagnostic

evaluation and plans for treatment, as well as assisting in bringing parent input into the individualized educational plan (IEP). In addition, the bilingual/bicultural paraprofessional can keep the family informed of the progress of the client or changes in the instructional program. In situations in which the client speaks English, but the family does not, the bilingual/bicultural paraprofessional is a valuable intermediary who keeps the family informed of changes in the client's communication skills the family cannot directly observe.

There are, no doubt, additional roles for the bilingual/bicultural paraprofessional in speech/language pathology that are not outlined here. It is apparent that this individual is becoming a necessary part of working with bilingual LEP and NEP clients. Since the majority of the trained speech/language clinicians in the United States speak only one language, training bilingual/bicultural paraprofessionals to assist in the rehabilitative process is helpful to professionals, to clients, and to the minority communities that need to be informed so that they can participate in the services available.

How Should Paraprofessionals Be Trained?

Given the premise that bilingual/bicultural paraprofessionals are needed and can be utilized, proper training is both necessary and complex. Setting, time, and curriculum can all be points of decision for those planning the training program. For example, training can take place in preservice workshops, at inservice meetings, or through academic courses in colleges and universities. There is no consensus on which approach is most effective. However, the training must be done before paraprofessionals are effective.

The ASHA guidelines of 1970 specified a general outline of the curriculum for training paraprofessionals, but did not specify the length of time that training programs should take. Guidelines did indicate that the duration of the program can vary from a few days to several weeks, depending on the nature of the work to be performed. The Committee on Supportive Personnel recommended that the training of paraprofessionals should be determined by the task to be performed and should be the responsibility of the organization that will employ them. Guidelines for the training curriculum included the following: (a) orientation regarding the significance of human communication, (b) ethical responsibilities of the professional clinician, client, and employing organization, (c) administrative structure of the speech and hearing program, (d) the types of tasks to be performed by the clinician, and (e) recognition and identification of client's responses.

The general function of the paraprofessional is to enhance the effectiveness of the speech/language pathology services; therefore, training should be confined to practical, relevant information that will help the paraprofessional function in that capacity. The training should be appropriate to the setting in which the paraprofessional will work and the duties to be performed. Training that is specific to a particular type of clientele or setting should be done within the organization in which the paraprofessional will work.

Paraprofessional training programs developed by Alpiner, et al. (1970) and by Scalero and Eskenazi (1976) include information in the following areas: (a) the profession of communicative disorders and the role of the speech, language, and hearing clinicians and their support personnel, (b) professional responsibilities and the code of ethics, (c) normal development of speech and language in children, contrasted with children who develop disorders in communication, (d) anatomy and physiology of the speech and hearing mechanism, (e) identification and treatment of speech, language, and hearing disorders, (f) evaluation of clients' progress, (g) administrative structure of the school district, and (h) the nature of second language acquisition.

In summary, the paraprofessional can perform a variety of functions and duties within a training program to provide necessary knowledge. The bilingual/bicultural paraprofessional, however, needs as much information as possible about communicative disorders, their diagnosis, and treatment, as well as specified training about the role of a bilingual specialist.

A Model Training Program

This proposed program includes objectives, rationales, and suggested areas for a preservice training program for bilingual/bicultural paraprofessionals in speech/language pathology. The first objective is related to bicultural sensitivity and is therefore presented in greater detail than the other objectives.

Objective I.
The trainees will identify the differences between their culture and that of mainstream America.

Rationale. While many bilingual/bicultural individuals understand that major differences exist between their culture and that of the dominant culture, they are often unaware of specific differences. Some believe that their lifestyle, values, and perspectives are not only different, but inferior to those of the dominant culture and must be modified. Assuming that one of the roles of bilingual/bicultural paraprofessionals is to serve as models for the communicatively handicapped client, it is necessary for them to become both knowledgeable and proud of their own culture, as well as know about the dominant culture.

Areas covered. Culture includes the attitudes, values, customs, and beliefs of a group of people. Important aspects of culture are religion, political and economic beliefs, dress, language, food, education, and social organization. When studying culture it is necessary to understand the structures of one group and how it compares with another. The following are some of the cultural factors that should be included in the training program for bilingual/bicultural paraprofessionals:

1. Language: Linguistic description and analyses are necessary features of a training program for bilingual/bicultural paraprofessionals. Both verbal and nonverbal aspects must be included. Verbal aspects should include descriptive information that highlights differences between their language and English in syntax, semantics, phonology, and prosody. Nonverbal aspects should include proxemics, chronemics, haptics, and kinesics. Such behaviors represent a large portion of the communicative process and cause many of the conflicts and clashes in cross-cultural communication. When individuals from different cultures interpret nonverbal information based on their own culture and experiences, communicative problems result.
2. Values: The variance of values should be discussed to highlight similarities and differences between the dominant culture and those cultures represented in the paraprofessional training program. Such training should emphasize differences in religion, attitudes toward education, family, long-term planning, promptness, age, handicapping conditions, traditions, authority figures, and competition. It is important that paraprofessionals utilize such information in assessment, counseling, and therapy.

Objective II.
The trainee will identify and describe the common speech, language, and hearing disorders.
Rationale. Paraprofessionals who will assist in the identification and remediation of communicative disorders must develop the ability to recognize the more common conditions that will be observed in the setting in which they will work.
Areas covered.
1. Normal speech and language development and behavior.
2. Second language acquisition, bilingualism, linguistic interference, code switching, and code mixing.
3. Characteristics and etiologies of speech disorders, including articulation, voice, and fluency; language disorders, including delayed language development and aphasia; and hearing disorders, including problems in acuity, discrimination, and processing.
4. Observation of behavior using videotapes of clients displaying various types of communicative disorders.

Objective III.

The trainee will help evaluate speech, language, and hearing of children and adults.

Rationale. One of the roles of the paraprofessional is to assist in the screening and diagnostic process; therefore, it is necessary to include in the training information about assessment of communication.

Areas covered.

1. Definitions of assessment terminology, such as diagnosis, diagnostic tests, screening tests, norms, and formal and informal assessment.
2. Demonstrations of the uses of formal and informal assessment procedures.
3. Interpretation of assessment results.
4. Use of assessment results in planning therapy.

Objective IV.

The trainees will develop skill in planning and implementing IEPs for communicatively handicapped individuals.

Rationale. An additional role of the paraprofessional is to implement IEPs developed by the speech/language clinician.

Areas covered.

1. Developing and implementing programmed instruction.
2. Preparing culturally relevant material for meeting therapy goals.
3. Evaluating success of therapy sessions.
4. Communicating results of speech and language evaluations to the client and family.

Objective V.

The trainee will identify by name and function those anatomical structures involved in communication.

Rationale. In order to work with communicatively handicapped individuals it is necessary to understand the basic anatomy and physiology of the speech mechanism.

Areas covered.

1. Structures of the respiratory, phonatory, articulatory, and auditory mechanisms.
2. An overview of the neuroanatomy and neurophysiology of speech and hearing.
3. Deviation in structure and function that could cause communicative disorders such as cleft lip and palate, aphasia, dysarthria, and vocal nodules.

Objective VI.
The trainee will demonstrate knowledge of second language acquisition in children.
Rationale. Paraprofessionals must function in situations where children are learning two languages. They must have an awareness of the methods of learning two language systems by children and the problems they encounter.

These recommended competencies are general guidelines and can be modified to fit the specific objectives of the training program. The content and extent of any training program for paraprofessionals are determined by the situation in which the paraprofessional will work and the duties they will perform.

What Are the Realities of Training and Utilization of Paraprofessionals?

Paraprofessionals have been trained and utilized for many years in a variety of settings. Universities, community agencies, hospitals, schools, and preschool programs such as Head Start have maintained a number of types of programs. The trained paraprofessionals salaried might be students, parents, nurses, teachers, occupational and physical therapists, aides, or peers. The roles of these individuals vary depending on the setting, but they do not and cannot take the place of trained speech/ language clinicians who have advanced credentials such as state licensure or clinical certification from the American Speech-Language and Hearing Association.

While paraprofessionals have served numerous useful functions, their use continues to be abused in some situations. For example, in the New York City public schools, paraprofessionals are hired to "liberate teachers from a wide range of noninstructional tasks" (Grossman, 1972, p. 2). The use of the term *liberate* forces teachers to utilize their aides in limited, noncreative ways, including being disciplinarians and babysitters. The successful use of paraprofessionals means that they should be given responsibilities within their abilities and the framework of their training. Abuses occur when paraprofessionals are assigned to work without direct supervision and frequent consultation with the speech/ language clinician. ASHA's Commission on Supportive Personnel has cautioned its members to avoid less than appropriate supervision of aides and misrepresentation of aides as speech/ language pathologists or audiologists (1979).

A number of disturbing hypothetical situations can be described in which paraprofessionals operate outside their training limitations to the detriment of the client. For example, if single word utterances in Spanish by a

4-year-old are accepted as evidence of "normal" expressive language by a shy child, a significant language delay might be missed. Multiple articulation problems may be considered to be dialectal when they are normal developmental errors or disorders. Speech patterns resulting from structural or functional disorders of the speech mechanism or from hearing loss may go unrecognized. Additionally, the professional is usually better trained to notice evidence of birth defects. Because of the significant parameters in communication, the paraprofessional should be carefully instructed and frequently monitored even when screening for speech, language, and hearing disorders.

Summary

Paraprofessionals in speech/language pathology have been trained and employed successfully for many years. They can provide valuable assistance in the identification and intervention of communicative disorders in children and adults. These paraprofessionals should be carefully trained and supervised. Bilingual/bicultural paraprofessionals can provide valuable assistance in communities where clients either do not speak English or speak limited English. They can assist in screening and diagnosing communicative disorders, planning and implementing the individualized educational plan, counseling the family, and contacting other community agencies.

Federal and state laws require that assessments of children's abilities be done in their native langauge. An immediate solution to compliance with the law is the training and employment of bilingual/bicultural paraprofessionals. The trained paraprofessional is then also available for delivering supervised services. The paraprofessional cannot supplant the speech/language clinician who has acquired expertise in communicative disorders, but can enhance the effectiveness of the clinical pathology program.

References

Alpiner, J., Ogden, J., and Wiggins, J.: The utilization of supportive personnel in speech correction in the public schools: A pilot project. *ASHA, 12*:599–604, 1970.

Berman, S.: Speech and language services on an Indian reservation. *Language, Speech, and Hearing Services in Schools, 7*:56–60, 1976.

Braunstein, M.: Communication aides: A pilot project. *Language, Speech and Hearing Services in Schools, 3*:32–35, 1972.

Carrier, J.:   A program of articulation therapy administered by mothers. *J Speech and Hearing Disorders, 5*:344–353, 1970.

Cloward, R.:   Teenagers as tutors of academically low-achieving children: Impact on tutors and tutees. In Allen, V.L. (Ed.): *Children as Teachers: Theory and Research on Tutoring.* New York, Academic, 1976.

Commission on Supportive Personnel: Guidelines on the role, training, and supervision of communication aides. *ASHA, 12*:78–80, 1970.

Commission on Supportive Personnel: ASHA Policy re: Supportive Personnel. *ASHA, 21*:419, 1979.

Costello, J., and Schoen, J.:   On the effectiveness of paraprofessionals and speech clinician as agents of articulation intervention using programmed instruction. *Language, Speech, and Hearing Services in the Schools, 9*: 118–128, 1978.

Cromwell, F.:   The development of occupational therapy assistants: History and Status Report. *ASHA, 16*:671–678, 1974.

Davies, D.:   Education profession development act: An inside perspective. In Gartner, A., Riessman, F., and Jackson, V. (Eds.): *Paraprofessionals Today, Volume I: Education.* New York, Human Sciences, 1977.

Dopheide, W., and Dallinger, J.:   Preschool articulation screening by parents. *Language, Speech, and Hearing Services in Schools, 7*:124–127, 1976.

Frith, G, and Teller, H.:   Using paraprofessionals in programs for hearing impaired children: a discussion of roles. *Language, Speech, and Hearing Services in Schools, 13*:215–220, 1982.

Galloway, H., and Blue, G.:   Paraprofessional personnel in articulation therapy. *Language, Speech, and Hearing Services in Schools, 6*:125–130, 1975.

Goodwin, D.:   The bilingual teacher aide: Classroom assets. *Elementary School J, 77*:265–267, 1977.

Groher, M.:   The experimental use of cross-age relationships in public school speech and language program. *Language, Speech, and Hearing Services in Schools, 7*:150–156, 1976.

Grossman, L.:   The misuse of paraprofessionals. *The Urban Review, 5*:2, 1972.

Hall, P., and Knutson, C.:   The use of paraprofessional students as communication aides in the schools. *Language, Speech, and Hearing Services in Schools, 9*:162–168, 1978.

Jelinek, J.:   A pilot program for training and utilization of paraprofessionals in preschools. *Language, Speech, and Hearing Services in Schools, 7*:119–123, 1976.

Lynch, J.:   Using paraprofessionals in a language program. *Language, Speech, and Hearing Services in Schools, 3*:82–87, 1972.

Pickering, M.:   Bilingual/bicultural education and the speech pathologist. *ASHA, 18*:275–279, 1976.

Pickering, M., and Dopheide, W.:   Training aides to screen children for speech and language problems. *Language, Speech, and Hearing Services in Schools, 7:*236-241, 1976.

Scalero, A., and Eskenazi, C.:   The use of supportive personnel in a public school speech and language program. *Language, Speech, and Hearing Services in Schools, 7:*150-158, 1976.

Sommers, R., Furlong, A., Rhodes, F., Fichter, G., Bowser, D., Copetas, F., and Saunders, Z.:   Effects of maternal attitudes upon improvement of articulation when mothers are trained to assist in speech correction. *J Speech and Hearing Disorders, 29:*126-132, 1976.

Index

Note: **Boldface indicates material in table or figure on given page.**